Pocket PC development in the enterprise

First and foremost I want to thank you, Hanna, my wife and eternal love. Without your support and love, my life (and definitely this book too) would be empty. And to Ludde, Frasse, Max, and Linus – you are Daddy's shining lights.

Christian

To Marie, my wife and love I want to forever live in your embrace, constantly fall in love with you and always drown in   your beauty.

To our children; Alexander and Rebecka, Dad loves you always!

Andy

Pocket PC Development in the Enterprise

Mobile Solutions with Visual Basic and .NET

CHRISTIAN FORSBERG AND ANDREAS SJÖSTRÖM

 Addison-Wesley

An imprint of **Pearson Education**

Harlow, England • London • New York • Reading, Massachusetts • San Francisco • Toronto
Don Mills, Ontario • Sydney • Tokyo • Singapore • Hong Kong • Seoul • Taipei • Cape Town
Madrid • Mexico City • Amsterdam • Munich • Paris • Milan

PEARSON EDUCATION LIMITED

Head Office:
Edinburgh Gate
Harlow CM20 2JE
Tel: +44 (0)1279 623623
Fax: +44 (0)1279 431059

London Office:
128 Long Acre
London WC2E 9AN
Tel: +44 (0)20 7447 2000
Fax: +44 (0)20 7240 5771

Website: www.it-minds.com
        www.aw.com/cseng/

———————————————

First published in Great Britain in 2002

© Pearson Education Ltd 2002

The rights of Christian Forsberg and Andreas Sjöström to be identified as Authors of this Work
have been asserted by them in accordance with the Copyright, Designs and Patents Act 1988.

ISBN 0-201-75079-1

British Library Cataloguing in Publication Data
A CIP catalogue record for this book can be obtained from the British Library

Library of Congress Cataloging in Publication Data
Applied for.

The programs in this book and the contents of the CD-ROM have been included for their
instructional value. The publisher does not offer any warranties or representations in respect of
their fitness for a particular purpose, nor does the publisher accept any liability for any loss or
damage arising from their use.

Many of the designations used by manufacturers and sellers to distinguish their
products are claimed as trademarks. Pearson Education Limited has made every
attempt to supply trademark information about manufacturers and their products mentioned
in this book.

10 9 8 7 6 5 4 3 2 1

Designed by Claire Brodmann Book Designs, Lichfield, Staffordshire.
Typeset by Pantek Arts Ltd, Maidstone, Kent.
Printed and bound in the UK by Biddles Ltd, Guildford.

The Publishers' policy is to use paper manufactured from sustainable forests.

Contents

Acknowledgements

This book is the result of many people's dedication. Our thanks go to all of you!

We would especially like to thank Michael Strang, Acquisitions Editor at Addison Wesley, for believing in us and in the book. You have done a remarkable job in making everything come together and your support helped us keeping deadlines. Thanks to everyone at Addison-Wesley for making this book happen!

We owe the deepest gratitude to Linda Richmond – our Queen Editor – for an astounding achievement in turning our attempts to get our message through into something understandable and enjoyable to read. Thanks for all the positive e-mails and for always being so supportive. If there were a Nobel Prize for patience, you would have been awarded it. And thanks also to Princess for lending us part of your time to help us out.

Big thanks to Ted Clark at Compaq for writing an excellent foreword and thanks to Cliff Weiss, Compaq, for all your support. A big round of applause to Compaq for the iPAQ Pocket PCs that follow us day and night, keeping our life and jobs in order, and for all the fun always in reach.

Thanks, Craig Peacock, Jason Dunn, and Frank McPherson, for helping us get started, for the tips on book writing and the moral support.

Thanks, Chris Muench, for recommending a great publisher and for excellent feedback when reviewing the book.

Kudos to Chris De Herrera for a solid tech review, valuable comments, and generous helpings of advice.

Many thanks to Mark Gentile, Dave Vanable, Mark Wade, Jim Sullivan, and everyone else at Odyssey Software for excellent support and good ideas that really have made the difference. The fact that you bring the readers a full license of a powerful tool in their Pocket PC toolbox is truly awesome.

Thanks to all our friends at Microsoft: Lenn Pryor, Derek Brown, Lilli Harwood, Steve Seroshek, David Rasmussen, Douglas Dedo, Vidur Luthra, and Phil Holden. A special thanks to Steven Lees for reviewing the .NET chapter.

Special thanks to our fellow contributing writers at PocketPC.com for all the inspirational and cool articles!

Thanks, Simon Fell, for sharing your SOAP knowledge and code with the rest of us.

Thanks to John Psuik at Developer One for the full version of your ScreenSnap product. We're sure there will be many great screenshots of cool Pocket PC applications created with it.

Thanks to Christopher Meyer and Stan Davis for writing the book *BLUR*. It has been a true inspiration in our lives.

Thanks to the staff at MSDN for your excellent job of providing superior developer content. Keep up the good work!

And this book would never have been possible without all the contributing members of the communities at **www.pocketprojects.com**, **www.pocketpc.com**, **www.devbuzz.com**, and the newsgroups at Microsoft. Thanks for being a source of inspiration and for the shared code snippets.

Thanks to Bill Gates for creating Microsoft.

And finally, thanks to all other authors for not writing the book we were looking for back in December 2000!

Andreas Sjöström and Christian Forsberg

Foreword

The past several years have given us giant leaps in personal productivity as a direct result of technology improvements. The trend continues through the explosive adoption of mobile and wireless technologies. The convergence of easy-to-use applications and advancements in mobile technology – both now and in the near future – portend tremendous growth and adoption of mobile, personal productivity tools. Mobility in combination with new applications will have a long lasting impact on the quality of our lives going forward. Ultimately the convergence of mobility and smart handheld devices brings commerce and other information to consumers, employees, and business partners anytime and anywhere.

Compaq is a leading global provider of technology and solutions, bringing a wealth of experience and innovation to customers all over the world. Compaq's mission of enabling human achievement and customer success by transforming information technology is dependent upon a dual strategic focus of building the business critical internet, and the continual redefinition of the access experience. Central to the achievement of those strategies is the investment in technologies that enable customers to harness the power and possibilities of the internet – everywhere, all the time.

In their book, Andreas and Christian provide the necessary linkage between the popular program development environments and the explosive growth potential exhibited by the Pocket PC platform. The key to continued growth and productivity in the smart handheld device market is the development of the next wave of applications.

Andreas and Christian take a unique approach by focusing on the enterprise and their view of the Pocket PC as a logical extension of the enterprise and the next access device. For clarity and ease of learning, the authors develop a series of applications focused upon a fictitious company. By following the examples, the reader becomes acquainted with the business processes and is walked through the code that brings those processes to the Pocket PC.

As a result, this book becomes an important contribution to the literature supporting the move towards smart handheld devices and the growth of Pocket PC as an enabling operating environment.

Enjoy!

Ted Clark
Vice President,
iPAQ Mobile Solutions
Compaq Computer Corporation

Introduction

Something has changed. Have you noticed?

You know how to build great solutions for your users: robust, scalable, user friendly, and maintainable enterprise applications; how to design a solid architecture with normalized databases, structured component models and even good-looking dialogs and web pages; you are the expert in satisfying the increasing demands of an ever-changing business. You are the system "carpenter" equipped with a solid toolbox of enterprise tools. You are the champ!

> Business demands integration between process and mobility, a demand that in turn drives integration between mobility and systems.

But now your users have begun to express a completely new requirement that you cannot solve with the tools you used before. Some of them purchased small gadgets to take along on business trips and customer visits, at first just as replacements for their calendars. They even found out how to get their e-mail onto those devices. But they soon wanted more.

They want to be able to perform their tasks and conduct business wherever they are. Business demands integration between process and mobility, a demand that in turn drives integration between mobility and systems. And *system integration* smells like a lot of development effort.

This book is intended to assist you in responding to these new demands with real, working mobile solutions. Your current skills and experience are not only an asset, they are prerequisites in building solid enterprise mobile applications. You have the opportunity to become a new mobile solutions hero. And we will help you become one.

The purpose of this book

The purpose of this book is to help you hit the ground running in building mobile solutions for your business *today*, based on the Windows for Pocket PC platform, and leveraging your existing enterprise design and developer skills. The book contains a significant amount of business-oriented content, spanning business case development, mobile trends, software development methodology, and mobile architecture, plus lots of sample code.

This book intentionally mixes the business and developer aspects of mobile development. We chose not to split the material into two separate parts because of our conviction that today's and tomorrow's heroes have to understand both.

You will be able to take advantage of your experience in building scalable architectures with the Microsoft platform as a foundation. The Pocket PC is the best choice, not just as a catchy marketing phrase; it's also a core element of the Microsoft platform. Core technologies, tools, and technologies that you already know are the same – from the server and all the way out to the Pocket PC device itself.

Based on our experiences, we have come to regard the Microsoft platform as a basis for creating state-of-the-art solutions for enterprise business problems.

Why we wrote this book

Mobile solutions will be a natural ingredient in most enterprise business operations. The developer efforts required to make this prediction happen are significant. Critical focus areas include optimization of skill and IT reuse as well as mobile technologies training.

During the fall of 2000, we looked around for a book about developing mobile solutions for enterprise companies aimed at experienced developers. We wanted to get a head start in this race. We did not find that book. During a late night e-mail exchange between us, a week before Christmas of 2000, we decided to write it ourselves.

The core idea for the book is to bring the good news to the millions of Visual Basic developers that they only need to make a small effort to be able to create mobile solutions – much in the same way and with the same tools that they already know. Visual Basic developers will be instrumental in extending existing systems, those that they have already developed, to be available anywhere – on a Pocket PC. In the mobile marketplace, some players have pushed the idea that mobile solutions are something isolated and "new," but as the web is now used as an extension of existing business models and systems, so will mobile solutions. If you want to take part in the wave of mobile development, this book is for you!

Pocket PC – the best device platform for the enterprise

We possess between us 25 years of experience in enterprise system development. During these years we have worked with everything from coding to building and testing solid architectures.

If there is anything that we have learned during these years, it's the importance of system and even application integration. In most enterprise projects, the majority of effort surrounds integration. Integration is mainly about extending systems and most often it is really about extending business processes. Mobile solutions extend business processes to be available to the workforce and other participants in business functions the market – anywhere. It means that the employees can access and even manipulate core business information just when they need it the most – immediately.

We are convinced that the Pocket PC is a premier platform to enable enterprise business solutions to be available anywhere. We intend to assist you in getting started with "business mobilization." During the last couple of years we have realized that the Pocket PCs (preceded by the earlier generation called Palm-size PCs) are useful for far more than organizing contacts, appointments, and e-mail. Pocket PCs consolidate technologies that enable you to take the knowledge and power in your business applications, and then use it wherever your employees are.

The Pocket PC has the capability to extend both business processes and enterprise applications to be available, literally, from the mobile employees' hands.

> ❝We are convinced that the Pocket PC is a premier platform to enable enterprise business solutions to be available anywhere. We intend to assist you in getting started with 'business mobilization.'❞

Who should use this book

So, who do we think that you are? We believe that you are an IT professional who has performed any of a number of roles, from system designer, to IT manager and decision maker, to manager or member of development teams, either in or for corporate environments. You probably have worked with most of the following tools and technologies from Microsoft:

- Windows (both on server and client)
- Transaction Server and/or Component Services (COM+)
- SQL Server
- Visual Studio (most importantly Visual Basic)
- Component Object Model (COM/DCOM)
- ActiveX Data Objects (ADO)
- Internet Information Server (IIS)
- ActiveX Server Pages (ASP)

And also some general methodology and technologies:

- Internet Technologies (HTTP, HTML, CSS, etc)
- Extensible Markup Language (XML)
- Unified Modeling Language (UML)

You probably work for one or with several large corporations using a number of applications built on the Microsoft platform. We hope that you like structured ways of approaching a problem and that your main focus is to support and even drive the business to which you provide IT solutions. And we assume, since you purchased this book, that you are actually planning to design and/or build a mobile solution yourself soon.

You are likely to have an interest in Pocket PCs, and probably even have a Pocket PC yourself. Having a Pocket PC device will help you in trying out the samples in this book. And it will also help you to understand the situation for your users. You will then be familiar with the different aspects of the smaller screen, stylus-based input, and limited memory.

So that's who we address this book to – generally anyone interested in developing solutions for the Pocket PC, for use in an enterprise environment. This book is for you.

Who we are

Some call us mad men. Others call us highly regarded and sought after senior consultants in the domains of corporate mobile solutions. In an industry where it seems to be fashionable to stay away from the developer craftsmanship, we regard ourselves as proud developers. We both work at the Swedish practice of Cap Gemini Ernst & Young and are both moonlighting as contributing writers at PocketPC.com (found at **www.pocketpc.com**).

I (Christian Forsberg) have been designing and implementing enterprise solutions based on Microsoft technologies for more than 15 years. I started programming in 1977 and am still a proud developer, now for the Pocket PC. I have worked with everything from game programming to field service support on Pocket PC and feel confident that the message of this book really works in real-life situations. I'm also a proud Pocket PC owner who does much of my e-mailing, e-book reading, internet browsing, and even writing on it. Some parts of this book are written on my Pocket PC. My non-Pocket PC life is spent with my love and wife, Hanna, and our children, Ludwig, Franz, Max, and Linus.

I (Andreas Sjöström) have more than 10 years of experience in system architecture design and software development. I enthusiastically began programming a Sinclair ZX81 back in 1982. When I was 13, I wrote an essay about happiness. The essay was about BASIC-programming. Much as this book, really! I specialize in mobile database development and back office integration. I live in Mullsjö, Sweden, together with my lovely wife Marie, and our two children, Alexander and Rebecka. I am, along with my family, active in the local church and lead a children's choir called Joysound.

You can visit us at the web site www.businessanyplace.net or send us e-mail at christian.forsberg@pocketpcwriter.com and andreas.sjostrom@pocketpcwriter.com.

Talk with us!

In closing, we'd like to let you know that Chapter 1 provides many resources for you, including an URL for a web site where you can communicate with us, ask us questions, and find updates for the information and code we've supplied here. We hope to hear from you, and look forward to working together with you in this exciting arena.

We're glad to be on your team. Well, now that we've all been introduced it's time to get to work.

Andreas Sjöström   Christian Forsberg

Examples, software from the CD, and resources you can use

1.1 Introducing ACME Copier Inc.

We will try to make the samples in this book come alive as much as possible by having them evolve around a fictitious company and its business processes. Hopefully, you will be able to reuse our ideas from the solution design and development discussions here.

We want to introduce to you a fictitious company called ACME Copier Inc. The ACME Copier samples can be found in Chapters 9 and 10. ACME Copier Inc. is a company that rents and leases out copier machines, faxes, and printers. Their customers are mid-size to large corporations and organizations.

ACME Copier's main source of income is their field service operation. Service engineers visit customers regularly to perform scheduled maintenance. When an ACME business machine breaks down, the customer calls ACME's customer service, which in turn forwards a service order to the field service operation.

Our samples will illustrate how ACME Copier improves the productivity within their field service operation.

Note

Perhaps you are thinking that we could have chosen a slightly more exciting sample theme. Mobile solutions are hot, and many predict new and fascinating mobile business opportunities. We are all for new cool and mind-boggling Pocket PC applications. However, the sample code we provide is likely to be more valuable for real life enterprise scenarios, based on field service processes – rather than based on something too narrow (such as MP3s and streaming video – something the Pocket PC indeed is capable of).

1.2   ACME Copier's architecture requirements

Pocket PC-based solutions are no different from other IT solutions in that they need to stand on firm and predefined system architecture principles. The field service management team at ACME Copier Inc. had, before the deployment of the Pocket PC solutions, articulated the following few principles that the solutions had to support:

- Improve the service engineer productivity by increasing the time spent in service order and scheduled maintenance work.
- Increase customer satisfaction by cutting lag time between the customer service call to when the service engineer shows up.
- Reduce customer service administration by removing all paper forms and notes carrying service order information.
- Reduce cost by improving service engineer daily routes through historical information, allowing ACME to plan them better.
- Enable decision support (type of equipment details, causes and frequency of failure, etc.).
- Pocket PC solutions must be easy to use.
- Pocket PC solutions must support both connected and disconnected scenarios.
- Must be a scalable solution that performs equally well for one service engineer as for thousands.
- Solution must integrate well with current and future IT architecture at ACME Copier Inc.
- Maximize development efficiency by leveraging skill set already present in the IT department.

You can read more about architecture principles in the Pocket PC Solution Definition Method in Chapter 3.

1.3   A day in the life of Anne

In Chapter 9, you will get to know Anne. She uses the Pocket PC solutions defined by the sample code.

Anne is a service engineer in the field service operation at ACME Copier Inc. A service engineer visits customers regularly to perform scheduled maintenance. When a copier machine, a fax or a printer breaks down, the customer calls customer service at ACME Copier Inc., which forwards a service order to a service engineer.

A typical day in Anne's professional life goes something like this:

In the morning Anne turns on her Pocket PC to check what equipment is up for scheduled maintenance and who the customers are. As she plans her route for the day, she dials up to the ACME Copier network to download any open service orders that urgently need attention.

The information Anne takes with her on her Pocket PC includes:

● Customer information – Addresses, phone numbers etc.

● Maintenance schedule – Equipment, type of maintenance

● Service order information – Symptoms, time of failure, equipment

● Inventory of spare parts – How many of each in service van

● Equipment information – Which customer has what copier, fax, and/or printer

● Equipment service logs – Who fixed what and when

Anne drives away to the first job in her service van in which she has the most commonly used spare parts. While on her first call fixing a broken printer, Anne uses her Pocket PC to note how long it takes, what spare parts she uses and what tasks she performs. When she is done, the customer signs the service order sheet and Anne closes the service order.

On her way to the next job, she wirelessly connects her Pocket PC to the network and uploads the completed service order for invoicing. Furthermore, she also checks to see whether or not any more new service orders have been registered during her first job.

Over at ACME Copier the incoming service order information is processed in a number of ways:

1 The service orders are billed the same day that they are completed.

2 The central warehouse for spare parts gets precise data regarding which service engineer needs which parts replenished.

3 The ACME Copier purchasing manager can draw accurate conclusions regarding the next year's copier, fax, and printer purchases by avoiding the failing models.

1.4   Resources, online and off

Along with the samples surrounding ACME Copier, you will be studying the sample code in Chapter 10 to see how the Pocket PC solutions support the customer's predefined architecture principles.

The sample code will illustrate:

- Pocket PC applications, written in eMbedded Visual Basic, working disconnected (off-line) as well as connected (online). Technologies that we will explore include ActiveX Data Objects for Windows CE (ADOCE), SQL Server for Windows CE, remote COM-components and databases, XML and SOAP (Simple Object Access Protocol) as well as third-party software from Odyssey Software and others.

- Web-based applications running on a Pocket PC using ASP, HTML, JScript, XML, XSL, and SOAP.

- Integration with Calendar and Contacts on the device, using the Pocket Outlook Object Model (POOM).

- And much, much more.

You will get to know ACME Copier and Anne better and thereby learn *Pocket PC Development in the Enterprise*. Along the way we will reveal some valuable programming tips and tricks. So buckle up and enjoy the ride!

1.5   What's on the CD

On the CD accompanying this book you will find:

- All the book samples in source code format
- Microsoft eMbedded Visual Tools 3.0
- Microsoft SQL Server 2000 for Windows CE 1.1 Trial Edition
- Software 309 PictureBox Control 2.7
- Odyssey Software CEfusion 3.5 Free Developer Enterprise Edition
- Odyssey Software ViaXML 1.1 Trial Edition
- Odyssey Software OSIUtil 1.0
- Microsoft Visual Studio 6.0 Service Pack 5
- Ezos EzWAP 2.0 Evaluation
- Larry Banks' Virtual CE
- Developer One Pocket ScreenSnap 5.0 (Full Version)
- Microsoft SOAP Toolkit 2.0
- Simon Fell's Pocket SOAP 0.9.1
- Microsoft Reader 1.5
- Word 2000 Microsoft Reader Add-in: Read in Microsoft Reader 1.0

As you read through the book, you will find that several samples and all of the source code (and more) shown in the book are also available on the CD. You will find information on where to find the sample code on the CD at the end of each section discussing a specific sample.

All the tools and other material on the CD enable you to get started right away. Most of them can be downloaded from the suppliers' various web sites, but by making these tools available to you on the CD, we are saving you a considerable amount of download time. Following are descriptions of the various tools.

 Tip

As mentioned earlier, another important tool that you will need if you plan to do serious Pocket PC development is a Pocket PC you can use yourself. It will help you in your work to understand the smaller device paradigm. When developing, you'll find a number of advantages to actually building and running your software directly on the device, its normal environment. Some differences exist in the emulator compared to an actual Pocket PC, and in fact, a number of things cannot be done in the emulator.

Microsoft eMbedded Visual Tools 3.0

Here are all the tools you need to start developing for the Windows powered devices. The eMbedded Visual Tools include eMbedded Visual Basic, eMbedded Visual C++, and the SDKs for the Pocket PC, Palm-size PC, and Handheld PC. More information can be found at:
www.microsoft.com/mobile/downloads/emvt30.asp

Microsoft SQL Server for Windows CE 1.1 Trial Edition

Microsoft SQL Server 2000 Windows CE Edition (SQL Server CE) is the compact database for rapidly developing applications that extend enterprise data management capabilities to devices. SQL Server CE has the familiar feel of SQL Server, with tools, APIs, and SQL grammar that minimize development time.

Additionally, the SQL Server CE engine exposes an essential set of relational database features – including an optimizing query processor and support for transactions and assorted data types – while maintaining a compact footprint that preserves precious system resources. Remote data access and merge replication, which work over HTTP and support encryption, ensure that data from enterprise SQL Server databases is reliably delivered and that this data can be manipulated off-line and synchronized later to the server. This makes SQL Server CE ideal for mobile and wireless scenarios. More information can be found at:
www.microsoft.com/sql/productinfo/ceoverview.htm

Software 309 PictureBox Control 2.7

The S309PictureBox.ocx provides a PictureBox ActiveX control that can display bitmap (.bmp and .2bp), GIF, JPEG, and XBM image files. It can display bitmap resources from resource files, including common bitmaps such as FileOpen and FileClose. It will allow you to capture and display an image of the physical screen as well as save an image as a bitmap file. And you'll find lots of other things. More information can be found at this web address: members.nbci.com/S309/

Odyssey Software CEfusion 3.5 Free Developer Enterprise Edition

Applications developed with CEFusion enable workers to access enterprise data in real time over any wireless LAN or WAN, wired, or dial-up connection. CEfusion is not an end-user application; it is a set of powerful tools and infrastructure for developing custom mobile enterprise applications. It offers secure real time access to critical data on an as-needed basis. Because Odyssey Software has optimized the software infrastructure for mobilization, your developers can focus on creating powerful applications optimized for your company's real world requirements. For information on how to access your free permanent single-user development license for CEfusion, see page 411.

Odyssey Software ViaXML 1.1 Trial Edition

ViaXML elevates the capabilities of the mobile application developer to a new level. Until now true interactions with the enterprise were platform dependent, usually required proprietary servers operated only in client-server mode, and didn't allow direct peer-to-peer interaction. ViaXML uses open XML standards, which eliminates these limitations while enabling a wide range of new mobile application possibilities.

Odyssey Software OSIUtil 1.0

This is a free utility that will help you with the memory leak in the eVB CreateObject function. It will also provide you with some Registry editing functionality.

Virtual CE – the authors' favorite utility!

When it comes to usable utilities, this one is especially useful. It's made by Larry Banks and called Virtual CE. As you might suspect, this utility makes it possible for you to watch and even interact with your Pocket PC from your PC. This is especially useful for doing presentations directly from your device but can also be an excellent tool to test your applications. The utility not only displays a copy of the device screen on the PC, you can even interact with it both using the mouse (simulating the stylus) and the keyboard. Yes, you read right, you can use the keyboard to enter things like long SQL statements, etc. If you get a registered version, you will also get some extra cool features like saving screenshots, recording macros, etc. You can install the demo version by starting \Software\BitBank\Virtual CE\ virtual_ce_demo.exe on the accompanying CD. Larry also encourages you to check out his site for new versions: www.bitbanksoftware.com/ce/

1.6   Other required software

And to try out all the samples, you will need the following commercial software:

- Microsoft Windows 2000 (we have been using Windows 2000 with Service Pack 1 to build the samples. You may need to make some changes to make it work on any other version of Windows)
- Microsoft Visual Basic 6.0
- SQL Server 2000

1.7   Installation

We assume that you have the above commercial software already installed. And if not, you should start by installing them as a first step.

Installing ActiveSync

To install the software you need to start with the basic connectivity software, ActiveSync. You can download it from www.microsoft.com/mobile/pocketpc/downloads/.

Installing eMbedded Visual Tools

Then you should install the development tools, and they can be installed by starting \Software\Microsoft\eVT\EN_WINCE_EMBDVTOOLS30.exe on the accompanying CD and follow the instructions. When prompted for the CD key, please enter TRT7H-KD36T-FRH8D-6QH8P-VFJHQ.

Installing SQL Server CE

Next, since many of the samples are dependent on the SQL Server database, you should also install it. The free evaluation edition can be installed by starting \Software\Microsoft\SQLCE\setup.exe on the accompanying CD and follow the instructions.

When you run the SQL Server CE setup, you choose whether you want to install server tools or client tools. Install client tools on your development system. If you plan to use either Remote Data Access (RDA) or Merge Replication, install server tools on your Internet Information Server (IIS) system.

There is no specific setup that installs SQL Server CE to your Pocket PC. Once you have installed the client tools on your desktop PC, you can add a reference to the Microsoft CE SQL Server Control 1.0 to your Pocket PC project. When you first run the project from eMbedded Visual Basic, the ADOCE 3.1 and SQL Server CE components will be copied over and registered onto your Pocket PC.

SQL Server CE can only be accessed through ADOCE 3.1 or later. ADOCE 3.1 installs during the Client Tools setup. For more information regarding installing ADOCE 3.1 you can read the Microsoft Developer Network (MSDN) article, *Adding the ADOCE Control to an Application*, which you can locate by searching the MSDN site at: msdn.microsoft.com/

To programmatically create and manage SQL Server CE databases you also need to add a reference to ActiveX Data Objects Extensions for Data Definition Language and Security (ADOXCE), an extension to the ADOCE objects and programming model. ADOXCE also makes it possible to create and modify tables, columns, and indexes. You will find more about this in Chapter 6.

Installing SQL Server CE Query Analyzer

SQL Server CE Query Analyzer (ISQL) is a Pocket PC application that lets you connect to and manage your SQL Server CE databases. ISQL is a useful tool for executing ad-hoc SQL statements directly on the Pocket PC. You install ISQL simply by copying the file isqlw_wce.exe for type of device (processor) from the directory **Program Files\Microsoft SQL Server CE\ ISQLWCE\Pocket PC\(processor type; Arm, MIPS, etc)** on your desktop PC.

Installing S309PictureBox

As some of the samples require the Software 309 PictureBox control, you can install it by starting **Software\Software309\PictureBox\S309 PictureBox_ PocketPC.exe** on the accompanying CD and follow the instructions.

Installing Odyssey Software CEfusion

Since you would probably like to test the server component integration samples, you will need to install Odyssey Software's CEfusion. You should have ActiveSync connected to your Pocket PC before you start the installation. It is also best if you have your license key ready before you install (see page 411), as it will be inserted in all samples during installation (requiring you to update them manually). You install it by starting **Software\Odyssey Software\CEfusion\cefusion350e.exe** on the accompanying CD and the setup will guide you through the installation. To get started, you just follow these instructions:

To start the CEfusion Services on your Windows NT/2000 computer:

1 Click the **Start** menu and select **Programs** > **CEfusion**, then click **Service Manager.**

2 To start a CEfusion service, first select the service from the list, and then click the **Start Service** button (looks like a VCR play button).

3 Repeat this for all services in the list.

And to configure the CEfusion client on your device:

4 Through the Control Panel or Settings interface, find and start the CEfusion properties applet.

5 Enter the TCP/IP address of your Windows 2000 computer, and then click **(OK).**

And finally, to run PocketQuery on your Windows CE device:

6 Tap **Start** > **Programs** > **Pocket Query**. This will run the PocketQuery application.

7 Tap **File** > **Open** and select the **Access Example.sql** file. This file contains an example of querying the example database included with CEfusion.

8 Tap the **Execute** button on the toolbar (looks like a VCR play button).

9 You should now see your query results in a grid!

10 The results are fully editable (add/modify/delete). To edit, double-click a cell that you wish to modify. This begins **Edit Mode** in the grid. You can continue changes to other cells on the current row using the keyboard or stylus. To commit or save the changes, navigate off the row (arrow up/down or click a different row). A confirmation dialog will appear, allowing you to continue the save operation or to cancel your changes.

11 Have fun!

For more information on installing CEfusion, please see the **readme.txt** file in the installation directory.

Installing Odyssey Software ViaXML

Odyssey Software's ViaXML provides a loosely coupled applications integration. Install it by starting **\Software\Odyssey Software\ViaXML\ viaxml110.exe** on the accompanying CD and the setup will guide you through the installation.

After the installation, these additional steps have to be taken:

1 For any files placed into the ASP folder (typically C:\Program Files\ Odyssey Software\ViaXML\ASP) that need to be modified (such as a database file): the security permissions need to be modified:

- Select the file using Windows Explorer.
- Right click and choose **Properties**.
- Select the **Security** tab.
- Click the **Add** button.
- Verify the **Look in:** combo box has your computer name visible.
- Locate **IUSR_MACHINENAME**, highlight it and click **Add**, then click **OK**.
- Back at the main screen, make sure the **Modify** right is checked for the new user.
- Click **OK**.

Follow the same steps on the ASP directory as well.

2 Check to make sure that a virtual directory has been created under IIS called ViaXML, i.e. C:\ProgramFiles\OdysseySoftware\ViaXML\ ASP

If it was not created, please do so now.

3 If you skipped entering the ViaXML license key, this key needs to be entered into the Example projects before use. Inside the projects, replace the constant string "XXX..." in the following line with your ViaXML License Key.

Const LICENSE_KEY = "XXXX-XXXX-XXXX-XXXX"

To request an evaluation license key, go to
http://www.odysseysoftware. com/viaxml_eval.html

Installing Odyssey Software OSIUtil

To install this utility library, you start \Software\Odyssey Software\ OSIUtil\OSIUTIL100.exe on the accompanying CD and the setup will guide you through the installation.

You can read more about distributing these components in Chapter 11.

1.8   Meet others on the internet

We truly encourage you to take part in the growing and very lively developer community for Pocket PC. You should check out web sites like:

● PocketProjects.com at www.pocketprojects.com
Great forums for both eVB and eVC developers. Lively discussions and loads of problems and solutions.

● Microsoft's own PocketPC.com at: www.pocketpc.com
A lot of developer content both from Microsoft and independent authors.

● DeVBuzz.com at www.devbuzz.com
Many code snippets and great developer articles. Also an opportunity to publish your software.

And newsgroups like (on the news server msnews.microsoft.com):

● microsoft.public.pocketpc.developer

● microsoft.public.windowsce.app.development

● microsoft.public.windowsce.embedded.vb

● microsoft.public.sqlserver.ce

1.9   Meet the authors on the internet

Everything changes, especially in our business. We would like to see this book as the beginning of Pocket PC-targeted enterprise development, a starting point for you to move forward in developing mobile enterprise solutions.

Since technology will change, the contents of the book will in time become outdated. We decided that a way to extend the life of the book is to put up a web site containing all the samples as well as news, comments on the book, etc. The idea is to be able to update samples as new technology becomes available. That's exactly what we have done at: www.businessanyplace.net

There, you can find a web site surrounding this book. You will be able to contact us and also comment on different parts of the book. You will find updated code samples from what you find in this book, reflecting changes in the architecture. You are most welcome to join us in our online discussions, collaborative projects, and other interesting ventures. See you there!

Extend the enterprise

In this chapter we're going to look at the forces in the marketplace, the changing environment in which businesses must do business, and we'll then focus on the potential this means for mobile solutions.

Speed: Everything happens faster in a sphere where information is exchanged digitally and people who need the information are connected to it. Customers can find the right vendors faster, businesses can interact with each other faster, companies face swifter competition and can respond more quickly to new challenges in the marketplace.

Mobile technologies contribute significantly to the speed of business in many ways. Companies can reach their customers with their proposal – regardless of where the customer is because mobile technologies are connecting and converging with the web. For corporate use, mobile solutions make it possible to get rid of unnecessary manual steps throughout business operations. Business processes meet mobility, and the system integration that occurs as a result extends existing back office systems to users wherever they are.

Value: Entire ranges of administrative activities and manual processing of collected data are on the verge of extinction. Proposals for goods and services become possible from anywhere in the world.

2.1   Leading us to mobile information systems

The past few years of internet-based business development has forced most large corporations to integrate technology aspects into their business agenda. The technology-driven opportunities to reach and interact with more customers and partners, improve operations, and cut unnecessary supply chain intermediaries have driven this trend. A proof of this trend is the common inclusion of CIOs and IT managers on the boards of directors, which injects the necessary technology skills to make right business decisions into corporate management.

The dot com bubble burst during the year 2000. As more and more dot com founders were thrown into unbelievable wealth, more and more venture capital seemed to gravitate towards even the wildest business plans. It seemed that the race was about market growth, but instead we know now it was about burning as much capital in as little time as possible. Only a few of these dot coms sobered up in time, while most of them have vanished and with them billions of venture capital dollars.

The online business winners seem to be large traditional enterprise companies who succeed in integrating core business processes and online connectivity. These companies had growth and profitability well before anyone even began to think about the New Economy.

However, while the New Economy does not necessarily guarantee sound financial planning and execution (though it should have been learned as a result of the dot com demise), it still is defined by the increasingly rapid trends such as:

- **Globalization** – Online business is instantly global. Competition, partners and customers know no geographical boundaries.

- **Digitalization** – The digitalization of information and content.

- **Innovation** – Business and technology innovation to gain competitive edge, growth, and profitability.

- **Convergence** – Because everything is moving towards a state of connectedness with the network, stand-alone objects connect and thereby converge with the web. For example, cell phones and personal digital assistants converge with the web.

- **Integration** – A significant system integration challenge is posed where core business processes meets the web.

These New Economy business and technology conditions drive one single attribute: speed. Everything happens faster when everything – communications, business transactions, and information – takes place digitally and in a connected state.

Obviously mobile technologies add tremendously to the speed of business, in many ways. More importantly, corporate back office (people and systems) as well as any connected mobile worker can be made available at the point of mission critical activity, leading to freely exchanged internal and external (customers and partner) interaction. The digitalization of communication will not lead to the end of normal voice telephone calls from the field to the back office. But messaging, such as e-mail or specific knowledge management systems, is appropriate when the person out in the field needs to reach a group of people, for example a group of specialists.

> ❝These New Economy business and technology conditions drive one single attribute: speed. Everything happens faster when everything – communications, business transactions, and information – takes place digitally and in a connected state. ❞

So now we come to the point of the discussion: software development must respond to this new business environment. Our trade has been radically affected by the intensified conditions of the New Economy.

Note

We choose to say "intensified conditions" instead of "new conditions." Development projects that we were engaged in, well before the term "the New Economy" was invented, were also conducted in time constraints. Nothing new here. Perhaps we should even say "the Intensified Economy." If you want to read some real New Economy insights we can recommend these books:

- *BLUR: The Speed of Change in the Connected Economy*, by Stanley M. Davis, Christopher Meyer
- *Business @ the Speed of Thought: Succeeding in the Digital Economy*, by Bill Gates, Collins Hemingway (Contributor)

Development projects that previously took a year to finish must now be completed in three months or less – and involve even more complexities. Development life cycles are changing. The traditional "waterfall"-development practice where a significant amount of time was spent in writing functional and technical requirements long before actual development took place, has now largely been replaced by new development cycles, for example Rapid Application Development (RAD), Cap Gemini Ernst & Young's Iterative Application Development (IAD), and Rational Unified Process (RUP).

The two fundamental differentiators between the RAD, IAD, and RUP styles of development, in comparison with the "waterfall" software development life cycle, are that they have built in mechanisms for controlling scope, time, and cost; but most importantly they force a tight relationship between individuals with business knowledge and software developers. Key elements in delivering the right solutions rapidly act as the active and creative workshops where the users and developers meet regularly to define, prioritize, and design solutions. Our experience is that mobile solutions will not be well designed or received by the users if they have not been involved in the actual design.

So, the reality is that our solution development skills and practices are undergoing rapid change. In business where *technology is the business*, this is even truer. The more we learn about the business aspects of software development, the faster we can move. The faster we can move, the more we can do business. World-class developers have already learned about and realized business-driven aspects of software development. It is clear that this trend must continue.

❝World-class developers have already learned about and realized business-driven aspects of software development. It is clear that this trend must continue.❞

Perhaps we are stating the obvious, but it seems important to say it: the rapid development of mobile technologies demands that business decision makers no longer may neglect technology competence. Despite the tightening of the relationship between business and technology, it is disturbing at times to see how some managers, salespeople, business consultants, and project managers almost seem to take pride in not understanding technology. Corporations that do not address this attitude will experience a serious disadvantage in the marketplace.

❝The heroes of today's and tomorrow's corporations are individuals who are either business savvy developers or technology savvy business decision makers (or best of all, a combination of these backgrounds) – with a focus on the benefits of mobile computing.❞

While mobile solutions still are in their infancy, the core technologies driving them are not. This combination promises success to those businesses that move quickly. The Pocket PC platform is designed as a mobile, yet integrated, part of a larger system architecture. Although the Pocket PC platform lives on the leading edge of new, sometimes not-so-proven technologies such as Bluetooth connectivity, mobile speech recognition, and video; it is very much a part of Microsoft's well-proven blueprint; Microsoft's Web Solution Platform (formerly known as Windows DNA) and .NET.

The heroes of today's and tomorrow's corporations are individuals who are either business savvy developers or technology savvy business decision makers (or best of all, a combination of these backgrounds) – with a focus on the benefits of mobile computing.

2.2   Vision for mobile solutions

The vision for mobile solutions is to put business at the fingertips of customers, partners, and employees. In one short sentence: Mobile solutions add "anywhere capabilities" to enterprise core processes and systems.

The key word is *availability*. If a product is not available, your customer cannot buy it. Even worse, if your competitor's product is available, and not yours, you lose revenue as well as market share. From a business intelligence point of view, if vital data for decision-making is not available when it needs to be, the risk of making wrong decisions is obvious. Mobile solutions are about making information and functionality available anywhere and at anytime.

What we know now about online business clearly shows that the most competitive product does not necessarily win. The winning combination is the high quality product and superb service, both integrated online. In the mobile marketplace companies will find new ways to add competitive edge to their offerings by making both products and service available to their customers from anywhere, and thereby building an ever-closer relationship with the customer.

An example of this is the Swedish company Fagerhult. Fagerhult is one of Northern Europe's leading manufacturers of lighting systems and luminaires for offices, industries, hospitals, and public areas. Fagerhult provides their

66 The vision for mobile solutions is to put business at the fingertips of customers, partners, and employees. In one short sentence: Mobile solutions add 'anywhere capabilities' to enterprise core processes and systems. 99

Figure 2.1   Product information and ordering from the Pocket PC

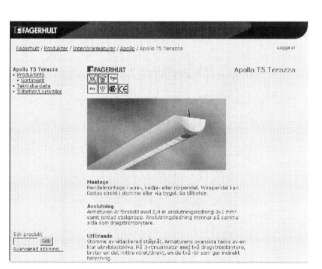

customers with online availability product information and ordering. This means that a customer can obtain important product information and order anytime, but only from where there is a live connection to the internet. The Pocket PC has a built-in web browser, Pocket Internet Explorer, which means that customers with Pocket PCs can use Fagerhult's web site wirelessly in much the same way they do from their regular desktop PC.

To increase their availability even more, they are now looking into the possibilities of adding a mobile, off-line channel to their offerings.

This type of mobile, off-line channel enables customers and partners to reach necessary product information and ordering facilities at the actual point of need, for example a construction site.

Enterprise information systems were really hot in the early 1990s. These systems were meant to pull together data from multiple data sources to support decision-making and planning. With few exceptions these projects did not succeed very well in meeting their objectives.

> 66 Mobile solutions will add significant value to existing IT investments as they increase the availability of business critical information to the individuals who need it, wherever they happen to be. 99

Since then products and technologies have matured and business intelligence solutions based on data and web warehousing, data mining, and digital dashboards are now common in enterprise companies. Mobile solutions will add significant value to existing IT investments as they increase the availability of business critical information to the individuals who need it, wherever they happen to be. Mobile business intelligence software is very likely to become the killer Pocket PC application within corporations.

Billions of users and millions of dollars? Or vice versa?

Mobile solutions can be divided into two main types:

- **Mobile commerce (m-commerce)** for the selling and buying of goods using mobile terminals. Growth and revenue are the two most important factors in this stream.
- **Mobile enterprise solutions** that extend corporate (internal and external) processes. Operations efficiency is the most important factor in this stream.

The m-commerce stream is the most spoken of in media and gets the most headlines. It is not unexpected because as soon as there is a new phenomenon in the IT-industry that may generate revenue analyst firms line up to major news agencies. With the motto: "The higher prediction, the larger headlines," they seem to try to outbid each other. Sometimes it is difficult to remember if they mean billions of users and millions of dollars, or vice versa – or both!

Is mobile commerce happening? Definitely. Regardless of how many millions or billions, Table 2.1 provides at least a hint about where we are going. The predictions were made late in the year 2000.

Table 2.1   Predictions about mobile use

Analyst	No. of Users Predicted	Revenue Prediction	Projected Year
Ovum Ltd.	**500 million** users worldwide will use mobile e-commerce.	Mobile e-commerce will result in **$200 billion** total revenues.	2005
Strategy Analytics	The number of wireless internet subscribers will grow from 6.6 million in 1999 to **400 million**.	The global market for m-commerce is expected to reach **$200 billion**.	2003–2004
Forrester Research *Many Devices, One Consumer*	Three-quarters of U.S. households will have at least one "internet-capable" device.		2005
British wireless carrier Vodaphone	More than **200 million** Europeans (85 percent of the market) will have WAP phones.		2003
Cap Gemini Ernst & Young		Mobile e-business revenues in Europe will reach **$70 billion**.	2005

This book is not about mobile commerce (also known as m-commerce) despite all these users and dollar amounts. We believe that Pocket PCs and other mobile devices will be used in traditional commerce as well as in new, innovative business models. Products and services that can be obtained and provided from anywhere at anytime, are likely to be involved in mobile commerce. However, mobile commerce will not, to any larger extent, happen anytime soon – something the analyst firms seem to agree upon. In contrast, mobile solutions implemented for improved efficiency and faster turnaround times are in use already today.

There are primary reasons why m-commerce will not happen anytime soon:

> However, mobile commerce will not, to any larger extent, happen anytime soon – something the analyst firms seem to agree upon. In contrast, mobile solutions implemented for improved efficiency and faster turnaround times are in use already today.

- Habit – Even "traditional" internet commerce geared towards the end consumer struggles with trying to break old "in-person"-shopping habits. Mobile commerce has the same challenge: how to get the consumer comfortable with using a mobile device to make purchases, breaking habits and getting used to new ones takes time.

- **Immature technologies** – Wireless networks are not yet readily available everywhere. Where they do provide coverage, the bandwidth is severely limited leading to frustrating wait times and significant communications cost. WAP over promised and under delivered throughout its entire architecture – a clear example of immature technology in the mobile industry.

- **Few user-friendly and affordable mobile devices** – The Pocket PCs are the most user-friendly mobile devices to date. There is definitely room for improvement, but the platform is well ahead of its competition. Pocket PCs need to come down in price, continue the convergence with mobile telephony and most importantly become readily available in the retail channel.

Our advice is, from the business side of mobile solutions, to focus on what brings value now – not tomorrow. The company that successfully implements mobile solutions for improved efficiency is in many ways well prepared for tomorrow's mobile revenue streams. Not only has this company been able to improve its efficiency through the use of mobile computing, but also its readiness, decision-making, experiences, and infrastructure are already in place when m-commerce takes off!

The other of the two types of mobile solutions, and what the rest of this book is all about, is the "mobile enterprise solutions."

What drives the mobile solution growth?

There are a number of driving factors and trends behind the growth of mobile solutions. Figure 2.2 illustrates some of the most significant.

To stay competitive a company has to continuously improve its offerings and its operations. Growth in mobile solutions is seen as largely due to the desire of businesses to gain the competitive lead, obtain new revenue channels, as well as improve productivity and efficiency for a workforce that is increasingly mobile.

A major driving factor behind mobile solutions is the convergence between the internet and mobile devices. Microsoft mobile platform strategy favors the view that, in the mix of products resulting from this ongoing convergence, one type of device will not fit all needs. During 2001 we saw the strategy span across a wide range of devices:

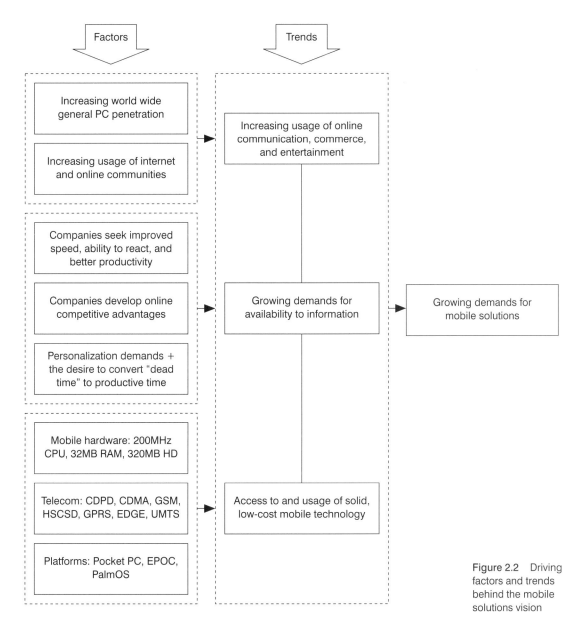

Figure 2.2   Driving factors and trends behind the mobile solutions vision

- Simple cell phones, with thin WAP and web micro browsers (Sony CMD-Z5, etc.)
- Cell phones with near Pocket PC-like functionality (such as the Microsoft product code-named "Stinger")
- Pocket PCs with built-in cell phones (Sagem WA3050, Mitsubishi Trium Mondo, etc.)

Figure 2.3 Mobile devices converge with each other and with the internet

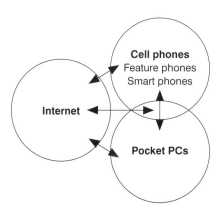

In your work designing and developing solutions you must never lose sight of the user. This is true regardless of whether you plan to design a mobile consumer solution for the masses or a solution aimed at only a few people in one company department. When you combine this awareness of the user with the understanding of the pros and cons of each type of device and protocol, you are well prepared to design your solution platform. Based on these statements we ask you to consider the following:

> **However, mobile does not exclusively mean WAP. There is only one internet, and it is *the* internet.**

As cell phones and Pocket PCs converge, don't be too focused on the "WAP people." The "WAP people" refers to the WAP phone manufacturers, carriers, and cell phone network operators, and all those who used the last two years hyping WAP as *the* "Mobile Internet" technology. However, mobile does not exclusively mean WAP. There is only one internet, and it is *the* internet. In most people's minds the internet means the web and, in all relevant aspects, the internet experience is based on the web. The WAP backlash that the industry headed into during 2000 is partly due to this highly questionable marketing by "the WAP people."

The internet penetration (percentage of population using the internet) is in most western countries more than 50 percent. The combination of the high internet penetration and the increasing number of mobile phones users is driving the demand for mobile access to products and services. It is understandable that the "WAP world" wishes to capitalize on this ongoing convergence, but at this time the "mobile internet" WAP isn't mature enough to deliver on its promises.

We concur that WAP can effectively be used for simple, mass market, consumer oriented services. However, the inherent limitations of WAP such as poor user interface, inferior input facilities as well as the fundamental platform issues including the requirement of new hardware, gateways, tools, and technologies, are severely impacting the feasibility of WAP.

Also consider that most mobile enterprise solutions require support for disconnected scenarios. This means that the solution has to provide functionality outside of wireless coverage and hence server connection. WAP does not cut it for many enterprise solutions.

The key conclusion is not that you should not consider WAP. The key conclusion is that whatever mobile platform you intend to use to realize a mobile solution has to embrace a multi-channel approach when dealing with the different types of mobile clients. Multi-channel architecture supports multiple types of devices, protocols, and content formats. In succeeding chapters you will get the real details about how to deal with multi-channel issues.

In contrast to WAP, the Pocket PC supports the real online internet (web) you and your users know, via Internet Explorer for the Pocket PC, WAP (using third-party browsers) as well as off-line support for disconnected usage. The Pocket PC platform, although it is not yet sold in comparable volumes as cell phones and cheaper digital PIMs, is a premiere platform from the perspective of the enterprise mobile solutions.

> "The Pocket PC platform, although it is not yet sold in comparable volumes as cell phones and cheaper digital PIMs, is a premiere platform from the perspective of the enterprise mobile solutions."

2.3 What exactly *are* mobile enterprise solutions?

During the past year, we've met hundreds of corporate clients and worked through a number of business and mobile technology workshops. In one of our most recent workshops a gentleman raised his hand and asked: "What *is* a mobile solution?" At times there is a risk of taking too many terms and definitions for granted. The question was sincere and the time it took to provide the definition was well spent for all workshop participants. It is important to sometimes stop for a minute to consider even what seems to be very basic. This is true especially in areas dominated by hype and prophesies rather than reality and what's viable today.

Our definition of a mobile solution in the enterprise is by no means a scientific or industry standard. We derive the definition from the sum of the mobile projects that we've been involved in.

> *A mobile solution is technology enabling a user to digitally participate in business processes regardless of location.*

A mobile solution is technology enabling a user to *digitally* participate in business processes regardless of location. The mobile solution may support wireless connectivity, although it does not have to. It does not require wired connectivity, although it might.

Note

From a business solution standpoint, a mobile solution is likely to encompass strategy and process support – not just technology. Keep in mind, though, that technology is *the* key enabler.

To be able to be online from anywhere, using unlimited wide area wireless bandwidth is a commonly depicted scenario. But since widespread wireless use won't be realized very soon we emphasize that mobile solutions should not have to rely on being constantly online. A mobile platform for your solution needs to support disconnected scenarios. The future will be *both online and off-line, just as today.*

Another very important factor in mobile solutions is the ability to enable *information needs at anytime, from anywhere.* Wireless networks are not ubiquitous. So, in order to maximize the value of a mobile solution, from a connectivity standpoint, you need to include both local off-line as well as remote online access.

There has been a significant shift in the attitude towards mobile devices just in recent months and the introduction of the Pocket PC has been a deciding factor in this shift. The shift is about whether a mobile device is just a digital calendar or if it is a vital element of an enterprise extension of process and system. The Pocket PC embraces both connected and disconnected scenarios, which mean that the platform adheres to the value-adding factor: *information available at anytime, from anywhere.*

> *Rolling out Pocket PCs will bring mobile calendar, e-mail, and note taking capabilities to a work force, but these do not drive business benefits. A true mobile mindset considers the Pocket PCs to be portable 'containers' for mobile solutions, not just regarded as digital calendars and notebooks.*

Rolling out Pocket PCs will bring mobile calendar, e-mail, and note taking capabilities to a work force, but these do not drive business benefits. A true mobile mindset considers the Pocket PCs to be portable "containers" for mobile solutions, not just regarded as digital calendars and notebooks.

Field service

This book's sample code illustrates one of the most easy-to-understand business processes; field service. Field service is about fixing things in a planned maintenance schedule or because of a breakdown situation. The efforts involved have to be carefully noted, in terms of steps taken, the time and effort required, as well as parts used. At the end of the process, an invoice is usually created and the customer receives the invoice.

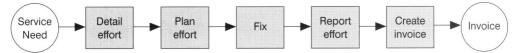

Figure 2.4 Generic field service process

Field technicians everywhere around the globe, with or without mobile solutions, perform these general functions. A mobile solution supports their work and information needs, the chain of events necessary to their tasks, and enables the field technician to be digitally a part of all these events. In addition, the field technician can play an active, connected role in processes such as record keeping, billing, accounting, and customer service. For example, just after the service need has been detected, by schedule or by a customer call, the most experienced field technician, equipped with a Pocket PC, can from anywhere play a crucial role in determining the efforts required before they are committed.

For example, a mobile solution can, from a field service core perspective, provide the field technician with exact stock levels or expected availability of parts when the technician is out in the field. It can also estimate installation times for the part, and thus accurate expected completion times can be given to the customer. For more complex routines the mobile solution can even provide step-by-step instructions to the field technician.

Once the work is done, the mobile solution can be used to note the parts replaced and the time required. Once transmitted to the office, the completed work order immediately triggers sending an invoice to the customer, with no extra administration. A digital dataflow means faster turnaround.

The more information systems can capture business data at the point of origin and in every interaction with worker, customer, and partner, the more value they provide. Mobile solutions are key enablers to more effective business processes and better customer service, since they speed up and simplify entire processes from beginning to end.

These features do not only enable the field technician to play an active role in the business processes wherever he or she may be; they enable the rest of the company to participate in the actual field service activities, as well. The field technician can, using a Pocket PC, consult with product experts via the corporate network, in real time. No longer is it just the lonely field technician at the customer's site. The collective knowledge of the entire team of experienced

> 66 The field technician can, using a Pocket PC, consult with product experts via the corporate network, in real time. No longer is it just the lonely field technician at the customer's site. The collective knowledge of the entire team of experienced specialists can be there too. 99

specialists can be there too. The data collected out in the field can, in real-time, be analyzed by managers and responsible supervisors. Service levels can be upheld and monitored on minute-by-minute basis for excellent customer satisfaction.

Note

Our professional experience indicates that a mobile solution in field service leads to:

- A 30 to 40 percent reduction in field service back office support.
- Two- to three-day decrease in invoice cycle.
- Improvement of 15 to 20 percent in field service productivity.

The digitalization of data collection, processing, and management is driven by the fact that a number on a piece of paper is a one-way ticket to nowhere, while a figure stored digitally is the beginning of strategic thinking. This is an old truth within the entire IT industry, but it is not until the user is enabled to capture, use, and easily share data and information from anywhere that we can close the circle.

Business operations go mobile

Field service is one of many common but highly relevant types of business operations where mobile solutions will provide significant value. Among these other types of business operations we want to highlight uses in these workgroups and industries:

- **Sales force** – the sales team could access vital data about their customers on a Pocket PC with up-to-date information, wherever they happen to be. Accurate product, order, and stock level information could be communicated to the customer during meetings at the customer's site. Orders could be taken and processed immediately, resulting in a significant reduction in stock held once a mobile solution has been implemented. As with field service, we see a 15 to 20 percent reduction in sales force back office support using a mobile sales force solution. The sales force productivity is likely to increase because of fewer back-to-base visits. But most importantly the digitalization of customer information turns it into a corporate asset – not just the asset of individual salespeople.

- **Manufacturing and production** – Manufacturing and production planning, in any industry, is an extremely intense business. Production tuning constantly preoccupies engineers and production managers, as well as IT specialists. Regardless of how smooth other parts of an enterprise company in a manufacturing business run, profitability is severely hurt if the actual manufacturing does not run well. More accurate production and scheduling decisions can be made when data is available in real-time. Eliminating paper forms and digitizing data capture in these scenarios prove to be very valuable. A production plant is an ideal location for connecting Pocket PCs using a wireless LAN. The geographical limitations of a wireless LAN are not an issue when the users stay within a given location. Production details can be captured on the floor and transmitted from the Pocket PC wirelessly to the number crunching back office systems. Updated machine and staff schedules, stock levels, and the next steps in production cycles are easily available from anywhere on the floor.

- **Research and development** – Mobile solutions in research and development (R&D) address much the same issues as for manufacturing and production but with even more intensity. The manual management of forms and test scores are still prevalent in the systematic R&D approach in the medical, technical, chemical, and biological labs. That more than 70 percent of all data errors in corporate databases can be blamed on the manual entering of paper-based data is a pretty strong business case in itself for a mobile solution in the lab environment. Researchers can then spend more time in qualitative analysis instead of doing double entry paper work.

- **Health care** – IT efforts in health care is a huge business. IT spending in this sector, in the U.S. for 2001, is projected at $30 billion according to Dataquest, a technology consulting firm. This is up from $15 billion in 1997. Mobile health care solutions provide practitioners with instant access to patient records, medication history, lab values, chart notes, from anywhere.

Most apparently, point-of-care digital data access and record keeping means less paper work for practitioners and more time available for patients. Mobility bridges the gap between practitioners and patient information databases. The scenes in which mobile health care applications can be implemented are numerous, as are the types of users.

Automatic alerts based on newly updated patient information can be transmitted and received by connected hospital staff. Paper-based patient records that were once updated during ward rounds can be made immediately available throughout the hospital, as data is captured using a connected Pocket PC. In many countries, there is a trend towards providing treatment in the patient's home whenever possible. Commonly, the mobile nurses carry patient records on paper. After each day, the nurse spends a significant amount of time re-entering the patient data at the hospital – an activity that could be eliminated if the nurse had captured the patient data digitally in the first place.

> The reason why mobile solutions in the enterprise hold such solid promise is that they enable today's activities to take place more efficiently and more effectively, anywhere. "

The reason why mobile solutions in the enterprise hold such solid promise is that they enable today's activities to take place more efficiently and more effectively, anywhere. Furthermore, we believe that the first wave of mobile solutions will not revolutionize businesses or systems. Rather, they will extend existing processes and systems by making them available to a mobile workforce.

2.4   What does this mean for me?

Think about your own business for a while. Where can mobile solutions add value in your own business? The following questions will be helpful as you ponder this important question:

Paper-based forms

1 List five vital activities in your company that rely on paper-based forms and manual data collection.

2 Write down how many individuals who will be involved in processing the paper-based data on its way to corporate IS/IT systems.

3 List the three most important benefits that would be derived if these forms were made digital and available online, in real-time, from anywhere.

Business operations

1 Describe scenarios in which mobile availability of systems and business processes can add efficiencies in your organization.

   – Do processes change or simply move faster because of increased mobility?
   – How much time can be saved using a mobile solution in these scenarios?

2 Define knowledge management processes in your company where you can connect the need for the knowledge and information, at the precise time and place it is needed, using a mobile solution.

3 How can you enable your company's management to make better decisions?

   – Describe what key indicators and reports make a difference if they could be available anytime and from anywhere.

Customer and partner questions

Start with the assumption that your customer and partner want to reach your services or products from anywhere. The idea is to make services and products available to customers anytime, any place.

1 List the services and information that is *regularly* sought by your customers and partners.

2 Describe the competitive advantage your business would have if your offerings were available without limitation of time and place.

Regardless of the conclusions that you reach by working through these questions we urge you not to start with the scenario most difficult to implement. Instead follow this path:

- Pick the no-brainer and break it down into small pilot projects.
- Put together a core team with two business-oriented colleagues that are knowledgeable about the part of the business that you wish to "mobilize"; include yourself and two fellow developers.
- Make sure that you can deliver the solution within one month. This means that you have to manage the scope of the project really well.
- Use the system architecture blueprint found in this book's sample code.

2.5   Conclusion

You will walk on well-trod paths if you choose to go through these lists of questions and follow the steps above. The next chapter tells you how to systematically plan, design, and develop your own successful Pocket PC mobile enterprise solution.

Learning Pocket PC development from an enterprise perspective

In this chapter we will describe the solution definition methodology and the approach we recommend when embarking on a Pocket PC-targeted solution. After a brief examination of the architecture for a mobile application, you'll find guidelines and additional considerations that can be incorporated into your standard team practices.

3.1   It all begins with good system architecture

We found an old picture from early 1999 describing the overview of the Windows DNA platform (see Figure 3.1).

Most of the thinking in this picture still applies. Note especially that in the presentation tier there is already a small thing looking much like a Pocket PC, even if the Pocket PC can be both a "thin" (online) and a "rich" (off-line) client.

The idea behind this architecture was that presentation, business, and data logic should be separated. The business logic tier implements our business logic in the form of modular components, and in the data tier we persist our data in numerous ways. The presentation tier handles user interaction in a number of different ways. It could be anything from a traditional, rich (fat) client executable to a simple (thin) web page in a browser.

The placement of the Pocket PC client in the presentation tier might mislead you that all this book is about is the programming of a new client

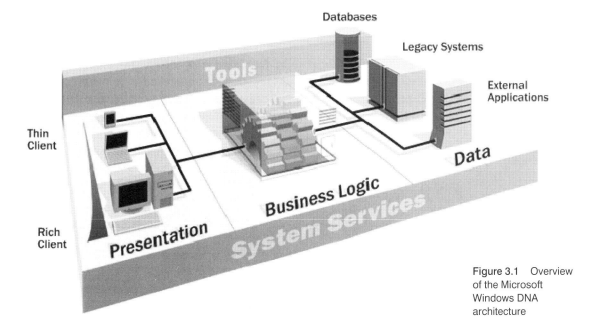

Figure 3.1 Overview of the Microsoft Windows DNA architecture

as only a presentation tier component. To a certain extent it is true: The Pocket PC is just another client along with an increasing number of other clients. However, to build enterprise applications we have to consider the whole picture. Pocket PCs span all the way from the data tier to the presentation tier. All enterprise applications start with a solid architecture covering all the tiers; a mobile application will only extend this architecture to cover mobile clients capable of connecting to this complete architecture.

The attentive reader will also notice an interesting detail in the picture. The business logic tier is connected to all the presentation tier clients. This means that the same components in the business logic tier will connect to the various clients in much the same way. Not very many business logic components today have this capability, allowing numerous clients to connect to the same business logic components in a unified way. This type of architecture is generally called *component based*. The reason why component-based development is so important is that we do not want to implement new components in the business logic tier for each added client. As more and more clients are added, we have to consider ways to connect various clients to the same business logic and data.

> "All enterprise applications start with a solid architecture covering all the tiers; a mobile application will only extend this architecture to cover mobile clients capable of connecting to this complete architecture."

With mobile solutions added to this picture, we want to call this architecture **multi-channel** component-based architecture. The addition of multi-channel is important as it highlights that the communication between client and component can occur over different protocols and use different content formats. The same or similar content is transformed to fit different clients. This transformation is the key in a multi-channel strategy. You can read more about multi-channel architectures in Chapter 8.

> **Note**
>
> The term *multi-channel strategy* derives from the view that businesses in the new economy will not consider adding a new technology on a replacement "or/else" basis, but rather on a "both/and" view. This means that we will be well prepared to add new technology, especially when talking about new clients, if we consider providing client-independent data from our business logic components. A key enabling technology here is Extensible Markup Language (XML).

Let us take a quick tour through the architecture. The basic attributes of the mobile platform as a whole mean that it is meant to support:

● Development of distributed applications

● Integration with existing systems

● A common component model through all tiers

● Choice of the programming language to be used.

The presentation tier offers a choice to develop everything from traditional Windows applications to web applications viewed through a simple web browser. A number of levels between those extremes are enabled through scripting (JavaScript, VBScript, DHTML, XML DOM, etc.) and client components (Java Applets, ActiveX controls, etc.).

The application logic tier offers a number of services for component (COM+, resource and transaction management) and message handling (MSMQ, XML; application integration). Here is also the support for web applications (Internet Information Services; WWW, FTP, ASP, and so forth). You can read more about accessing server components from Pocket PC in Chapter 7.

The data tier offers the availability of many types of data sources. Based on earlier API-based standards (ODBC) Microsoft has developed a more general and component-based (ADO/OLE-DB) way of accessing data sources. The data sources can be relational database, but could as well be the e-mail system, a directory (LDAP) or the basic file system. Today, there is also a built-in support for XML. You can read more about Pocket PC databases in Chapter 6.

The basic system services are services for networks, communication, and security. Built-in directory services (Active Directory) and a set of solid and integrated administration tools also comprise the package. And you'll find support in all the development tools (Microsoft Visual Studio) offering the possibility to develop parts of the system for all three tiers. This is focused on supporting an iterative and team-based process for component-based development. The tools offer a native way of utilizing the built-in functionality in the system services and the various products.

> 66 As we go through the architecture you will notice that much the same technology is used in the Pocket PC platform. You are capable of writing both rich client applications as well as using Internet Explorer for the Pocket PC as a thin client. 99

As we go through the architecture you will notice that much the same technology is used in the Pocket PC platform. You are capable of writing both rich client applications as well as using Internet Explorer for the Pocket PC as a thin client. Through third-party tools, you can use the business logic implemented in components as well as in other applications services. As you even have access to the middleware components for data access (ADOCE/OLE-DB) you are well prepared to work with various kinds of data sources – locally on the device (Access and SQL Server for Windows CE) as well as distributed (like a SQL Server 2000 database).

With some third-party add-on tools, like Odyssey Software's ViaXML, you can even have peer-to-peer access, in other words, Pocket PC to Pocket PC. You can read more about things to come in Chapter 12.

You have access to some of the same basic system services for networking, communication, and security. When it comes to the development tools, there is currently a set of separate tools for Pocket PC-based development.

The tools to target the Pocket PC are called Microsoft eMbedded Visual Tools and are derived but stand-alone from the tools provided in Microsoft Visual Studio 6.0. The tools included are eVB (Microsoft eMbedded Visual Basic 3.0) and eVC (Microsoft eMbedded Visual C++ 3.0). The IDE in eVB is very similar to that experienced with VB (Microsoft Visual Basic 6.0). The event-driven programming model is the same. The forms and controls paradigm is the same and most of the basic language syntax is the same. This means that the possibility to reuse interface designs and even code that you have built already is huge. You can actually copy and paste the code from existing VB applications into eVB and you will be off building your first mobile application in a snap. You can read more about these tools in Chapter 4 and also how to get started using them in Chapter 5.

Note

The most common language used to design and develop corporate solutions is Visual Basic. This is the reason you will not find any Visual C++ code in this book. However, in some projects and at times (although very rarely), we need to go beyond the capabilities of Visual Basic. So, make sure you retain your Visual C++ skills!

> **Our main message is that what you already know is the most important part of building well-designed mobile solutions.**

Our main message is that what you already know is the most important part of building well-designed mobile solutions – you know the Windows DNA platform (or Web Solution Platform as it has recently been renamed by Microsoft). You have the skills to create solid architectures and you already know the tools to implement the applications. You are ready to go, and we will guide you along.

3.2   IT architecture bridges the gap between business and technology

Mobile: Second wave of integration

Increasing numbers of businesses go online to reap the fruits of connectivity and global presence. The convergence between business processes and online connectivity drives the first major wave of integration in the New Economy. The software development projects supporting integration between business and web have proved system integration to be a critical success factor. Since most businesses today use information systems to support their internal and external operations, going online includes the integration of web applications and back office information systems.

> **The convergence between business processes and online connectivity drives the first major wave of integration in the New Economy.**

From a "business-meets-mobility" point of view, there is a lot to learn from past experiences when business first met the web. Clearly, the integration between business process and mobility drives the second wave of integration in the New Economy. From a business perspective, the major goal of a mobile solution is to enable each user and the entire business to operate and function – anywhere. Once again, since most businesses already use information systems to support their internal and external operations; the effort of going *mobile* includes the integration of mobile solutions and back office information systems.

According to the report "Best of European e-commerce" from Forrester Research, 45 percent of the costs in e-commerce projects are related to systems integration. Don't let it surprise you that integration costs will play a major part in your projects. This means that you should carefully examine what can be reused from recent business and system integration efforts within past web-development projects. Reuse and development efficiency require careful planning. These critical aspects, along with many more, can and should be addressed in a business and technology blueprint – an IT system architecture plan.

Evolution instead of revolution

This book is not about a revolution. Going mobile does not mean a revolution for most corporations. The real power of a corporate, mobile solution is based on a "business as usual" approach.

Processes will improve, availability will increase, competitive advantages will be gained; but rather in an evolution format than a revolution. The value of an enterprise mobile solution increases with its ability to provide a natural "anywhere extension" of existing business processes.

An IT architecture study is an essential part of a mobile solutions project to ensure a successful implementation. Business and technology aspects of the mobile evolution are carefully studied and defined before any code gets written.

> **"** Processes will improve, availability will increase, competitive advantages will be gained; but rather in an evolution format than a revolution. The value of an enterprise mobile solution increases with its ability to provide a natural 'anywhere extension' of existing business processes. **"**

3.3   Pocket PC solution definition method

This book introduces the Pocket PC solution definition method as a structured approach for guiding the project preparations from early explorations of Pocket PC technologies, through business analysis, to a documented business case, prototype, and project plan. A development and implementation project can be initiated immediately after the solution definition process is finished. In fact, it is a full development and implementation project that is meant to actually build the Pocket PC solution, the Pocket PC solution definition efforts should be held on an overview level.

A mobile solution project needs to be staffed by one project manager, one workshop facilitator, at least three people with experience and knowledge about the business, one IT architect, and one Pocket PC technical lead. The IT architect and Pocket PC technical lead can be one and the same person.

The Pocket PC solution definition process emphasizes business as well as technology aspects of the solution at an early stage. The method uses parallel IT architecture design processes to enable the results to be achieved rapidly after the full Pocket PC solution definition has been completed.

Figure 3.2 The Pocket PC solution definition method

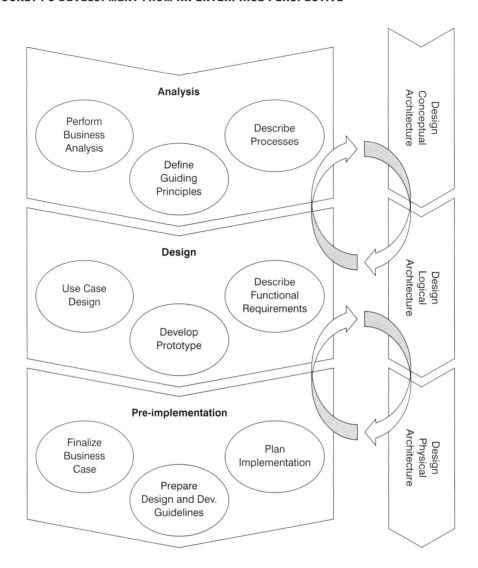

The Pocket PC solution definition method (Figure 3.2) offers the ability to analyze, visualize, and prepare for the opportunity to design and develop a Pocket PC solution for a chosen scenario. As you can see, the IT architecture efforts run parallel to the Pocket PC solution definition, although the architecture process communicates and works with the main activities in the Pocket PC solution definition.

Pocket PC solution definition steps

The main activity in each step in the Pocket PC solution definition is a one-day workshop where the entire project team meets. This means that you will need at least three one-day workshops to finish. It is important that the workshop facilitator is well prepared before each workshop. It is a good idea to allow one to two weeks between each workshop, because of the efforts required in between.

1. Analysis

The project team has most likely already established an idea about where a Pocket PC solution can add value to the business. The questions in the upcoming section *What Does This Mean For Me?* may help define the business context of the Pocket PC solution.

The business analysis step prepares for the actual definition of the Pocket PC solution, and develops vital insights about the business issues, objectives, and priorities.

The objectives of the first workshop are to:

- Describe the business context for the Pocket PC solution.
- Define the scope of the processes (current and future) that need to be supported.
- Prepare the architecture design activities for the Pocket PC solution by defining guiding principles. The architecture efforts need the business context information gathered here to start the conceptual architecture cycle.

Since this is the first workshop, it is not certain that everyone in the project team is aware of all the capabilities of a Pocket PC solution. Since it is necessary to understand what it can do for your business before everyone begins focusing on the particular solution at hand, it is recommended to spend the first two hours walking through the value of the Pocket PC mobile platform, such as you read earlier in this chapter. This should be done on a conceptual level, explaining what can be achieved – instead of explaining all the technical details about the platform.

The next topic in the workshop is about defining the business context. It is important to know where and what the businsess issues and challenges are, *and* what are the cost and revenue aspects will be.

During the workshop the team should agree on the scope of the processes that need to be supported, on a business activity and individual actor (role) level.

By defining guiding principles the team identifies the business objectives that are to drive the development of the solution and solve the business problem(s) identified. Guiding principles address business and technology challenges and form the basis of the solution. Examples of guiding principles can be:

- Improved field force productivity by *x* percent
- Decreased back office manual labour by *x* hours per week
- Faster billing process by *x* days
- Increased job satisfaction by *x* percent
- Maximized reuse of existing IT infrastructure – or efficient replacement and upgrade of existing IT infrastructure
- Improved system performance by *x* seconds per page view
- Improved scalability
- And so on

Table 3.1   Analysis workshop deliverables

A documented business context for the Pocket PC solution
Identification of the processes supported by the solution
A prioritized list of principles that the solution must adhere to
First deliverables of the conceptual architecture

2. Design

Hold the second workshop in the next step, to work on the design for the solution. Documentation from the first workshop includes what the solution needs to address. The conceptual architecture cycle has begun, the architect should be present to gain further input from this second workshop.

Describe functional requirements

The map of processes and activities produced during the first workshop can help the group identify what the high level functional requirements are and where each software feature needs to be available. The project team jointly identifies what back office systems need to be integrated with the new mobile solution.

The "high" in high level functional requirements indicates that the team should spend no more than three to four hours documenting the functional requirements. These are then used when adding more detail in the use case design. The workshop facilitator assists the team in describing the Pocket PC user, back office user, and other roles' use cases. The use case documentation should include a high level user interface representation.

At the conclusion of the workshop session, the technical lead will have the documentation necessary to, within two to three days, put together a Pocket PC-targeted prototype that illustrates the design of the solution.

The deliverables of this workshop then move to the conceptual and logical architecture cycles.

Table 3.2　Design workshop deliverables

Functional requirements
Use case documentation
Prototype completed
Finalized conceptual architecture
First deliverables of the logical architecture

3. Pre-implementation

The purpose of this workshop and step is to prepare development and implementation of the Pocket PC solution that has been defined and built by now in a prototype state.

The workshop begins with the technical lead demonstrating the Pocket PC solution prototype. The workshop facilitator collects the feedback from the rest of the team. If necessary, amendments to the prototype are planned during this workshop.

The business case quantifies the solution's value propositions and motivates the development of the defined solution. Clearly, this is where many great ideas fail. At the end of the day, someone will have to fund the project. Usually this someone will not spend any money unless a great looking business case is presented. Therefore the team has to spend the time to put together the business case. The business case should include quantified tangible and intangible benefits and the costs (very tangible) of the defined solution and hopefully show a worthwhile bottom line benefit.

The team needs to outline what the next steps are, the timeline, milestones, and determine the deliverables, and what resources will be required. Overview design and development guidelines are produced. The results of the outline and guidelines will feed into the creation of the Pocket PC solution project plan.

Table 3.3   Pre-implementation workshop deliverables

Business case

Overview development and implementation plan

Design and development guidelines

Finalized logical architecture

Finalized physical architecture

IT architecture in the Pocket PC solution definition method

Systematic efforts are required to reach to an IT architecture that is designed to support core business processes and solve real business issues. As stated earlier, a successful design for mobile solution has to include multi-channel strategy.

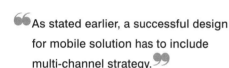As stated earlier, a successful design for mobile solution has to include multi-channel strategy.

The special signature features of an architecture that includes a multi-channel strategy are the need to implement *channel adaptation services* and most often also *user profile services*.

- *Channel adaptation services* provide availability to information systems and content to different types of devices. Each type of device is regarded as a channel and the IT architecture has to determine how the information system functionality and content gets adapted to each channel, in the aspects of screen size, input, local data store facilities, and so on.

- A *user profile* spans the channels and device types currently available to each user. The profiles are fundamental to selecting the modes of interaction with the user.

The driving idea behind a multi-channel strategy is that corporate information systems have to be available across a wide range of mobile devices.

UMTS Forum articulates the following about the multitude of channels.

"Critical success factors for creating a mobile data mass market include access to all types of information in a format appropriate to each type of terminal and the right diversity of products (including terminals) to accommodate all types of users and usage."   Source: UMTS Forum, Report No 11

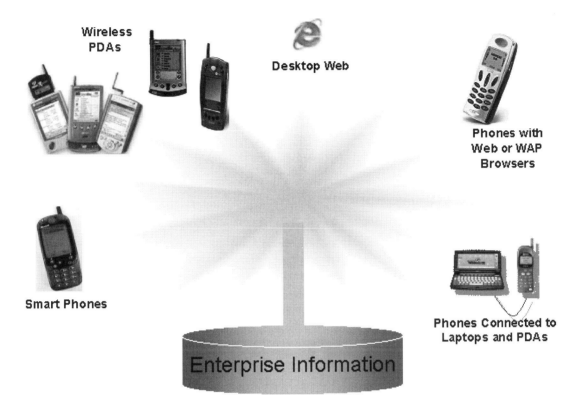

Figure 3.3
Information systems
availability across
many mobile channels

The systematic approach to defining a business supporting IT architecture includes the grouping of the architecture design activities into three distinct and separate cycles:

- **Conceptual Architecture Cycle** – The objective of the conceptual architecture cycle is to answer the question *"What* needs to be designed and developed to meet the business requirements?"* Business principles and strategies are gathered during this cycle.

- **Logical Architecture Cycle** – The objective of the Logical Architecture Cycle is to answer the question *"How* should the architecture be designed and developed to meet the business requirements?"* Required information system resources are defined during this cycle.

- **Physical Architecture Cycle** – The objective of the physical architecture cycle is to answer the question *"With what* should the architecture be designed and developed to meet the business requirements?"* Required products, standards, and technologies are defined during this cycle.

Conceptual architecture cycle

The conceptual architecture cycle answers the question: "*What* needs to be designed?" The business principles and objectives that the solution must address are the basis for answering the question. Some common mobile business principles and objectives are:

- Productivity improvements
- Revenue growth
- Customer offer improvements
- Cost reduction
- Elimination of double data entry
- Increase velocity in communication
- Provide up-to-date information to workforce
- Value-add through personalization
- Ease of use

The documentation of the functional requirements and use cases takes place during the design phase of the Pocket PC solution definition. The core idea in IT architecture is to document how these defined principles and objectives are supported. The first exercise is to map the functional requirements and use case to the defined business principles. The results of such an exercise can look like something like Figure 3.4:

Each use case is mapped to online, off-line, or online *and* off-line support when using the application.

This exercise helps focus the solution to address only the identified business principles. If there is a use case that is difficult to map to a business principle, it is likely superfluous. This type of matrix should be used throughout the three IT architecture cycles to minimize the risk of producing a solution that is technically perfect but still inadequate for the business.

The conceptual architecture cycle also deals with technology principles. Some common mobile technology principles are:

- **Performance** – The function must always be completed within the desired duration (response time).
- **Scalability** – Needs to perform well under load.
- **Development efficiency** – Reuse components already installed and leverage developers' existing skills.
- **Availability** – The function must always be available.
- **Fast restore** – Restoration of corrupted data must be finished as soon as possible.

Use Case	Online/ Off-line	Productivity Improvements	Revenue Growth	Customer Offer	Cost Reduction	Double Data Entry	Communication Speed	Up-to-date Information	Personalization
Mobile field technician									
Download service order	Online	X					X	X	
Complete service order	Off-line					X			
Create service order	Off-line		X			X			
Synchronize service orders	Online	X			X	X	X	X	
Customer									
Online access to service orders	Online		X	X	X		X	X	X
Back office staff									
Create service order	Online	X			X	X		X	
Assign service order to technician	Online	X			X	X	X	X	

Figure 3.4   Mapping use cases to business principles

- **Operational considerations** – The solution needs to be supported and run by defined help desk functions.
- **Content transparency** – Content should be accessible from any device type.
- **Flexibility** – Minimize architectural impact of new releases of supporting information systems.
- **Buy versus Build** – Maximize use of off the shelf software.
- **Interoperability** – Information exchange based on internet standards.
- **Testability** – Components must be tested without interference of the production system.
- **Data up-to-date** – Data must always be up-to-date.

It is important to quantify both the business and technology principles in order to make it possible to measure how they actually are met.

Regardless of how hot and cool Pocket PC solutions are, you need to carefully plan how to run and support the solution. The aspects of running and supporting the mobile solution are also addressed during the conceptual architecture cycle. These are some likely operational considerations:

Table 3.4   Operational considerations

Configuration management		
	Configuration scope	What will be included in the configuration and what is excluded?
	Detail level	Which level of detail is to be used when recording configuration data?
	Tools	Tools to be used to record the configuration.
Incident management		
	Organization	Which organization form will be (is) implemented for the help desk?
	Prioritizing	How will priorities be assigned to incidents? Which forms of escalation are required?
Change management		
Request for change procedure outline		What are the required procedures for change management requests?

cont.

Software distribution

Release strategy	What is the required number of releases per period? What will happen with urgent changes that have to be distributed between releases, or off schedule?
Software distribution strategy	How will software be distributed?

Capacity management

Capacity management approach	To what level of detail should capacity management be approached?
Capacity management organization	Which processes will be implemented: capacity planning, performance management, resource management, demand management, workload management, application dimensioning?

Availability management

Availability management approach	How will availability management be approached?

Cost management

Cost management approach	How will the costs be passed on to the users: real usage prices, distribution of costs per department / user, or other method?

Contingency planning

Contingency planning approach	To what level of detail should contingency planning be approached?
Risks	What are the most significant risks?
Threats	What are the most significant threats?
Vulnerabilities	What are the most significant vulnerabilities?
Counter measures required	Which counter measures are required and have to be implemented?

Security management

Security management approach	How is security management approached or organized: centralized, decentralized, distributed, combinations? Which policies and strategy statements are applicable?

Finally, the conceptual model is visualized in a diagram that includes the users, information systems, where the functionality is available, and what the information flow looks like.

Logical architecture cycle

The logical architecture cycle is about answering the question: "*How* should the solution be designed?" The answer is given by identifying the services that has to be implemented to meet the business and technology principles. Our experience is that these services can be divided into two categories:

- **Common information system architecture services** – These are services that information systems have used and implemented since the Dark Ages of software development.
- **Specific mobile and multi-channel architecture services** – These are new services that are defined by the challenges of mobile access to information systems.

Among the common information system architecture services you will find the following:

- **Integration Services** – Extending processes and systems drives system integration. Integration establishes relationships between parts or entire information systems. Component, messaging, database, and other types of middleware products play a major role in implementing services such as push, pull, log, and integration management.
- **Connectivity Services** – Various types of wireless and wired connectivity.
- **Protocol Services** – Examples are HTTP, WAP, TCP/IP, and so on
- **Security Services** – Authentication, access control, confidentiality, integrity, non-repudiation.
- **Data Store Services** – Disconnected scenarios drive mobile and local data stores.

Note

The reason behind identifying logical information system services first, before choosing products and technologies, is to make sure that the most appropriate products and technologies are chosen based on all known business and technology aspects that need to be supported. The earlier a product and technology is chosen, the larger the risk is that they will limit the solution's ability to meet its requirements. This book is about the Pocket PC platform. Therefore the mobile device is already chosen. The reason that this choice is made early on is that the Pocket PC platform is, current aspects considered, the most viable platform for building mobile enterprise applications.

The specific Mobile and Multi-Channel Architecture Services are:

- **Channel Adaptation Services** – Prepare existing content with different presentations in the various channels.
- **User Profile Services** – The profiles are fundamental to selecting the modes of interaction with the user.

The logical architecture is usually illustrated in three main diagrams:

1 Distribution view

2 Integration view

3 Security view

The *distribution view* contains the users and their locations; servers and their location and information flow between them.

The *integration view* contains the servers and the specific integration services that need to be implemented in and through them.

The *security view* contains the users and their locations, the servers and their locations, the networks that connect the servers with the clients, and most importantly, where each specific type of security service must be implemented. This means that for each architecture element such as server, network, access point, client, and so on, you need to specify what security service is implemented; authentication, access control, confidentiality, integrity, and non-repudiation.

Physical architecture cycle

The physical architecture cycle answers the question: *"With what* should the solution be designed?" It is finally time to put some product names into the architecture.

During the physical architecture cycle you define what products physically implement the logical services: integration mechanisms, information storage environments, physical security specifications, and physical governance specifications.

The major development efforts will be about integrating existing infrastructure that already supports the business, with mobile technologies. The benefits are significant when you leverage the integration between the Pocket PC platform and the framework of products and technologies found in Microsoft's .NET and Microsoft's Web Solution Platform (formerly known as Windows DNA).

The enterprise IT shop that has done its homework has already begun implementing Microsoft's Web Solution Platform for building scalable and

> **"**The reason that this choice is made early on is that the Pocket PC platform is, current aspects considered, the most viable platform for building mobile enterprise applications.**"**

66In short, the system architecture, which defines the Pocket PC as an application client using application logic and databases from a central back-end network of resources, promotes reuse and integration efficiency.99

modular applications. By leveraging these investments and practices, IT shops can get a head start in their mobile development projects.

In short, the system architecture, which defines the Pocket PC as an application client using application logic and databases from a central back-end network of resources, promotes reuse and integration efficiency. The underlying operating system in the Pocket PC (Windows CE 3.0) is integrated with core Microsoft technologies and development tools. The application development tools and languages (eMbedded Visual Tools) are almost identical to ones already existing in the framework of the Web Solution Platform, making the Pocket PC platform ideal for creating mobile solutions in the enterprise.

An overview of the physical architecture description can look something like Table 3.5.

Table 3.5 Physical architecture description

Service		Product / Technology
Development tools		
	Server side	Visual Studio, Visual Studio.NET
	Client side	eMbedded Visual Tools, Visual Studio.NET
Connectivity standards		
	Wireless network	GSM, GPRS, CDPD, CDMA, etc.
	Wired network	Ethernet, Token Ring, etc.
Integration technologies		
	Component technologies	COM+, CLR
	Messaging	MSMQ
	Middleware	Odyssey Software
	Remote access to services and components	SOAP, Web Services, CEfusion, ViaXML, etc

Channel adaptation methods	
Content transformation	XML/XSL, .NET Mobile Forms

Protocol standards	
Wireless	TCP/IP, WAP
Wired	TCP/IP, HTTP

Device data store	
Local relational databases and message queues	SQL Server CE, MSMQ, CEfusion, Object Store, Sybase Anywhere, Oracle Lite, etc.

Security technologies	
Server access control	Firewalls, etc.
device access control	Power on password, smart cards, fingerprint, application passwords
Authentication	Integrated network authentication, application passwords
Confidentiality/integrity	SSL, CryptoAPI, SQL Server CE encryption, Softwinter Sentry 2020, etc.

The physical architecture is usually illustrated in four main diagrams:

1 Distribution view

2 Integration view

3 Security view

4 Deployment view

In essence, these are similar to the logical architecture views, with the addition of the product and technology definitions.

3.4   Parting words about the Pocket PC solution definition method

While the method we've described here is not a silver bullet to building corporate Pocket PC solutions, it does provide you with some basic, common-sense advice that will hopefully prepare you for beginning a successful mobile solution project. Regardless if or how you use the method it contains some heads-up issues that need to be addressed before pulling together costly development resources.

Tools of mobile trade

In this chapter we will look at:

- New tools in your toolbox.
- Differences between the new tools and the ones you've worked with in the past.

You will readily recognize most of what you will see in the mobile development tools – not because you have built many mobile applications before, but because you are used to the Microsoft development tools.

The most important part of a platform for a developer is the programming language. In the new tools that you will learn to know, you will find familiar tools like Visual Basic. Even if there are some differences in the implementation, the core of the tool is the same and all the code you have already written is reusable even in your new tools. You will actually leverage more on what you already know and have done than you will learn and reinvent. This is indeed the Microsoft theme for mobile development, in contrast to many other tool suppliers who expect you to believe that mobile by definition means a brand new set of skills. That is important if you set out to solve an urgent problem rather than wanting to leisurely explore new technology just for fun. In this chapter you will find that you can do both at the same time.

> 66 You will actually leverage more on what you already know and have done than you will learn and reinvent. 99

4.1   Extending your toolkit

As an enterprise developer focusing on the Microsoft toolset, you probably have Visual Studio installed on your PC. The main part of Visual Studio is the development IDE (Integrated Development Environment) and of course the compilers. You also get version control and a number of other tools that come with the toolset. Also, since you are a structured developer you probably have a number of tools for modeling your architectures and systems. Hopefully, you are using UML (Unified Modeling Language) and a UML-enabled tool to document the design for what you intend to do, and to provide documentation for what you have already done. You probably have a methodology for software development and a number of tools associated with that methodology. You have a working toolset.

We tell you this for a reason. We want you to know that to build mobile Pocket PC enterprise solutions you still need your current tools. What you will do is extend your current toolset to include the tools that you need to make your enterprise applications "go mobile." There is no shift of platform or the way you work with development. There is not even a shift in programming language. It's your home ground. The new tools that you need, will not only build on the knowledge that you already have, they even look similar. The main tool for Pocket PC development is called eMbedded Visual Tools, or eVT for short. This is the Visual Studio for Pocket PC developers and it is the tool that you will get to know in this chapter. We think that you will agree that we have not added something new at all to your toolbox, but extended it with something that you almost already know.

4.2   The new tools

When you installed the eVT (eMbedded Visual Tools) you discover that you have the option to install a number of different platforms SDK (Software Development Kits). Even though we will be covering only the Pocket PC SDK here, there are two additional platforms that you can target when developing with eVT. They are: Handheld and Palm-size PCs. In eVT you can build solutions for all of these platforms, but you will have to take device capabilities (screen size, etc.) into account to build applications for multiple devices.

Tip

Even though Pocket PCs have several of these capabilities standardized (screen size is 320 × 240 pixels, etc.) you have to take into account that the different Pocket PC devices have different capabilities. Our recommendation is that if you have users with multiple devices, you should have at least one of each kind when you develop, test, and deploy your applications.

As you will discover the platform SDK for Pocket PC includes an emulator that you can use to test your applications without having a physical device at your disposal. However, as we have pointed out before, we strongly recommend that you have a real Pocket PC for many reasons.

eMbedded Visual Basic

Because most enterprise developers use Visual Basic, we will be providing information in this book primarily to help them. However, much of what is said can be applied to developers using Visual C++ who are moving to eMbedded Visual C++ as well. Another reason for focusing on eVB is that there are already books for eVC programming on Pocket PC. If we may make a recommendation, go and get Chris Muench's *The Windows CE Technology Tutorial* (ISBN: 0-201-61642-4).

A new and familiar IDE

So, let's fire up the new eVB IDE by choosing **Start** > **Programs** > **eMbedded Visual Tools** > **eMbedded Visual Basic 3.0.** After you have selected a project type. For now, just select **Windows CE for the Pocket PC project.** Figure 4.1 shows what you should see.

Hopefully this is a view that you are familiar with. As you see, the form-drawing metaphor is still there. The control toolbox, the project explorer, the properties, and immediate windows are all there. All the things you know are still true. You start developing by creating a number of forms, using a number of controls. Then, create some modules, and you can instantly test how the program runs by compiling and running it. Let's do that!

First, start off by putting a button on the form and enter some simple code, like:

```
Option Explicit
Private Sub Command1_Click()
  MsgBox "Hello!"
End Sub
```

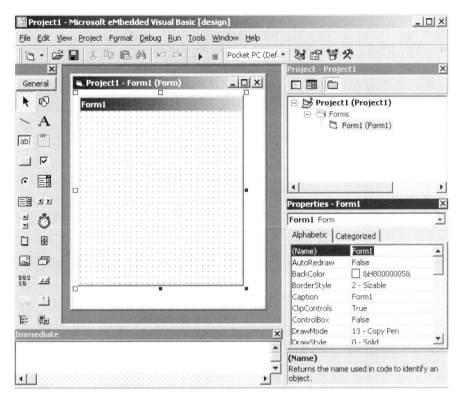

Figure 4.1
eMbedded Visual
Basic IDE

```
Private Sub Form_OKClick()
   App.End
End Sub
```

And then you just press the **run** (▶) icon on the toolbar. The emulator will start and the form will load. When you press the button, you will get the message box with a greeting for you.

Take a moment and be amazed of the fact that you have just launched a mobile application. You are now formally a part of the mobile developer community – be proud! After that you can end the program by tapping the (**OK**) button in the top right corner of your form. If you have a real device and you want to run the same application on the device, just change the ComboBox in the middle of the Standard toolbar of the IDE from **Pocket PC Emulation** to **Pocket PC (Default Device)** and hit the ▶ button again.

Intermediate runtime files

Let us take a moment to consider what really happened behind the scenes. When you pressed the ▶ button in the eVB IDE the first thing that happened was that your program was compiled into a file with the extension

.vb (probably **Project1.vb**). That file, combined with the required runtime files, was then transferred to the device (real or emulated) and then the application was launched. You might wonder why there was not an **.exe** extension on the compiled file, and you probably guessed right. The eVB compiler does not create natively executable files for the Pocket PC. Instead, it creates a semi-compiled script file that is passed to the runtime executable (pvbload.exe in the **Windows** folder).

 Tip

If you are using the emulator, and if during install of the Platform SDK you didn't change the default install folder, you will find the file system root of the device on your hard disk at **C:\Windows CE Tools\wce300\MS Pocket PC\emulation\palm300**. So if you are looking for a file in the **Windows** folder of the emulator device, you can find it at **C:\Windows CE Tools\wce300\MS Pocket PC\emulation\palm300\Windows.**

The eVB compiler is mainly based on VBScript and therefore have some limitations compared to VB 6.0 that we will come back to later in this chapter. And the next thing you might be wondering is, where did the different files that were transferred go? Well, if you didn't change anything before launching the application, the **Project1.vb** file was placed in the **Windows****Start Menu**\ folder. That means that the application is accessible from the Start menu of the device. You can check this by pulling the Start menu down and it will most probably include a **Project1** entry.

Note

Throughout this chapter we are referring to the project as the default name, **Project1**, but of course you would use something more relevant to name for your project. In all references to **Project1**, you will simply have to replace it with your selected project name (and sometimes folder).

Project Properties window

You would most probably like to store the application in a folder of your choice. To change the default destination let us open up the Project Properties dialog (by selecting the menu option **Project > Project1 Properties**). It will look something like Figure 4.20.

As you can see the path we were looking for can be found in the **Remote Path** text box. Normally, you would change this value to any folder under the **Program Files** folder. Note that you have to specify the complete path including the filename of the compiled file (**Project1.vb**). Since we are here let us examine some other new settings compared with VB 6.0. In the same group (Remote Settings) as the Remote Path you also find **Run on Target**, which has the same function as the ComboBox in the Standard toolbar of the IDE.

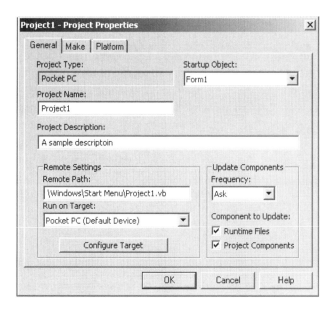

Figure 4.2   Project
Properties dialog

There is also another new group called **Update Components** where you can
specify how the controls, runtime, and the project files (intermediate and
related documents) are transferred to the device (real or emulator). Here you
can also control how the controls are transferred to the device. If you select
to update components (**Frequency** selection **Always** or **Ask**), the controls will
be transferred and registered on the device when you start the application.
Another option to transfer (and register) controls on your Pocket PC is to
use the **Component Manager** (see separate section below).

 Tip

When controls are transferred to the Pocket PC they will be copied for each instance
that they occur – in every form! For a large application, this can take some time and
therefore we recommend that you run the application with **Frequency** set to **Always**
once (or each time you add a control) and when you have compiled the application
(and thereby transferred the controls to the device) you can switch to **Never** to prevent long waits for each compilation (and transfer of controls).

There are some other new options on the **Platform** tab in the Project
Properties dialog to set the default form size and the default target device.
Then, there are a few things that are missing that can be found on **Make**
tab. For example, there is no option to select an application icon. If you
consider that the compiler is not really creating an executable (exe) file,
this may not be so strange. There is no way to include an icon (resource)
that the operating system can extract into the compiled file. So what icon

do you get? Well, since the extension **.vb** is associated with the runtime executable (pvbload.exe) the icon is extracted from this file and it looks much like the icon on VB 6.0. However, in Chapter 11 you will find a solution to this problem by using a launcher application written with eMbedded Visual C++.

Options dialog

Use the eVB **Options** dialog to configure project and environment settings. You find it by choosing **Tools > Options**.

Use the eVB **Options** dialog to configure project and environment settings. You find it by choosing **Tools > Options**. Let's go through the tabs and talk about some of the changes you will note, as compared to your previous work with Visual Basic (see Figure 4.3).

Figure 4.3   Options window

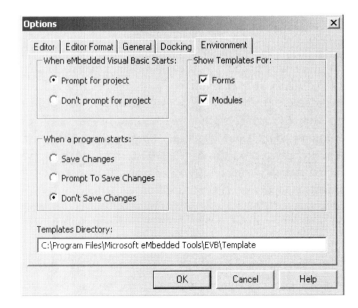

The first two tabs (**Editor** and **Editor Format**) are identical to what you have in VB 6.0.

● However, on the third tab, **General**, all the options for error trapping and compilation on demand are not available. This means that you don't have the option to stop the execution if you have implemented error handling, unless you have set debugging break points.

● In the **Docking** tab you may notice that the **Locals** and **Form Layout** windows are missing. The **Form Layout** window is not really a big loss, since most screens you will create will be run in full screen on the device.

You may very much miss the **Locals** window since it is so valuable to easily and quickly track values of both variables and properties. However, considering the communication needed between the PC and the device to make this information available, there is some logic as to why this feature was not implemented.

- On the **Environment** tab you can also see that there are a number of templates, and thereby project components, missing in eVB. You can only have forms or standard modules. Enterprise developer that you are, the biggest issue is of course that the class modules are missing. This important part of VB 6.0 enables us to write *n*-tier application with presentation in forms, logic in classes and data in a database is missing. We will get back to how to work without this later in this chapter.

- An obvious consequence of missing class modules and the lack of a means to create executable files is the fact that we cannot create (ActiveX) DLLs or custom controls.

- The last difference, the missing MDI Form option is no problem at all, since the concept would not work very well on the small screen of a Pocket PC device.

Controls

If you start examining the toolbox with controls, you'll soon see that the basic set of controls is somewhat reduced compared to VB 6.0. The most important and common controls (Label, TextBox, etc.) are included but the VB 6.0 standard controls for Pictures and File handling have been placed in their own components that you have to include yourself. The optional controls as you see in Figure 4.4 appear in the **Components** dialog (which you get by selecting the menu option **Project > Components...**).

Most of the controls will be familiar to you, but there are also some new ones to mention.

Intrinsic control

The intrinsic, or built-in, controls are the ones that you get when you open a new eVB project without adding any other controls to it. Compared to what you are used to in VB 6.0, you may be missing a number of controls. Table 4.1 gives a list of the different controls in eVB and how they correspond to the VB 6.0 controls.

Figure 4.4
Components dialog

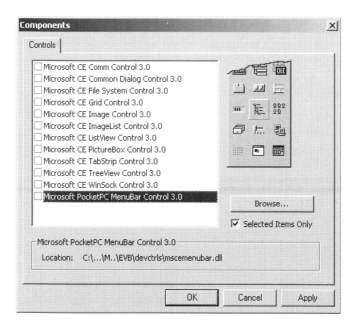

Table 4.1   Controls in common between VB 6.0 and eVB

Control	VB 6.0	eVB
Shape	Intrinsic	Intrinsic
Line	Intrinsic	Intrinsic
Label	Intrinsic	Intrinsic
TextBox	Intrinsic	Intrinsic
Frame	Intrinsic	Intrinsic
CommandButton	Intrinsic	Intrinsic
CheckBox	Intrinsic	Intrinsic
OptionButton	Intrinsic	Intrinsic
ComboBox	Intrinsic	Intrinsic
ListBox	Intrinsic	Intrinsic
HScrollBar	Intrinsic	Intrinsic

VScrollBar	Intrinsic	Intrinsic
Timer	Intrinsic	Intrinsic
PictureBox	Intrinsic	DLL
Image	Intrinsic	DLL
DriveListBox	Intrinsic	–
DirListBox	Intrinsic	–
FileListBox	Intrinsic	–
Data	Intrinsic	–
OLE	Intrinsic	–
Comm	DLL	DLL
CommonDialog	DLL	DLL
File and FileSystem	Built into VB	DLL
Grid	DLL	DLL
ImageList	DLL	DLL
ListView	DLL	DLL
MenuBar	– (ToolBar)	DLL
TabStrib	DLL	DLL
TreeView	DLL	DLL
WinSock	DLL	DLL

As you can see, most of the important controls are still there. If we are talking enterprise applications, our guess is that MenuBars, Labels, TextBoxes, ComboBoxes, CommandButtons, ListViews, and a few CheckBoxes and OptionsButtons will cover most of what you want to do in your applications. As you can see, the MenuBar has no exact match in VB 6.0 (the closest is the ToolBar or possibly the CoolBar), why we will talk more about that control in the next chapter. Another change is that the file manipulation functionality, both for file access (open, input, etc.) and file manipulation (kill, dir, etc.), have been removed from the core language and moved into a separate control that, in turn, actually contains two controls. We will go into this deeper in the next chapter.

Form object

Since you are already coding, let us look at an odd thing in the first code snippet at the beginning of this chapter. As you saw, we responded to an event called **Form_OKClick** and this is a new event. It is related to the new Form property **ShowOK** that controls if there should be an **OK** button (in a circle) at the far right on the form caption in runtime. This new feature has simply one purpose – to save screen space for more important things than OK command buttons.

Another new property on the form is the **SIPVisible** property. As you may be aware, SIP stands for soft input panel and is the means by which your users can input information into your applications. And as you may also be aware, there are several different input panels that you can choose from:

- A character recognizer for handwritten information.
- Tap with a stylus on a software keyboard on-screen.
- Type all over the screen with the stylus. (In order for handwriting to be converted to typewritten information, when writing all over the screen, the user would have to install the free **Transcriber** software.)

To resume, the **SIPVisible** property indicates if the SIP should be visible when the form loads. Another related property is **SIPBehavior** that dictates how the SIP will be activated. It can be activated manually by the user (**vbSIPUser**), or it can occur automatically when the focus is put on a control that enables input, like a TextBox control (**vbSIPAutomatic**) or it could be constantly visible (**vbSIPAlways**).

Another new property is the **FormResize** property. It determines how (or if) the form will be resized after it is loaded. It can be set to size the form as large as possible and resize the form as soon as the SIP is visible (**vbFormFullSIPResize**), to put the SIP on top of it when visible (**vbFormFullNoResize**), or show the form in the size defined at design time or as changed during runtime (**vbFormUserSize**).

A notable difference in the way that you load new forms is that all forms are modeless. The user can always switch to another form by selecting it in the Start > Settings > System > Memory > Running Programs window on the device. Therefore, even if you can add the **vbModal** parameter to the **Show** method on a form, this parameter will be ignored.

Another difference is that you cannot unload a form in runtime. If a form is loaded it will remain in memory until the application is ended. If you want to prevent your users from selecting another form in your application than the one you want them to interact with (compare with the VB 6.0 ShowInTaskBar property on the Form), you will have to use the **Me.Hide** method in your forms code for closing the form (usually this is done in the **Form_OKClick** event code).

A side effect of this is that you have to reset all controls either before the form is shown or before it is hidden. For example, you have a form for searching with one search argument (TextBox) and a results list (ListView). When you have made a search and are about to close (hide) the form, you should clear both the contents of the TextBox and the ListView. The other alternative is to always set these default empty values each time you load the form.

Remote Tools

Let us look at a completely new feature of the IDE called Remote Tools. You access them by selecting the menu option **Tools > Remote Tools**. The main purpose of these tools is to access system information on the Pocket PC. The more interesting Remote Tools for eVB developers are:

- **Registry Editor** – Makes it possible for you to edit the registry on the device.
- **Zoom** – With Zoom you can capture the screen of the device and save or print the resulting bitmap.
- **Configure Platform Manager** – Manage all your devices (even the emulator) connections, etc.
- **Control Manager** – manage which controls are installed on the device.

In the menu you also find the *Application Install Wizard*. You will find more about that tool in Chapter 11.

When you have installed eVT, you will only be able to access the Remote Tools from within eVB (or eVC), but it is often convenient to access these tools directly from the Start menu. We have therefore included the necessary shortcuts on the accompanying CD in folder **\Tips\eVT Tools Shortcuts**. The most important shortcuts you need are shown in Table 4.2. Let's just take a short tour of these tools.

Table 4.2   Shortcuts and target application files

Shortcut	Target
Registry Editor	"C:\Windows CE Tools\BIN\CEREGEDT.EXE"
Zoom	"C:\Windows CE Tools\BIN\CEZOOM.EXE"
Control Manager	"C:\Windows CE Tools\BIN\CECTLMGR.EXE"
App Install Wizard	"C:\Program Files\Microsoft eMbedded Tools\EVB\INSTWZRD.EXE"

Registry Editor

This tool is very similar to its PC equivalent and you can create, update, and delete registry entries (keys) much in the same manner. It also looks much like the Registry Editor that you are used to (see Figure 4.5).

Figure 4.5 Windows CE Remote Registry Editor

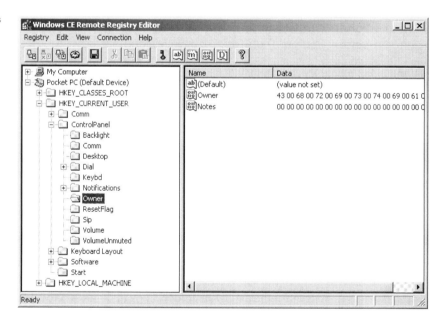

An interesting feature is that you can connect to the registry on multiple machines (different devices) as well as the registry on your PC. You can export registry keys, but unfortunately you cannot import keys. To import keys, there are several third-party tools that you can use (like PHM Registry Editor at www.phm.lu/Products/regedit.asp).

Zoom

This tool can be used to capture screen shots from your device (see Figure 4.6).

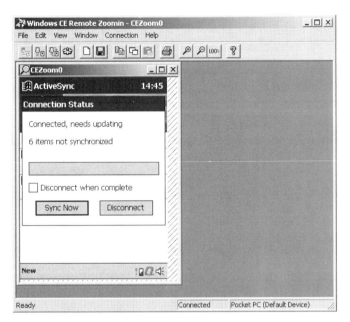

Figure 4.6   Windows CE Remote Zoomin

Even if there are better tools for this purpose, you can do quite a lot with this simple application. You can capture multiple screens and you can save them in bitmap (.bmp) format. You can even print the screen shots directly from this application. The ability to copy a screen shot to the clipboard is also quite useful.

Platform Manager

The Platform Manager can be accessed from several different places in eVT. You can access it from eVB via the menu option **Tools > Remote Tools**. In the Platform Manager you can configure the devices that your system are aware of. All the devices configured in Platform Manager can be selected as target platform for running eVB programs. For each device you select which transfer protocol that the IDE should use to connect to the device. For physical devices, you have the transport options shown in Figure 4.7.

The emulator only uses TCP/IP and to speed development using a physical device you should use TCP/IP for it as well. This is a very powerful tool to test your connection between your PC and the Pocket PC.

Figure 4.7 Platform
Manager tool

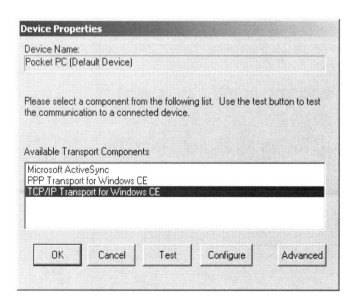

Control Manager

This is the tool where you manage the controls installed on your device. It is shown in Figure 4.8.

Figure 4.8 Windows
CE Control Manager

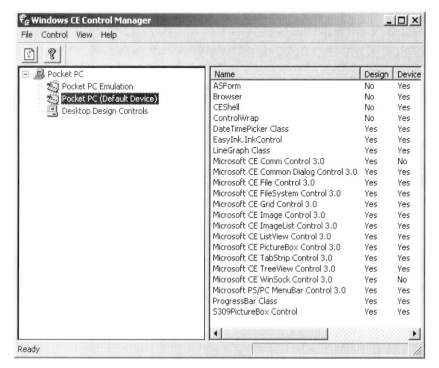

You can see that each control can be available as Desktop Design Controls usable from eVB and also installed on the device. You can add and remove (install and uninstall) controls on each device and you can even add new controls from here.

Debugging

When you want to debug your eVB applications, it is very similar to how you do this in VB 6.0. You set breakpoints where you want. Then you can step through the code as usual. However, there are a few differences that you have to take into account when debugging:

- No change of code

  In contrast to what you might be used to, you cannot change the code during debug of an eVB application. If you need to make any changes, you will simply have to stop the execution and do the changes before you can continue debugging again.

- No skipping over code

  You are not able to skip over execution of any lines of code during debugging. If you need to have this capability you could declare a variable that you set to set to **True** or **False** depending on what you want to do. And then you insert a simple **If** statement based on this variable around the code that you might want to step over.

- No stepping back

  Just as stepping over lines of code, you are not allowed to step back to an already executed line of code when debugging.

- No Debug object

  You cannot use the **Debug.Print** statement in your eVB code. You will not get any error message, but you will not have the desired output in the immediate windows, so there is not much of a point in using it.

- Issue with IntelliSense in immediate windows

  A form that contains controls does not display the code completion for those controls unless the fully qualified path to the control is given.

Some language/syntax differences

In this section, we will discuss some of the differences that we have discovered when developing applications for the Pocket PC. You may also check the Microsoft Knowledge Base articles at **http://support. microsoft.com/ support/kb/articles/Q260/0/80.ASP** for more issues.

● **No class modules**

So, how do you solve the lack of class modules? Well, the short simple answer is – you don't! If you want to layer your application and separate presentation and logic you have to find a custom way to do it.

One simple solution is to put common logic in modules with public functions and "subs" acting as public members of the "class." Let us say that you have some business logic for a Customer, like validation. You could then create a module called **clsCustomer** and implement a public **Validate** function in it. In a form you can then call **clsCustomer.Validate** with the control values as arguments. This is not really either object oriented or component oriented but could work for simple needs. An overall goal is to minimize the need for business logic on the device since it will probably have to be implemented on the server anyhow. The solid answer is that in the not too distant future, we will most probably see this in the next generation of development tools.

● **No User-Defined Types**

In eVB there is no support for UDTs (User Defined Types). We don't know how much you are accustomed to using this functionality, but it usually is more useful when you want to define enumerated values for fields in a database. The substitute for UDTs here is to use public constants instead. The solution is not as neat as it is with UDTs, but it works anyway.

Another important use of UDTs is for calling Windows CE APIs. Many API calls have defined structures (as they are called in eVC) and the only solution for you in eVB is to create strings of bytes matching the binary representation of the UDT that you need. You will see how this is done in the next chapter when we call some APIs for using the DateTimePicker and ProgressBar controls. You do this by using a number of standard functions for converting long and integer values (most common data types in the API structures) to strings of bytes. You can read more about how it works in the excellent article **UDTs (User Defined Types) with VBCE!** by Antonio Paneiro at: **http://www.vbce.com/articles/udt/index.asp**

● **No Format function**

One of the functions that we miss the most in eVB is the **Format** function. However, the situation where you use this function the most is when you want to format date and time values. In eVB you have the function **FormatDateTime** to assist you with that and if you look in the online help, you will find how to use this important function. For number there is the **FormatNumber** function.

No ParamArray

In VB 6.0 you have the flexibility to add the **ParamArray** parameter at the end of a parameter list for a method. This functionality is not available in eVB. What you have to do instead is add your own variant array as the last parameter. In the implementation of the function, it will look very similar to what you are used to, but it is the calling side that will change. Here is an example of how such a call could look:

```
Dim lavParameters(2) As Variant

' Set parameters
lavParameters(1) = "ThirdParameter"
lavParameters(2) = "ForthParameter"

' Make call
MsgBox = AnyMethod("FirstParameter", "SecondParameter",
lavParameters)
```

And this will actually take you most of the way. It is not as pretty as using **ParamArray**, but it works.

No control arrays

In eVB you cannot create control arrays the way that you are used to in VB 6.0. A common situation is to determine which of the OptionButton controls in a group that is selected. And a plain **If** statement would be quite annoying, especially if you had many option buttons in the group. If you insert three option buttons on a form and name them **optChoice1**, **optChoice2**, and **optChoice3** and add a Command Button and name it **cmdOK**, the workaround to find the selected option could look like this:

```
Public poptChoice(3) As OptionButton
Public Sub Form_Load()

  Set poptChoice(1) = optChoice1
  Set poptChoice(2) = optChoice2
  Set poptChoice(3) = optChoice3

End Sub
Private Sub cmdOK_Click()

Dim i As Integer

  For i = 1 To 3
    If poptChoice(i).Value Then MsgBox i
  Next 'i

End Sub
```

And even if you solve one part of the problem (the long If statement), you will still have to respond to the events on each OptionButton if you want to respond to the user selecting one of the option buttons. You would probably put only one line of code in each event and that would be a call to a private method that handles the click response in one function or procedure.

● No Left function in forms

Due to a small bug in eVB, the **Left** function in a form is interpreted as **Me.Left** and there are two workarounds for this. The first is to use the **Mid** function instead, like this:

```
ls = Mid(ls,1,5) ' same as Left(ls,5)
```

The second is that since the problem is only related to forms, you can move the code to a module instead.

● Only strings from resource files

You may have noticed that it is only the **LoadResString** function that is documented in the online help for eVB and that means that you can only use strings from Resource files. You can create resource files in eVC and use them in eVB by adding them as a file as you are used to, but resources other than strings will not be usable from your eVB application.

● No With...End With statements

You cannot use the **With...End With** statement. The only workaround is to simply always use the object name. This is how you may have written this code in the past:

```
' NOTE: Cannot be done in eVB!
With cmbItems
  .Clear
  .AddItem "First"
  .AddItem "Second"
  .AddItem "Third"
  .ListIndex = 0
End With
```

Instead you will have to do this:

```
' This is the solution!
cmbItems.Clear
cmbItems.AddItem "First"
cmbItems.AddItem "Second"
cmbItems.AddItem "Third"
cmdItems.ListIndex = 0
```

4.3   Conclusion

You have seen that most of what you know from VB 6.0 is still there. The IDE looks the same and even if reduced in number, the most important controls are also there. The new tools, like the remote Registry Editor, you also recognize even if you will have to spend some time on a few of them. We have also looked at the most important differences in the VB language and we hope you are now ready to start using these tools.

Getting started and beyond

In this chapter we will:

- Take a walk through core elements of eMbedded Visual Basic (eVB). You will learn about the basic functionality built into the tools like form navigation, included controls, third-party controls, and even base system controls.

- Reveal some hidden tricks that give Pocket PC applications that extra twist. We will cover some useful techniques when building enterprise applications for the Pocket PC, like building a wizard, creating a splash screen, programming the Pocket Outlook Object Model (POOM), launching applications, and much more.

 Tip

The best hardware tip we can offer is to get an Ethernet adapter for your Pocket PC. A fast Ethernet connection allows you to develop and debug code directly on the Pocket PC device. You might otherwise soon go crazy with the slower serial and even USB speeds.

5.1   Introduction to Pocket PC development

By now you have learned that eMbedded Visual Basic 3.0 and Visual Basic 6.0 IDEs are similar, yet different. This chapter will provide you with tips and tricks and best practices related to application navigation, management of modules and forms, variable declarations, and graphical user interface (GUI).

Application navigation and GUI are two development aspects that differ between Pocket PC development and development you've done for the desktop PC. One of the primary reasons for this is the Pocket PC's smaller screen-size. As in real-life, real estate price goes up where there is lack of land. In a situation where we don't have a lot of screen real estate you need to carefully optimize it always bearing in mind usability and readability, and the few pixels available.

Multiple Document Interface (MDI) is out of the question on the Pocket PC. Everything is Single Document Interface (SDI), clearly because of the screen size limitation. To design a clear and crisp GUI: think backwards! The Pocket PC screen is small; therefore design big and with a lot of white space.

66The Pocket PC screen is small; therefore design big and with a lot of white space. 99

On the CD we have included a document from Microsoft called *"Ready for Windows Logo Program for Windows Powered Pocket PC Handbook for Software Applications."* This document provides software design guidelines for application developers targeting the Pocket PC platform.

Reading the document prepares you well in understanding the thinking that Microsoft suggests application developers adopt in order to present a common user experience throughout the platform and across applications. We advise you to consider the guidelines found in the document. However, many of the guidelines assume that you're developing an off-the-shelf application, rather than a corporate application. This can poorly affect what is important for an enterprise application, and what is not. In our own reading we've also found certain aspects that we disagree with. We will come back to these issues later.

5.2   Your first Pocket PC application

Follow these steps to create your first Pocket PC application. (See **Sample 5.1** on the CD.)

1 Start eMbedded Visual Basic 3.0.

2 Select the project type "Windows CE for the Pocket PC project."

You will feel right at home once you have opened a new Pocket PC project!

Figure 5.1   Selecting
the Pocket PC project
type

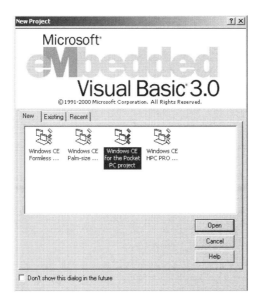

IIII➡ Tip

Before adding any controls or code, set the properties **Project Name, Form Name** and the **Form Caption**. The reason why it's a good idea to set **Project Name** and **Form Name** early on is because once you wish to save your project, you'll get the file naming right for your project from the very beginning. No more "project1.ebp" and "form1.ebf" in the default directory! **Form Caption** is an important property, since the Pocket PC user interface will regard it as the application name. In one and the same application, all forms should therefore have the same caption.

3 Add a Label, and a **CommandButton** control to the form.

4 Add the following code to the **CommandButton's Click** event:

```
Private Sub Command1_Click()
Label1.Caption = "Hello Mobile World!"
End Sub
```

5 Make sure that your Pocket PC is connected to your PC or select "Pocket PC Emulation" as the target.

6 Run the project.

The result is as shown in Figure 5.3. Even though this is a very basic sample, there are two relevant aspects to this project:

First, notice the **OK** button in the navigation bar. It is not far-fetched to believe that the **OK** button should be used to close the application. But

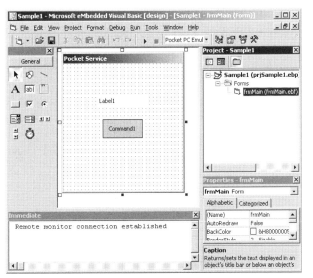

Figure 5.2   A pretty good start, don't you think?

Figure 5.3   "Hello Mobile World!" in one line of code

Microsoft does not want Pocket PC application developers to provide the user with a method that closes the application. Instead, Microsoft says that Pocket PC shell automatically closes idle applications, as more memory is needed. The following two paragraphs are copied from the document *"Ready for Windows Logo Program for Windows Powered Pocket PC Handbook for Software Applications."* Similar phrasings can be found in the eMbedded Visual Basic Help files.

Required: No user-exposed method for closing the application. The Pocket PC automatically closes the least recently used application(s) as more memory is needed. The goal of this is to free the user from needing to worry about managing memory. Thus, applications must not expose a method for the user to manually close or exit the application. Note that it is typical for documents/items within an application to have a means for closing (e.g. main application view is a list, items within the list may be opened or closed). When documents/items are opened and closed, the Pocket PC OK button should be used to close the document/item and return to the application list.

Recommended: Pocket PC OK button use and placement. The Pocket PC OK button should be used to close dialogs and document windows (not closing or exiting applications). When used, it should appear in the rightmost location on the NavBar. The Pocket PC OK button should only be used when there is no Cancel or other buttons that also close the current dialog or window. When other buttons are necessary (e.g. confirmation prompt, etc.), both OK and Cancel buttons should be in the client area of the window so that the user's choices are next to each other (instead of one in the NavBar and the other in the client area) to avoid confusion.

Isn't it nice of Microsoft to care so much about what the user worries about regarding managing memory? We understand that usability aspects have driven these guidelines, but respectfully disagree. Users have since the Dark Ages learned to close applications, and they still are required to do so in current desktop and server versions of Windows. The vast number of user postings in public newsgroups about the lack of manual methods to close applications testifies that we users want control, not lack of control. The dreaded seven-tap process that is necessary to close an application drives quite a few people crazy:

Start > Settings > System > Memory > Running Programs > Application > Stop

Figure 5.4   This is not a very user-friendly way of closing applications

We recommend that you do expose a method to close your application. Either use the menu bar control and **File Exit**, or simply use the **OK** button. In fact, even Microsoft uses **File Exit** in their own Pocket PC application SQL Server CE Query Analyzer (ISQL).

To allow the user to close the application by tapping the **OK** button, add the following lines of code to your project:

```
Private Sub Form_OKClick()
    App.End
End Sub
```

*We recommend that you do expose a method to close your application. Either use the menu bar control and **File Exit**, or simply use the **OK** button. In fact, even Microsoft uses **File Exit** in their own Pocket PC application SQL Server CE Query Analyzer (ISQL).*

The **App**-object's **End** method terminates the application.

 Tip

Be aware that it does take a tad longer to restart an application rather than switching to it. This might lead you to decide not to implement application termination. On the other hand, the limited amount of RAM is a factor that will have you leaning towards implementing application termination. This is simply a matter of a case-by-case decision.

The second aspect to observe with this simple example, is that the **Form Caption** appears in the **Navigation Bar** as if it is the application name. The Pocket PC memory management also identifies the application by the **Form Caption**. You should therefore avoid switching the captions of the forms in your application unless you want to confuse the user about which application is actually running.

Designing the Pocket PC user interface

User interface design is really not a major topic in this book but even so we would like to highlight some key things to keep in mind. Designing a great application user interface is a challenge. The challenge intensifies on a Pocket PC as it has no keyboard and the screen is smaller.

If you are a developer, history disqualifies you as a graphical user interface designer. It hurts as much as it is true! In any significant software project you should make sure that the appropriate user interface design skills are present to make GUI calls. Having said that, you as a developer need to be aware of two significant Pocket PC GUI topics: application navigation and input methods. You'll need to master different methods of accepting input, including the built-in soft input panel (SIP).

In any significant software project you should make sure that the appropriate user interface design skills are present to make GUI calls. Having said that, you as a developer need to be aware of two significant Pocket PC GUI topics: application navigation and input methods.

Tip

You will find more details on design and development of web-based application targeted at Pocket PCs in Chapter 8.

Your Pocket PC application has to adopt a Single Document Interface (SDI), which means that only one document or form can be visible at the same time. You will therefore need to learn all about showing and hiding **Forms**, **Frames**, and using **TabStrips**.

The user is more efficient in entering and manipulating data using controls such as **ListBoxes**, **ComboBoxes**, **Checkboxes**, and **Option Buttons** than using the SIP. Where you could have gotten away with providing just a simple text box for data input in a traditional PC application, you need to think twice before forcing the user to use the SIP to enter data into your application. First consider using list boxes, drop-down combo boxes, check boxes, option buttons, slide controls, scroll bars, and so on. Once you have decided to use the SIP, you need to ensure that the SIP does not cover the input fields, such as text boxes, when it pops up.

When designing the user interface, a great general rule of thumb is leverage! Study the built-in Pocket PC applications; Pocket Excel, Pocket Word, Calendar, and not least of all, Settings. Spend some time investigating how these applications:

● Allow the user to navigate within the application.

● Group tasks together using Wizards, **Frames**, and **TabStrips**.

● Use header labels to indicate where the user currently is in the application.

● Use **OK**, **Cancel**, and the Form **OK** buttons.

● Manage to get input fields out of the way of the SIP.

● Use a lot of white space to accomplish a clean, crisp look and feel.

Your user has already learned to use these applications or is likely to spend some time learning them. By designing your application to behave in a similar fashion as the built-in application you can leverage on this learning.

User interface – Settings

Observe in the screenshots in Figure 5.5.

● Application name stays **Settings** throughout the exercise.

● The use of **TabStrips** to group the tasks.

● The use of the header label to indicate what task is currently active (**Buttons**, **Owner Information**).

- The use of lists, check boxes, and option buttons (other parts of Settings) for one-tap input.
- The use of the Form **OK** button to close the task.

Figure 5.5 Learning UI design from Settings!

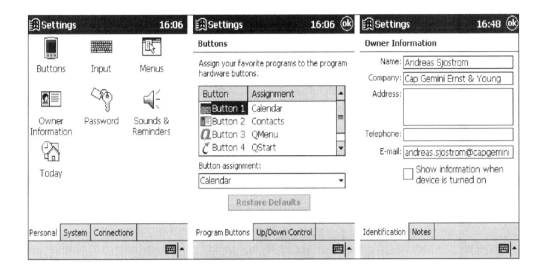

User interface – Settings (new connection)

(The screenshots in Figure 5.6 are taken from where the user can create a new modem connection.)

Observe in the screenshots in Figure 5.6:

- Application name stays **Settings** throughout the exercise.
- The use of a wizard to structure the input from the user. This is a great way to collect input because it both presents a logical grouping of information as well as it automatically addresses the screen size issue as it spreads across multiple screens.
- That the input fields are positioned in the upper part of the form so that the SIP does not hide them when it is used.
- The use of the header label to indicate what task is currently active (**NewConnection**).
- The use of drop-down lists for two-tap input.
- The use of standard wizard **Cancel**, **Back**, and **Next** buttons.

User interface – Pocket Excel

Observe in the screenshots in Figure 5.7:

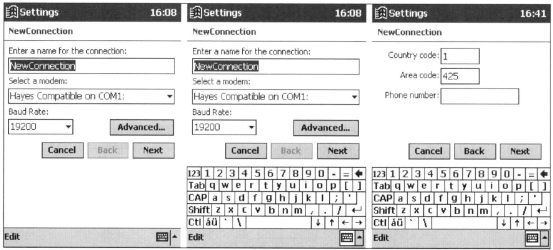

Figure 5.6   Learning
UI design from
Settings!

- Application name stays **Pocket Excel** throughout the exercise.

- The use of **TabStrips** to group the tasks.

- The use of the header label to indicate what task is currently active (**Format Cells**, **Insert Cells**).

- The frequent use of lists, check boxes, and option buttons for one-tap input.

- The use of the form's **OK** button to close the task.

Figure 5.7   Learning
UI design from Pocket
Excel!

- That the use of **OK** and **Cancel** *excludes* the use of the **OK** button on the top right.

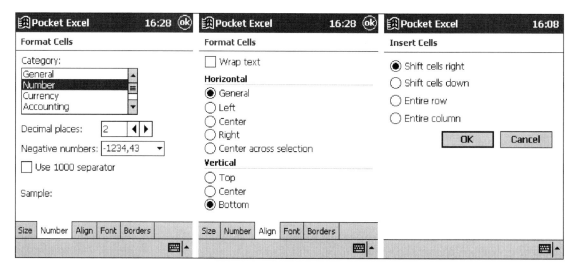

Application navigation

The first event that fires up when opening a form is **Form_Load**. Once the form loads it stays resident in memory until the application terminates because Windows CE does not support the **Form Unload** statement or event. This means that the more forms your application needs, the more memory it will consume. Memory is a scarce resource even though Pocket PCs have 16 MB RAM or more. A great Pocket PC application is one that doesn't eat up all those megabytes just because they are there. It takes just one RAM-hungry application to get an unhappy user.

The lack of support for the **Unload** statement affects the way you structure the actual code. The code in the **Form_Load** event runs just once, when the form is first loaded. You therefore need to put code that needs to run every time the form becomes visible some other place than in the **Form_Load** event.

The SDI nature of a Pocket PC application requires you to hide the forms that are not visible to the user. If one form is used to call another, and the calling form is not hidden, it results in the appearance of two applications running. You need to have figured out a plan to manage the calling, showing, and hiding forms before having come too far in your Pocket PC development project.

Figure 5.8   Two Pocket Service applications running? No, I forgot to hide the calling form!

Managing Pocket PC forms

The following sample (see **Sample 5.2** on the CD) illustrates how to deal with these and other related issues. We will have a form (**frmMain**) call another form (**frmServiceOrders**). The **frmServiceOrders** displays a **ListBox** populated with service orders. The user can then tap to close the form, and return to the form **frmMain**.

Figure 5.9 frmMain
in all its glory!

... and the code behind the form:

```
' ****************************
' Implements the Main form
' ****************************
' Form FileName: frmMain.ebf
' Creator:       Andreas Sjostrom
' Created:       2001-03-14
' ****************************
' Version   Date   Who  Comment
' 00.00.000 010314 ASJ  Created
' ****************************

Option Explicit

Private Sub Form_Load()
' Loads the form. Executes once, when the form is loaded.
' Known bugs:
' Version   Date   Who  Comment
' 00.00.000 010315 ASJ  Created
' ****************************

End Sub
Private Sub cmdView_Click()
' Open the Service Orders form
' Known bugs:
' Version   Date   Who  Comment
' 00.00.000 010314 ASJ  Created
' ****************************

    ' Call the frmServiceOrders form
    frmServiceOrders.ShowForm (Me)
End Sub
```

```
Private Sub Form_OKClick()

' Handle the Form OK click event
' Known bugs:
' Version   Date    Who   Comment
' 00.00.000 010315  ASJ   Created
'*****************************

    App.End

End Sub
```

The form **frmServiceOrders** is called when the user taps the **View…** button.

Figure 5.10   Service Orders!

To call this form we use a custom built **ShowForm** method. The **ShowForm** method accepts a Form object as parameter. The form object tracks the calling form. In this example, the current form (**frmMain**) is sent to the **frmServiceOrders.ShowForm** using the **Me** reference. This is how the **frmServiceOrders** code looks like:

```
'*****************************
' Implements the Service Orders form
'*****************************
' Form FileName: frmServiceOrders.ebf
' Creator:      Andreas Sjostrom
' Created:      2001-03-14
'*****************************
' Version   Date    Who   Comment
```

```
' 00.00.000 010314 ASJ  Created
'****************************

Option Explicit

' Private variables
Private pfrmParent As Form

Private Sub Form_Load()
' Loads the form. Executes once, when the form is loaded.
' Known bugs:
' Version    Date    Who  Comment
' 00.00.000 010315 ASJ  Created
'****************************

End Sub

Public Sub ShowForm(ByVal ParentForm As Form)

' Only function that is called from the outside to start up the
form.
' IN: ParentForm, parent form
' Known bugs:
' Version    Date    Who  Comment
' 00.00.000 010314 ASJ  Created
'****************************

    ' Set parent form
    Set pfrmParent = ParentForm

    ' Call to turn the form invisible
    MakeInvisible (Me)

    ' Load the form's controls
    pLoadControls

    ' Call to turn the form visible
    MakeVisible (Me)

    ' Hide the parent form
    pfrmParent.Hide

End Sub

Private Sub pLoadControls()

' Load controls.
' Known bugs:
' Version    Date    Who  Comment
' 00.00.000 010315 ASJ  Created
```

```
'*****************************
' Variables
Dim strItem As String
Dim intCounter As Integer

    For intCounter = 0 To 200
        strItem = "Service Order: " & CStr(intCounter)
        lstServiceOrders.AddItem strItem
    Next intCounter

End Sub

Private Sub pResetControls()

' Reset controls.
' Known bugs:
' Version   Date    Who   Comment
' 00.00.000 010315 ASJ  Created
'*****************************

    ' Clear the listbox
    lstServiceOrders.Clear

End Sub

Private Sub Form_OKClick()

' Handle the Form OK click event
' Known bugs:
' Version Date Who Comment
' 00.00.000 010315 ASJ Created
'*****************************

    ' Reset the controls of this form
    pResetControls

    ' Show the parent form (as it was left before calling the
child form)
    pfrmParent.Show
    ' Hide this form
    Me.Hide

End Sub
```

The form displays and the user can tap the **OK** button to hide the form and
return to **frmMain**. The sub **pResetControls** resets and empties the form's
controls. Avoid introducing bugs related to adding the same items to lists
and column headers to **ListViews**, by resetting the controls when you leave
a form. Moreover, in case a control, for example a **ListView** or **ListBox**, holds

a large amount of data, free up that memory by clearing the contents from the control.

You can see that we have chosen not to place any code in the **Form_Load** event. It is good practice to have little or no code in the **Form_Load** event because the code in **Form_Load** executes only the first time the form is shown, i.e., loads. You are bound to introduce bugs into your application if you at any point assume that the Form_Load code executes any more than after the first time. Furthermore, you will likely want to reset and load controls, not just the first time the form loads, but every time the form displays.

We place all relevant action in the **ShowForm** method:

1 Set the private variable **pfrmParent** so that we may know and use the calling form later.

2 The call to **MakeInvisible** hides the form and turns the mouse pointer into an hourglass. The reason why the form is made invisible is that generally the loading of the form's controls executes faster if they are not visible.

3 The **pLoadControls** is a private sub that populates the **ListBox**. This is where you would populate all of the form's controls.

4 **MakeVisible** makes the form visible and restores the mouse pointer. The hourglass indicates to the user that something is happening while populating of the form's controls.

5 The calling form (**frmMain**) is concealed.

If you need somewhere to place the code that needs to execute every time a form is activated you can still use the **Form_Activate** event. The benefits of using a custom **ShowForm** method include the ability to pass variables when making a call to a form.

```
' Set parent form
Set pfrmParent = ParentForm

' Call to turn the form invisible
MakeInvisible (Me)

' Load the form's controls
pLoadControls

' Call to turn the form visible
MakeVisible (Me)

' Hide the parent form
pfrmParent.Hide
```

General code is put in a module. This project has only the two subs
MakeVisible and **MakeInvisible**.

```
'****************************
' General declarations and functions
'****************************
' FileName: basGlobal.bas
' Creator:  Andreas Sjostrom
' Created:  2001-03-14
'****************************
' Version   Date   Who  Comment
' 00.00.000 010313 ASJ  Created
'****************************
Option Explicit

' Private variables
Private pfrmCurrentForm As Form

' Misc constants
Public Const vbHourGlass = 11
Public Const vbArrow = 1

Public Sub MakeInvisible(ByVal CurrentForm As Form)
'****************************
'Makes the form invisible and turns on hourglass
'
'Parameters:
'CurrentForm, form to hide
'
'Return:
'N/A
'
'History:
' Version   Date   Who  Comment
' 00.00.000 010124 AS   Created
'****************************

    Set pfrmCurrentForm = CurrentForm
    ' Show hourglass
    Screen.MousePointer = vbHourGlass

    ' Make invisible
    pfrmCurrentForm.Visible = False

End Sub
```

```
Public Sub MakeVisible(ByVal CurrentForm As Form)
'****************************
'LoadMenu
'Makes the form visible and restore mousepointer
'
'Parameters:
'currentForm, form to show
'
'Return:
'N/A
'
'History:
' Version   Date   Who  Comment
' 00.00.000 010124 AS   Created
'****************************

    Set pfrmCurrentForm = CurrentForm

    ' Make visible
    pfrmCurrentForm.Visible = True

    ' Show form
    pfrmCurrentForm.Show

    ' Restore mousepointer
    Screen.MousePointer = vbArrow

End Sub
```

This sample can be used as a rule of thumb in terms of calling, loading, showing, hiding, and returning back to forms.

Framing a wizard

Microsoft introduced the use of wizards in their applications about ten years ago. One of the first applications to make use of wizards was Microsoft Excel 3.0 with the first implementation of the Chart Wizard. The purpose of the Chart Wizard was, and still is, to make chart creation user-friendlier. Microsoft succeeded in dramatically reducing the number of support calls related to chart creation by having the wizard group the various chart properties into a number of sequential steps and lead the user through them.

Your Pocket PC application can make use of the same concept, and thereby combine the increased user-friendliness with the opportunity to group a number of controls onto more than form – something badly needed with the small screen-size.

An efficient way to build a Pocket PC wizard is to use **Frames**. By creating a frame for each wizard step and then showing and hiding these frames, you will gain the appearance of a wizard using just one form.

 **Tip**

You may consider the technique of using frames instead of forms altogether throughout your application. The benefits include a snappier and less memory-consuming application. The drawbacks include a messier development environment, because the IDE is not designed to facilitate this approach. You also will have to programmatically manage the multiple form logic yourself.

The following sample (see **Sample 5.3** on the CD) illustrates how to use **Frames** to build a wizard in a Pocket PC application. The wizard sample will assist the user, a field technician, to collect the customer's signature and level of satisfaction. The sample will finish by displaying all collected data on a separate form.

Tapping the **Finish** button starts the wizard that is designed to close a service order.

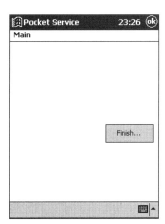

Figure 5.11   Let's begin the magic!

The first step in the wizard is to choose the particular service order on which to collect customer information (see Figure 5.12).

The wizard uses three buttons; **Cancel**, **Back**, and **Next**. The user can cancel the wizard at any time, and thereby return to the first form. The **Back** and **Next** buttons are enabled and/or disabled appropriately.

The second step is where the field technician gains the customer's signature and name (see Figure 5.13).

Figure 5.12
Selecting appropriate
Service Order

Figure 5.13   The
customer signs off the
Service Order

Use a normal **PictureBox** control for recording the signature by storing the x- and y-coordinates. Note that the **Back** button is now enabled. Each form has **SIPBehavior** property that controls how and when the SIP pops up. The property can be set to the values:

- **vbSIPUser** – The user manually brings up the SIP.
- **vbSIPAutomatic** – The SIP is brought up automatically whenever the user positions the cursor in a field that accepts input.
- **vbSIPAlways** – The SIP is always brought up whenever this form is activated.

Figure 5.14 shows how this form has set the **SIPBehavior** property to **vbSIPAutomatic**, which means that the SIP will pop up soon as the user taps the Customer name text box.

The field technician obtains the customer's response about their level of satisfaction in the last step, as you see in Figure 5.15. By using

Figure 5.14   The SIP pops up, but does not hide the Customer name TextBox

OptionButtons the user can enter level of customer satisfaction. Note that the caption of the **Next** button has changed to **Finish** indicating that this is the last step.

Figure 5.15   How satisfied is your customer?

Once the user is finished, all the data collected is displayed in the Wizard Results screen as you see in Figure 5.16. This form redraws the signature, based on the coordinates, and echoes the rest of the collected data, as well.

The following code hides behind the first form, **frmMain.**

```
'*****************************
' Implements the Main form
'*****************************
' Form FileName: frmMain.ebf
' Creator:       Andreas Sjostrom
' Created:       2001-03-14
'*****************************
```

Figure 5.16   The results from the Wizard!

```
' Version    Date    Who   Comment
' 00.00.000 010314 ASJ   Created
'****************************

Option Explicit

' Private variables
Private pfrmParent As Form

Private Sub Form_Load()

' Loads the form. Executes once, when the form is loaded.
' IN:
' Known bugs:
' Version    Date    Who   Comment
' 00.00.000 010315 ASJ   Created
'****************************

End Sub

Public Sub ShowForm(ByVal ParentForm As Form)

' Only function that is called from the outside to start up the
form.
' IN: ParentForm, parent form
' Known bugs:
' Version    Date    Who   Comment
' 00.00.000 010315 ASJ   Created
'****************************

    ' Set parent form
    Set pfrmParent = ParentForm
```

```
    ' Call to turn the form invisible
    MakeInvisible (Me)

    ' Reset the controls
    pResetControls

    ' Load the form's controls
    pLoadControls

    ' Call to turn the form visible
    MakeVisible (Me)

    ' Hide the parent form
    pfrmParent.Hide
End Sub

Private Sub pLoadControls()

' Load controls.
' Known bugs:
' Version   Date   Who  Comment
' 00.00.000 010315 ASJ  Created
'*****************************

End Sub

Private Sub pResetControls()

' Reset controls.
' Known bugs:
' Version   Date   Who  Comment
' 00.00.000 010315 ASJ  Created
'*****************************

End Sub

Private Sub cmdFinish_Click()

' Open the Service Orders form
' Known bugs:
' Version   Date   Who  Comment
' 00.00.000 010314 ASJ  Created
'*****************************

    ' Call the frmFinishWizard form
    frmFinishWizard.ShowForm (Me)

End Sub
```

```
Private Sub Form_OKClick()

' Handle the Form OK click event
' Known bugs:
' Version   Date    Who  Comment
' 00.00.000 010315 ASJ  Created
'****************************

    App.End
End Sub
```

The wizard form **frmFinishWizard** is called when the user taps the **Finish** button. The method **frmFinishWizard.ShowForm** (**Me**) is used as we have already discussed.

The most significant code in the wizard form is in the private sub **pStepInWizard**. The sub **pStepInWizard** is called every time the user taps the "**Next**" and "**Back**" button and it manages how the frames becomes visible and invisible.

```
Private Sub pStepInWizard(ByVal blnNext As Boolean)

' Sub that moves the Wizard
' IN: blnNext is TRUE for Next and FALSE for Back
' Known bugs:
' Version   Date    Who  Comment
' 00.00.000 010314 ASJ  Created
'****************************
' Variables
Dim intCounter As Integer

    ' Save current frame
    Select Case pintCurrentFrame
    Case FRA_SERVICEORDERS
        ' Store the selected Service Order in private variable
        pintServiceOrder =
lstServiceOrders.ItemData(lstServiceOrders.ListIndex)
        fraServiceOrders.Visible = False

    Case FRA_SIGNATURE
        ' Store the customer name in private variable
        pstrCustomerName = txtCustomerName.Text

        ' Make sure there is a customer name!
        If Len(pstrCustomerName) = 0 Then
            MsgBox "Enter the customer name!", vbInformation,
App.Title
```

```
        Exit Sub
     End If

     ' Make sure there is a signature!
     If Not pblnCustomerSignature Then
        MsgBox "The customer signature is lacking!",
vbInformation, App.Title
        Exit Sub
     End If

     ' Get signature string, and store in private variable
     pstrSignature = pSaveSignatureToString

     fraSignature.Visible = False
  Case FRA_CUSTOMER
     ' Store satisfaction in private variable

     If optAnnoyed Then pstrCustomerSatisfaction = "Annoyed"
     If optDissatisfied Then pstrCustomerSatisfaction =
"Dissatisfied"
     If optSatisfied Then pstrCustomerSatisfaction =
"Satisfied"
     If optVerySatisfied Then pstrCustomerSatisfaction =
"Very Satisfied"

     fraCustomer.Visible = False

End Select

' Next step in Wizard
If blnNext Then
   pintCurrentFrame = pintCurrentFrame + 1
Else
   pintCurrentFrame = pintCurrentFrame - 1
End If

' Show next frame
Select Case pintCurrentFrame
Case FRA_SERVICEORDERS
   cmdCancel.Enabled = True
   cmdBack.Enabled = False
   cmdNext.Caption = "Next >"
   lblStep.Caption = pvntWizardStepsCaption(pintCurrent
Frame)

   fraServiceOrders.Visible = True
```

```
        Case FRA_SIGNATURE
            cmdCancel.Enabled = True
            cmdBack.Enabled = True
            cmdNext.Caption = "Next >"
            lblStep.Caption = pvntWizardStepsCaption(pintCurrent
    Frame)

            fraSignature.Visible = True

        Case FRA_CUSTOMER
            cmdCancel.Enabled = True
            cmdBack.Enabled = True
            cmdNext.Caption = "Finish"
            lblStep.Caption = pvntWizardStepsCaption(pintCurrent
    Frame)

            fraCustomer.Visible = True

        Case FINISHED
            ' Wizard is completed!
            ' Build array to pass to the form frmWizardResults
            pvntResults(0) = pintServiceOrder
            pvntResults(1) = pstrCustomerName
            pvntResults(2) = pstrSignature
            pvntResults(3) = pstrCustomerSatisfaction

            ' Reset the controls
            pResetControls

            ' Call frmWizardResults form
            frmWizardResults.ShowForm Me, pvntResults

        End Select

    End Sub
```

In the last few rows of code, the wizard results get packed into an array, **pvntResults**, and passed to the form **frmWizardResults**.

Some of the **PictureBox** code that tracks and stores the coordinates was initially shown at a Microsoft conference in a SQL Server CE demo. A benefit of handling signatures like this is that you can store the signature using an efficient Text data type instead of having to deal with binaries and bitmaps.

There is code in the form **frmWizardResults** that reads the coordinates from a string the array **pvntResults** and redraws the signature. This is how it works:

```
Private Sub pLoadSignatureFromString(SignaturePath As String)

' Loads the signature
' Known bugs:
' Version    Date    Who   Comment
' 00.00.000 010315 ASJ   Created
'*****************************
' Variables
Dim iCurrentX As Integer
Dim iCurrentY As Integer
Dim iNextSemiColonX As Integer
Dim iNextSemiColonY As Integer
Dim iPreviousSemiColonX As Integer
Dim iPreviousSemiColonY As Integer
Dim intSignaturePoint As Integer
Dim sXPath As String
Dim sYPath As String
Dim sSignaturePath As String

    ' Set path
    sSignaturePath = SignaturePath

    ' Load the signature path into the coordinate arrays.
     sXPath = Mid(sSignaturePath, 1, InStr(1, sSignaturePath,
"|", vbTextCompare) - 1)
     sYPath = Right(sSignaturePath, Len(sSignaturePath) -
InStr(1, sSignaturePath, "|", vbTextCompare))

     iNextSemiColonX = InStr(1, sXPath, ";", vbTextCompare)
     iNextSemiColonY = InStr(1, sYPath, ";", vbTextCompare)
     iPreviousSemiColonX = 1
     iPreviousSemiColonY = 1

     Do While iNextSemiColonX <> 0
        iCurrentX = Mid(sXPath, iPreviousSemiColonX,
iNextSemiColonX - iPreviousSemiColonX)
        iCurrentY = Mid(sYPath, iPreviousSemiColonY,
iNextSemiColonY - iPreviousSemiColonY)

    ' Begin by checking if there is enough room to add this new
    ' coordinate to the arrays used to store the points. If
    ' there is not enough room extend it.
        If (mintCoordinatesCountCustomer >=
UBound(mintXCoordinatesCustomer)) Then
```

```
            ReDim Preserve
mintXCoordinatesCustomer(mintCoordinatesCountCustomer + 500)
            ReDim Preserve
mintYCoordinatesCustomer(mintCoordinatesCountCustomer + 500)
        End If

    ' Add this point into the signature point array.
        mintXCoordinatesCustomer(mintCoordinatesCountCustomer)
= CInt(iCurrentX)
        mintYCoordinatesCustomer(mintCoordinatesCountCustomer)
= CInt(iCurrentY)
        mintCoordinatesCountCustomer =
mintCoordinatesCountCustomer + 1

    ' Parse out the next point.
        iPreviousSemiColonX = iNextSemiColonX + 1
        iPreviousSemiColonY = iNextSemiColonY + 1
        iNextSemiColonX = InStr(iPreviousSemiColonX, sXPath,
";", vbTextCompare)
        iNextSemiColonY = InStr(iPreviousSemiColonY, sYPath,
";", vbTextCompare)
    Loop

    ' Redisplay the signature path.
        For intSignaturePoint = 0 To mintCoordinatesCountCustomer
- 1

    ' Is this the start of a new segment of the signature path?
        If mintXCoordinatesCustomer(intSignaturePoint) = -1
Then
            mintLastXCustomer = -1
            mintLastYCustomer = -1
    ' This is just part of an existing segment so add it to the
display.
        Else
        iCurrentX = mintXCoordinatesCustomer(intSignaturePoint)
        iCurrentY = mintYCoordinatesCustomer(intSignaturePoint)
        If (mintLastXCustomer = -1) Then mintLastXCustomer =
iCurrentX
        If (mintLastYCustomer = -1) Then mintLastYCustomer =
iCurrentY
        picCustomerSignature.DrawLine mintLastXCustomer,
mintLastYCustomer, iCurrentX, iCurrentY, vbBlack
        mintLastXCustomer = iCurrentX
```

```
        mintLastYCustomer = iCurrentY
      End If
    Next

    ' The signature is now loaded. Set it up so that it appears
    ' as if the user has just picked up their stylus.
      mintLastXCustomer = 0
      mintLastYCustomer = 0
      mintCoordinatesCountCustomer = intSignaturePoint

  End Sub
```

The coordinates are publicly declared and globally available in the project:

- mintCoordinatesCountCustomer
- mintLastXCustomer
- mintLastYCustomer
- mintXCoordinatesCustomer
- mintYCoordinatesCustomer

If you were looking to improve this sample, it would probably include the removal of these global variables and introduction of a new set of data in the array **pvntResults.**

MenuBar control

You will most likely include the MenuBar control in all your projects. This control enables you to implement menus into your applications. The closest match to a VB 6.0 control is the Toolbar control. Unfortunately there is no visual interface (Properties dialog) for working with menus, so the only way to do this is to create menu options in code. Let us take a break from our exploring and code some more. The following code (see **Sample 5.4** on the CD) implements a simple menu:

```
Dim mnuMain As MenuBarMenu

  ' Add Main Menu
Set mnuMain = mnuBar.Controls.AddMenu("Menu", "mnuMain")
mnuMain.Items.Add 1, "mnuMainOptions", "Options..."
mnuMain.Items.Add 2, , , mbrMenuSeparator
mnuMain.Items.Add 3, "mnuMainAbout", "About..."
mnuMain.Items.Add 4, "mnuMainExit", "Exit"
```

If you put a MenuBar control on your form, name it **mnuBar**, and put the above code in the **Form_Load**, and click the Run icon, you will see that you have created a menu in the bottom bar of the device screen, as seen in Figure 5.17.

Figure 5.17 Simple MenuBar sample

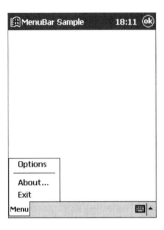

Just to close the loop, put the following code into the same form:

```
Private Sub mnuBar_MenuClick(ByVal Item As MenuBarLib.Item)

    Select Case Item.Key
      Case "mnuMainOptions"
        MsgBox "Options"
      Case "mnuMainAbout"
        MsgBox "About"
      Case "mnuMainExit"
        App.End
    End Select

End Sub
```

If you click Run now, your required code is in place to respond to menu options. So far, we have covered most of what you need to know about the MenuBar control.

Sometimes, you may want to do more advanced things; so therefore we will go through some of the more advanced uses of the MenuBar control. First of all, you will probably want to create more than one menu (even if it can't take you very far). Here is a code sample doing just that:

```
Dim mnuMain As MenuBarMenu
Dim mnuTools As MenuBarMenu
```

```
' Add Main Menu
Set mnuMain = mnuBar.Controls.AddMenu("File", "mnuMain")
mnuMain.Items.Add 1, "mnuMainAbout", "About..."
mnuMain.Items.Add 2, "mnuMainExit", "Exit"

' Add Tools Menu
Set mnuTools = mnuBar.Controls.AddMenu("Tools", "mnuTools")
mnuTools.Items.Add 1, "mnuToolsOptions", "Options..."
```

If you would like to create a cascading menu, here is an example of that:

```
Dim mnuMain As MenuBarMenu

' Add Menu
Set mnuMain = mnuBar.Controls.AddMenu("Menu", "mnuMain")
mnuMain.Items.Add 1, "mnuToolsMap", "Options"
  mnuMain.Items(1).SubItems.Add 1, "mnuToolsMapZoomFull",
"Toolbar"
  mnuMain.Items(1).SubItems.Add 2, "mnuToolsMapPanArrows",
"Status Bar"
  mnuMain.Items(1).SubItems(2).Checked = True
mnuMain.Items.Add 2, , , mbrMenuSeparator
mnuMain.Items.Add 3, "mnuMainAbout", "About..."
mnuMain.Items.Add 4, "mnuMainExit", "Exit"
```

Notice how you can use CheckBoxes in menu options since we have enabled the check box for one of the menu options in the cascading menu. If we move further on, we can see how to include a button on the menu bar. This is the code to do that:

```
Dim mnbOptions As MenuBarButton

' Add Image
imlButtons.Add App.Path & "\properties.bmp"

' Connect MenuBar and ImageList
mnuBar.ImageList = imlButtons.hImageList

' Add Button
Set mnbOptions = mnuBar.Controls.AddButton("mnbOptions")
mnbOptions.Image = 1
```

As you can see, you need to add an ImageList control to the form and name it **imlButtons**. You will also need to place the bitmap file in the folder where your **.vb** file is created on your device (real or emulated). We have therefore included the most common bitmaps (cut, copy, paste, Help, print, etc.) on the accompanying CD (in folder **Tips****Button Icons**).

Tip

The eVB Help file incorrectly instructs you to use **Set** MenuBar1. ImageList = ImageList1.hImageList, which will not work.

And to respond to menu button selections, you will do something like this:

```
Private Sub mnuBar_ButtonClick(ByVal Button As
MenuBarLib.MenuBarButton)

  Select Case Button.Key
    Case "mnbOptions"
      MsgBox "Button Pressed"
  End Select

End Sub
```

Figure 5.18
Advanced MenuBar
sample

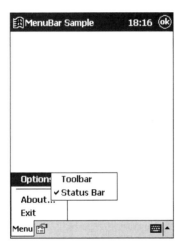

You can do a lot more with the MenuBar control, especially related to menu buttons. The buttons can act like check boxes; or they can be grouped as option buttons, and so forth. You have probably seen enough about the control to begin your own exploration of all its features.

A last comment on menus is that you can include the standard **New** menu, which is available for all applications on the Pocket PC by just setting the **NewButton** property of the MenuBar control to **True**. You will then have to implement a **mnuBar_NewClick** event to respond to the user tapping the **New** menu.

FileSystem control

As we mentioned before, this control is actually two different controls in the same file. When you select the FileSystem control in Components (**Project > Components**), you will have two new controls visible in the tool-box (the bar on the left). Let's examine them separately. We will start with the File control.

The File control is used for file access and if you drop a File control (name it **filAny**) and a TextBox control (name it **txtContents**) on a form, here is how you would open and read a file into the TextBox (see **Sample 5.5** on the CD):

```
filAny.Open "\My Documents\default.htm", fsModeInput, _
fsAccessRead
txtContents.Text = filAny.Input(filAny.LOF)
filAny.Close
```

And writing is very similar. Enter some text into the text box and you can save it with this code.

```
filAny.Open "\My Documents\test.txt", fsModeOutput, _
fsAccessWrite, fsLockWrite
filAny.LinePrint txtContents.Text
filAny.Close
```

One important detail is that this code will actually add an extra carriage return/line feed to the text written. So, if you use **filAny.Input** (**filAny.LOF**) the next time, you will have to remove the last two bytes before saving again.

If you want to include file access in your application, you probably will not add a visual control to your form (as we just did). You would probably create the file control in your code. The main reason for this is that it will save you memory to do so, and there is not very much you can do with the visual control on your form. Here is how the previous **Read** operation would look:

```
Dim loFile As File

  ' Create object
Set loFile = CreateObject("FileCtl.File")

  ' Read File
loFile.Open "\Windows\default.htm",, fsModeInput, fsAccessRead
Text1.Text = loFile.Input(loFile.LOF)
loFile.Close
```

There are some more to be said about file access, but the main point here is to make you aware of the fact that you should use this control instead of the native language components (**Open...For...As, Print #, Close**, etc) you are used to.

If we look at the other control, the FileSystem control, much of what you could do with VB 6.0 natively you now need this control to do. As with the File control, you could use this control as a visual control by adding it to a form. But since you would probably not add the visual control when writing your applications, we only show the code for creating the control yourself. Let's start by some basic file manipulation:

```
Dim loFileSystem As FILECTL.FileSystem

' Create object
Set loFileSystem = CreateObject("FileCtl.FileSystem")

' Copy a file
loFileSystem.FileCopy "\Windows\default.htm", "\My
Documents\test.htm"

' Rename (move) a file
loFileSystem.MoveFile "\My Documents\test.htm", "\My
Documents\test1.htm"

' Delete a file
loFileSystem.Kill "\My Documents\test1.htm"
```

And then let us just see how we can find all the directories in the **Program Files** folder and add them to a ComboBox (named **cmbDirs**):

```
Dim loFileSystem As FILECTL.FileSystem
Dim lsFileName As String

' Create object
Set loFileSystem = CreateObject("FileCtl.FileSystem")

' Get first item that matches path and is also a folder
lsFileName = loFileSystem.Dir("\Program Files\*.*",
fsAttrDirectory)

' Get the rest of matches
cmbDirs.Clear
Do While lsFileName <> ""
  cmbDirs.AddItem lsFileName
  lsFileName = loFileSystem.Dir
Loop

' Select first
If cmbDirs.ListCount > 0 Then cmbDirs.ListIndex = 0
```

And that concludes the point of this section – to show you that you already know how to perform file access and manipulation. Now this functionality is available through a control instead of built into the language with a syntax that is slightly different from what you may be used to.

ListView control

As an enterprise developer, the ListView may be the most important user interface control to master. If you can make your lists appear in an efficient way, your users will be more efficient. The ListView control is very capable and here we will only cover the most important parts for enterprise application development. We will also look into some of the things you can do with some hard-core programming beyond what the documentation tells you (see **Sample 5.6** on the CD).

Okay, so let us start with the basic stuff. Start up a new eVB project and add the ListView control in the Components dialog (**Project > Components**). Then add a ListView control to the form and name it **lvwItems**. Even if the control can handle four different views, we will now only look at the view where each item appears on a separate row with additional column. This mode is called **Report** view. You can enable this mode by setting the **View** property to **lvwReport** (3). When you have done that, you can add the following code to the **Form_Load** event:

```
Dim litm As ListItem

' Clear and add ListView headings
lvwItems.Sorted = False
lvwItems.ColumnHeaders.Clear
lvwItems.ColumnHeaders.Add 1, , "No", 800
lvwItems.ColumnHeaders.Add 2, , "Description", 2000
lvwItems.ColumnHeaders.Add 3, , "Price", 500, lvwColumnRight

' Clear and fill item list
lvwItems.ListItems.Clear
Set litm = lvwItems.ListItems.Add(, , "11111")
  litm.SubItems(1) = "Multipurpose Paper"
  litm.SubItems(2) = "50"
Set litm = lvwItems.ListItems.Add(, , "22222")
  litm.SubItems(1) = "Toner 6-pack"
  litm.SubItems(2) = "200"
Set litm = lvwItems.ListItems.Add(, , "33333")
  litm.SubItems(1) = "Toner 2-pack"
  litm.SubItems(2) = "80"
```

```
Set litm = lvwItems.ListItems.Add(, , "44444")
  litm.SubItems(1) = "Standard Paper"
  litm.SubItems(2) = "35"
Set litm = lvwItems.ListItems.Add(, , "55555")
  litm.SubItems(1) = "Standard Paper"
  litm.SubItems(2) = "35"
```

When you run the code, you will get the expected list of items with headings. One obvious thing you would probably like to do is to be able to sort on different columns. Add the following code to the form:

```
Private Sub lvwItems_ColumnClick(ByVal Index As Long)

  If lvwItems.SortKey = Index - 1 Then
    If lvwItems.SortOrder = lvwAscending Then
      lvwItems.SortOrder = lvwDescending
    Else
      lvwItems.SortOrder = lvwAscending
    End If
  Else
    lvwItems.SortOrder = lvwAscending
    lvwItems.SortKey = Index - 1
  End If
  lvwItems.Sorted = True

End Sub
```

Now when you run the code, you will be able to sort by tapping each column name. Do one tap for ascending and another for descending sort. Additional taps will simply toggle between ascending and descending sort. Easier than you may have thought, wasn't it?

> 66 However, full row select is still in the Pocket PC basic control that the eVB control is using. This is probably something you would want in every application. 99

You may have noticed by now what happens if you select an item in the list. Only the first column gets highlighted and you cannot select rows by tapping on any other column but the first. In VB 6.0 you have probably used the **FullRowSelect** property to enable the users to tap anywhere on the row to select it. Also, when selected, the whole row is marked as selected. This is not implemented in the ListView control that comes with eVB. However, full row select is still in the Pocket PC basic control that the eVB control is using. And since this is probably something you would want in every application, here is what you have to do to make it work anyway. First, you have to add some declarations and constants (preferably a code module, i.e. with the extension **.bas**):

```
Public Declare Function GetFocus Lib "coredll" () As Long
Public Declare Function SendMessage Lib "coredll" Alias
"SendMessageW" (ByVal hWnd As Long, ByVal wMsg As Long, ByVal
wParam As Long, ByVal lParam As Long) As Long
Public Const LVM_GETEXTENDEDLISTVIEWSTYLE = &H1037
Public Const LVM_SETEXTENDEDLISTVIEWSTYLE = &H1036
Public Const LVS_EX_FULLROWSELECT = &H20 ' applies to report
mode only
```

And the code to actually set the property is best placed in a separate public
function (in the same code module):

```
Public Sub SetFullRowSelect(hWnd As Long)
  Dim lStyle As Long
  lStyle = SendMessage(hWnd, LVM_GETEXTENDEDLISTVIEWSTYLE, 0,
0)
  lStyle = lStyle Or LVS_EX_FULLROWSELECT
  Call SendMessage(hWnd, LVM_SETEXTENDEDLISTVIEWSTYLE, 0,
lStyle)

End Sub
```

As you can see, we need to have the window handle (**hWnd**) for the control
to do this. If you check the properties available, you will see that there is no
such property on the ListView control. Well, that is why we included the
declaration for the Windows CE API **GetFocus** in the code above. This API
returns the window handle (hWnd) of the control that currently has the
focus. Now, here's what we need to do to set the ListView to enable
FullRowSelect:

```
' Set FullRowSelect
lvwItems.SetFocus
SetFullRowSelect GetFocus()
```

If you put the above code in the form with the ListView control, you can
now tap anywhere on the rows, to select the full row (see Figure 5.19).

If you do not want to set the column widths yourself, you can make the
ListView control simulate what happens when you double-click the column
separator – the column auto-sizes. You can do this by calling a method that
looks like this (with the necessary declarations first):

```
Public Const LVM_SETCOLUMNWIDTH = &H101E
Public Const LVSCW_AUTOSIZE = -1
Public Const LVSCW_AUTOSIZE_USEHEADER = -2

Public Sub AutoSizeColumns(lvw As ListViewCtrl)
```

Figure 5.19   ListView
sample

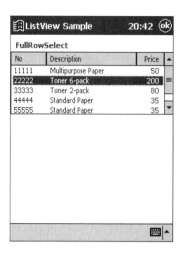

```
' Autosize all columns in ListView.
' IN: lvw, ListView control
' Known bugs:
' Version    Date    Who  Comment
' 00.00.000  010205  CFO  Created
'*********************************************************

***************

  Dim l As Long
  Dim hWnd As Long

  ' Get ListView control windows handle
  lvw.SetFocus
  hWnd = GetFocus()

  ' Autosize columns
  For l = 0 To lvw.ColumnHeaders.Count - 1
    Call SendMessage(hWnd, LVM_SETCOLUMNWIDTH, l,
LVSCW_AUTOSIZE)
  Next

End Sub
```

But remember that you have to fill the ListView control before you auto-size the columns. If you want to auto-size the columns according to the column header text (which you can do as soon as the headers are set), you just change the last parameter to **LVSCW_AUTOSIZE_USEHEADER**. You make the call to this method like this:

```
AutoSizeColumns lvwItems
```

Another similar example is to enable CheckBoxes in a ListView control. This is also easily available in the VB 6.0 ListView control (by setting property **Checkboxes** to True) and you can easily check the state of each ListItem with the **Checked** property. The ListView control in eVB lacks this implementation and therefore we have to use the same approach as for enabling the FullRowSelect. First, we have to add some declarations and constants:

```
Public Declare Function SendMessageString Lib "coredll" Alias
"SendMessageW" (ByVal hWnd As Long, ByVal wMsg As Long, ByVal
wParam As Long, ByVal lParam As String) As Long
Public Const LVM_GETITEMSTATE = &H102C
Public Const LVM_SETITEMSTATE = &H102B
Public Const LVS_EX_CHECKBOXES = &H4
Public Const LVIS_STATEIMAGEMASK = &HF000
```

And to enable CheckBoxes in the ListView, we could use the following public function:

```
Public Sub SetCheckBoxes(hWnd As Long)

  Dim lStyle As Long

  lStyle = SendMessage(hWnd, LVM_GETEXTENDEDLISTVIEWSTYLE, 0,
0)
  lStyle = lStyle Or LVS_EX_CHECKBOXES
  Call SendMessage(hWnd, LVM_SETEXTENDEDLISTVIEWSTYLE, 0,
lStyle)

End Sub
```

If you add another ListView control and name it **lvwCheckBox** you can enable CheckBoxes for it with the following code:

```
' Set check boxes
lvwCheckBox.SetFocus
SetCheckBoxes GetFocus()
```

Because the property on the ListItem (Checked) is also not available, we must add some more functions to obtain and set the checked state for each item. Here is the code to obtain the checked state for an item:

```
Public Function GetCheckState(hWnd As Long, Index As Long) As
Boolean

GetCheckState = CInt((SendMessage(hWnd, LVM_GETITEMSTATE, Index
- 1, LVIS_STATEIMAGEMASK) / 2 ^ 12) - 1) > 0

End Function
```

As when you enable CheckBoxes on the ListView, we need to pass the window handle and the currently selected item in the ListView. And here is the code to do that:

```
lvwCheckBox.SetFocus
MsgBox GetCheckState(GetFocus(),
lvwCheckBox.SelectedItem.Index)
```

And to set the checked state for each item, we have to add some more functions:

```
Public Sub SetCheckState(hWnd As Long, Index As Long, State As
Boolean)

  Dim lsLVITEM As String
  Dim llResult As Long
  Dim liStateValue As Integer

  ' Set state value
  If State Then
    liStateValue = &H2000
  Else
    liStateValue = &H1000
  End If

  ' Set simulated UDT LVITEM values
  lsLVITEM = LongToBytes(0) & LongToBytes(0) & LongToBytes(0) & _
             LongToBytes(liStateValue) & _
             LongToBytes(LVIS_STATEIMAGEMASK) & _
             LongToBytes(0) & LongToBytes(0) & _
             LongToBytes(0) & LongToBytes(0) & LongToBytes(0)

  ' Set state
  llResult = SendMessageString(hWnd, LVM_SETITEMSTATE, Index -
1, lsLVITEM)

End Sub
Public Function LongToBytes(ByVal Value As Long) As String

  Dim lsHex As String
  Dim i As Long
  lsHex = Right("00000000" & Hex(Value), 8)
  For i = 1 To 7 Step 2
    LongToBytes = ChrB(CInt('&H' & Mid(lsHex, i, 2))) &
LongToBytes
  Next
```

```
End Function
Public Sub ClearAllCheckState(hWnd As Long)

  Dim lsLVITEM As String
  Dim llResult As Long

  ' Set simulated UDT LVITEM values
  lsLVITEM = LongToBytes(0) & LongToBytes(0) & LongToBytes(0) & _
             LongToBytes(&H1000) & _
             LongToBytes(LVIS_STATEIMAGEMASK) & _
             LongToBytes(0) & LongToBytes(0) & _
             LongToBytes(0) & LongToBytes(0) & LongToBytes(0)

  ' Set state
  llResult = SendMessageString(hWnd, LVM_SETITEMSTATE, -1,
lsLVITEM)

End Sub
```

Above, we are using a special way of simulating UDTs with strings that you
will see more of later in this chapter. Note that the item index is zero-
based in when using the Windows API **SendMessageString**. That is why we
have to subtract 1 from the Index value passed as the third parameter. And
when you pass –1 as the third parameter, you see that the status changes
for all items in the ListView. And here is how it would look like to call
these functions:

```
' Set check box of currently select item
lvwCheckBox.SetFocus
Call SetCheckState(GetFocus(),lvwCheckBox.SelectedItem.Index,
True)

' Clear check box of currently select item
lvwCheckBox.SetFocus
Call SetCheckState(GetFocus(),lvwCheckBox.SelectedItem.Index,
False)

' Clear all checkboxes
lvwCheckBox.SetFocus
Call ClearAllCheckState(GetFocus())
```

In Figure 5.20 you'll see that we have selected the second item in the
ListView and then we tapped the **Get** button to get the message that the
selected item is checked.

Figure 5.20   ListView
checkbox sample

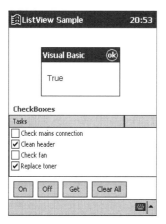

> 66 The ListView control can be used as a visually appealing menu. 99

Before we leave the ListView control, we will show you that it can be used as a visually appealing menu (see **Sample 5.7** on the CD).

1 Start a new eVB project, add a ListView control.

2 Name it **lvwItems**.

3 Set the **View** property on that ListView to **lvwIcon** (0) to show each item in the list as an icon instead of a row.

The ListView control cannot contain images itself, so it has to be connected to an ImageList control. We will therefore have a look at the ImageList control for a moment. If you add an ImageList control on a new form and name it **imlIcons**, you can add images to that control with the following code:

```
' Load images
imlIcons.Add App.Path & "\image1.bmp"
imlIcons.Add App.Path & "\image2.bmp"
imlIcons.Add App.Path & "\image3.bmp"
ImageList1.Add App.Path & "\image4.bmp"
```

Provided that the image files are located in the same folder as the **.vb** file on the device (real or emulated), the images will load. And the images in the ImageList control will be numbered 1, 2, 3, etc. This is what we need to use these images in a ListView control. If we add a ListView control to the same form, we could then add the following code:

```
Dim litm As ListItem

' Connect ListView and ImageList
lvwItems.Icons = imlIcons.hImageList

' Create ListItems
```

```
lvwItems.ListItems.Clear
Set litm = lvwItems.ListItems.Add(, , "First", 1)
Set litm = lvwItems.ListItems.Add(, , "Second", 2)
Set litm = lvwItems.ListItems.Add(, , "Third", 3)
Set litm = lvwItems.ListItems.Add(, , "Forth", 4)
```

As you can see, we start by linking the ListView to the ImageList control by setting the **Icons** property on the ListView to the **hImageList** property on the ImageList. And then we remove all previous items in the ListView and then add new items to it. We are now using the fourth parameter to the **Add** method on the ListItems collection. This parameter selects the number of the image to connect to each item from the ImageList control.

> ▦▶ **Tip**
>
> When you create the images, all items will need to be the size of the first image added to the ImageList. To make a good-looking menu, you should make sure that all images are the same size (width and height).

To complete the logic, you could add the following code:

```
Private Sub lvwItems_ItemClick(ByVal Index As Long)
  Select Case Index
    Case 1
      ' do something
    Case 2
      ' do something else
    .

    .

    .
  End Select

End Sub
```

This is all you have to do to create your nice looking menu of images (icons). Figure 5.21 shows an example of a real-world application for sales-people at Cap Gemini Ernst & Young using this technique.

The images in Figure 5.21 are sized 75×75 pixels each. That is an ideal size if you want the ListView to align the menu choices in two columns as you see in Figure 5.21. If you want a more standard-looking view of your menu (like the **Start > Programs** folder on your Pocket PC), you should create images that are sized as normal icons (32×32 pixels). You will then get three items on each row.

Figure 5.21 ListView
as menu sample

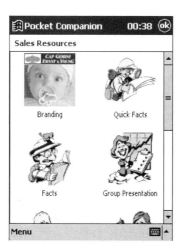

And what you have seen so far is probably the majority of what you need to include in your applications. The ListView is a very capable control and if you want to explore more of the "hard-core" features of this control, you have more to discover.

This sample is actually the complete application provided with permission from Cap Gemini Ernst & Young.

HScrollBar and VScrollBar controls

You might wonder why we have dedicated a section of our book for these controls. When was the last time that you used them in your VB 6.0 applications? Well, probably some time ago. And the use of these controls might not be what you expect since we will not talk about them as scrollbars. Rather, we will use them as input assistance.

> 66 And the use of these controls might not be what you expect since we will not talk about them as scrollbars. Rather, we will use them as input assistance. 99

One of the most important considerations when writing the user interface for Pocket PC applications is that the data input must be as efficient as possible. We cannot afford to have the user entering everything from the SIP (keyboard, character recognizer, etc.) because it is not very user-friendly and time consuming for the user. We need ways to turn as many of the SIP inputs as possible into stylus taps. When it comes to entering numeric values into TextBox controls, the scrollbars can actually be used as the VB 6.0 **UpDown** control (see **Sample 5.8** on the CD). Let's examine Figure 5.22 to see how this could look.

As you can see, we can use both the VScrollBar and the HScrollBar controls to accomplish what we want to do. If we start with the more

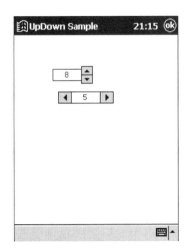

Figure 5.22
ScrollBars simulating
UpDown sample

traditional use of the UpDown control, you can add a VScrollBar name **vscUpDown** to the right of a TextBox control named **txtNumber**. And then you could add this code to the **Form_Load** event:

```
vscUpDown.Max = 1
vscUpDown.Min = 10
vscUpDown.SmallChange = 1
vscUpDown.Value = vscUpDown.Max
```

Notice that the **Max** property holds the lower bound and **Min** the upper. Also you would have to add the following code:

```
Private Sub txtNumber_LostFocus()

  vscUpDown.Value = CInt(txtNumber.Text)

End Sub
Private Sub vscUpDown_Change()

  txtNumber.Text = vscUpDown.Value

End Sub
```

If you do not want to include the user's ability to enter values manually, set the **Enabled** property to **False** on the TextBox. You can also remove the **txtNumber_LostFocus** event code above. This way you don't even have to handle the validation of upper and lower boundaries.

The code for the HScrollBar named **hscUpDown** looks much the same:

```
hscUpDown.Min = 1
hscUpDown.Max = 10
hscUpDown.SmallChange = 1
hscUpDown.Value = hscUpDown.Min
```

But as you can see the upper and lower bounds are more logical. The event code is almost identical. If you add another TextBox named **txtAmount**, you can place this control on top of the HScrollBar control. Since the HScrollBar should be placed behind the TextBox, you have to explicitly right-click the HScrollBar control and select the context-sensitive menu option **Send To Back**.

Using TabStrips

Microsoft Windows users are now very familiar with **TabStrips**. **TabStrips** were introduced about the same time as wizard, in the early 1990s. The functional difference between TabStrips and a wizard is that the **TabStrip** allows the user to choose the order to enter data, whereas the wizard takes the user through a set of predefined steps.

These two methods share the objective of facilitating a logical grouping of data. They even share the preferred way to technically implementing the grouping.

66 However, the **TabStrip** control is not a container. So in order to show and hide groups of controls you need to use a **Frame**, just as you would when implementing a Wizard. 99

However, the **TabStrip** control is not a container. So in order to show and hide groups of controls you need to use a **Frame**, just as you would when implementing a Wizard.

Included in eMbedded Visual Basic is a **TabStrip** component. In order to use the control, you need to add it to your project.

Figure 5.23 (see **Sample 5.9** on the CD) consists of a form from ACME Copier's Pocket Service Application project. The sample lets the field technician work with Customer information that is logically grouped into Address, Phone, Contacts, and Comments.

Figure 5.23   The Address Tab

The **TabStrip** can be configured to appear as normal tab strips or as buttons by using the property **Style**.

Figure 5.24   The Address Tab using tabButtons style

Through the code, each tab strip is associated to a frame. When the user taps on a tab, the code turns the associated frame visible and renders the other frames invisible.

Figure 5.25   The Phone Tab

The code that turns the frames visible and invisible is put in the TabStrip click event:

```
Private Sub tabStrip_Click()

' Handle tab selection.
' Known bugs:
' Version    Date    Who   Comment
' 00.00.000 010205 CFO   Created
'*****************************

  ' Respond to tab click
    If tabStrip.Tabs(1).Selected Then
    fraTab1.Visible = True
    fraTab2.Visible = False
    fraTab3.Visible = False
    fraTab4.Visible = False
  ElseIf tabStrip.Tabs(2).Selected Then
    fraTab1.Visible = False
    fraTab2.Visible = True
    fraTab3.Visible = False
    fraTab4.Visible = False
  ElseIf tabStrip.Tabs(3).Selected Then
    fraTab1.Visible = False
    fraTab2.Visible = False
    fraTab3.Visible = True
    fraTab4.Visible = False
  ElseIf tabStrip.Tabs(4).Selected Then
    fraTab1.Visible = False
    fraTab2.Visible = False
    fraTab3.Visible = False
    fraTab4.Visible = True
  End If

End Sub
```

PictureBox control

The PictureBox control is a familiar control, but with some new limitations. It can only handle pictures in the standard Windows bitmap format. Also, the supported bitmap format can have a maximum of 256 colors in the palette. If you are using the standard Paint program in Windows, you have to select the **256 Color Bitmap** option when saving the file. This means that if you have a picture in JPEG (Joint Photographic Experts Group) or GIF (Graphics Interchange Format) format, you have to import (menu option **Edit > Paste From**) the picture into Paint and then save it in the correct format to use in your eVB application. We will come back to this issue when we talk about a third-party control called **S309PictureBox** later in this chapter.

You also have to handle the design of pictures in a new way.

- First of all, you cannot paste a picture from the clipboard directly into the **Picture** property of the PictureBox control as you may be used to. Instead, you have to enter the path of a file, or at least the file name, where the picture is stored.

- When you set the **Picture** property of the **PictureBox** control, the picture will not be shown in the control on your form. The **Picture** property will only be resolved during runtime. If you want to try out entering a file-name in the **Picture** property, you have to place the picture file in the folder where the running program can access it.

- If you enter just the name of the picture file, the running program will look for it in the root folder of the device (real or emulator). The normal situation is that you reference the picture files as Related Documents. You do that by choosing to add a file (**Project > Add File...**) and selecting the picture file. Make sure that you have checked the **Add As Related Document** in the lower left of the Add File dialog. This means that the pictures will be copied to the same path as you have selected as target for your compiled intermediate file (probably something like **\Program Files\Project1\Project1.vb** which you select in **Project Properties**. You access this via the menu option **Project > Project1 Properties**).

S309PictureBox control

As we mentioned before, there are some obvious limitations with the standard PictureBox control. The most important limitation of the standard PictureBox control is the fact that it can only handle 256-color standard Windows bitmaps. Bitmap files are an uncompressed format that creates large files, and that is something you want to avoid on a Pocket PC with its limited memory.

> "The most important limitation of the standard PictureBox control is the fact that it can only handle 256-color standard Windows bitmaps."

Most of your picture files (at least ours) are *not* in standard Windows bitmap format – they are either in JPEG or GIF format since they come from all those web applications that you have probably built for some years. The most obvious consequence of this is that you would have to convert all those files into bitmap format and that is not a fun task – you have more important things to do! Another is the fact that bitmap files are significantly larger in size than a corresponding JPEG or GIF file (a typical file is more than double the size in bitmap format).

Due to the limitations of the standard PictureBox control we have included a third-party control called **S309PictureBox** on the accompanying CD. This control has the following features:

- Display bitmap (bmp and 2bp), GIF, JPEG, and XBM image files.
- Display bitmap resources from resource files, including common bitmaps such as FileOpen and FileClose.
- Capture and display an image of the physical screen.
- Save an image as a bitmap file.
- Display and animate playing cards like the ones used in the Solitaire game provided with Windows CE.
- Clip, invert colors, mirror, resize, and rotate an image.
- Display an image with a transparent color.
- Provide access to individual pixels in the image.
- Specify colors using RGB or QBColor notation.
- Overlay one image on top of another.
- Draw lines, rectangles, circles, polygons, and round rectangles.
- Change the color depth of an image.
- Refresh the desktop wallpaper.
- Better support for drawing.
- Better support for 65,536 color displays.
- Support drawing text.
- Support command button emulation.
- Support label emulation.
- Use scroll bars.
- Display icon resources from executable files, resource files, and icon (*.ico) files.
- Support for tap and hold event.

And of course the most important feature is the support for JPEG and GIF files. The use of the S309PictureBox control is very similar to using the standard PictureBox control. Here are some additional tips on using the S309PictureBox control:

- If your image does not load, try setting the property .ImageLoadBuffer Size = 4096.
- Use .DrawMouseMoveLine or .DrawMouseMoveLineEx methods in the _MouseDown, _MouseMove, and _MouseUp events to draw smother lines with the stylus.
- Set the property .Visible = True in code for each S309PictureBox to get it to display even if you have set it in design mode.
- Set property .AutoSize = False in the code prior to loading an image. If you need to AutoSize the control see the next item.

- If you need the S309PictureBox to auto-size itself you will need to set the property. .AutoSize = True and have a _VBCEAutoSize event for the control and set the .Height and .Width properties in the event procedure.

```
Private Sub S309PictureBox1_VBCEAutoSize(ByVal nWidth As Long,
ByVal nHeight As Long)
  S309PictureBox1.Width = nWidth
  S309PictureBox1.Height = nHeight
End Sub
```

- When using the .Height and .Width properties outside of the VBCEAutoSize event, you will need to subtract six pixels in order for eVB to display it in the correct dimensions.
- The .Hide, .Show, and .Refresh methods do not work with eVB.
- You can find an updated list of tips on using the S309PictureBox control at: members.nbci.com/s309/PictureBox2/S309PictureBox_tips.html

Let us look in practice what the S309PictureBox control can do. We have ported one of the example projects provided with the control to an eVB application and when it is run, it is shown in Figure 5.26 (see **Sample 5.10** on the CD).

In Figure 5.26, we have loaded a picture (GIF) from the first page of the web site **www.PocketPC.com**, captured the screen with the application itself, and then used the mirror function (magnifying glass button) to mirror it horizontally.

Figure 5.26
S309PictureBox
sample

With the S309PictureBox sample application you can:

- Open any picture file with the extensions supported by the control (*.2bp, *.bmp, *.gif, *.jpg, *.jpeg, *.jpe, *.xbm).
- Save the picture in bitmap (.bmp) format.
- Use predefined button images as buttons.
- Mirror a picture (horizontally and/or vertically).
- Rotate a picture.
- Align a picture (stretch, center, etc.).
- Get information about a picture (size, color depth).
- See a picture in full screen.
- Invert colors in picture.
- Add scrollbars to picture.
- Capture the screen.

As you can see this application is very useful. With only about 300 lines of code in this demo, it can really be used for doing many things. Actually, the screen shot in Figure 5.26 was made by the sample application. You will actually be able to write your own screen capture application, sell it, and get rich! If you do write your own screen capture software, please let us know and we will spread the news.

Let's see the code for doing the screen capture. This advanced functionality is accomplished with this code:

```
picBox.CaptureScreen
```

It is really too easy! But the fact is that the only screen capture we can do at the moment is of the running demo application. You might get tired of getting identical screen shots all the time. To make this a usable application, you will need to implement a way to activate this screen capture application from any other of your Pocket PC applications. And a suitable solution would be to assign one of the hardware buttons to do just that. That is actually the solution that many of the commercial products have chosen. We have included an example of how it is done later in this chapter.

If you look carefully, you will see another interesting feature; you can use images for buttons that are already on your Pocket PC. The button images are stored in the Pocket PC ROM (read-only memory). You can use them to provide buttons in your applications that look like the standard applications from Microsoft and others. To initialize such a button, which is actually an S309PictureBox control named **btnSave**,

66You can use images for buttons that are already on your Pocket PC. 99

you use the following code:

```
btnSave.AutoSize = True
btnSave.BorderStyle = 1
btnSave.Appearance = 1
btnSave.CommonBitmapType = S309_STD_ENABLE ' =1
btnSave.CommonBitmapID = STD_FILESAVE ' =8
btnSave.Visible = True
```

And you can use the following code to rotate the image:

```
picBox.Rotate = 90 ' degrees
picBox.RotateImage
```

Use this code to invert the colors:

```
picBox.Invert = True
picBox.InvertImage
```

To mirror an image:

```
picBox.Mirror = 1 ' Horizontal
picBox.MirrorImage
```

To load a picture from a file:

```
picBox.Picture = FileName
```

To save the picture to file, you just:

```
picBox.SaveImageToFile FileName, 0 ' bitmap
```

The only file format currently available for saving picture is bitmap (.bmp).

 Tip

If you get some spare time, you might even explore the ability that this control has to show all playing cards. With this ability, you would easily put together your favorite card game.

Suppose that you would like the picture loaded to resize to fit in the S309PictureBox control. This will happen as soon as you show a picture of a product or person and is a very common business scenario. The code to do this is:

```
Dim liImageWidth As Integer
Dim liImageHeight As Integer
Dim liPictureWidth As Integer
Dim liPictureHeight As Integer
Dim ldRatio As Double
```

```
S309PictureBox1.Visible = True
S309PictureBox1.Picture = "\Program Files\Test\picfile.jpg"

liImageWidth = S309PictureBox1.ImageWidth
liImageHeight = S309PictureBox1.ImageHeight

liPictureWidth = S309PictureBox1.Width / 15
liPictureHeight = S309PictureBox1.Height / 15

If (liImageWidth / liPictureWidth) > (liImageHeight /
liPictureHeight) Then
  ldRatio = liImageWidth / liPictureWidth
  liImageWidth = Int(liImageWidth / ldRatio)
  liImageHeight = Int(liImageHeight / ldRatio)
Else
  ldRatio = liImageHeight / liPictureHeight
  liImageWidth = Int(liImageWidth / ldRatio)
  liImageHeight = Int(liImageHeight / ldRatio)
End If
S309PictureBox1.ResizeWidth = liImageWidth
S309PictureBox1.ResizeHeight = liImageHeight
S309PictureBox1.ResizeImage
```

And this way you will always have a picture that is fully visible when it is resized, no matter if the resize have been made due to the width or the height of the picture.

You have already seen that this control is loaded with practical uses. We encourage you to explore its capabilities further.

Date/Time Picker control

As you probably have noticed, there is no DateTimePicker control included with eVB. And as we mentioned before it's very desirable to minimize what the user has to enter through the SIP. We want to convert SIP entries to stylus taps and when it comes to dates, it can really be a hassle to enter dates by using the SIP. As with some of the other things that you want to do that are not included in eVB, you have to use Windows CE API calls with all its obstacles (lack of UDTs, and so forth).

> ❝It can really be a hassle to enter dates by using the SIP. ❞

To create a date and time picker yourself (see **Sample 5.11** on the CD), you can start with a blank form. Add a Frame control, name it **fraDatePick**, and add the following code to a code module:

```
Option Explicit

' Variable to pass the Window Handler
Private DateTimePickCtl_hWnd As Long

' Constants
Private Const DATETIMEPICK_CLASS = "SysDateTimePick32"
Private Const ICC_DATE_CLASSES = &H100&

Private Const WS_BORDER = &H800000
Private Const WS_CHILD = &H40000000
Private Const WS_VISIBLE = &H10000000

Private Const SWP_NOZORDER = 4

' DateTimePicker Messages
Private Const DTM_GETSYSTEMTIME = &H1001
Private Const DTM_SETSYSTEMTIME = &H1002
Private Const DTM_GETRANGE = &H1003
Private Const DTM_SETRANGE = &H1004
Private Const DTM_SETFORMAT = &H1032
Private Const DTM_SETMCCOLOR = &H1006
Private Const DTM_GETMCCOLOR = &H1007
Private Const DTM_GETMONTHCAL = &H1008
Private Const DTM_SETMCFONT = &H1009
Private Const DTM_GETMCFONT = &H1010

' DateTimePicker styles
Private Const DTS_UPDOWN = &H1             ' use UPDOWN instead of MONTHCAL
Private Const DTS_SHOWNONE = &H2           ' allow a NONE or checkbox selection
Private Const DTS_SHORTDATEFORMAT = &H0    ' use the short date format (app must
                                           '    forward WM_WININICHANGE messages)
Private Const DTS_LONGDATEFORMAT = &H4     ' use the long date format (app must
                                           '    forward WM_WININICHANGE messages)
Private Const DTS_TIMEFORMAT = &H9         ' use the time format (app must forward
                                           '    WM_WININICHANGE messages)
Private Const DTS_APPCANPARSE = &H10       ' allow user entered strings (app MUST
                                           '    respond to DTN_USERSTRING)
Private Const DTS_RIGHTALIGN = &H20        ' right-align popup instead of
                                           '    left-align it
Private Const DTS_NONEBUTTON = &H80        ' use NONE button instead of checkbox

' Month Calendar color attributes
```

```
Private Const MCSC_BACKGROUND = 0   ' Background color (between months)
Private Const MCSC_TEXT = 1         ' Dates within a month
Private Const MCSC_TITLEBK = 2      ' Background of the title
Private Const MCSC_TITLETEXT = 3    ' Text within the calendar's title
Private Const MCSC_MONTHBK = 4      ' Background of a month
Private Const MCSC_TRAILINGTEXT = 5 ' The text color of header & trailing days

' API Declares
Declare Function SetWindowPos Lib "Coredll" (ByVal hwnd As Long, ByVal
hWndInsertAfter As Long, ByVal x As Long, ByVal y As Long, ByVal cx As Long,
ByVal cy As Long, ByVal wFlags As Long) As Long
Declare Function SendMessageString Lib "Coredll" Alias "SendMessageW" (ByVal hwnd
As Long, ByVal wMsg As Long, ByVal wParam As Long, ByVal lParam As String) As
Long
Declare Function SendMessage Lib "Coredll" Alias "SendMessageW" (ByVal hwnd As
Long, ByVal wMsg As Long, ByVal wParam As Long, ByVal lParam As Long) As Long
Declare Function CreateWindowEx Lib "Coredll" Alias "CreateWindowExW" (ByVal
dwExStyle As Long, ByVal lpClassName As String, ByVal lpWindowName As String,
ByVal dwStyle As Long, ByVal x As Long, ByVal y As Long, ByVal nWidth As Long,
ByVal nHeight As Long, ByVal hWndParent As Long, ByVal hMenu As Long, ByVal
hInstance As Long, ByVal lpParam As String) As Long
Declare Function InitCommonControlsEx Lib "Commctrl" (ByVal
LPINITCOMMONCONTROLSEX As String) As Boolean
Public Sub DateTimePickCtl_Load(hwndOwner As Long, g_hinst As Long, cLeft As
Long, cTop As Long, ByVal cWidth As Long, ByVal cHeight As Long, ByVal Style As
Long)

   Dim udtINITCCEX As String 'To hold INITCOMMONCONTROLSEX udt
   Dim udtRECT As String: udtRECT = Space(8) 'Reserve 16 bytes for RECT udt

   ' Create INITCOMMONCONTROLSEX udt...
   udtINITCCEX = setINITCOMMONCONTROLSEX(8, ICC_DATE_CLASSES)
   ' ...and initialize Common Controls
   Call InitCommonControlsEx(udtINITCCEX)

   ' Create the month calendar (resize it later)
```

```
DateTimePickCtl_hWnd = CreateWindowEx(0, DATETIMEPICK_CLASS, "", WS_BORDER +
WS_CHILD + WS_VISIBLE + Style, 0, 0, 0, 0, hwndOwner, vbNull, g_hinst, vbNull)

  ' Resize the control
  Call SetWindowPos(DateTimePickCtl_hWnd, vbNull, cLeft, cTop, cWidth, cHeight,
SWP_NOZORDER)

End Sub
Public Function DateTimePickCtl_SetColor(iColor As Long, clr As Long) As Long

  ' Set colors to draw control
  DateTimePickCtl_SetColor = SendMessage(DateTimePickCtl_hWnd, DTM_SETMCCOLOR,
iColor, clr)

End Function
Public Function DateTimePickCtl_SetFormat(ByVal FormatString As String) As Long

  ' Set colors to draw control
  DateTimePickCtl_SetFormat = SendMessageString(DateTimePickCtl_hWnd,
DTM_SETFORMAT, 0, FormatString)

End Function
Public Function DateTimePickCtl_GetDateTime() As Date

  Dim wYear As Integer, wMonth As Integer, wDayOfWeek As Integer, wDay As Integer
  Dim wHour As Integer, wMinute As Integer, wSecond As Integer, wMSecond As
Integer
  Dim udtSYSTEMTIME As String

  udtSYSTEMTIME = Space(8) ' Reserve 16 bytes for SYSTEMTIME udt

  ' Get the date currently selected
  Call SendMessageString(DateTimePickCtl_hWnd, DTM_GETSYSTEMTIME, 0,
udtSYSTEMTIME)

  ' Read SYSTEMTIME udt items...
  Call getSYSTEMTIME(udtSYSTEMTIME, wYear, wMonth, wDayOfWeek, wDay, wHour,
wMinute, wSecond, wMSecond)
  ' ...and convert them to a Date value
  DateTimePickCtl_GetDateTime = DateSerial(wYear, wMonth, wDay) +
TimeSerial(wHour, wMinute, wSecond + wMSecond / 1000)
```

```
End Function
Public Sub DateTimePickCtl_SetDateTime(ByVal Value As Date)

  Dim wYear As Integer, wMonth As Integer, wDayOfWeek As Integer, wDay As Integer
  Dim wHour As Integer, wMinute As Integer, wSecond As Integer, wMSecond As
Integer
  Dim udtSYSTEMTIME As String

  udtSYSTEMTIME = Space(8) ' Reserve 16 bytes for SYSTEMTIME UDT

  wYear = Year(Value)
  wMonth = Month(Value)
  wDayOfWeek = Weekday(Value)
  wDay = Day(Value)
  wHour = Hour(Value)
  wMinute = Minute(Value)
  wSecond = Second(Value)
  wMSecond = 0

  ' Read SYSTEMTIME udt items...
  Call setSYSTEMTIME(udtSYSTEMTIME, wYear, wMonth, wDayOfWeek, wDay, wHour,
wMinute, wSecond, wMSecond)

  ' Set the current date to be selected
  Call SendMessageString(DateTimePickCtl_hWnd, DTM_SETSYSTEMTIME, 0,
udtSYSTEMTIME)

End Sub
Private Function DateTimePickCtl_GetMinReqRect(prc As String) As Long

  ' Get minimum size required to display a full month
  DateTimePickCtl_GetMinReqRect = SendMessageString(DateTimePickCtl_hWnd,
MCM_GETMINREQRECT, 0, prc)

End Function
Public Sub getSYSTEMTIME(ByVal str As String, ByRef wYear As Integer, ByRef
wMonth As Integer, ByRef wDayOfWeek As Integer, ByRef wDay As Integer, ByRef
wHour As Integer, ByRef wMinute As Integer, ByRef wSecond As Integer, ByRef
wMSecond As Integer)

  ' Read SYSTEMTIME UDT components
  wYear = BytesToInteger(MidB(str, 1, 2))
  wMonth = BytesToInteger(MidB(str, 3, 2))
```

```
  wDayOfWeek = BytesToInteger(MidB(str, 5, 2))
  wDay = BytesToInteger(MidB(str, 7, 2))
  wHour = BytesToInteger(MidB(str, 9, 2))
  wMinute = BytesToInteger(MidB(str, 11, 2))
  wSecond = BytesToInteger(MidB(str, 13, 2))
  wMSecond = BytesToInteger(MidB(str, 15, 2))

End Sub
Public Sub setSYSTEMTIME(ByRef str As String, ByVal wYear As Integer, ByVal
wMonth As Integer, ByVal wDayOfWeek As Integer, ByVal wDay As Integer, ByVal
wHour As Integer, ByVal wMinute As Integer, ByVal wSecond As Integer, ByVal
wMSecond As Integer)

  ' Set SYSTEMTIME UDT components
  str = IntegerToBytes(wYear) & _
        IntegerToBytes(wMonth) & _
        IntegerToBytes(wDayOfWeek) & _
        IntegerToBytes(wDay) & _
        IntegerToBytes(wHour) & _
        IntegerToBytes(wMinute) & _
        IntegerToBytes(wSecond) & _
        IntegerToBytes(wMSecond)

End Sub
Private Function getRECT(ByVal RECT As String, ByRef RECTleft As Long, ByRef
RECTtop As Long, ByRef RECTright As Long, ByRef RECTbottom As Long) As Long

  ' Read RECT UDT components:
  ' Type RECT
  ' Left As Long
  ' Top As Long
  ' Right As Long
  ' Bottom As Long
  ' End Type

  RECTleft = BytesToLong(MidB(RECT, 1, 4))
  RECTtop = BytesToLong(MidB(RECT, 5, 4))
  RECTright = BytesToLong(MidB(RECT, 9, 4))
  RECTbottom = BytesToLong(MidB(RECT, 13, 4))

End Function
Private Function setINITCOMMONCONTROLSEX(ByVal dwSize As Long, ByVal dwICC As
Long) As String
```

```
' Build INITCOMMONCONTROLSEX UDT:
' Type LPINITCOMMONCONTROLSEX
' dwSize As Long
' dwICC As Long
' End Type

  setINITCOMMONCONTROLSEX = LongToBytes(dwSize) & LongToBytes(dwICC)
End Function
Function LongToBytes(ByVal Value As Long) As String

  Dim lsHex As String, i As Integer

  lsHex = Right("00000000" & Hex(Value), 8)
  For i = 1 To 7 Step 2
    LongToBytes = ChrB(CInt("&H" & Mid(lsHex, i, 2))) & LongToBytes
  Next

End Function
Function BytesToLong(ByVal Value As String) As Long

  Dim lsHex As String, i As Integer

  For i = 1 To 4
    lsHex = Hex(AscB(MidB(Value, i, 1))) & lsHex
  Next
  BytesToLong = CLng("&H" & lsHex)

End Function
Function IntegerToBytes(ByVal Value As Integer) As String

  Dim lsHex As String, i As Integer

  lsHex = Right("0000" & Hex(Value), 4)
  For i = 1 To 3 Step 2
    IntegerToBytes = ChrB(CInt("&H" & Mid(lsHex, i, 2))) & IntegerToBytes
  Next

End Function
Function BytesToInteger(ByVal Value As String) As Integer

  BytesToInteger = CLng("&H" & Hex(AscB(MidB(Value, 2, 1))) &
Hex(AscB(MidB(Value, 1, 1))))

End Function
```

You then start the form (in the **Form_Load** event) by creating the control:

```
DateTimePickCtl_Load fraDatePick.hwnd, App.hInstance, 0, 0,
  fraDatePick.Width / 15, fraDatePick.Height / 15, 0
```

The reason we have to divide by **15** is that we are using the default **ScaleMode** on the Form, which is **Twip** (1). You have now created something similar to Figure 5.27.

Figure 5.27
DatePicker sample

And to set the format of the control you can use the following code:

```
DateTimePickCtl_SetFormat "MM'/'dd'/'yy"
```

The date format string can contain the same tokens as defined in the **GetDateFormat** Microsoft Windows CE API. See the Help file for eVT for a complete reference. Table 5.1 has a list of the most important tokens.

Table 5.1   Date tokens

Value	Description
d	Day of month as digits with no leading zero for single-digit days.
dd	Day of month as digits with leading zero for single-digit days.
ddd	Day of week as a three-letter abbreviation.
dddd	Day of week as its full name.

Value	Description
M	Month as digits with no leading zero for single-digit months.
MM	Month as digits with leading zero for single-digit months.
MMM	Month as a three-letter abbreviation.
MMMM	Month as its full name.
y	Year as last two digits, with no leading zero for years less than 10.
yy	Year as last two digits, with a leading zero for years less than 10.
yyyy	Year represented by full four digits.

If you want to use the control as a time picker instead, just create the control (in the **Form_Load** event) with this code instead:

```
DateTimePickCtl_Load fraDatePick.hwnd, App.hInstance, 0, 0, _
    fraDatePick.Width / 15, fraDatePick.Height / 15, _
    DTS_TIMEFORMAT
```

When you have selected any of the time parts (hour, minute, or second), you can use the up and down arrows to increment or decrement the value. As with the date entry, you can change the display format with code such as:

```
DateTimePickCtl_SetFormat "hh"':'mm' 'tt"
```

The time format string can contain the same tokens as defined in the **GetTimeFormat** Windows CE API. See the Help file for eVT for a complete reference. Table 5.2 has a list of the most important tokens.

Table 5.2   Time tokens

Value	Description
h	Hours with no leading zero for single-digit hours; 12-hour clock
hh	Hours with leading zero for single-digit hours; 12-hour clock
H	Hours with no leading zero for single-digit hours; 24-hour clock
HH	Hours with leading zero for single-digit hours; 24-hour clock

m	Minutes with no leading zero for single-digit minutes
mm	Minutes with leading zero for single-digit minutes
s	Seconds with no leading zero for single-digit seconds
ss	Seconds with leading zero for single-digit seconds
t	One character time marker string, such as A or P
tt	Multicharacter time marker string, such as AM or PM

You can now build a date string from the selected date (or time) with code like this:

```
Dim x As Date
x = DateTimePickCtl_GetDateTime
MsgBox "Current date is: " & _
        Month(x) & "/" & _
        Day(x) & "/" & _
        Year(x)
' or
'       Hour(x) & ":" & _
'       Minute(x) & ":" & _
'       Second(x)
```

And you set the date (or time) with code like:

```
Dim x As Date
x = DateSerial(1965, 9, 23) ' or x = TimeSerial(14, 23, 13)
DateTimePickCtl_SetDateTime x
```

You can even change the background color of the month view, by:

```
DateTimePickCtl_SetColor MCSC_MONTHBK, vbRed
```

As you can see the usage is very straightforward and if you spend some time entering date and time values you will see the benefit of not having to enter the values via the SIP.

If you for some reason find the above a bit hard-core, you should think about obtaining a ready-made control for eVB called vbceDateTimePicker. You find the control at: **www.vbce.com/vbceDateTimePicker/**

ProgressBar control

As a developer you always expect things to run at the speed of thought. If you are developing for PCs, you may be used to the fantastic speed of modern processors. When developing for Pocket PCs, there are things that take more time than you might expect. This is partly because the processor speed is not comparable with your PC (yet) and partly because many operations, like communication, are dependent on bandwidth, which is not yet what we would wish.

When you test your application you may realize that a certain operation takes too long just to let the screen freeze. The first idea would be to show the hourglass cursor. This simple line of code will do the trick:

```
Screen.MousePointer = 11 ' vbHourGlass
```

And if you declare a global constant called vbHourGlass and assign the value **11** to it, your code looks even better (then you should also add a vbArrow constant set to **1** for restoring the cursor).

Even if this is a great way of solving the problem and has also been used extensively by other Pocket PC developers, there are still situations where even the hourglass can appear annoying. Your users may start asking questions like "Is it still running?" or "Should I make a soft reset?" even if everything is all right with your application. However, the delay may be perfectly normal and necessary, such as waiting for a connection to be established or the response from a web server.

❝A progress bar not only shows your users that something is happening, it also shows how fast something is happening. ❞

That is when you should consider a progress bar. A progress bar not only shows your users that something is happening, it also shows how fast something is happening. That helps your users to predict when to expect the operation to be finished. Somehow, it will even keep them occupied just following the progress bar, as it seems to have a calming effect on many people.

If there are multiple operations, each of which are time consuming, do not hesitate to use more than one progress bar; one for the overall operation and one for each sub operation. This method has been used successfully for many years by installation application developers.

To create a progress bar yourself (see **Sample 5.12** on the CD), you can start with a blank form. Add a Frame control; size the frame control to a size that will fit a progress bar nicely. Then, add the following code to a code module:

```
Option Explicit

' Variable to pass the Window Handler
Private ProgressBarCtl_hWnd As Long
```

```
' Constants
Private Const PROGRESS_CLASS = "msctls_progress32"
Private Const ICC_PROGRESS_CLASS = &H20

Private Const WS_BORDER = &H800000
Private Const WS_CHILD = &H40000000
Private Const WS_VISIBLE = &H10000000

Private Const SWP_NOSIZE = &H1
Private Const SWP_NOMOVE = &H2
Private Const SWP_NOZORDER = &H4
Private Const SWP_FRAMECHANGED = &H20 ' The frame changed: send
WM_NCCALCSIZE

Private Const GWL_STYLE = (-16)
Private Const GWL_EXSTYLE = (-20)

' ProgressBar Messages
Private Const PBS_SMOOTH = &H1
Private Const PBS_VERTICAL = &H4
Private Const PBM_SETRANGE = &H401
Private Const PBM_SETPOS = &H402
Private Const PBM_DELTAPOS = &H403
Private Const PBM_SETSTEP = &H404
Private Const PBM_STEPIT = &H405
Private Const PBM_SETRANGE32 = &H406 ' lParam = high, wParam =
low
Private Const PBM_GETRANGE = &H407 ' wParam = return (TRUE ?
low : high). lParam = PPBRANGE or NULL
Private Const PBM_GETPOS = &H408

' API Declares
Declare Function SetWindowPos Lib "Coredll" (ByVal hWnd As
Long, ByVal hWndInsertAfter As Long, ByVal x As Long, ByVal y
As Long, ByVal cx As Long, ByVal cy As Long, ByVal wFlags As
Long) As Long
Declare Function SendMessageString Lib "Coredll" Alias
"SendMessageW" (ByVal hWnd As Long, ByVal wMsg As Long, ByVal
wParam As Long, ByVal lParam As String) As Long
Declare Function SendMessage Lib "Coredll" Alias "SendMessageW"
(ByVal hWnd As Long, ByVal wMsg As Long, ByVal wParam As Long,
ByVal lParam As Long) As Long
Declare Function CreateWindowEx Lib "Coredll" Alias
"CreateWindowExW" (ByVal dwExStyle As Long, ByVal lpClassName
```

```
As String, ByVal lpWindowName As String, ByVal dwStyle As Long,
ByVal x As Long, ByVal y As Long, ByVal nWidth As Long, ByVal
nHeight As Long, ByVal hWndParent As Long, ByVal hMenu As Long,
ByVal hInstance As Long, ByVal lpParam As String) As Long
Declare Function InitCommonControlsEx Lib "Commctrl" (ByVal
LPINITCOMMONCONTROLSEX As String) As Boolean
Declare Function SetWindowLong Lib "Coredll" Alias
"SetWindowLongW" (ByVal hWnd As Long, ByVal nIndex As Long,
ByVal NewLong As Long) As Long
Declare Function GetWindowLong Lib "Coredll" Alias
"GetWindowLongW" (ByVal hWnd As Long, ByVal nIndex As Long) As
Long
Public Sub ProgressBarCtl_Load(hwndOwner As Long, g_hinst As
Long, ByVal cLeft As Long, ByVal cTop As Long, ByVal cWidth As
Long, ByVal cHeight As Long, ByVal Smooth As Boolean)

  Dim lStyle As Long
  Dim udtINITCCEX As String ' To hold INITCOMMONCONTROLSEX udt
  Dim udtRECT As String: udtRECT = Space(8) ' Reserve 16 bytes
for RECT udt

  ' Create INITCOMMONCONTROLSEX udt...
  udtINITCCEX = setINITCOMMONCONTROLSEX(8, ICC_PROGRESS_CLASS)
  ' ...and initialize Common Controls
  Call InitCommonControlsEx(udtINITCCEX)

  ' Set Style
  If Smooth Then lStyle = PBS_SMOOTH

  ' Create the month calendar (resize it later)
  ProgressBarCtl_hWnd = CreateWindowEx(0, PROGRESS_CLASS, "",
WS_BORDER + WS_CHILD + WS_VISIBLE + lStyle, 0, 0, 0, 0,
hwndOwner, vbNull, g_hinst, vbNull)

  ' Resize the control
  Call SetWindowPos(ProgressBarCtl_hWnd, vbNull, cLeft, cTop,
cWidth, cHeight, SWP_NOZORDER)
End Sub
Private Function ProgressBarCtl_SetRange(ByVal MinValue As
Integer, ByVal MaxValue As Long) As Long

  ' Set range
  ProgressBarCtl_SetRange = SendMessage(ProgressBarCtl_hWnd,
PBM_SETRANGE32, MinValue, MaxValue)
```

```
End Function
Private Function ProgressBarCtl_SetPos(ByVal PosValue As
Integer) As Long

  ' Set pos
  ProgressBarCtl_SetPos = SendMessage(ProgressBarCtl_hWnd,
PBM_SETPOS, PosValue, 0)

End Function
Private Function setINITCOMMONCONTROLSEX(ByVal dwSize As Long,
ByVal dwICC As Long) As String

  ' Build INITCOMMONCONTROLSEX UDT:
  ' Type LPINITCOMMONCONTROLSEX
  ' dwSize As Long
  ' dwICC As Long
  ' End Type

  setINITCOMMONCONTROLSEX = LongToBytes(dwSize) &
LongToBytes(dwICC)

End Function
Private Function LongToBytes(ByVal Value As Long) As String

  Dim lsHex As String, i As Integer

  lsHex = Right("00000000" & Hex(Value), 8)
  For i = 1 To 7 Step 2
  LongToBytes = ChrB(CInt("&H" & Mid(lsHex, i, 2))) &
LongToBytes
  Next

End Function
```

As you can see, many functions are in common with the DatePicker that we discussed earlier. If you want to use both the DatePicker and a ProgressBar, you have to make sure there are no duplicate functions, variables, or constants in the project.

Now, you start the form (in the **Form_Load** event) by creating the control:

```
ProgressBarCtl_Load fraProgressBar.hWnd, App.hInstance, 0, 0, _
  fraProgressBar.Width / 15, fraProgressBar.Height / 15, False
```

And set the range of the ProgressBar:

```
ProgressBarCtl_SetRange 1, 100
```

Finally, to make something happen, add a Timer control, name it **timProgress**, and the following code:

```
' Private variable
Private x As Integer
Private Sub timProgress_Timer()

   ' Increase counter and reset if max
   x = x + 1
   If x > 100 Then x = 1

   ' Set new pos
   ProgressBarCtl_SetPos x

End Sub
```

You have now created something similar to Figure 5.28.

Figure 5.28
ProgressBar sample

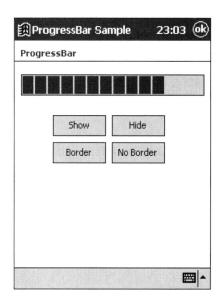

If you want a smooth ProgressBar to be shown, you create the control with the following code instead:

```
ProgressBarCtl_Load fraProgressBar.hWnd, App.hInstance, 0, 0, _
    fraProgressBar.Width / 15, fraProgressBar.Height / 15, True
```

If for some reason you find the above a bit hard-core, you can obtain a ready-made control for eVB called vbceProgressBar. You find the control at: www.vbce.com/vbceProgressBar/

5.3   And beyond

In the rest of this chapter we will look at how you can give your applications some additional polish and desirable features.

Go full screen and gain screen real estate

The screen size dominates application navigation and user interface design on the Pocket PC, and any mobile device for that matter. You can gain valuable screen real estate by utilizing the entire screen by removing the menu and task bar and thereby gaining access to all the 240 × 320 pixels. These extra pixels may prove to be valuable in many scenarios including displaying maps, blueprints, and other graphics, as well as when creating games.

> "You can gain valuable screen real estate by utilizing the entire screen by removing the menu and task bar and thereby gaining access to all the 240 x 320 pixels. "

The following sample code (see **Sample 5.13** on the CD) illustrates how to use the Pocket PC resource files **coredll.dll** and **aygshell.dll** to get a **Form** to go full screen:

Here are the Windows CE API declarations needed to make a form go full screen:

```
' Functions in Coredll
Declare Function ShowWindow Lib "Coredll" (ByVal hwnd As Long,
ByVal nCmdShow As Long) As Long
Declare Function FindWindow Lib "Coredll" Alias "FindWindowW"
(ByVal lpClassName As String, ByVal lpWindowName As String) As
Long
Declare Function MoveWindow Lib "Coredll" (ByVal hwnd As Long,
ByVal x As Long, ByVal y As Long, ByVal nWidth As Long, ByVal
nHeight As Long, ByVal bRepaint As Long) As Long
Declare Function SetForegroundWindow Lib "Coredll" (ByVal hwnd
As Long) As Boolean

' Function in aygshell
Declare Function SHFullScreen Lib "aygshell" (ByVal
hwndRequester As Long, ByVal dwState As Long) As Boolean
```

You make use of these declarations by having the following lines of code run when the form is activated. You can use either the **Form_Activate** event or the method of using **ShowForm** and **pLoadControls**, explained earlier in this chapter.

```
Dim lWindow

    lWindow = FindWindow("menu_worker", "")
    ShowWindow lWindow, SW_HIDE

    lWindow = FindWindow("HHTaskBar", "")
    ShowWindow lWindow, SW_HIDE

    SetForegroundWindow Me.hwnd
    SHFullScreen Me.hwnd, SHFS_HIDESIPBUTTON + SHFS_HIDETASKBAR
  + SHFS_HIDESTARTICON
    MoveWindow Me.hwnd, 0, 0, 240, 320, 0
```

The following code has to run to turn on the task bar again, before switching to another form and before closing the application:

```
Dim lWindow

    lWindow = FindWindow("HHTaskBar", "")
    ShowWindow lWindow, SW_SHOW
    SHFullScreen hwnd, SHFS_SHOWSTARTICON
```

The results are given in Figure 5.29.

Figure 5.29   The start up form is Full Screen!

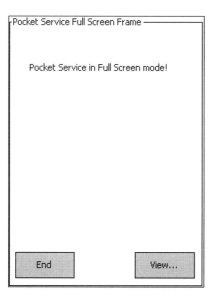

When the "View" button is clicked, a normal form opens (see Figure 5.30).

Figure 5.30   The **View** button was clicked to open a second form...

This form's **OK** button closes the form and returns to the full screen form.

Using Pocket Outlook

Pocket Outlook is, from a Microsoft application standpoint, not a true application, and normally they do not make any references to "Pocket Outlook" in the Pocket PC user community. Instead Microsoft refers to the different applications such as Inbox, Calendar, Tasks, and Contacts. It is only to us, the developer community, that Microsoft chooses to call Pocket Outlook by its right name; Pocket Outlook.

 Tip

POOM (Pocket Outlook Object Model) includes access to Contacts, Tasks, and Calendar. It does not include access to the Inbox. The Mail API provides a C/C++ interface and allows you to read, modify, and create messages or folders, but not to send the messages. You can instead put messages in the Outbox and if you are connected through ActiveSync the incoming and outgoing messages will exchange through your host connection. We illustrate the possibility to use Pocket Internet Explorer's "mailto": support in the ACME Copier Inc. samples described in Chapter 10.

To use, display, and manipulate data in Pocket Outlook you need the Pocket Outlook Object Model SDK. From a Pocket PC perspective, the **POOM SDK** is really just the resource file **pimstore.dll** and the Word-document **pocket outlook object model.doc**. The resource file pimstore.dll is preinstalled on all Pocket PCs, so you are ready to go straightaway. You don't need to run a specific **POOM SDK** setup. We have put the document "pocket outlook object model.doc" on the CD for your reference.

The following links provide more information, tips, and tricks regarding the **POOM SDK**:

● support.microsoft.com/support/kb/articles/Q265/7/71.ASP

● www.microsoft.com/MOBILE/pocketpc/stepbystep/evbpoom.asp

● msdn.microsoft.com/library/techart/poomsdk.htm

Add a reference (**Project > References** in eVB) to **pimstore.dll** by using the path \Windows CE Tools\wce300\MS PocketPC\emulation\palm300\windows\pimstore.dll.

From an enterprise application perspective it is not likely that you will want to replace the Pocket Outlook applications on your users' Pocket PCs with your own version of these applications. But because your users will likely use the Pocket Outlook applications and store vital data using them, you can leverage and make use of the Pocket Outlook data using the **POOM SDK**.

The sample code found in **Sample 5.14** on the CD illustrates how to use the POOM to reach the Calendar, Tasks, and Contact information stored on the Pocket PC. By using two frames, the user can switch between viewing Calendar Appointments, Contacts, and Tasks; and creating a new service order. The Service Order is stored as new appointment with a user set **Subject** and **Body**. The Service Order / Appointment is associated with the Customer / Contact by concatenation of Body text and Contact name. The sample project includes the declarations of the POOM constants.

A preferred way to integrate your data entities with Pocket Outlook data would be to store the unique object id (oids) that each Pocket Outlook data element is identified with and associate it with your data entities in SQL Server CE. Read more about SQL Server CE in Chapter 6.

The user can choose the type of Pocket Outlook data to view, by using the **View** menu (see Figure 5.31).

The first **Frame** includes a **ListView** that gets populated with the chosen type of Pocket Outlook data.

The following code snippet populates the ListView with Contacts:

```
' Set Contacts folder
Set pItems =
pOLA.GetDefaultFolder(olFolderContacts).Items

' Set the listview headers
    lvwPOOM.ColumnHeaders.Add , , "Contact", 1200
    lvwPOOM.ColumnHeaders.Add , , "Company", 800
```

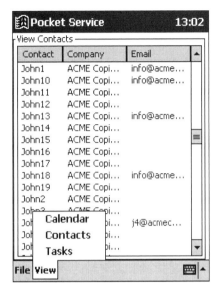

Figure 5.31 Viewing
Contacts in Pocket
Service

```
lvwPOOM.ColumnHeaders.Add , , "Email", 1150

' Loop through the contacts
For intCounter = 1 To pItems.Count
    Set pContact = pItems.Item(intCounter)

        ' Set the unique oid as the key!
        Set litm = lvwPOOM.ListItems.Add(, "K" &
CStr(pContact.oid), pContact.FileAs)
                litm.SubItems(1) =
pContact.CompanyName
                litm.SubItems(2) =
pContact.Email1Address
        Next intCounter

    Set pItems = Nothing
    Set pContact = Nothing
```

The **File** menu includes a **New Service Order...** command that shows
the second **Frame**. The user can create new Service Order that gets saved as
a new **Appointment** with the **Customer** / **Contact** concatenated into the
Body text (see Figure 5.32).

The list of customers is read from Pocket Contacts. The following code
creates the **Appointment**:

Figure 5.32 Creating a new service order as an appointment

```
Dim pAppointment As PocketOutlook.AppointmentItem

    Set pAppointment = pOLA.CreateItem(olAppointmentItem)

    ' Set appointment properties
    pAppointment.Subject = txtSubject.Text
    pAppointment.Body = cmbCustomer.Text & ": " & txtBody.Text

    pAppointment.Start = Now
    pAppointment.End = Now

    pAppointment.Save
    Set pAppointment = Nothing
```

The new **Appointment** is available from Pocket Calendar:

Restrict method

When working with the **POOM**, you will need to take a closer look at a valuable method in the collection **PocketOutlook.Items**; the **Restrict** method. The **Restrict** method is used to filter the items in the collection.

The **Restrict** method uses a string as restrict clause. The clause is constructed in a Boolean format using the properties of the current set of items. Clauses can be combined using AND and OR. Comparison operators can be one of <, <=, >, >=, =, or <>. An example of a valid call to the **Restrict** method is:

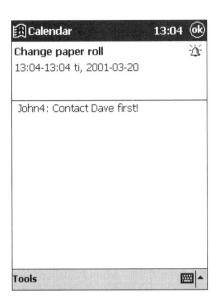

Figure 5.33   The
Service Order just
created from Pocket
Service!

```
pItems.Restrict ("[Start] > " & Chr(34) & Date - 1 & Chr(34) &
" and [IsRecurring] = True")
```

5.4   Launching applications

As you have seen there are a number of things you can do even if it is not
natively possible from eVB. One such thing is the possibility to launch an
application as you did with the **Shell** command in VB 6.0. There is no such
command in eVB and if you want to use the Windows CE API
CreateProcess, you have the problem with eVB's lack of UDTs. Let's start off
with the declarations we need (you would probably want to put these in a
code module or check out **Sample 5.15** on the CD):

```
Declare Function MyCreateProcess Lib "coredll" Alias
"CreateProcessW" (ByVal lpApplicationName As String, ByVal
lpCommandLine As String, ByVal lpProcessAttributes As Long,
ByVal lpThreadAttributes As Long, ByVal bInheritHandles As
Long, ByVal dwCreationFlags As Long, ByVal lpEnvironment As
Long, ByVal lpCurrentDirectory As Long, ByVal lpStartupInfo As
Long, ByVal lpProcessInformation As String) As Long
Declare Function MyGetLastError Lib "coredll" Alias
"GetLastError" () As Long
```

```
Declare Function MyCloseHandle Lib "coredll" Alias
"CloseHandle" (ByVal hObject As Long) As Long
```

And this is the public function that you need to do the launch.

```
Public Function Shell(ByVal Application As String, ByVal
Parameters As String) As Long

  Dim lsPI As String, llResult As Long, lhProcess As Long,
lhThread As Long

  lsPI = LongToBytes(0) & LongToBytes(0) & LongToBytes(0) &
LongToBytes(0)
  llResult = MyCreateProcess(Application, Parameters, 0, 0, 0,
0, 0, 0, 0, lsPI)
  If llResult <> 0 Then
      lhThread = BytesToLong(MidB(lsPI, 5, 4))
      Call MyCloseHandle(lhThread)
      lhProcess = BytesToLong(MidB(lsPI, 1, 4))
      Call MyCloseHandle(lhProcess)
      llResult = 0
  Else
      llResult = MyGetLastError()
      If llResult = 0 Then llResult = -1
  End If
  Shell = llResult

End Function
```

You will also need these two "helper" functions:

```
Private Function LongToBytes(ByVal Value As Long) As String

  Dim lsHex As String, i As Integer

  lsHex = Right("00000000" & Hex(Value), 8)
  For i = 1 To 7 Step 2
    LongToBytes = ChrB(CInt("&H" & Mid(lsHex, i, 2))) &
LongToBytes
  Next

End Function
Private Function BytesToLong(ByVal Value As String) As Long

  Dim lsHex As String, i As Integer
```

```
  For i = 1 To 4
    lsHex = Hex(AscB(MidB(Value, i, 1))) & lsHex
  Next
  BytesToLong = CLng("&H" & lsHex)

End Function
```

When you have all this in a code module, here is what you will use to launch an application:

```
Dim llResult As Long
llResult = Shell("peghelp", "soltr.htm")
If llResult <> 0 Then MsgBox "Shell() error: " & llResult
```

The above launches the Help file for the Solitaire game. If you want to launch another eVB application, you would do something like this:

```
llResult = Shell("pvbload", "\Program Files\Test\Project1.vb")
```

And now you can launch other applications from your eVB applications.

Getting owner information

Sometimes you would like to get hold of the owner information already stored in the Pocket PC registry. For example, when you want to provide default values for name and e-mail address, you might want to provide the information that the user has already entered.

As you know, you can update the user's owner information by choosing **Start > Settings > Personal > Owner Information**. And the values in that form are stored in only two registry keys. They are located at **HKEY_CURRENT_USER\ControlPanel\Owner** and the first, **Owner**, contain most of the owner information (name, address, etc.) and the other, **Notes**, contains the notes that the user have entered. Even if these values are stored as binary values, they are actually strings (in Unicode format). The **Notes** key can be read directly into a string. The **Owner** key can too, but you will only get the owner name. If you want to retrieve the other values (telephone, address, e-mail, etc.), the **Owner** key has to be split up since it contains multiple values at fixed positions. You can use the following code to extract the different pieces of owner information (see **Sample 5.16** on the CD):

```
Dim lreg As OSIUTIL.Registry
Dim ls As String

' Get Owner Information
Set lreg = CreateObject("OSIUtil.Registry")
lreg.OpenKey hKeyCurrentUser, "ControlPanel\Owner", False
On Error Resume Next
ls = lreg.GetValue("Owner")
If Err = 0 Then ' Value in registry
  txtName.Text = ls
  txtCompany.Text = Mid(ls, 37)
  txtAddress.Text = Mid(ls, 73)
  txtTelephone.Text = Mid(ls, 259)
  txtEmail.Text = Mid(ls, 284)
End If
On Error GoTo 0
lreg.CloseKey
Set lreg = Nothing
```

You can see that we can use the **Mid** function to start reading at specific positions in the string. The bytes between the different owner information fields are filled with null (zero) values. And eVB will therefore interpret the first null value as the end of the string and only copy the relevant characters to each control.

 Tip

We have used the free OSIUtil utility library provided by Odyssey Software (which you find on the accompanying CD) to read the registry, but you could do this with basic Windows CE API calls as well.

And as you might guess, you could use the following code to get the **Notes** fields:

```
Dim lreg As OSIUTIL.Registry
Dim ls As String

' Get Owner Information Notes
Set lreg = CreateObject("OSIUtil.Registry")
lreg.OpenKey hKeyCurrentUser, "ControlPanel\Owner", False
On Error Resume Next
ls = lreg.GetValue("Notes")
```

```
If Err = 0 Then MsgBox "Notes: " & ls
On Error Goto 0
lreg.CloseKey
Set lreg = Nothing
```

When you run the code, it looks like Figure 5.34.

Figure 5.34
Ownerinfo sample

So the next time that you need to provide a default value for the user's name, e-mail address, etc., you know how to help her save some stylus taps (or other actions).

Capture application launch buttons

There are situations when you may like to use the application launch buttons (also referred to as hardware buttons) on your device to ease navigation in your application. It could be a great addition to a tabbed screen where you switch tabs with the keys as well as the stylus (see **Sample 5.17** on the CD). You first have to declare a number of constants and a Windows CE API (probably in a module):

```
Public Const APPKEY1 = 193
Public Const APPKEY2 = 194
Public Const APPKEY3 = 195
Public Const APPKEY4 = 196
Public Const APPKEY5 = 197
```

```
Public Declare Function SHSetAppKeyWndAssoc Lib "aygshell.dll"
(ByVal bVk As Long, ByVal hwnd As Long) As Boolean
```

The way you capture the keys, is simply to call the API with the form that should receive the key messages. It looks like this:

```
' Capture buttons
SHSetAppKeyWndAssoc APPKEY1, frmHWKeys.hwnd
SHSetAppKeyWndAssoc APPKEY2, frmHWKeys.hwnd
SHSetAppKeyWndAssoc APPKEY3, frmHWKeys.hwnd
SHSetAppKeyWndAssoc APPKEY4, frmHWKeys.hwnd
SHSetAppKeyWndAssoc APPKEY5, frmHWKeys.hwnd
```

The form name here is **frmHWKeys** and if you have put the above code in the **Form_Load** event and added a Label control (and named it **lblKey**), you could see that it works by putting this code in the **Form_KeyPress** event:

```
Select Case KeyAscii
  Case APPKEY1
    lblKey.Caption = "1"
  Case APPKEY2
    lblKey.Caption = "2"
  Case APPKEY3
    lblKey.Caption = "3"
  Case APPKEY4
    lblKey.Caption = "4"
  Case APPKEY5
    lblKey.Caption = "5"
End Select
```

And before you end your application (or leave the form), you should reset the key associations. The code to do this is:

```
' Release buttons
SHSetAppKeyWndAssoc APPKEY1, 0
SHSetAppKeyWndAssoc APPKEY2, 0
SHSetAppKeyWndAssoc APPKEY3, 0
SHSetAppKeyWndAssoc APPKEY4, 0
SHSetAppKeyWndAssoc APPKEY5, 0
```

> ❝Different devices have different support for this functionality simply because they have a different number of hardware buttons.❞

Remember that different devices have different support for this functionality simply because they have a different number of hardware buttons. If you stick with the first four, they are supported on most devices. This could increase the usability of your application, and there are many uses that you might have. You could use two buttons to step forward (Next) and Back in a wizard, or you could use them to make selections, as long as there are no more than four options. You might even use this feature to switch between different parts of your application.

Scrollable forms

If you want to get more information into a form, you might want to make your forms scrollable. This is not natively supported in eVB, so we will have to do our own implementation of this (see **Sample 5.18** on the CD). If you start by creating a Frame control and name it **fraForm**. Beside it place a VScrollBar control and name it **vsbForm**. You can then put some controls (use at least one TextBox control) on the **fraForm** Frame control. We then create a private method to manage the scrollbar. It looks like this:

```
' Scrollbar height with or without SIP
Const SB_HEIGHT_SIP = 2820
Const SB_HEIGHT_NOSIP = 4020

Private Sub pResizeScrollBar()
    ' Is SIP active
  If Me.SIPVisible Then
    ' Scrollbar size
    vsbForm.Height = SB_HEIGHT_SIP
    ' Scrolling size
    vsbForm.Max = fraForm.Height - SB_HEIGHT_SIP
  Else
    ' Scrollbar size
    vsbForm.Height = SB_HEIGHT_NOSIP
    ' Scrolling size
    vsbForm.Max = fraForm.Height - SB_HEIGHT_NOSIP
  End If

  ' Scroll size
  vsbForm.SmallChange = vsbForm.Max / 10
  vsbForm.LargeChange = vsbForm.Max

End Sub
```

You have to call this method both from the **Form_Load** event and the **vsbForm_Change** event. Then you are done. Figure 5.35 shows how it will look.

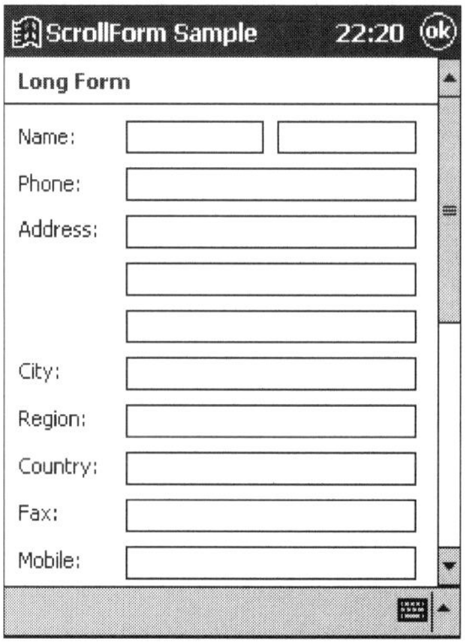

Figure 5.35
Scrollable forms
sample at the top of
the form

You can fit in a lot of information on one form by doing this. Check out what happens when we scroll all the way down (see Figure 5.36).

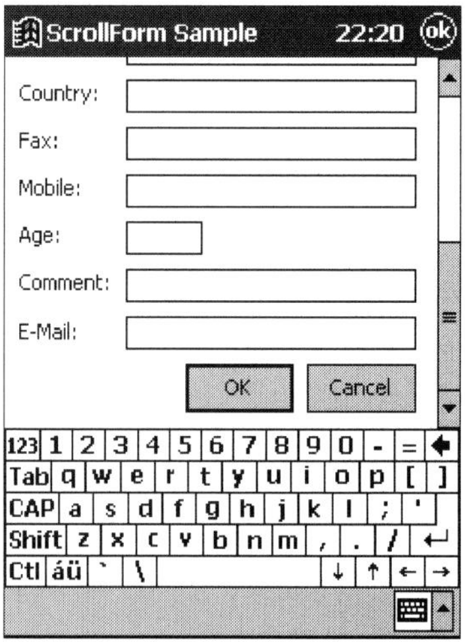

Figure 5.36
Scrollable forms
sample with form
scrolled down

66 This means that you can even edit fields that are at the bottom of the form, something that is not possible if you have a normal-size form where the SIP will cover the lower part when it appears. 99

You can see that when the SIP appears, the scroll bar is resized. This means that you can even edit fields that are at the bottom of the form, something that is not possible if you have a normal-size form where the SIP will cover the lower part when it appears.

But setting the form property **SIPBehavior** to **vbSIPAutomatic** (1) will result in the SIP disappearing as soon as you tap the scroll bar. Instead set it to

vbSIPUser (0). The downside is that the user has to turn the SIP on and off herself. We are sure that you could find a solution if you really want the SIP to be automatic.

5.5   Memory check

Sometimes it is interesting for you to check available memory (see **Sample 5.19** on the CD). In that case, then you can use the following code (with necessary declaration first):

```
Declare Function GlobalMemoryStatus Lib "coredll.dll" (ByVal
strBuffer As String) As Long

Dim ls As String

' Call memory status API
ls = LongToBytes(32) & Space(32)
GlobalMemoryStatus ls

' Memory load in percent
MsgBox BytesToLong(MidB(ls, 5, 4))
```

And you also need these two helper functions:

```
Private Function LongToBytes(ByVal Value As Long) As String

  Dim lsHex As String, i As Integer
  lsHex = Right("00000000" & Hex(Value), 8)
  For i = 1 To 7 Step 2
    LongToBytes = ChrB(CInt("&H" & Mid(lsHex, i, 2))) &
LongToBytes
  Next

End Function
Private Function BytesToLong(ByVal Value As String) As Long

  Dim lsHex As String, i As Integer

  For i = 1 To 4
    lsHex = Hex(AscB(MidB(Value, i, 1))) & lsHex
  Next
  BytesToLong = CLng("&H" & lsHex)

End Function
```

And the number you get is the percentage of program memory used. It will change if the automatic memory management allocates more or less program memory. However, it will give an indication of how much program memory you have left. You could then warn your users if the memory runs low when they are using your application.

5.6   Programming Help files

The normal way to access Help on a Pocket PC, is by selecting **Help** at the **Start** menu. Depending upon where you are, different things will happen. The rule as always is to look at other applications (preferably the applications from Microsoft like Pocket Word and Pocket Excel) to know how to handle user interface issues. In your eVB application, when the user selects Help from the Start menu, the **From_HelpClick** event on the currently active form will be called. There are a number of things that you can do when this happens (show a message box, etc.), but if you want to conform to the standard that other applications use, you should open a Help file with a context-sensitive topic (probably concerning the current form). Then you have two main options:

- Use the CommonDialog control
- Start the Help engine yourself

If you choose to use the CommonDialog control, you will have to have at least one form in the application that has a CommonDialog in it. If you have a CommonDialog control on a from called **frmMain**, you can use the following code from any form to start the Help system (see **Sample 5.20** on the CD):

```
frmMain.CommonDialog1.HelpFile = "soltr.htm"
frmMain.CommonDialog1.HelpCommand = 1
frmMain.CommonDialog1.HelpContext = "play"
frmMain.CommonDialog1.ShowHelp
```

The above example will show the Help file for the Solitaire game that comes with all Pocket PCs and it also shows the "play" topic. When you want to jump to a specific topic, you must set the **HelpCommand** property to **1**. If you set the **HelpFile** property when you load the **frmMain** form, and if you use the **Tag** property on each form to set the topic to go to, you could add a function to a module similar to:

```
Public Sub ShowHelp(ByVal Topic As String)

    frmMain.CommonDialog1.HelpFile = "soltr.htm"
    frmMain.CommonDialog1.HelpCommand = 1
    frmMain.CommonDialog1.HelpContext = Topic
```

```
    frmMain.CommonDialog1.ShowHelp

End Sub
```

And you would only have to add this line of code to each form:

```
Private Sub Form_HelpClick()

    ShowHelp Me.Tag

End Sub
```

If you do not want to be dependent on the CommonDialog control, you can choose to launch the Help engine directly using the technique we learned in the "Launching applications" section above. If you use the **Tag** property on each form the way we described above, the common function (in a module) would look like this:

```
Public Sub ShowHelp(ByVal Topic As String)

    Shell "peghelp.exe", "soltr.htm#" & Topic

End Sub
```

And you could use the same code in each form (the **ShowHelp Me.Tag** code above).

If you have a TabStrip control in your form, and would like to have context-sensitive Help depending on which is the currently selected tab, you could use the following code:

```
Private Sub Form_HelpClick()

    ShowHelp Me.Tag & tabStrip.SelectedItem.Key

End Sub
```

If you have the TabStrip **Key** property on each tab set to something like First, Second, etc., and you have a form with the **Tag** property set to Main, you would name the different topics in the Help file to MainFirst, MainSecond, etc.

If you want to learn more about Help files and how to create them, please see Chapter 11.

5.7   Regaining the challenge

A story for you:

In 1998 a couple of young Swedes left an internet start-up to begin their own business in the mobile space. In the first newspaper article about them and their new company (many more have followed), they were asked why they left lucrative web development and started doing something that at the time seemed to be very uncertain. Their response was quite unexpected:

> Web development is not a challenge anymore. Developing for mobile devices is a real challenge due to the memory and GUI constraints.

They were looking for challenges and adventure!

Developing for mobile devices such as the Pocket PC is still a challenge, even though the developer toolset, technologies, and the market in general has matured significantly since 1998. In many ways we have taken a step backwards in comparison with developing for normal PCs. We may no longer take 1 GHz, gigabytes of RAM and 800 × 600 displays for granted. Instead, real developer craftsmanship is required. By leveraging our skills in tools and languages, we can use eMbedded Visual Tools and Pocket PCs to efficiently craft some great mobile solutions.

Databases in motion

In this chapter we will look at:

- The use of databases on the Pocket PC.
- Technical information and code that you need to know to create the database applications to serve common business requirements.

We'll also examine some of the industry discussions so that you can decide for yourself the best course of action for your company's or clients' mobile solution.

6.1 Mobile solutions need mobile databases

The wireless era has just begun. Expect wireless coverage, bandwidth, and the cost aspects to improve, but mobile solutions will continue to require local data store capabilities. From an enterprise perspective, local data store capabilities need to be implemented through solid relational database management system (RDBMS) technologies. Microsoft SQL Server 2000 for Windows CE Edition enters the scene.

SQL Server 2000 Windows CE Edition

The Pocket PC strikes a mobile enterprise application "sweet spot." The Pocket PC inherently supports disconnected scenarios better than any other mobile device because of the fast CPU, memory capacity, and tight integration with the familiar Win32 API and server-side development tools. It supports both wired and wireless (WAN and LAN) connectivity with its built-in networking (TCP/IP) support and hardware extensions possibilities. On top of all this, the Pocket PC includes support for web content through Pocket Internet Explorer and wireless e-mail connectivity (POP3, IMAP4) using Pocket Inbox.

And that's what this chapter is all about: helping you implement powerful database systems that will support mobile workers using the Pocket PC. But before we go into the practice of design and implementation, let's first look at some of the controversy surrounding the combined use of local data stores and wireless capabilities.

6.2   The local data store and wireless debate

The local data store in mobile devices has for some in the wireless industry reached ideological heights. This is even more evident in markets where the majority of the population uses wireless networks.

This question is at the heart of the issues: Does the definition of a mobile solution include the support for local data store?

Wireless fundamentalists contend that a mobile solution is by definition wireless and always requires an online connection to a server. To enable a local store is from a solution definition perspective incorrect in the fundamentalists' opinion. We find advocates of the WAP environment asserting this view.

But our answer to the question whether mobile solutions should support local data stores, is, in short: Absolutely!

We don't want to make mobile solutions *exclusively* dependent on wireless coverage (which usually is poor), wireless bandwidth (which usually is poor), and wireless connectivity costs (which usually are high).

Instead we would like the business needs to dictate the dependencies, and if the business scenarios need to run outside wireless coverage, we need local data store capabilities.

Déjà vu? Definitely! It is the familiar thin client versus fat client debate, only with a wireless twist. We are witnessing the clash of five major forces, so ideology seems to be unavoidable. While observing the clash, keep in mind what economic interests each entity has on its agenda while wanting to cater for your mobile needs. Let's take a look at each of these delegations and their respective economic interest.

Delegation no 1: Wireless carriers

The wireless carrier's largest revenue stream is currently the "per minute" charges of voice communication. Voice communication will continue to be a large revenue stream for them. The new wireless networks such as GPRS and UMTS aim at increasing the bandwidth as well as enabling mobile devices to always be online (where there is wireless coverage). The most common rate model for data communication will most likely be based on to the amount of data transferred in the wireless network, not the elapsed time of the connection. However, we don't expect the overall wireless costs to decline. If the end customer doesn't pay for the large investments in these new wireless networks – then who will?

Granted that many significant "value adds" to mobile solutions require the use of these networks, we have to deal with the real life issues of poor coverage, low bandwidth, and the costs involved with using the network.

Do you believe that wireless carriers want you to think about business scenarios that occur outside their coverage? (Answer: Nope!)

Don't expect wireless carriers to discuss databases in handheld devices.

Delegation no. 2: Server hardware manufacturers

The server hardware manufacturers are the steel providers in the IT industry. As steel providers, they play an important role. Server hardware manufacturers have, in part, facilitated the recent years of massive increase in the internet's use.

Wireless connectivity is about to marry the web, providing new and fascinating opportunities. The boom of mobile devices is driving through the roof the number of potential wireless clients to the servers. Many corporate web applications will have to scale out, leading to new server hardware investments.

The server hardware manufacturers revenues increase with the quantity of steel they sell. It is not surprising that a steel providers' trademark expression is "The Network Is The Computer™." The more focus is placed on network dependencies, the better for a steel provider. However, while this ideology is not completely flawed in a wired world where connectivity is fast and almost free, it is irrelevant in a wireless perspective, because of limited coverage, poor bandwidth, and significant cost. To anyone pragmatically inclined regarding mobile solutions, a network is a network, and a computer is a computer.

> To anyone pragmatically inclined regarding mobile solutions, a network is a network, and a computer is a computer.

Do you believe server hardware manufacturers want you to think about business scenarios that occur beyond existing wireless coverage? (Answer: Not likely!)

Don't expect server hardware manufacturers to discuss databases in handheld devices.

Delegation no. 3: Cell phone and wireless infrastructure manufacturers

A cell phone is typically used for voice communication, so voice communication does not require local data storage. WAP phones are cell phones equipped with a WAP browser. Since the WAP browser model is identical to the web browser model it represents an implementation of a thin client that works only if there is an online connection to a server. A thin client does not require local data storage capabilities. So, regardless of what type of cell phone is thrown into the debate it does not support local data store to any relevant degree. We expect most cell phone manufacturers to soon wake up and realize that it makes a lot of sense to base their products on platforms that support disconnected scenarios. When these products are designed and manufactured, even cell phone manufacturers will get their mobile story right.

The economic interests of wireless infrastructure manufacturers are apparent: Their revenue increases with the need of their server infrastructure.

Do you believe that cell phone manufacturers want you to think about business scenarios that occur outside wireless coverage and thus need local data store capabilities? (Answer: No way!)

Do you believe that wireless infrastructure manufacturers want you to think about business scenarios that occur outside wireless coverage? (Answer: Don't think so!)

Don't expect cell phone and wireless infrastructure manufacturers to discuss databases in handheld devices either.

Delegation no. 4: PC manufacturers

The explosion of wireless connectivity is driven by the convergence of cell phones and other handheld devices. The PC manufacturers are late to the party. However, in their arrival they bring 20-plus years of building PCs, and some (for example, Compaq and Hewlett-Packard) have already successfully brought strong PDAs to the marketplace.

There is no contradiction between wireless and local data store capabilities to a PC manufacturer. Their pragmatic approach brings us devices that work both wirelessly connected as well as disconnected. In fact, in the relationship with cell phone manufacturers, they have the upper hand, as it is the PC manufacturers that have proven core skills to keep a platform together. We frequently see new partnerships being established between PC manufacturers and cell phone manufacturers leading to new exciting hybrids.

The platforms brought to the market by the PC manufacturers have inherent support for local data store capabilities.

Do you believe PC manufacturers want you to think about business scenarios that occur outside wireless coverage? (Answer: Sure – and they will support you when you do become wirelessly connected as well!)

Delegation no. 5: Software makers

Software runs on servers. Software runs on clients. Software does not care if it is executed on a server CPU or on a mobile device CPU.

Regardless of whether a mobile device needs wireless connectivity or local data store capabilities, the software maker provides the client and server side software necessary.

At first glance, it may seem as if a software maker will want to optimize their software for disconnected scenarios in order to sell licenses to each and every mobile device. However, the past few years of internet-based business have shown that they have the creativity to design licensing models based on the amount of client connections to the server. This means that, in general, software makers have no inherent extremist ideological approach regarding the issue of local data store capabilities.

If anything, the last 15 years in the IT industry prove that regardless of direction in computing it is the software makers that make everything come together. This is going to be true in the convergence of the web, cell phones, and PDAs as well.

Do you believe that software makers want you to think about business scenarios that occur outside wireless coverage? (Answer: Why not? They will even support you when you can connect wirelessly!)

Final words on the local data stores and wireless debate

This debate will most likely intensify as wireless networks are continuously rolled out and standardized. The purpose of listing the key forces that are active in the current events is to provide a basis of analysis. Our conclusion is that the optimal approach to the debate is to focus on the real life business and technology challenges you face today. Make the most of wireless connectivity and let your business needs define the use of mobile, wireless, and disconnected features.

6.3   SQL Server CE – the specification

So let's get back to the real purpose in this chapter and take a look at the newest member in the Microsoft family of database products: SQL Server 2000 Windows CE Edition (SQL Server CE). SQL Server CE is the younger sibling to SQL Server 2000, and Microsoft's first real relational database for Pocket PCs.

Pocket PCs have a built in OLE DB provider called CEDB or the Object Store. Pocket Outlook uses CEDB to store its data. Developers can use CEDB features for use with simpler database tasks. Because SQL Server CE delivers better performance, a richer feature set, and better connectivity options it is better suited to take on the requirements of corporate Pocket PC applications.

SQL Server CE manages the challenges of two potentially conflicting goals: a rich feature set and a low memory footprint. The footprint ranges between 1 and 3 MB depending on which processor and connectivity option is used. The following is a feature set overview:

- SQL grammar is compatible with SQL Server 2000. This includes SQL Aggregate functions such as MAX, MIN, SUM, COUNT, and AVG.
- Supported data types include TINYINT, SMALLINT, INTEGER, BIGINT, REAL, NUMERIC, FLOAT, BIT, BINARY, VARBINARY, IMAGE, and the UNICODE character data types NATIONAL CHARACTER, NATIONAL CHARACTER VARYING, NTEXT MONEY, DATETIME, and UNIQUEIDENTIFIER.
- 32 indexes per table, multicolumn indexes.
- NULL support.
- Nested transactions.
- 128-bit data encryption.
- Data Definition Language: Create databases, alter tables, referential integrity, and default values.
- Data Manipulation Language: INSERT, UPDATE, and DELETE.
- Support for SELECT: SET Functions (aggregates), INNER/OUTER JOIN, Subselect, GROUP BY/HAVING.
- Scrollable and forward-only cursors.
- Remote data access (RDA) to SQL Server 6.5 and above.
- Merge replication with SQL Server 2000.
- Relay functionality for network connectivity through ActiveSync.

Data access overview

The similarities of the Pocket PC's data access architecture to the desktop/server side are evident. Microsoft has designed Pocket PC versions of the well-known ActiveX Data Objects (ADO) and OLE DB objects. Figure 6.1 illustrates that a Windows developer can leverage programming skills based on desktop/server-side development experiences.

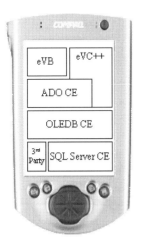 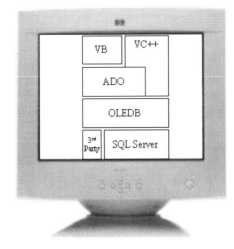

Figure 6.1   Pocket PC data access architecture

Both SQL Server 2000 and SQL Server CE are OLE DB providers. A developer can reach SQL Server data using similar ADO and OLE DB object implementations.

SQL Server CE has two native methods of reaching remote SQL Server databases:

1 Remote Data Access

2 Merge replication

We will discuss both methods in detail later in this chapter.

The similarities are significant, but so are the differences. The main differences from a system architecture perspective are related to the platform's vastly different scalability goals. The server version, SQL Server 2000, is optimized to handle a large number of concurrent users while maintaining performance and scalability. The Pocket PC is by definition a single user environment, so SQL Server CE is a single user database. SQL Server CE is therefore loaded by the application as a normal DLL instead of being implemented as something like a server service.

The next chapter will illustrate both similarities and differences.

File locations on the development PC

The SQL Server CE files listed in Table 6.1 are installed on the development PC, in the default folder \Program Files\Microsoft SQL Server CE folder.

Table 6.1   File locations on the development PC

Location	Contents
\Device	Each subfolder contains Ssce10.dll, Ssceca10.dll, Sscecw10.dll, Ssceinet.dll, and Sscesock.dll. These subfolders also contain DllRegister.exe, a tool that registers the other DLLs.
\Encryption	Rsaenh.dll that implements the security features of SQL Server CE.
\Inc	Contain include files for use with Microsoft eMbedded Visual Basic and Microsoft eMbedded Visual C++.
\Lib	The library Ca_mergex.lib for the SQL Server CE ActiveX objects. A single type library (Ca_mergex.tlb) is located in the root of this folder. It describes the SQL Server CE RDA, replication, and engine objects.
\Relay	The SQL Server CE Relay extension to ActiveSync (SSCERelay.exe).
\Redist	A series of subfolders containing the components that you may need to include together with your application when you have finished it and are ready to deploy it.

Internet Information Services

The SQL Server CE files listed in Table 6.2 are installed on the Internet Information Services (IIS). Microsoft Data Access Components (MDAC) 2.6 must also be installed on the IIS. The IIS can be located on the development PC.

Table 6.2: SQL Server CE file locations and contents

Location	Contents
\Program Files\Microsoft SQL Server CE\Server	SQL Server CE Server Agent component (sscesa10.dll)
\Program Files\Microsoft SQL Server CE\Server	SQL Server CE replication component (sscerp10.dll)
\Program Files\Microsoft SQL Server\80\com	SQL Server CE replication components

ActiveSync software

The SQL Server CE files given in Table 6.3 should be installed on a PC running ActiveSync system. The ActiveSync system can be located on the development PC.

Table 6.3: SQL files for ActiveSync

Location	Contents
\Program Files\Microsoft SQL Server CE\	SQL Server CE Relay component (SSCERelay.exe)

Table 6.4: Files for the Pocket PC

File(s)	Location	Category	Requirement
Ssce10.dll,	\Program Files\Microsoft SQL Server CE\Device*processor family\processor type*	SQL Server CE	Required. Must be registered.
Ssceca10.dll	\Program Files\Microsoft SQL Server CE\Device\processor *family\processor type*	SQL Server CE	Required for RDA or replication. Must be registered.
Sscecw10.dll and Rsaenh.dll	\Program Files\Microsoft SQL Server CE\Device\processor *family\processor type*	SQL Server CE	Required if your database is encrypted. Rsaenh.dll is located in the \Encryption folder. Sscecw10.dll must be registered.
Msdadc.dll and Msdaer.dll	\Windows CE Tools\dataaccess31*wce300\ processor type*	ADO	Required. Must be registered.
Msdaeren.dll	\Windows CE Tools\dataaccess31\ *wce300\processor type*	ADO	Required. Msdaeren.dll is the English version of the ADOCE error DLL and will work on devices of all languages. For localized ADOCE error messages, substitute the Msdaerxx.dll that corresponds to the language setting of your device.

Adoceoledb31.dll	\Windows CE Tools\dataaccess31\ *wce300\processor type*	ADO	Required for ADO.
Adoce31.dll	\Windows CE Tools\dataaccess31\ *wce300\processor type*	ADO	Required for ADO. Must be registered.
Adoxce31.dll	\Windows CE Tools\dataaccess31\ *wce300\processor type*	ADO	Required for ADO. Must be registered.
isqlw_wce.exe	\Program Files\Microsoft SQL Server CE\ISQLWCE\Pocket *PC* *processor type*	ISQL	The Query Analyzer (ISQL) application
mfcce300.dll	\Program Files\Microsoft SQL Server CE\ISQLWCE\Pocket *PC* *processor type*	ISQL	Required for ISQL.
olece300.dll	\Program Files\Microsoft SQL Server CE\ISQLWCE\Pocket *PC* *processor type*	ISQL	Required for ISQL.

You can choose to manually copy the required files and register them using DLLRegister, or have eMbedded Visual Basic automatically register the components as you reference them in your projects.

6.4   Introduction to Mobile SQL

SQL Server CE Query Analyzer

❝Developers will most likely use ADO(X)CE, Remote Data Access or merge replication to programmatically design, develop, and manage SQL Server CE databases which we cover later in this chapter.❞

SQL Server CE Query Analyzer (ISQL) is the only Pocket PC application that ships with SQL Server CE. Query Analyzer provides a client side graphical user interface for database administrators (DBAs) and developers to manage SQL Server CE databases and their respective objects.

Developers will most likely use ADO(X)CE, Remote Data Access or merge replication to programmatically design, develop, and manage SQL Server CE databases which we cover later in this chapter. Even so, Query Analyzer provides valuable means to develop and debug SQL statements interactively. The main reason why we'll spend some time digging around core SQL Server CE features is that it is not uncommon to see Visual Basic developers develop code to do things that the database engine inherently supports and executes with greater performance. This includes searching, updating, and deleting records. There is a Swedish saying that goes: "What you don't have in your brain, you have in your feet!" In the context at hand this means that smarter database developers get more done using less code, or more efficient code.

 Tip

Databases in corporate Pocket PC-targeted solutions will most likely be dependent on central remote databases. The use of Remote Data Access or merge replication is likely to play a major role in SQL Server CE implementations. Databases and tables are often created as a result of using Remote Data Access or merge replication, rather than manually creating them using Query Analyzer.

Query Analyzer can be used from the Pocket PC itself or from the emulator. Since Pocket PCs lack a built-in keyboard (unless you have obtained an external Pocket PC keyboard) it makes a lot of sense to use the development PC's keyboard to work with Query Analyzer. You can use the development PC's keyboard by either …

a) using a remote control application such as "Remote Control for Windows CE" or Visual CE (included on the accompanying CD) and use the Pocket PC remotely, or

b) installing and using Query Analyzer in the emulator.

 Tip

To pass SQL statements over to your Pocket PC for manual execution in Query Analyzer you can copy and paste them into Microsoft Outlook Notes. Then use ActiveSync to synchronize to your Pocket PC. You can then copy and paste the SQL statements into Query Analyzer.

You need to connect to a database before you can run any SQL, Data Definition Language (DDL) or following Data Manipulation Language (DML) statements in Query Analyzer. To get going with the examples below, you can create a database from the graphical user interface in Query Analyzer (which is the only database management functionality that has a GUI implementation in SQL Server CE) (see Figure 6.2).

You can start running DDL, DML, and SQL statements once you are connected to a database. Figure 6.3 shows that the Query Analyzer user interface is divided into two panes. The upper pane is where you run your statements. The lower pane is split into two tabs: a) the **Rowset**-tab that will display the results and b) the **Messages**-tab where **Elapsed times** and **Error messages** display.

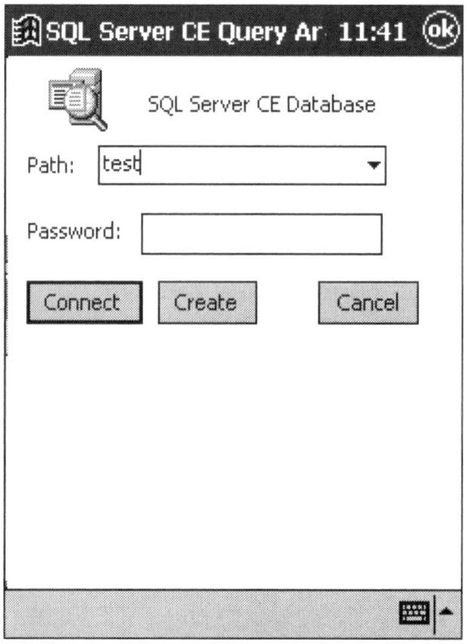

Figure 6.2   Creating a database in Query Analyzer

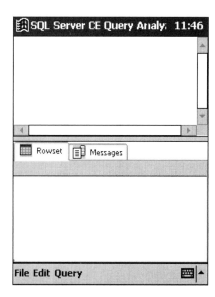

Figure 6.3   Query Analyzer user interface

Data Definition Language

The Data Definition Language (DDL) is used to manage databases, tables, and indexes. It is possible to use DDL from Query Analyzer, but ADOCE and ADOXCE are the objects through which database management usually occurs.

SQL Server CE supports the following DDL statements:

- CREATE DATABASE
- CREATE TABLE
- ALTER TABLE
- CREATE INDEX
- DROP INDEX
- DROP TABLE

Creating a database

Use the **CREATE DATABASE** statement to create a SQL Server CE database. A SQL Server CE database is physically implemented as one single file using a default .SDF-extension. You specify where the database is stored when creating the database.

CREATE DATABASE syntax:

```
CREATE DATABASE "database_name"
    [DATABASEPASSWORD 'database_password'
        [ENCRYPTION {ON|OFF}]
    ]
    [COLLATE collation_name comparison_style]
```

To specify the database sort order you use a setting called Locale Identifier (LCID). LCID is available from the ADOXCE Catalog object.

Examples

```
CREATE DATABASE "PSA.sdf"
```
The database will be created in the Pocket PC root folder since no path is provided.

```
CREATE DATABASE "\My Documents\PSA.sdf"
```
The database will be created in the folder \My Documents\.

```
CREATE DATABASE "\My Documents\PSA.sdf" COLLATE
Finnish_Swedish_CI_AS
```
The database will use Finnish Swedish collation.

```
CREATE DATABASE "\My Documents\PSA.sdf" DATABASEPASSWORD 'pwd'
ENCRYPTION on
```
The database will be password protected and encrypted.

If you try to connect to a password-protected database without supplying a password, you will receive an error message as shown in Figure 6.4.

Figure 6.4
Remember your
passwords!

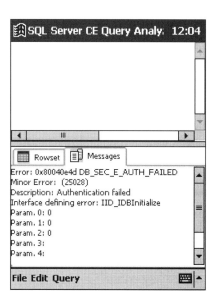

 Tip

SQL Server CE does not support a **DROP DATABASE** statement. If you want to delete an entire database, you need to delete the .SDF file. This can be done from eVB using the **FileSystem** control.

Creating tables

Much of SQL Server CE functional capacity becomes evident when looking at what is supported in the **CREATE TABLE** statement. By reading through the syntax below you will see that:

- Declarative Referential Integrity (DRI) is supported because tables can be created to have Primary and Foreign keys, and tables can use Unique columns, as well as be set to reference each other.
- A column can be set to use an Identity property.
- A column can be set to use **ROWGUIDCOL** and the uniqueidentifier datatype.
- Cascading **UPDATE** and **INSERT** statements are supported.

Here is **CREATE TABLE** syntax:

```
CREATE TABLE table_name
    ( { < column_definition > | < table_constraint > } [ ,...n
]
    )
```

```
< column_definition > ::=
    { column_name data_type }
    [ { DEFAULT constant_expression
        | [ IDENTITY [ ( seed , increment ) ]
        ]
     } ]
    [ ROWGUIDCOL ]
    [ < column_constraint > [ ...n ] ]

< column_constraint > ::=
    [ CONSTRAINT constraint_name ]
    { [ NULL | NOT NULL ]
        | [ PRIMARY KEY | UNIQUE ]
        | REFERENCES ref_table [ ( ref_column ) ]
        [ ON DELETE { CASCADE | NO ACTION } ]
        [ ON UPDATE { CASCADE | NO ACTION } ]
    }

< table_constraint > ::=
    [ CONSTRAINT constraint_name ]
    { [ { PRIMARY KEY | UNIQUE }
        { ( column [ ,...n ] ) }
        ]
    | FOREIGN KEY
        [ ( column [ ,...n ] ) ]
    REFERENCES ref_table [ ( ref_column [ ,...n ] ) ]
        [ ON DELETE { CASCADE | NO ACTION } ]
        [ ON UPDATE { CASCADE | NO ACTION } ]
    }
```

The following data types are supported:

- bigint (INT 8)
- integer (INT 4)
- smallint (INT 2)
- tinyint (INT 1)
- bit
- numeric (p, s)
- money
- float(n)
- real
- datetime

- nchar(n)
- nvarchar(n)
- ntext
- binary(n)
- varbinary(n)
- image
- uniqueidentifier

For more information regarding data types you can execute the following SQL statement from Query Analyzer:

```
SELECT * FROM INFORMATION_SCHEMA.PROVIDER_TYPES
```

Replacing the PROVIDER_TYPES with the following retrieves additional SQL Server CE information regarding the current database:

```
COLUMNS
INDEXES
KEY_COLUMN_USAGE
PROVIDER_TYPES
TABLES
TABLE_CONSTRAINTS
```

Examples

```
CREATE TABLE Customer (CustomerID int, Name nvarchar(30))
```

Creates a Customer table.

```
CREATE TABLE Customer (CustomerID int PRIMARY KEY, Name nvar-
char(30))
```

Creates a Customer table with a **Primary Key**.

Figure 6.5 illustrates what happens when trying to insert a record with the same value in the **Primary Key** field.

```
CREATE TABLE Customer (CustomerID int IDENTITY (1,1) PRIMARY
KEY, Name nvarchar(30))
```

Creates a Customer table with an **Identity Primary Key**, as you can see in Figure 6.5.

```
CREATE TABLE Customer (CustomerID uniqueidentifier ROWGUIDCOL
CONSTRAINT pkCustomerID PRIMARY KEY, Name nvarchar(30) NOT NULL)
```

The above code creates a Customer table with a **Primary Key**, called pkCustomerID, which uses a **uniqueidentifier** data type. Name column must not be **NULL**.

Figure 6.6 illustrates the example in Query Analyzer including an **INSERT** and **SELECT** statement that uses the Customer table.

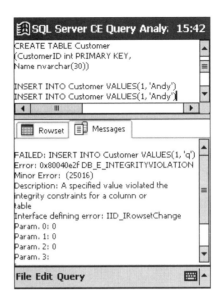

Figure 6.5
Declarative referential
integrity fights back!

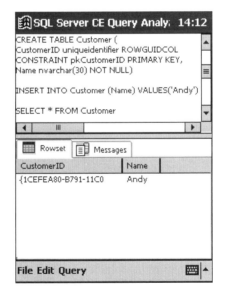

Figure 6.6   CREATE
TABLE rock and roll

Note

The GUID for the CustomerID field is automatically generated for you. This happens
because we specified ROWGUIDCOL on the field.

```
CREATE TABLE POrder (OrderID int, OrderDate datetime)
```

The above statement creates a POrder table.

```
CREATE TABLE POrder (
OrderID uniqueidentifier ROWGUIDCOL PRIMARY KEY,
CustomerID uniqueidentifier,
OrderDate datetime NOT NULL)
```

Creates a POrder table with a **Primary Key** that uses the **uniqueidentifier** datatype. OrderDate must not be **NULL**.

Altering tables

Use the **ALTER TABLE** statement to change the existing table definition. The syntax is therefore similar to the **CREATE TABLE** statement.

ALTER TABLE syntax:

```
ALTER TABLE table_name
{ [ ALTER COLUMN column_name
    {DROP DEFAULT
    | SET DEFAULT constant_expression
    | IDENTITY [ ( seed , increment ) ]
    }
| ADD
    { < column_definition > | < table_constraint > } [ ,...n ]
| DROP
    { [ CONSTRAINT ] constraint_name
    | COLUMN column }
] }

< column_definition > ::=
    { column_name data_type }
    [ [ DEFAULT constant_expression ]
        | IDENTITY [ ( seed , increment ) ]
    ]
    [ROWGUIDCOL]
    [ < column_constraint > ] [ ...n ] ]

< column_constraint > ::=
    [ CONSTRAINT constraint_name ]
    { [ NULL | NOT NULL ]
        | { PRIMARY KEY | UNIQUE }
        | REFERENCES ref_table [ ( ref_column ) ]
        [ ON DELETE { CASCADE | NO ACTION } ]
        [ ON UPDATE { CASCADE | NO ACTION } ]
    }
```

```
< table_constraint > ::=
    [ CONSTRAINT constraint_name ]
    { [ { PRIMARY KEY | UNIQUE }
        { ( column [ ,...n ] ) }
        | FOREIGN KEY
        [ ( column [ ,...n ] ) ]
        REFERENCES ref_table [ ( ref_column [ ,...n ] ) ]
        [ ON DELETE { CASCADE | NO ACTION } ]
        [ ON UPDATE { CASCADE | NO ACTION } ]
    }
```

Examples

```
ALTER TABLE POrder ADD CONSTRAINT FK_Order_Customer FOREIGN KEY
(CustomerID) REFERENCES Customer (CustomerID)
```

Alters the POrder table to include a **FOREIGN KEY** constraint that references the column CustomerID in the Customer table.

Figure 6.7 illustrates the error that occurs when attempting to insert a row into the POrder table with a CustomerID value that does not exist in the Customer table. In this example, there is not a CustomerID with the value of 3 in the Customer table.

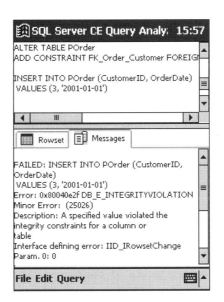

Figure 6.7 Foreign key constraint in action

```
ALTER TABLE POrder ADD CONSTRAINT FK_Order_Customer FOREIGN KEY
(CustomerID) REFERENCES Customer (CustomerID)
ON DELETE CASCADE
ON UPDATE CASCADE
```

Alters the POrder table to include a **FOREIGN CONSTRAINT** includes the declaration of cascading **UPDATE** and **INSERT**.

The constraint will automatically:

- Delete records in the POrder table if corresponding records are deleted in the Customer table.
- Update records in the POrder table if corresponding records are updated in the Customer table.

Dropping tables

You can drop tables by using the **DROP TABLE** statement.

DROP TABLE syntax:

```
DROP TABLE table_name
```

Examples

```
DROP TABLE Customer
```

Drops the Customer table.

 Tip

To drop a table that is referenced declaratively by another table you must first either drop the reference using **ALTER TABLE** or drop the referenced table altogether.

Creating indexes

To design indexes is a natural next step after having created tables. The purpose of indexes is to increase performance of data retrieval from the database and to maintain uniqueness of the indexed columns.

Appropriate index candidates are columns:

- Containing a number of duplicate value
- Frequently used in **ORDER BY** clauses
- Used in range searches
- Other than the primary key referenced in join clauses

When designing indexes keep in mind the following SQL Server CE index restrictions:

- A maximum of 32 indexes per table.
- A maximum of 10 columns in an index.
- Only the first 510 bytes of data can be indexed in any column. Columns of type **ntext** and **image** cannot be indexed.

⫸ Tip

If you plan to create tables and populate them with data before your application will use the tables, it is a good idea to wait to create indexes until the data resides in the tables. INSERT, UPDATE and DELETE statements generally are more time consuming if an index has to be maintained while they are executed.

CREATE INDEX syntax:

```
CREATE [ UNIQUE ] INDEX index_name
    ON table ( column [ ASC | DESC ] [ ,...n ] )
```

Examples

The following example (see Figure 6.8) uses a table called ptdVote. The table has 3,000 records.

First, we will run a **SELECT** with a **WHERE** clause and without an index:

```
SELECT * FROM ptdVote
WHERE votedesc = 'Andy3000'
```

The result is back four seconds later. The table has only one record that matches the criteria.

We will create the following index and then run the same query:

```
CREATE INDEX idxVoteDesc ON ptdVote (votedesc)
```

The result is back in less than *one* second. Additionally, the index increased the performance of a **SELECT** statement with an **ORDER BY** clause by more than 30 percent.

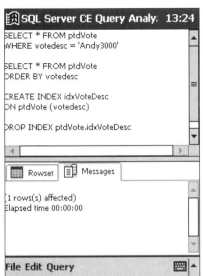

Figure 6.8   Sub second results using indexes

Dropping indexes

You can drop indexes from the database by using the **DROP INDEX** statement.

DROP INDEX syntax:

```
DROP INDEX table_name.index_name
```

Examples

The following drops the index idxVoteDesc.

```
DROP INDEX ptdVote.idxVoteDesc
```

Data manipulation language

The data manipulation language (DML) is used to manipulate data in database tables. As with DDL, it is possible to use DML from Query Analyzer, but ADOCE and ADOXCE are the objects through which data manipulation usually occurs.

SQL Server CE supports the DML statements **INSERT**, **UPDATE**, and **DELETE**.

Inserting data

The DML statement **INSERT** that is used to insert new records into tables supports using **DEFAULT**, **NULL**, expressions, and derived tables.

INSERT syntax:

```
INSERT [ INTO]
    table_name [ ( column_list ) ]
        { VALUES
        ( { DEFAULT | NULL | expression } [ ,...n] )
        | derived_table
        }
```

Examples

A Customer table with two columns (CustomerID and Name) will be used in these examples:

```
INSERT INTO Customer (CustomerID, Name) VALUES(1, 'CustName')
```

Using qualifying column names, as you see above.

```
INSERT INTO Customer VALUES(2, 'CustName')
```

Without qualifying column names. The **VALUES** columns have to match the actual table columns.

```
INSERT INTO Customer VALUES(3, DEFAULT)
```

Using the **DEFAULT** property. In this example, the **DEFAULT** value is "NewCustomer."

```
INSERT INTO Customer(CustomerID, Name)
    SELECT CustomerID, Name
    FROM NewCustomer
```

Using **SELECT** from a second table.

The results after these INSERT statements are illustrated in Figure 6.9.

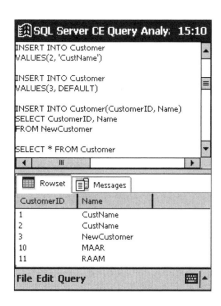

Figure 6.9   The rowset from the **SELECT** statement

Updating data

The DML statement **UPDATE** is used to update records. You need to specify which table is to be updated, which columns with which values, and the records that are to be updated (using the **WHERE** clause).

UPDATE syntax:

```
UPDATE table_name
    SET
    { column_name = { expression | DEFAULT | NULL } } [ ,...n ]
    [ WHERE < search_condition > ]
```

Examples

```
UPDATE Customer SET Name = 'Not So Common Name' WHERE
CustomerID < 5
```

Updates the customer name for all customers with CustomerID less than 5.

```
UPDATE Customer SET Name = 'A Very Common Name'
```

Updates all the customers' names.

```
UPDATE POrder SET Invoice = Invoice * 0.95, OrderDate = DEFAULT
WHERE CustomerID = 1
```

The customer with CustomerID 1 gets a better price. This statement updates the Invoice amount (a 5 percent discount) and sets the OrderDate to the defined **DEFAULT** of that column.

Deleting data

The **DELETE** statement is used to delete records. If the **WHERE** clause is omitted, all records are deleted.

DELETE syntax:

```
DELETE
    [ FROM ] table_name
    [ WHERE < search_condition > ]
```

Examples

```
DELETE FROM POrder
```

This deletes all orders in POrder.

```
DELETE FROM Customer WHERE CustomerID > 3
```

This deletes customers with CustomerID greater than 3.

Retrieving data

At the core of SQL Server CE is the support for Structured Query Language (SQL). Use the **SELECT** statement when querying data in SQL databases. To master the ins and outs of the **SELECT** statement is to master database development.

The **SELECT** statement is constructed using the clauses:

- SELECT
- FROM
- WHERE
- GROUP BY
- HAVING
- ORDER BY

SELECT FROM

The **SELECT** statement supports **DISTINCT**, table aliases, expressions in columns and column aliases. A **SELECT** statement must have a **FROM** clause in SQL Server CE.

The **FROM** clause supports **INNER**, **LEFT (OUTER)** and **RIGHT (OUTER)** joins, but not **FULL (OUTER)** joins. SQL Server CE does not support joins expressed as "*=" and "=*".

Inner joins are used if you want to retrieve records from both tables that match the join condition. Records that do not match with a record from the other table are not returned.

Outer joins return all records from at least one of the tables. All records are returned from the left table referenced with a left outer join. All records are returned from the right table referenced in a right outer join.

SELECT FROM syntax:

```
SELECT [ ALL | DISTINCT ] < select_list >

< select_list > ::=
    { *
    | { table_name | table_alias }.*
    | { column_name | expression } [ [ AS ] column_alias ]
    } [ ,...n ]

FROM { < table_source > } [ ,...n ]

< table_source > ::=
    table_name [ [ AS ] table_alias ]
    | < joined_table >

< joined_table > ::=
    < table_source > < join_type > < table_source > ON

<search_condition >
    | ( < joined_table > )

< join_type > ::=
    [ INNER | { { LEFT | RIGHT } [ OUTER ] } ] JOIN
```

Examples

The following examples are based on the Customers, Orders, and Order Details tables in the Northwind Traders database. The tables were first pulled down to the Pocket PC using the Remote Data Access method. More on that later in this chapter!

```
SELECT * FROM Customers
```

Returns all columns and all records from the Customers table.

Tip

Because Pocket PCs have a limited amount of RAM, you should consume just the amount of memory that your applications really needs. The **SELECT** * consumes more memory than **SELECT** col1, col2, etc.

```
SELECT OrderID, Shipname, ShipCountry FROM Orders
```

Returns the OrderID, Shipname, ShipCountry columns from the Orders table.

```
SELECT C.CustomerID,
C.CompanyName,
O.OrderID,
O.OrderDate,
O.ShipCountry
FROM Customers AS C
INNER JOIN Orders AS O
ON C.CustomerID = O.CustomerID
```

Returns records from the Customers and Orders table where CustomerID matches on both sides. This query ran 50 percent faster after having created the following index:

```
CREATE INDEX idxOrders ON Orders (CustomerID)
```

```
SELECT C.CustomerID,
C.CompanyName,
O.OrderID,
O.OrderDate,
O.ShipCountry
FROM Customers AS C
LEFT JOIN Orders AS O
ON C.CustomerID = O.CustomerID
```

Returns ALL customers (CustomerID and CompanyName) even if they do not exist in the Orders table.

WHERE, GROUP BY, HAVING and ORDER BY

The **WHERE** clause provides a search condition to the rowset. Intelligently designed **WHERE** clauses are very efficient for improving performance in database applications, since a lesser number of records returned is a win in communication and data management overhead.

GROUP BY groups records together and is often used in conjunction with aggregate functions. The SQL Server CE support of aggregate functions is a welcome benefit for CEDB developers. The following aggregate functions are supported:

- AVG
- COUNT
- MAX
- MIN
- SUM

HAVING is similar to the **WHERE** clause. The important difference is that **HAVING** is implemented after **GROUP BY**, whereas **WHERE** is implemented before. This means that records that pass the **WHERE** search conditions is part of the **GROUP BY** operation. The result of the **GROUP BY** operation is filtered through the **HAVING** clause.

ORDER BY sorts the rowset in ascending or descending order.

 Tip

ORDER BY, DISTINCT, and **GROUP BY** operations consume more memory than other operators. Use them only when you really need them!

Syntax

```
[ WHERE < search_condition >]
[ GROUP BY group_by_expression [ ,...n ] ]
[ HAVING < search_condition > ]
[ ORDER BY { order_by_expression [ ASC | DESC ] } [ ,...n] ]
```

Examples

```
SELECT CustomerID, CompanyName, Country
FROM Customers
WHERE (Country = 'Sweden' OR Country = 'Germany')
ORDER BY CompanyName
```

Returns customers from Sweden and Germany, ordered by CompanyName.

```
SELECT OrderID, SUM(UnitPrice * Quantity) AS Value
FROM OrderDetails
GROUP BY OrderID
ORDER BY Value DESC
```

Returns all Orders and the respective sum of each product unit price times quantity. The result is sorted so that orders with the highest value come first.

```
SELECT OrderID,
SUM (UnitPrice * Quantity) AS Value
FROM OrderDetails
GROUP BY OrderID
```

```
HAVING SUM(UnitPrice * Quantity) > 10000
ORDER BY Value DESC
```

Returns the same records as the previous query, but the **HAVING** clause filters away orders with a value that is less than 10,000.

Date functions

SQL Server CE provides five date functions: **DATEADD**, **DATEDIFF**, **DATENAME**, **DATEPART**, and **GETDATE**. These functions provide the means to retrieve and manipulate date values.

Syntax

```
GETDATE ( )
DATEADD (datepart, number, date)
DATEDIFF (datepart, startdate , enddate)
DATENAME (datepart, date)
DATEPART (datepart, date)
```

Examples

```
SELECT OrderID,
OrderDate,
DATEADD(week, 1, OrderDate) AS NewDate
FROM Orders
```

Returns OrderDate and a calculated column NewDate that is given a date value one week greater than the OrderDate.

```
SELECT OrderID,
OrderDate,
DATEDIFF(ww, OrderDate, RequiredDate) AS WeekDiff
FROM Orders
```

Returns OrderDate and the difference between OrderDate and RequiredDate expressed in number of weeks.

```
SELECT OrderID,
RequiredDate,
DATENAME(dw, RequiredDate) AS WeekDay,
DATEPART(ww, RequiredDate) AS Week
FROM Orders
```

Returns RequiredDate, the weekday and week number of RequiredDate.

```
INSERT INTO Customer (Name, InsertDate) VALUES ('Andy',
GETDATE())
```

Inserts a new customer record with InsertDate being today's date.

6.5   Using SQL Server CE from eMbedded Visual Basic

SQL Server CE is, as an OLEDB provider, available from eMbedded Visual Basic through ADOCE. The object model of ADOCE is similar to that of server side ADO, which means that you will be able to leverage both your skills and existing server side code. However, ADOCE does have some limitations in comparison with server side ADO due to the limited amount of memory. The limitations include the lack of:

- Asynchronous queries
- Collection objects
- Command and Parameter objects
- Disconnected Recordsets
- Dynamic creation of Recordsets
- Multiple queries (Recordset.NextRecordset)
- Property object
- Recordset persistence (Recordset.Save)

Data definition language through ADOXCE and ADOCE

Databases, tables, and indices can be created programmatically with eVB just as from Query Analyzer. Before we go into ADOCE it is vital to remember that you will most likely work with the Remote Data Access and Replication objects that provide methods that swiftly create tables and indexes from remote SQL Servers. The majority of the database management occurs through these objects, but from time to time you will need to pass DDL and DML statements directly to your SQL Server CE database.

All database items can be managed using the objects in ADOXCE. These are the objects that are available through ADOXCE:

- Databases (Catalogs)
- Tables
- Columns
- Indexes
- Keys
- Properties

In the following examples we will use the ADOXCE Catalog object's Create method to create databases. Tables and indexes will be created using the ADOCE Connection object's Execute method. The sample code can be found in **Sample 6.1** on the CD.

Creating a database

It is important to decide the following aspects regarding the database, before creating it:

1 **The name and location of the database.** You can store the database anywhere on your Pocket PC, including on secondary storage such as Compact Flash cards.

2 **Whether the database should be password protected.** Password protects the database.

3 **Whether the database should be encrypted.** The encryption used is a 128-bit encryption, which stops the database from being read as clear text.

4 **What Locale Identifier should be used.** The Locale Identifier specifies the database sort order. You cannot change the sort order, once the database is created, unless you compact the database into a new physical database. This chapter will provide more information on this subject.

The following code sample creates a SQL Server CE database. It creates a database called PPCDE.sdf.

```
' Variables
Dim paca As ADOXCE.Catalog

' Create the ADOXCE Catalog object
Set paca = CreateObject("ADOXCE.Catalog.3.1")

' Create a database
paca.Create "Provider=Microsoft.SQLSERVER.OLEDB.CE.1.0;
Data Source=\PPCDE.sdf"
```

You can encrypt and password protect the database by adding database password and encryption parameters to the **Create**-method:

```
' Create an encrypted database and password protected
'paca.Create "Provider=Microsoft.SQLSERVER.OLEDB.CE.1.0;
Data Source=\PPCDE.sdf;SSCE:Database Password='pwd';SSCE:
Encrypt Database=TRUE"
```

The following creates a database with Locale Identifier 2077. The Locale Identifier 2077 specifies Swedish sort order. The default Locale Identifier 1033 (U.S. English) is used if it is omitted in the **Create**-statement.

```
' Create a database with a locale identifier of 2077
' paca.Create "Provider=Microsoft.SQLSERVER.OLEDB.CE.1.0;
Data Source=\PPCDE.sdf;Locale Identifier=2077"
```

Connecting to a SQL Server CE database

Use the ADOCE **Connection**-object to connect to a SQL Server CE database. The following example declares and creates a variable as a **Connection**-object:

```
Dim paco As ADOCE.Connection
Set paco = CreateObject("ADOCE.Connection.3.1")
```

You need to include the ADOCE version number when calling the **CreateObject** method to create a reference to the ADOCE 3.1 control. SQL Server CE can only be accessed through ADOCE 3.1 or later.

The Connection object's methods and properties are available once it is created.

Once the **Connection** object is created, you can use the properties and methods of the **Connection** object to open, close, and manipulate a connection. The following code shows how to open a connection to a database by using the **Open** method:

```
Set paco = CreateObject("ADOCE.Connection.3.1")
paco.ConnectionString =
"Provider=Microsoft.SQLSERVER.OLEDB.CE.1.0; data
source=\Northwind.sdf"
paco.Open
```

The **Open** defaults to using the CEDB provider if the provider parameter in the source string is omitted. Since we never want to go back to the "Dark Ages of CEDB," we need to specify the SQL Server CE provider string when opening a SQL Server CE database. See the code above.

Managing tables

You can use the **Catalog** object in ADOXCE to create and manage tables, or you can choose to pass DDL statements through ADOCE using the **Connection**-object. The following sample illustrates a sub used to create tables and add table constraints using the **Connection** object.

```
Public Sub CreateTables()

' Creates tables
' Known bugs:
' Version    Date     Who   Comment
' 00.00.000  010205   ASJ   Created
'***************************************************************
' Variables
Dim strCreateTableSQL As String
```

```
' Open connection
paco.Open CONNECTION_STRING

' ********** Create tables ****************
' Create table Customer
strCreateTableSQL = "CREATE TABLE Customer (CustomerID
uniqueidentifier ROWGUIDCOL CONSTRAINT pkCustomerID PRIMARY
KEY,"
strCreateTableSQL = strCreateTableSQL & " Name nvarchar(30)
NOT NULL)"

' Execute SQL statement
paco.Execute strCreateTableSQL

' Create table POrder
strCreateTableSQL = "CREATE TABLE POrder ("
strCreateTableSQL = strCreateTableSQL & " OrderID
uniqueidentifier ROWGUIDCOL PRIMARY KEY,"
strCreateTableSQL = strCreateTableSQL & " CustomerID
uniqueidentifier,"
strCreateTableSQL = strCreateTableSQL & " Quantity int NOT
NULL,"
strCreateTableSQL = strCreateTableSQL & " OrderDate
datetime DEFAULT GetDate() NOT NULL)"

' Execute SQL statement
paco.Execute strCreateTableSQL

' Add foreign key constraint
strCreateTableSQL = "ALTER TABLE POrder ADD CONSTRAINT
FK_Order_Customer FOREIGN KEY (CustomerID) REFERENCES Customer
(CustomerID)"

' Execute SQL statement
paco.Execute strCreateTableSQL

' Close connection
paco.Close

End Sub
```

This sample constructs the DDL statements by concatenating strings into the **strCreateTableSQL** variable. The variable is then used in the Connection object's **Execute** method.

As you can pass any supported DDL statements through the Connection object, you can even programmatically create indexes to speed up database access on the run.

Tip

Observe in the above code that the Connection object **paco** is not declared in the sub, nor is it set to **Nothing** (Set paco = Nothing) at the end. Instead, the Connection object is declared in a module as a public object, and the object is instantiated using a **CreateObject**-statement in the Form_Load event. The reasons behind this design are to avoid the infamous **CreateObject** memory leaks that often occur at the **CreateObject**-call, and to gain performance. The Pocket PC application is single user environment by definition, which means that the scalability issues with that would be prevalent in a server side setting are not relevant. The performance gain is about a third of a second for each **CreateObject**-call. If performance is of extreme importance, you might even consider keeping a connection open throughout the entire application. This design is utterly flawed in a server side setting, but this pragmatic approach is based on the fact that more than one person cannot use your Pocket PC application at one time anyway. A critical and relevant concern to this design, however, is that no other application can connect to that database as long as you keep the connection open. This issue has a severe impact on the multitasking nature of the Pocket PC – so use this design only in critical situations. Finally, it is worth noting that the **CreateObject** memory leak can be worked around by using the **OSIUtil.dll** from Odyssey Software, which is included on the CD-ROM.

Data manipulation language through ADOCE

The server side ADO exposes through its Recordset object methods the ability to insert, update, and delete records. These methods are: **AddNew**, **Update**, and **Delete**.

These methods are also available from ADOCE. A significant difference to keep in mind is that the recordset must be opened referencing a base table in order for these methods to work. ADOCE does not allow **AddNew**, **Update**, and **Delete** based on a recordset opened using an SQL statement.

The following code shows how to insert a record into a table using **AddNew**. The code moves on to find a specific record to update that record. Finally, a record is deleted.

```
    ' Open connection and recordset
    paco.Open CONNECTION_STRING
    pars.Open "Customer", paco, adOpenDynamic,
adLockOptimistic, adCmdTableDirect

    ' Add new customer
    pars.AddNew "Name", "New Customer"
    pars.Update

    ' Find customer and update
    pars.MoveFirst
```

```
pars.Find "Name = 'Customer 2'"
If Not pars.EOF Then pars.Update "Name", "Customer Two"

' Delete record
pars.MoveFirst
pars.Find "Name = 'Customer 1'"
If Not pars.EOF Then pars.Delete

' Close recordset and connection
pars.Close
paco.Close
```

⟶ Tip

The code above is very familiar to any ADO programmer. The ADO and ADOCE **Recordset** objects expose a number of functional interfaces. We have become comfortable with these interfaces, and rightly so. However, never forget that SQL Server and SQL Server CE are set-oriented relational databases capable of handling direct DML statements (**INSERT**, **UPDATE**, and **DELETE**). Make sure that you don't fall into bad programming habits inherited from the old mainframe days where sequential text files were opened up and looped through at every lookup, update, and delete. To open a recordset, just for the purpose of finding a record to update or delete it is far from optimal from a performance point of view. Make sure you treat SQL Server CE as the relational database it is by using **INSERT**, **UPDATE**, and **DELETE** statements appropriately.

From an ADOCE **Recordset** point of view, indexes are only exposed on base tables. This means that when you use the ADOCE **Recordset** object's **Index** property with the **Seek** to search and retrieve data from SQL Server CE you need to include the property **adCmdTableDirect** (as in the sample above) in order to leverage the benefits of existing indexes. The following sample creates and uses an index to locate a specific customer record.

```
' Open connection
paco.Open CONNECTION_STRING

' Create an index
paco.Execute "CREATE INDEX idxCustomer ON Customer (Name)"

' Apply the index
pars.Index = "idxCustomer"

' Open the recordset
pars.Open "Customer", paco, adOpenStatic, adLockOptimistic,
adCmdTableDirect

' Find customer and update
pars.Seek "Customer 2", adSeekFirstEQ
If Not pars.EOF Then pars.Update "Name", "Customer Two"
```

```
' Close recordset and connection
pars.Close
paco.Close
```

Transactions

A fundamental aspect to database programming is the use of transactions. A transaction is an atomic series of SQL and DML statements that are guaranteed to be executed or aborted as one single statement. Consider the scenario where you transfer money from one bank account to another. (Have you heard this one before, or what?)

The transfer consists of a withdrawal from one account and a deposit into another. Your money is lost if an error would occur in between the withdrawal and the deposition had the transfer not been designed as an atomic transaction. However, the withdrawal would have been rolled back if the withdrawal and deposit had both been placed into a single transaction.

The following code performs the same operations as the previous sample. Observe where the beginning of the transaction is. The transaction is committed only if there is a customer with the name of "Customer 1." If there is no customer with that name, then the **AddNew** and **Update** calls will be rolled back.

```
      ' Open connection and recordset
      paco.Open CONNECTION_STRING
      pars.Open "Customer", paco, adOpenDynamic,
  adLockOptimistic, adCmdTableDirect

  paco.BeginTrans

      ' Add new customer
      pars.AddNew "Name", "New Customer"
      pars.Update

      ' Find customer and update
      pars.MoveFirst
      pars.Find "Name = 'Customer 2'"
      If Not pars.EOF Then pars.Update "Name", "Customer Two"

      ' Delete record
      pars.MoveFirst
      pars.Find "Name = 'Customer 1'"
      If Not pars.EOF Then
          pars.Delete

          ' Commit the transaction
          paco.CommitTrans
  Else
```

```
        ' Abort the transaction
        paco.RollbackTrans
    End If

        ' Close recordset and connection
        pars.Close
        paco.Close
```

The code below achieves the same data manipulation using DML statements, instead of using ADOCE Recordset methods.

```
    ' Open connection
    paco.Open CONNECTION_STRING

    ' Add new customer
    paco.Execute "INSERT INTO Customer (Name) VALUES ("New
Customer')"

    ' Find customer and update
    paco.Execute "UPDATE Customer SET Name = 'Customer Two'
WHERE Name = 'Customer 2'"

    ' Delete record
    paco.Execute "DELETE FROM Customer WHERE Name = 'Customer 1'"

    ' Close connection
    paco.Close
```

The subtle yet significant difference between these **UPDATE** and **DELETE** statements compared to the Recordset methods in the previous example is that they will update or delete all records matching the criteria. The Recordset methods as designed in the example will delete only the current record. Only if the column used in the **WHERE** clause were unique, then the result would be identical.

A similar approach is taken in the sample project when tables are populated with sample data. As you can see, the **For-Next** loop executes the DML statements in the array **strSQL**. If you are the optimizing type, you will notice that the sample code could have been designed more efficiently by moving the string concatenations into the loop. We chose to put them outside to make it easier to replace the predictable data with more non-generic data.

```
Public Sub PopulateTables()

' Populates tables
' Known bugs:
' Version    Date    Who  Comment
' 00.00.000  010205  ASJ  Created
'**************************************************************
```

```
' Variables
Dim strSQL(3) As String
Dim intCounter As Integer

    ' Open connection
    paco.Open CONNECTION_STRING

    ' Insert customer data
    strSQL(0) = "INSERT INTO Customer (Name) VALUES ('Customer
1')"
    strSQL(1) = "INSERT INTO Customer (Name) VALUES ('Customer
2')"
    strSQL(2) = "INSERT INTO Customer (Name) VALUES ('Customer
3')"

    ' Run through the SQL and execute!
    For intCounter = 0 To 2
        paco.Execute strSQL(intCounter)
    Next intCounter

     ' Close connection
     paco.Close

End Sub
```

Retrieving data through ADOCE

Data access is all about passing SQL statements to the database and retrieving the results. First, take a look at the following ADOCE **Recordset** "Rules of Thumb" that relate to optimizing performance and minimizing memory requirements:

1 The ADOCE **Recordset** should be opened using the cursor type **adOpenForwardOnly** (if you don't need scrollability) and the lock type **adLockReadOnly** (if you don't need to change any data).

2 Make sure that the Recordset only returns the records that you need. Use the **WHERE** clause wisely.

3 Use indexes on columns frequently in **WHERE** clauses, **ORDER BY**, or **JOIN** to improve performance significantly.

4 **DISTINCT**, **GROUP BY**, and **ORDER BY** consume memory. Use only when you must.

The code below includes four examples of SQL statements being passed to SQL Server CE using the Recordset's **Open** method.

Example 1 is a simple **SELECT** from the Customer table.

Example 2 retrieves records from the table POrder and sorts them in descending order by order date.

Example 3 performs an **INNER JOIN** between the tables Customer and POrder.

Example 4 returns the number of orders and total amount quantities by each customer.

```
paco.Open CONNECTION_STRING

' Example 1
strSQL = "SELECT CustomerID, Name FROM Customer"
pars.Open strSQL, paco, adOpenForwardOnly, adLockReadOnly

' Close recordset
pars.Close

' Example 2
strSQL = "SELECT OrderID, OrderDate, Quantity FROM POrder"
strSQL = strSQL & " ORDER BY OrderDate DESC"
pars.Open strSQL, paco, adOpenForwardOnly, adLockReadOnly

' Close recordset
pars.Close

' Example 3
strSQL = "SELECT C.Name, O.OrderDate, O.Quantity"
strSQL = strSQL & " FROM Customer C INNER JOIN POrder O"
strSQL = strSQL & " ON C.CustomerID = O.CustomerID"
pars.Open strSQL, paco, adOpenForwardOnly, adLockReadOnly

' Close recordset
pars.Close

' Example 4
strSQL = "SELECT C.Name, COUNT(O.OrderID) OrderCount,
SUM(O.Quantity) OrderQuantity"
    strSQL = strSQL & " FROM Customer C INNER JOIN POrder O"
    strSQL = strSQL & " ON C.CustomerID = O.CustomerID"
    strSQL = strSQL & " GROUP BY C.Name"
    strSQL = strSQL & " ORDER BY OrderQuantity DESC"
    pars.Open strSQL, paco, adOpenForwardOnly, adLockReadOnly

    ' Close recordset
    pars.Close

    ' Close connection
    paco.Close
```

The sample (**Sample 6.1** on the CD) also implements a simple user interface. It lists the customer and order records, and enables the user to add new orders to each customer (see Figure 6.10).

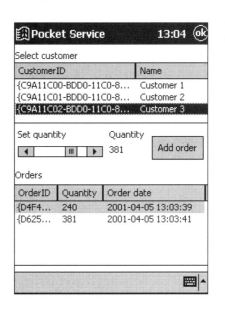

Figure 6.10
Customer and orders

To add a new order, the user selects the appropriate customer, specifies the quantity using the scrollbar, and then taps **Add order**. This is the code behind the **CommandButton's Click** event.

```
Private Sub cmdOrder_Click()
' Add order
' Known bugs:
' Version    Date    Who   Comment
' 00.00.000 010315 ASJ   Created
'*****************************
' Variables
Dim strSQL As String

    ' Open connection and recordset
    paco.Open CONNECTION_STRING
    pars.Open "POrder", paco, adOpenDynamic, adLockOptimistic,
adCmdTableDirect

    ' Add new order
    pars.AddNew
      pars("CustomerID") = Mid(lvwCustomer.SelectedItem.Key, 2)
      pars("Quantity") = scrQuantity.Value
    pars.Update

    ' Close recordset and connection
    pars.Close
    paco.Close
```

```
                       ' Call update POrder listview
                       pRefreshOrderList (Mid(lvwCustomer.SelectedItem.Key, 2))
               End Sub
```

The recordset opens the POrder table as a base table. The new record is inserted using the **AddNew** method. The POrder table's Primary Key is a uniqueidentifier defined as a ROWGUIDCOL, which means that the value in this column is set automatically.

The Order **ListView** refreshes once the new order has been inserted into the POrder table. The sub **pRefreshOrderList** manages the **ListView** and requires the **CustomerID** as parameter. The action behind this bold assertion:

```
Private Sub pRefreshOrderList(CustomerID As String)
' IN: CustomerID
' Known bugs:
' Version   Date    Who  Comment
' 00.00.000 010315 ASJ  Created
'*****************************
' Variables
Dim litm As ListItem
Dim strSQL As String

       ' Clear ListView list
       lvwOrder.ListItems.Clear
       lvwOrder.Sorted = False

       ' Make listview invisible to improve performance
       lvwOrder.Visible = False

       ' Set SQL
       strSQL = "SELECT OrderID, Quantity, OrderDate"
       strSQL = strSQL & " FROM POrder INNER JOIN Customer ON""
       strSQL = strSQL & " Customer.CustomerID =
POrder.CustomerID"
       strSQL = strSQL & " WHERE POrder.CustomerID = '" &
CustomerID & "'"

       ' Open connection and recordset
       paco.Open CONNECTION_STRING
       pars.Open strSQL, paco, adOpenForwardOnly, adLockReadOnly

       ' Populate list view
          Do While Not (pars.EOF Or pars.BOF)
              Set litm = lvwOrder.ListItems.Add(, "K" &
pars("OrderID"), pars("OrderID""))
                    litm.SubItems(1) = pars("Quantity")
```

```
            litm.SubItems(2) = pars("OrderDate")
        pars.MoveNext
    Loop

' Close recordset and connection
pars.Close
paco.Close

' Set full row select
lvwOrder.SetFocus
SetFullRowSelect GetFocus()

' Make first order default
If lvwOrder.ListItems.Count > 0 Then lvwOrder.SelectedItem
= lvwOrder.ListItems(1)

' Make listview visible
lvwOrder.Visible = True

End Sub
```

You can see more ADOCE sample code and learn more about working with ADOCE throughout the rest of this book.

Compacting a database

The SQL Server CE database grows and grows and grows. The database grows the more records you insert into the database (pretty obvious!), but SQL Server CE doesn't release memory as you delete records. You need to compact the database to reclaim the memory. The SQL Server CE's **Engine** object has a method called **CompactDatabase** that compacts an existing database into a new one. While creating the new database, you can change database password, sort order, and encryption settings – something you cannot do any other way.

It is a good idea to compact the database regularly and to do that without the knowledge of the user. A common scenario is to have the application monitor the available Pocket PC memory. At a given threshold the application automatically performs the compacting. Take a look at the code below:

```
Public Sub CompactDB()
' Compact database
' Known bugs:
' Version   Date   Who  Comment
' 00.00.000 010205 ASJ  Created
'**********************************************************
```

```
' Variables
Dim engSQL As SSCE.Engine
Dim fileDatabase As FILECTL.FileSystem

    On Error Resume Next

    ' Create engine object
    Set engSQL = CreateObject("SSCE.Engine.1.0")

    ' Create the FileSystem object
    Set fileDatabase = CreateObject("FILECTL.FileSystem")

    ' Backup the original database
    fileDatabase.FileCopy "\PPCDE.sdf", "\PPCDE_Backup.sdf"

    If Err <> 0 Then
        Exit Sub
    End If

    ' Compact the original database into temporary
    engSQL.CompactDatabase CONNECTION_STRING,
"Provider=Microsoft.SQLSERVER.OLEDB.CE.1.0; Data
Source=\PPCDE_Temp.sdf"

    ' Delete the original database
    fileDatabase.Kill "\PPCDE.sdf"

    ' Move the temporary database to the original file name
    fileDatabase.MoveFile "\PPCDE_Temp.sdf", "PPCDE.sdf"

End Sub
```

The database is first backed up (it is wise to do this first if you have enough RAM!). If anything fails during the subsequent operations, you still have the backup. This is what happens after the backup:

● The database is compacted into a temporary database.

● The original database is deleted.

● The temporary database is renamed back to the original filename.

6.6 ███ Reaching remote database servers

SQL Server CE natively supports two different methods (object models) of reaching remote database servers:

1 Remote Data Access (RDA) – Supports SQL Server version 6.5 and later.

2 Merge replication (MR) – Supports SQL Server 2000 only.

Both RDA and merge replication work across an HTTP connection to a Microsoft Internet Information Server. Two agents enable the communication between SQL Server CE and SQL Server: the SQL Server CE Client Agent and the SQL Server CE Server Agent (an ISAPI DLL).

RDA is, from an eVB angle, implemented in the SQL Server CE engine as a component that is created using the following syntax:

```
Set pRDA = CreateObject("SSCE.RemoteDataAccess.1.0")
```

Merge replication is, from an eVB angle, implemented in the SQL Server CE engine as a component that is created using the following syntax:

```
Set pREP = CreateObject("SSCE.Replication.1.0")
```

Merge replication or Remote Data Access?

It is vital to identify the differences between merge replication and RDA since both, from a conceptual level, enable remote SQL Server connectivity.

The goals for RDA are to facilitate data access to earlier versions of SQL Server and to support scenarios when merge replication is, for any reason, not desired.

The RDA method is more limited than merge replication but is more straightforward to set up and use because you don't have to bother with defining SQL Server publication. RDA uses the **RemoteDataAccess** object to pull table data from the server and push changes back to the server. In addition to this, the RDA Object has a **SubmitSQL** method that passes SQL statements to the server. In essence, the client controls the communication.

The **RemoteDataAccess** method **Push** passes data from the Pocket PC to the remote server, when using RDA. The data is pushed unconditionally into the remote server's tables, overwriting any changes made after the data was first pulled. RDA should only be used in scenarios where you either can partition the data between unique users or where conflicts never happen. Referential integrity has to be programmatically implemented when RDA is used. RDA is likely to communicate faster over the wire because less data is transferred.

Merge replication is based on SQL Server 2000 merge replication and uses the SQL Server 2000 publication/subscription model. Merge replication is therefore faster to develop for than RDA since you can manage an entire database with single calls to the **Replication** object.

To manage data with RDA each table needs its own set of calls to the **RemoteDataAccess** object. The referential integrity implemented in the remote database server as constraints and indexes are transferred to the SQL Server CE database when using merge replication. Data can be partitioned at the remote server, when designing the publications.

RDA and merge replication support any network connection based on TCP/IP including both wired as well as wireless connections. SQL Server CE 1.1 introduced the support for connecting to remote servers through ActiveSync and the desktop PC. The feature is called SQL Server CE Relay is based on the peer point-to-point protocol (PPP_PEER). Before the release of SQL Server CE 1.1, you had to configure and use a Pocket PC network adapter or a modem in order to reach remote SQL Servers from the Pocket PC. The Relay feature makes it possible to reach remote SQL Servers with the Pocket PC connected to a desktop PC, or with an ActiveSync connection using infrared, a serial, or USB cradle.

Database integration philosophy

Before we dive into the database RDA and merge replication database integration design, we'd like to highlight some significant aspects involved in database integration.

Modern system architecture separates presentation, logic, and data. Software clients use common components in the business logic layer, which in turn reads and writes data in the data layer. The common business logic layer implements rules about, for example, how customers, orders, and products relate to each other. These rules are not the declared database relationships (one-to-one, one-to-many, etc.), but are higher-level rules such as what customer type gets the better price.

The rule is in general that software clients should never establish links directly to the data source. Well-designed architecture implements business logic on application servers and separates the presentation layer from the data. The advantages are better scalability; possible application logic reuse across applications; and improved ability to design and develop new clients.

The relationship between a Pocket PC client and a central database should, to adhere to this architecture thinking, be implemented through an application server – not through a defined relationship between the local, mobile database and the remote, central database. The next chapter is a walkthrough on how to achieve remote connectivity to database servers through components.

Why should you then consider database integration using RDA or merge replication? Development and conflict-resolution management efficiency! The built-in support for merge replication makes it really easy to get a mobile client going with live data. It is tempting, and sometimes appropriate, to use features that quickly push and pull data from and to the remote server to identical table structures on the Pocket PC. The fact that those merge replication features in SQL Server 2000 provide replication management tools makes it even more tempting.

A common situation that needs to be managed in any project where many users access the same data (concurrency) is what happens when two or more users change the same data at the same time. This situation occurs much more often when using a mobile platform with support for disconnected scenarios.

For example, imagine two users downloading the same customer data. While disconnected they both make changes to the customer. The first user changes the customer discount percentage from 5 percent to 10 percent and then merges the customer data. The second user had just met with the customer and taken a product order using the 5 percent discount level. What should happen when the second user wants to merge the customer and order data? Should the 5 percent or the 10 percent rebate level be applied to the order, to which the customer already agreed? As you can understand, these conflicts have to be managed. Business rules rather than technology aspects (such as time stamps, etc.) should drive the conflict resolution.

Merge replication implemented by SQL Server CE integrates with the SQL Server Reconciler in the remote SQL Server 2000 database and can thereby automatically make use of the built-in conflict-resolving functionality.

A well-balanced architecture may make use of database-to-database relationships such as merge replication if it is combined with the use of business layer logic. This can happen if, for example, the data is first merged to and from the Pocket PC and then committed as a result of components being triggered by the merge.

If you implement merge replication without the use of business logic components, you must realize that the mobile client in the Pocket PC is firmly coupled with the remote database structure. This solid coupling introduces maintenance vulnerability because as soon as changes occur in the backend database, perhaps due to a system upgrade, the Pocket PC client has to be upgraded as well.

Configuring the server for replication

These are the steps necessary to configure the server for replication (using anonymous access):

1 Create folder C:\InetPub\wwwroot\sqlce.

2 Copy C:\Program Files\Microsoft SQL Server CE\Server\sscesa10.dll to C:\InetPub\wwwroot\sqlce.

3 Register: Regsvr32 C:\InetPub\wwwroot\sqlce\sscesa10.dll.

4 Create virtual directory sqlce pointing at C:\InetPub\wwwroot\sqlce with Execute Permissions=Script and Executables and Anonymous access.

5 Set Modify rights to IUSR_<machinename> for folder C:\InetPub\www-root\sqlce.

6 Set up IUSR_<machinename> as an integrated Login in SQL Server with database rights.

The SQL Server CE Books Online provides additional details!

Using Remote Data Access

The **RemoteDataAccess** object has three methods:

- **Pull** – Pulls data from the remote SQL Server
- **Push** – Pushes data back from the Pocket PC
- **SubmitSQL** – Passes SQL statements to the remote SQL Server

To initiate the database integration using RDA, you first have to pull down tables from the remote server to the Pocket PC. The **Pull** method retrieves data by passing a **SELECT** statement to the remote server. You partition the data you want to have pulled by using an appropriate **WHERE** clause. The **Pull** method creates a table in SQL Server CE and populates it with the data that is returned by the remote server. You define the name of the table that the **Pull** method creates. The table must not exist in the SQL Server CE database before you execute the **Pull** method. This means that you first have to drop the table, before you call the **Pull** method.

Use the **Push** method on tables that have been created by the **Pull** method and that have been declared to track changes. When you push data to the remote server, the data is unconditionally inserted and remote server data updated. Since the local table in SQL Server CE must not exist before calling the **Pull** method, it is a pretty good idea to first push the data to the remote server before dropping it. The local data will otherwise get lost.

The fact that the **Push** statement unconditionally changes data in the remote SQL Server poses a concurrency challenge that might lead you to consider other options, such as the merge replication method. However, it's possible to address the concurrency challenges even when using RDA. It is common in implementations using RDA that the new tables are created to manage the Push and Pull. These tables are placed in front of the production tables and the data that is then pushed and pulled from the Pocket PC reaches the production tables through SQL Server triggers. The triggers can contain logic to manage replication and concurrency issues. A slightly different theme to this approach is to make calls to COM components after the **Push** method has completed, using Odyssey Software CEfusion or ViaXML, or even using SOAP and Web Services. You can read more about these options later in the book.

⠿ **Tip**

Make sure that you specify all Primary Key columns in the **SELECT**-statement used in the **Pull** method. The **Push** method will fail if you don't include all Primary Key columns. Also, table names that include spaces are not enjoyable to work with, as you will have to place double quotes around the table name in each statement. The Northwind Traders database (included in the SQL Server setup) used in these samples has a table called "Order Details" (including the space in between "Order" and "Details." Is that a bad idea, or is it a bad idea?

The **Push** method fails if the table includes a **ROWGUIDCOL** column. If you have declared a **ROWGUIDCOL** column as Primary Key, you are toast. The support for Primary Key **ROWGUIDCOL's** is on our wish list for SQL Server CE 2.0.

The following code pulls the Customer, Order, and Order Details tables from the Northwind database in SQL Server. (See **Sample 6.2** on the CD.)

```
Public Sub PullData()

' Pull data from SQL Server
' IN:
' Known bugs:
' Version   Date    Who   Comment
' 00.00.000 010315 ASJ   Created
'*****************************
' Variables
Dim pRDA As SSCE.RemoteDataAccess
Dim strSQL As String

On Error Resume Next

    ' Show hourglass
    Screen.MousePointer = vbHourGlass

    ' Push data
    PushData

    ' Create the RDA Object
    Set pRDA = CreateObject("SSCE.RemoteDataAccess.1.0")

    ' Set RDA properties
    pRDA.InternetURL =
"http://z0000048/sscereplication/sscesa10.dll"
    pRDA.LocalConnectionString = "Data Source=\northwind.sdf"

    ' Drop the tables
    paco.Open CONNECTION_STRING
```

```
        paco.Execute "DROP TABLE " & pstrDoubleQuote & "Order
  Details" & pstrDoubleQuote
        paco.Execute "DROP TABLE Orders"
        paco.Execute "DROP TABLE Customers""
        paco.Close

        ' Pull the tables
        pRDA.Pull "Customers", "SELECT CustomerID, CompanyName,
  ContactName, rowguid FROM Customers", "Provider=sqloledb;Data
  Source=z0000048;Initial Catalog=Northwind;user
  id=guest;password=", TRACKINGOFF
        pRDA.Pull "Orders", "SELECT CustomerID, OrderID, OrderDate,
  RequiredDate, Freight, rowguid FROM Orders",
  "Provider=sqloledb;Data Source=z0000048;Initial
  Catalog=Northwind;user id=guest;password=", TRACKINGOFF
        pRDA.Pull "Order Details", "SELECT OrderID, ProductID,
  Quantity, UnitPrice FROM [Order Details]",
  "Provider=sqloledb;Data Source=z0000048;Initial
  Catalog=Northwind;user id=guest;password=", TRACKINGON,
  "tblErrOrderDetails"

        If pRDA.ErrorRecords.Count > 0 Then
          ShowErrors pRDA.ErrorRecords
        End If

        ' Destroy the RDA Object
        Set pRDA = Nothing

        ' Restore mouse pointer
        Screen.MousePointer = vbArrow

  End Sub
```

First the tables are pushed to the remote SQL Server. The **On Error Resume Next** is vital in this code. To complete the code, you will have to catch the **Err** object after every statement. In this example, the **On Error Resume Next** statement ensures that the code will work even if the tables first do not exist in SQL Server CE. This is the case before the first **Pull**. Observe the string management punishment for using a space in the "Order Details" table! It is also important to see that the **SELECT** statement that fetches the Order Details data does not include the **ROWGUIDCOL**. We include **ROWGUIDCOL** in Customers and Orders because the sample does not update these tables.

By using the **TRACKINGON** parameter in the **Pull** method, SQL Server CE tracks all changes to the Pocket PC Customer table. When the **Push** method is used, the changes update the table on the remote server. The last parameter in the **Pull** method specifies a local table name to store error messages from RDA errors. Figure 6.11 illustrates running a **SELECT**-statement on the error table. We have obviously tried pushing a table, with a **ROWGUIDCOL**, from the Pocket PC to the remote server.

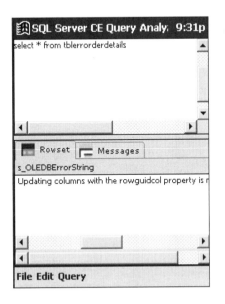

Figure 6.11   Using the RDA error table

The user can select customer, order, and order details in the following UI, once the data has been pulled to the Pocket PC. A new quantity can be entered and the local database is then updated (see Figure 6.12).

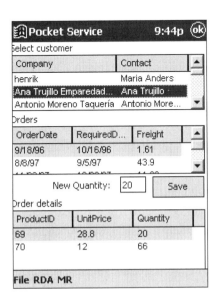

Figure 6.12   The sample is not likely to win a user interface contest

The following code pushes changes back to the remote SQL Server.

```
Public Sub PushData()
' Push data from SQL Server CE
' IN:
' Known bugs:
' Version   Date   Who  Comment
' 00.00.000 010315 ASJ  Created
'****************************
' Variables
Dim pRDA As SSCE.RemoteDataAccess

On Error Resume Next

    ' Create the RDA Object
    Set pRDA = CreateObject("SSCE.RemoteDataAccess.1.0")

    ' Set RDA properties
    pRDA.InternetURL =
"http://z0000048/sscereplication/sscesa10.dll"
    pRDA.LocalConnectionString = "Data Source=\northwind.sdf"

    ' Push the tables
    pRDA.Push "Order Details", "Provider=sqloledb;Data
Source=z0000048;Initial Catalog=Northwind;user
id=guest;password="

    If pRDA.ErrorRecords.Count > 0 Then
        ShowErrors pRDA.ErrorRecords
    End If

    ' Destroy the RDA Object
    Set pRDA = Nothing

End Sub
```

The **SubmitSQL** method can be used to pass SQL-statements to the remote database server for immediate execution. From a data perspective, statements passed by **SubmitSQL** can update or delete records, not return any records. You can change data in any table in the remote database, not only those that possibly have been pulled down to the Pocket PC.

This line of code updates the UnitPrice in the Products table for products that belong to a specific category:

```
    pRDA.SubmitSQL "UPDATE Products SET UnitPrice = UnitPrice *
1.1 WHERE CategoryID = 4", "Provider=sqloledb;Data
Source=z0000048;Initial Catalog=Northwind;user
id=guest;password="
```

RDA is a well-packaged method of reaching remote SQL Servers. The simple object model and topology make it possible to get going quickly. For an enterprise solution RDA offers both a quick implementation as well as programmatic control of the data being passed back and forth.

Using merge replication

Merge replication is built on the SQL Server Publish, Distribute, and Subscribe engines. These are the basic steps involved in setting up a mobile merge replication scenario:

1 Create a SQL Server publication on the remote SQL Server.

2 Subscribe to that publication from your Pocket PC.

3 Make changes on the Pocket PC and on the remote SQL Server.

4 Merge changes between the Pocket PC and the remote SQL Server.

5 Manage any conflicts from the remote SQL Server.

The built-in SQL Server wizards make it pretty straightforward to get going.

Create a SQL Server publication

The first step is to create a SQL Server Publication on the server for the database that you want to make available to the Pocket PC. You can initiate the Publication creation from SQL Server Enterprise Manager (see Figure 6.13).

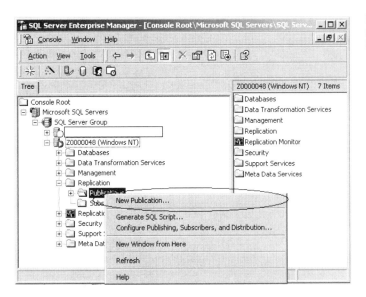

Figure 6.13   Start by creating the Publication!

The "Create Publication Wizard" will start when you select "New Publication." The wizard will walk you through:

● Selecting which database you wish to work with. In this sample we use Northwind.

● Choosing what type of publication. In this sample we will use "merge replication."

● Defining what types of subscribers should be supported. Make sure you select "Devices running SQL Server CE."

● The tables in the database that should be included. We use Orders, Customers, and Order Details.

● Define horizontal (which columns) and vertical (which rows) filters. In this example, we use no filters.

Subscribe to the publication

Once the publication is created, you need to programmatically subscribe to it from the Pocket PC. The merge replication architecture is from a connectivity point of view similar to that of RDA. The following code illustrates how to set up the subscription.

```
Public Sub CreateMerge()
' Create subscription
' Known bugs:
' Version    Date    Who    Comment
' 00.00.000 010315 ASJ    Created
'****************************
' Variables
Dim pMR As SSCE.Replication
Dim strSQL As String

CONNECTION_STRING = "Provider=Microsoft.SQLSERVER.OLEDB.CE.1.0;
Data Source=\NorthwindMerge.sdf"

On Error Resume Next

    ' Create the MR Object
    Set pMR = CreateObject("SSCE.Replication.1.0")

    ' Set MR properties
    pMR.InternetURL =
"http://z0000048/sscereplication/sscesa10.dll"
    ' Set Publisher properties.
    pMR.Publisher = "Z0000048"
```

```
        pMR.PublisherLogin = "sa"
        pMR.PublisherPassword = ""
        pMR.PublisherSecurityMode = DB_AUTHENTICATION
        pMR.PublisherNetwork = DEFAULT_NETWORK
        pMR.PublisherDatabase = "Northwind"
        pMR.Publication = "SQLNorthwind"

        'Set Subscriber properties.
        pMR.Subscriber = "Pocket PC"
        pMR.SubscriberConnectionString = CONNECTION_STRING

        ' Create the subscription
        pMR.AddSubscription CREATE_DATABASE
        ' Initiate MR
        pMR.Initialize
        pMR.Run
        pMR.Terminate

        ' Destroy the MR Object
        Set pMR = Nothing

    End Sub
```

The key statements to observe are the **AddSubscription, Initiate, Run,** and **Terminate.** The **AddSubscription** statement establishes the subscriber relationship to the server side publication. In this instance, the **CREATE_DATABASE** option is used which first creates the local SQL Server CE database. If the database already exists, you can use the option **EXISITING_DATABASE.**

The statements **Initiate, Run,** and **Terminate** are always run in this order. In conjunction they perform the actual merge replication. The entire subscription is pushed to the Pocket PC the first time these statements are performed. As you can see, merge replication works with all the server side defined tables at the same time. You don't have to specify each table to be replicated as everything happens through the same set of statements.

Make and merge changes

The sample project is designed to work with two local SQL Server CE databases; one for RDA and one for merge replication: Both methods connect to the same remote database and work with the same server side tables. You switch method by choosing the **Pull** command on the RDA menu or the **Merge** command on the merge replication menu (see Figure 6.14).

The sample allows you to make changes to the Quantity column in the Order Details table, and then merge those changes back to the remote SQL Server.

Figure 6.14
Choosing Merge
Replication

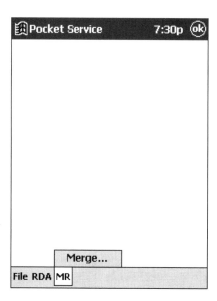

All you need to do to merge with the remote SQL Server is to instantiate the
Replication-object again and run the **Initiate**, **Run**, and **Terminate** methods:

```
Public Sub Merge()
' Update subscription
' Known bugs:
' Version   Date   Who   Comment
' 00.00.000 010315 ASJ   Created
'****************************
' Variables
Dim pMR As SSCE.Replication
Dim strSQL As String

CONNECTION_STRING = "Provider=Microsoft.SQLSERVER.OLEDB.CE.1.0;
Data Source=\NorthwindMerge.sdf"

On Error Resume Next

    ' Create the MR Object
    Set pMR = CreateObject("SSCE.Replication.1.0")

    ' Set MR properties
    pMR.InternetURL =
"http://z0000048/sscereplication/sscesa10.dll"

    ' Set Publisher properties.
    pMR.Publisher = "Z0000048"
    pMR.PublisherLogin = "sa"
    pMR.PublisherPassword = ""
```

```
    pMR.PublisherSecurityMode = DB_AUTHENTICATION
    pMR.PublisherNetwork = DEFAULT_NETWORK
    pMR.PublisherDatabase = "Northwind"
    pMR.Publication = "SQLNorthwind"

    'Set Subscriber properties.
    pMR.Subscriber = "Pocket PC"
    pMR.SubscriberConnectionString = CONNECTION_STRING

    ' Initiate MR
    pMR.Initialize
    pMR.Run
    pMR.Terminate

    ' Destroy the MR Object
    Set pMR = Nothing

End Sub
```

SQL Server 2000 replication features

The most significant architectural difference between RDA and merge replication is that while RDA is controlled from the client; merge replication is
controlled from the remote SQL Server. SQL Server 2000 has a very rich set
of features to manage the publications, subscribers, and any potential conflicts. In addition, the Performance Monitor can be used to monitor the
traffic between the Pocket PC and the server. The following features are
useful Replication Tools available from the SQL Server Enterprise Manager:

- **Replication Monitor** – Provides a view on ongoing events
- **Publication Properties** – Controls the actual contents of Publication
- **Merge Agent History** – Provides a merge replication overview on past events
- **Replication Conflict Viewer** – Controls how to manage replication conflicts

6.7   Conclusion

SQL Server CE provides the Pocket PC with strong local data store capabilities.
The connectivity to remote SQL Servers enables many enterprise applications
to go mobile. We expect SQL Server CE to become the mobile database of
choice. Fundamental database features are supported, remote connectivity
options are solid, and it is not hard at all to begin implementing it.

7

Corporate infrastructure hits the road

In this chapter we'll discuss how to interact with servers in corporate systems, to achieve the highest performance and scalability possible for your mobile solutions. We'll particularly look at Odyssey Software's CEfusion offerings as a way to achieve these goals.

7.1   No Pocket PC is an island

In an ever-progressing evolution, we've come a long way from mainframe and client/server architecture to *n*-tier and component-based development architecture. The purpose of component-based development is to address the core challenges in modern *n*-tier and multi-channel development. These challenges include significantly stronger demands of scalability, manageability, reusability, and development efficiency. Designing and developing distributed information systems today involves therefore a great deal of object-orientation and component-based design. Component-based development is a vital approach to software development because it enables the reuse or customization of existing components from commercially available sources.

Mobile solutions are rarely stand-alone. Instead, they often depend on other existing systems. The more you can reuse existing corporate infrastructure, the faster you can deliver the right solution. Leverage existing corporate infrastructure and you can hit the ground running.

Component-based development builds solutions that satisfy business needs quickly, preferably by using existing bodies of code, rather than developing every individual element. It involves designing the right set of primary components from which to build families of systems, including the harvesting of existing components. Instead of focusing on functions within one system the objective is to assume a component perspective, allowing for the executables to support more than one system.

A modular system architecture makes reuse possible on a larger scale, enabling systems to be composed from existing parts, off-the-shelf third-party parts, and a few new parts that address the specific domain and glue the other parts together. Microsoft's component object model (COM) offers a platform on which component-based architectures can be implemented. In .NET the Common Language Runtime (CLR) for fine grain integration and Web Services for coarse grain integration, replace the role of COM.

Coupled with the practice of developing software iteratively, component-based architecture complements perfectly the continuous evolution of a system's architecture. Using component-based architectures offers a number of solutions to the root causes of typical software development issues.

- User interface, business logic, and data stores are isolated from each other enabling the evolution of each layer individually.
- Improved means of achieving scalability since the architecture can scale out to multiple servers, for example, by implementing the business logic and data store on different servers.
- Components facilitate resilient architectures.
- Modularity enables a clear separation of concerns among elements of a system that are subject to change.
- Leveraging standardized frameworks and commercially available components facilitates reusability.
- Components provide a natural basis for configuration management.
- Visual modeling tools provide automation, for example through model-to-code-to-model round tripping, for component-based development.

Corporate mobile solutions intensify, by volumes, the importance of component architectures. Projects with the goal to design, develop, and implement a mobile solution have a significant advantage when it's possible to reuse existing components. The advantage includes faster analysis, design, and development cycles as well as a better shot at implementing a solution that is

> "Corporate mobile solutions intensify, by volumes, the importance of component architectures. Projects with the goal to design, develop, and implement a mobile solution have a significant advantage when it's possible to reuse existing components."

scalable. Most mobile development projects are not likely to stand on their own, where business process as well as information systems are designed from scratch. The more you can reuse from existing corporate infrastructure, the faster you can deliver the right solution.

7.2   Mobile middleware

The combination of the explosion of the number of mobile devices sold and the benefits of mobile solutions in the enterprise creates a hot new technology marketplace: mobile middleware. A number of products and technologies in this category have been introduced during the years 1999 and 2000 alone. The obvious fact that not much of the global market for mobile middleware has to be taken to make wealth has inspired many gold diggers – mature as well as immature.

We want to express a word of caution in these early days of this new technology marketplace. Outrageous licensing models and unproven technology are warning signs – especially in combination! Pay attention to recent case studies, client testimonials, and demand at least five large implementations (more than 500 users) before spending any large amount of time evaluating mobile middleware.

Microsoft has a couple of gaps in their own technologies for corporate Pocket PC solutions. These holes include the lack of connectivity to server components, network shares, message queues, and databases (other than SQL Server) from eVB. We expect these gaps to be addressed eventually in ways described in Chapter 12.

However, corporate mobile solutions cannot wait. We have therefore chosen to walk you through a proven and capable third-party middleware framework from Odyssey Software – CEfusion.

Note

There is no conflict between using SQL Server CE and Odyssey Software. They do different things, as you will soon discover!

7.3   Odyssey Software CEfusion architecture

Odyssey Software is a leading technology provider in the mobile middleware market. Odyssey was the first company to provide enterprise development tools and infrastructure for Windows CE. The framework of technologies in the CEfusion middleware integrates with core Microsoft technologies such as OLE DB data sources, COM+, MSMQ, file and printing services, and scripting. CEfusion works great even on wireless infrastructure.

Note

This book includes a free developer license for Odyssey CEfusion 3.5. We recommend that you install it to be able to use the sample code for this chapter.

CEfusion consists of four major building blocks. These building blocks are the glue between the Pocket PC application and the corporate infrastructure. Figure 7.1 depicts these four building blocks.

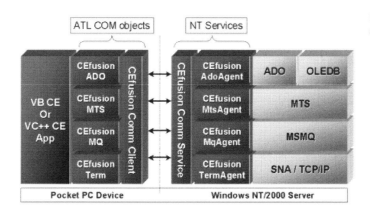

Figure 7.1   CEfusion architecture overview

These are the building blocks (from left to right):

1 Pocket PC: **CEfusion Client Components** are ATL (Active Template Library) COM objects. They are invoked from eVB as any other COM-object.

2 Pocket PC: **CEfusion Client**. This ATL COM component is responsible for establishing and keeping the connection to the remote server.

3 Remote server: **CEfusion Communications Server**. This software is run as an Windows NT or Windows 2000 service and is responsible for managing the connection to the Pocket PC. It also invokes the appropriate CEfusion Server Agent.

4 Remote server: **CEfusion Server Agents**. These agents as Windows NT and Windows 2000 services. They initiate and communicate with each type of element in the network infrastructure.

From a developer perspective it is clear that seamlessness has been a major design goal of the agent architecture. In essence, the agents act as proxy mechanisms between the Pocket PC application and the corporate infrastructure. The actual agent programming provides the notion that you are actually writing code directly against the remote server.

Seamlessness is an extremely important aspect in mobile middleware. The market is still in its infancy and proprietary "lock-in" therefore seems particularly harmful. A benefit to using CEfusion is that the agents are constructed, often at runtime, to be nearly identical to their server side counterparts. For example, an instantiated MTS Agent exposes the exact same interface as its server side COM component, making it possible to use any server side COM component from the Pocket PC application. This enables the migration to future native Microsoft solutions.

The flexibility of the CEfusion agents has lead many developers to regard CEfusion as the "Swiss Army knife" of Pocket PC development.

The communication between the CEfusion Client and Communications Server is based on TCP/IP, which means that you can use any wired and wireless connectivity method supported by the Pocket PC platform. Remote connectivity in general and mobile middleware in particular is heading towards HTTP-based connectivity. If you need HTTP-based connectivity to be able to work through firewalls you can read more about Odyssey Software ViaXML and SOAP and Web Services in Chapter 12. There still is a technical advantage to TCP/IP based connectivity in low bandwidth scenarios because it is not burdened by the HTTP-overhead.

Note

CEfusion works through ActiveSync, as well.

Using CEfusion Service Manager

The Communications Server and Server Agents are managed through a server side application called CEfusion Service Manager. CEfusion Service Manager lets you:

- Configure the networking aspects of the Communications Server including TCP/IP, NetBIOS, and IPX/SPX settings.

- Configure Reconnect-options that provide client state mechanisms, which enable the Communications Server to re-establish a connection to a client if it was lost.

- If desired, configure if the CEfusion components to start as Windows NT or Windows 2000 services.

- Start and stop the Communications Server and Server Agents.

- Allow the CEfusion Communications Server to communicate with CEfusion Service Agents running on other machines. This is commonly used for additional scalability and network architecture flexibility.

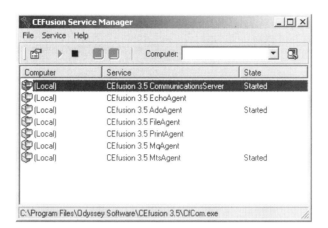

Figure 7.2   CEfusion
Service Manager for
Agent configuration

Starting Communications Server and Agents

The Communications Server and the appropriate Agents need to be started
in order for the Pocket PC to reach the network infrastructure through
CEfusion. Simply clicking the **Start Service** button starts these components.
A valuable feature throughout the development cycles is the ability to start
any of these components in Console or Debug mode. These modes run in a
command window and output calls from the Pocket PC and the responses
from the server side components. Figure 7.3 illustrates the Communications
Server being run in debug mode while using the Pocket Query application,
included with CEfusion.

Figure 7.3   Running
the Communications
Server in Debug-
mode

```
CEfusion 3.5 CommunicationsServer [DEBUG]
Copyright(C) 1995-2001  Odyssey Software, Inc.  All Rights Reserved
Starting CEfusion 3.5 CommunicationsServer in debug mode. (Version 3.5.0.0)
Checking license key...OK
License Type: Site license
Maximum licensed users: 300
Initializing sockets...OK
Press <Ctrl+C> to stop.
[Connection 10000184 open] [Users = 1/300]
>02.OpenAgent ADO
<02 000 CEfusion 3.5 AdoAgent
>15.ADO.OC (220) [Provider=SQLOLEDB;..Data Source=(local);..Initial Catalog=Pubs
;..User ID=sa;..Password=;,.,15,30]
<15 000 (478) Provider=SQLOLEDB.1;User ID=sa;Initial Catalog=Pubs;Data Source=(l
ocal);Use Procedure for Prepare=1;...
>20.ADO.OR (118) [1,select * from titles..order by title_id,1,3]
<20 000 (668) [False,False,1,3,title_id,200,BU1032,title,200,The Busy Executive'
s Database Guide,type,129,business    ,pub_id,129,1389,price,6,19,99,advance,6,5
000,royalty,3,10,ytd_sales,3,4095,notes,200,An overview of available database sy
stems with emphasis on common business applications. Illustrated...,pubdate,135,
1991-06-12]
>31.ADO.GR (28) [1,20]
<31 000 (6568) [False,True,<empty>,<empty>,<empty>,<empty>,<empty>,<empty>,<empt
y>,<empty>,<empty>,<empty>,10,18,BU1032,The Busy Executive's Database Guide,busi
ness    ,1389,19,99,5000,10,4095,An overview of available database systems with
emphasis on common business applications. Illustrated...,1991-06-12,BU1111,Cooki
```

In Figure 7.3 you can see that the server side ADO Agent is used to connect to the server side Pubs database. A SELECT-statement is passed and the records returning over the server back to the Pocket PC are visible in clear text. Great for debugging!

 Tip

Make sure that CommunicationsServer and the appropriate agents are started when running the samples in this chapter.

Configure the Pocket PC

You configure the CEfusion Client from the CEfusion properties applet which can be found on the Pocket PC under the System tab in Settings (see Figure 7.4).

Figure 7.4   CEfusion Client properties

CEfusion Properties   09:44   ok

CEfusion Connection Settings

TCP/IP Address: 169.254.80.31|

TCP/IP Port: 25250

Connect Timeout: 10

Receive Timeout: 30

The settings you need to set are:

● TCP/IP address for the remote server running the Communications Server
● TCP/IP port for the remote server running the Communications Server
● Connection Time out (in seconds)
● Receive Time out (in seconds)

 **Tip**

You may need to soft reset your Pocket PC if you don't see the CEfusion Control Panel Applet in the Control Panel.

Using Pocket Query

Pocket Query is an application included with CEfusion. Pocket Query uses the ADO Agent to establish a remote connection to any OLE DB source defined on the server. You can pass SELECT statements interactively from Pocket Query, get the results back, and edit the data on the fly from the Pocket PC. The application is a simple illustration of what you can do with CEfusion.

Follow these steps to start using Pocket Query and make some changes to the now well-known table Order Details in the Northwind database:

1 Start Pocket Query found in the Programs folder.

2 Tap **File > Open** and select the **SQL Server Example.sql** file.

3 Change the connect string to **Northwind**, to replace **pubs**.

4 Enter the Query string **SELECT * FROM [Order Details]**.

5 Tap the **Execute** button on the toolbar.

The results are now visible, and editable, in the View tab (see Figure 7.5).

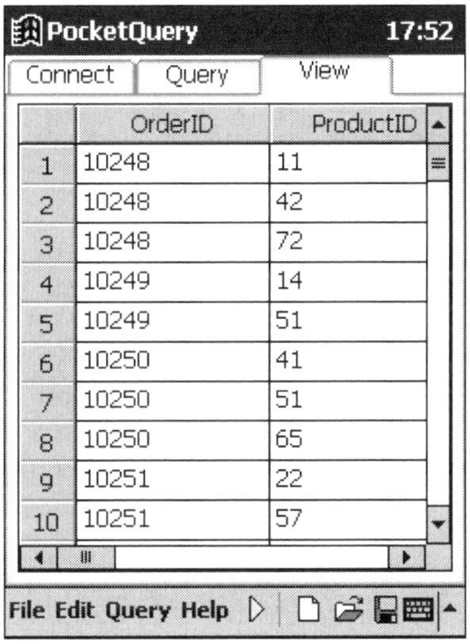

Figure 7.5   The Order Details table in Pocket Query. Editable!

Using CEfusion Client Agents from eMbedded Visual Basic

You use the CEfusion Client Agents in eMbedded Visual Basic as any other COM-component. To use any of the Client Agents in your project you need to declare reference to them. Notice the CEfusion Agents in the References dialog box in Figure 7.6.

Figure 7.6   Checking
the Agents

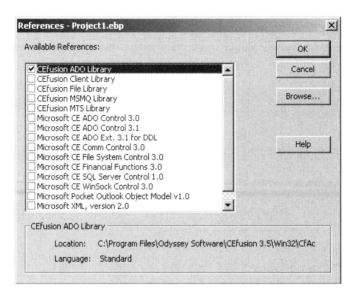

In this illustration we have checked the ADO Agent (**CfAdo**). Once this is done it is possible to view the **CfAdo** objects, methods, and properties in the Object Browser. The eMbedded Visual Basic's IntelliSense also kicks in as soon as you start to reference the **CfAdo** object in code.

The following lines of code illustrate declaring and creating the CEfusion Agents in eVB.

```
' Declaring variables
Dim cfCEfusion As CEFUSION.CfClient2
Dim cfMTS As cfMTS.Object
Dim CfMq As CfMq.MsgQueue
Dim cfcnADO As CFADO.Connection
Dim cfrsADO As CFADO.Recordset
Dim cfFile As cfFile.Transfer

' Creating CEfusion objects
Set cfCEfusion = CreateObject("CEFUSION.CfClient2")
Set cfMTS = CreateObject("cfMTS.Object")
Set CfMq = CreateObject("CfMq.MsgQueue")
Set cfcnADO = CreateObject("CFADO.Connection")
Set cfrsADO = CreateObject("CFADO.Recordset")
Set cfFile = CreateObject("CFFILE.Transfer")
```

As you can see, there are no magic tricks in this code. Just plain and simple **CreateObject**!

Note

Odyssey Software has informed us that the CEfusion 3.6 release will also register the components with Platform Manager so that they are automatically downloaded and registered on the device during debugging. They will then be included in any installation programs built with the eMbedded Visual Basic App Install Wizard.

Using the MTS Agent

The MTS Agent is probably the most important of the CEfusion agents. This agent makes it possible for you to utilize business logic (COM components) from eVB that you have implemented on the server. Instantiating COM-components on the server from the Pocket PC using eVB is actually not possible to do from out-of-the-box. You cannot call server-side components directly from eVB without a middleware like this. The chance that you choose to call your server components with their previously implemented business logic is significant. You now have a tool to make all that knowledge and effort available to your Pocket PC users. You are ready to extend your business logic to anywhere. We will start right away with showing you a common scenario, getting data from a server component down to the Pocket PC using the **MtsAgent** object.

Getting data from server components

We will start by looking at how you can get data from your server components to your Pocket PC. To make the following samples work, please make sure that you have both the CEfusion Communications Server as well as the MtsAgent started in the CEfusion Service Manager (**Programs > CEfusion 3.5 > Service Manager**). The Service Manager screen should look something like Figure 7.7.

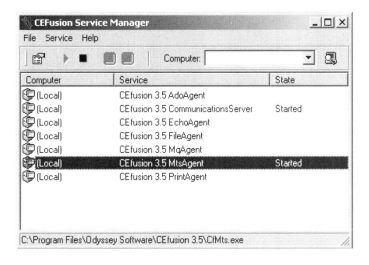

Figure 7.7   Starting up the Agents

And you should also make sure that you have the correct IP address of your server configured on the Pocket PC (**Start > Settings > System > CEfusion**).

Okay, then you are ready to start using the MtsAgent (see **Sample 7.1** on the CD). The code to create the connection to the server in eVB looks like this:

```
Private pcfoCatalog As CFMTS.Object

' Create the server object
Set pcfoCatalog = CreateObject("CFMTS.Object")
pcfoCatalog.ObjectName = "PPDE.Catalog"
```

As you can see, we have to make a reference (**Project > References**) to the **CEfusion MTS Library** to make the CFMTS.Object type library available. And after we have created the object, we have to set the **ObjectName** property. This property tells the MTS Agent what object to create on the server. After you do this, the variable (**pcfoCatalog**) will act as a proxy for the server object. All the methods that the server object has, will be available directly from this variable. For example, if you have a method on the server object with the name **GetAllArray**, you could call this method with the code:

```
ReturnValue = PcfoCatalog.GetAllArray()
```

To close the connection, you simply set this object to **Nothing**, like this:

```
Set pcfoCatalog = Nothing
```

Now we are ready to do some work. Let us start by looking at the simplified server implementation:

```
Public Function GetAllArray() As Variant

    Dim laco As Connection
    Dim lars As Recordset

    ' Create objects
    Set laco = CreateObject("ADODB.Connection")
    Set lars = CreateObject("ADODB.Recordset")

    ' Open Connection
    laco.CursorLocation = adUseClient
    laco.ConnectionString = CONNECTION_STRING
    laco.Open

    ' Open Recordset
    lars.CursorType = adOpenKeyset
    lars.LockType = adLockReadOnly
    Set lars.ActiveConnection = laco
```

```
    lars.Open "SELECT * FROM Article"

    ' Return Recordset
    GetAllArray = lars.GetRows()

End Function
```

To make it more readable we have removed both the error and transaction handling from the code, and as you can see we return a Variant array from the **GetAllArray** method.

Note

When you transfer Recordsets using the **GetRows** method, there is a special case with fields of the type **NTEXT** as they will appear as the last field(s) in the Variant Array even if they were declared in another position in SQL Server. The simple workaround is to always put fields of the type **NTEXT** as the last fields in a table.

We will now see how this return value can be used to fill a ListView control. We have created a ListView control with the name **lvwRecordset** and we have set the columns with the following code:

```
' Clear and add ListView headings
lvwRecordset.ColumnHeaders.Clear
lvwRecordset.ColumnHeaders.Add 1, , "ArtNo", 750
lvwRecordset.ColumnHeaders.Add 2, , "Description", 1850
lvwRecordset.ColumnHeaders.Add 3, , "Price", 550,
lvwColumnRight
```

And with all set up, we just have to call the server object and fill the ListView like this:

```
Dim lvRows As Variant
Dim i As Integer
Dim litm As ListItem

' Clear and fill ListView from server object
lvwRecordset.ListItems.Clear
lvRows = pcfoCatalog.GetAllArray()
For i = 0 To UBound(lvRows, 2)
  Set litm = lvwRecordset.ListItems.Add(, , lvRows(1, i)) '
ArticleNo
  litm.SubItems(1) = lvRows(2, i) ' Description
  litm.SubItems(2) = lvRows(3, i) ' Price
Next 'i
```

After we have cleared any previous rows in the Listview, we go ahead and call the method **GetAllArray** on the server object (ProgID is **PPDE.Catalog** on the server). The return value is put in a simple Variant variable, and in this case it is a Variant array. We then loop through the rows on the array and insert the different column values into the ListView control.

We can see that the component (the **PPDE.Catalog** object) on the server is activated (spinning)(see Figure 7.8).

Figure 7.8 Server component activated

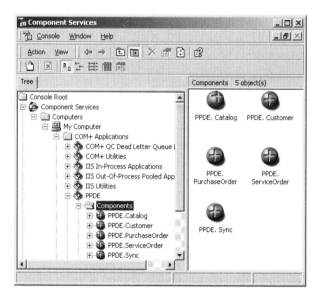

And on the Pocket PC, you can now get the data by pushing the **Array** button as illustrated in Figure 7.9.

Figure 7.9 ListView filled with Variant array data

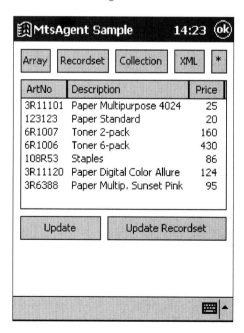

The reason why we started with the example of transferring Variant arrays from server objects (components) is because this is probably the most common way that you will transfer database information across to the device. Of course you could use a number of other ways to transfer Recordset data, but if we want to optimize on the minimum amount of data transferred, Variant arrays is the best option.

We have to consider the amount of data transferred because we often have low bandwidth between the server and the device, and we are often willing to pay the price of harder implementation. Variant arrays are not an optimal data container because they are very limited. As you saw above, there is no way to refer to the various fields with field names. You simply have to know in which order they appear. A good practice is to add a comment (as we did above) to make the code easier to read (as well as debug and maintain).

If we look at some of the other options that we have for transferring Recordset data, we could summarize the following:

- Variant array
- Recordset object
- Collection object
- XML data

We will look at these options in order. We have already looked at the option of using Variant arrays. The benefit is that it puts low demand on bandwidth and creates a truly stateless solution. Nothing will live on the server between calls from clients (Pocket PCs). The downside is that the code will be harder to read and maintain (as you have already seen above).

The obvious choice for an experienced developer who is familiar with Microsoft technologies is to keep object state in a Recordset. Even if somewhat "heavy," this is really the optimal construct when it comes to coding component-based solutions. You have a data holder that can even be moved over physical machine boundaries. When you return a plain ADODB.Recordset object to a Pocket PC using the MtsAgent, you will have a fully functional Recordset on the client, but you have to remember that everything you do with that Recordset will generate traffic to the server. The Recordset object will always live on the server, and the MtsAgent on the Pocket PC side will only be a proxy for that object. If we take the previous example, and use a Recordset instead, the simplified code on the server would look like this:

```
Public Function GetAll() As Variant

    Dim laco As Connection
    Dim lars As Recordset
```

```
' Create objects
Set laco = CreateObject("ADODB.Connection")
Set lars = CreateObject("ADODB.Recordset")

' Open Connection
laco.CursorLocation = adUseClient
laco.ConnectionString = CONNECTION_STRING
laco.Open

' Open Recordset
lars.CursorType = adOpenKeyset
lars.LockType = adLockReadOnly
Set lars.ActiveConnection = laco
lars.Open "SELECT * FROM Article"

' Disconnect Recordset from connection and close it
Set lars.ActiveConnection = Nothing
laco.Close

' Return Recordset
Set GetAll = lars

End Function
```

And on the client, we could have the following code:

```
Dim rs As CFMTS.Recordset
Dim litm As ListItem

' Clear and fill ListView from server object
lvwRecordset.ListItems.Clear
Set rs = pcfoCatalog.GetAll()
Do While Not rs.EOF
  Set litm = lvwRecordset.ListItems.Add(, ,
rs("ArticleNo").Value)
  litm.SubItems(1) = rs("Description").Value
  litm.SubItems(2) = rs("Price").Value
  rs.MoveNext
Loop
```

This code is easier to read than the previous Variant array example, but the cost is that we will interact with the server when we interact with the Recordset object. If you are willing to pay the price in bandwidth, this code will probably be easier to adapt to future programming styles on Pocket PC. And if you are reusing code from your server applications, the code probably already looks much like this. You just have to do some testing and find out how demanding this approach is for your application and decide if you can afford it. You should test both for demand of bandwidth but also demand on server load as all clients having objects (state) living on the server will demand more server capacity. It will not be a truly stateless solution.

There is another way of transferring Recordset data that provides as much information about the Recordset as you need. You could pack the Recordset into a Collection object (included in the Odyssey Software Utilities Library; OSIUtil), which will be retuned as a static or disconnected collection saving the bandwidth. You can then reference the collection on the client side to get at field information or the Variant array (GetRows) data through collection members. The simplified server implementation looks like this:

```
Public Function GetAllCollection() As Variant

  Dim laco As Connection
  Dim lars As Recordset
  Dim lcolPackage As OSIUTIL.Collection
  Dim lcolFields() As Variant
  Dim i As Integer

  ' Create objects
  Set laco = CreateObject("ADODB.Connection")
  Set lars = CreateObject("ADODB.Recordset")

  ' Open Connection
  laco.CursorLocation = adUseClient
  laco.ConnectionString = CONNECTION_STRING
  laco.Open

  ' Open Recordset
  lars.CursorType = adOpenKeyset
  lars.LockType = adLockReadOnly
  Set lars.ActiveConnection = laco
  lars.Open "SELECT * FROM Article"

  ' Fill Collection with fields and data
  Set lcolPackage = CreateObject("OSIUtil.Collection")
  If lars.Fields.Count > 0 Then
    ReDim lcolFields(lars.Fields.Count - 1)
    For i = 0 To UBound(lcolFields)
      Set lcolFields(i) = CreateObject("OSIUtil.Collection")
      lcolFields(i).Add lars.Fields(i).Name, "Name"
      lcolFields(i).Add lars.Fields(i).Type, "Type"
      lcolFields(i).Add lars.Fields(i).DefinedSize, "Size"
    Next
```

```
        lcolPackage.Add lcolFields, "RecordsetInfo"
    End If
    lcolPackage.Add lars.GetRows(), "RecordsetData"

    ' Return Collection
    GetAllCollection = lcolPackage

End Function
```

And you can add as many items as you like into the returned collection. You could add other information (meta-data) like record count and column totals. And you would use code on the client similar to this:

```
Dim lcolPackage As OSIUTIL.Collection
Dim lvRows As Variant
Dim i As Integer
Dim litm As ListItem

' Clear and fill ListView from server object
lvwRecordset.ListItems.Clear
Set lcolPackage = pcfoCatalog.GetAllCollection()
lvRows = lcolPackage("RecordsetData")
For i = 0 To UBound(lvRows, 2)
  Set litm = lvwRecordset.ListItems.Add(, , lvRows(1, i)) '
ArticleNo
  litm.SubItems(1) = lvRows(2, i) 'Description
  litm.SubItems(2) = lvRows(3, i) 'Price
Next 'i

' Show that we have meta-data too
MsgBox "First column name = " &
lcolPackage("RecordsetInfo")(0)("Name")
```

You can see the similarities with the Variant array sample above but with the new access to the field information that we show on the last line of the code above.

The last main option, using XML, is the choice for creating a more open and modern solution. As with the Recordset option, however, you will create more demand on bandwidth, as XML is a format that creates a lot of overhead. If you consider sending an article number, you would have XML looking something like this:

```
<ArticleNo>12345678</ArticleNo>
```

The length of the XML above is almost four times (!) the actual data (12345678) that you are sending. Of course, you could use a more efficient XML format, but you will still end up with a considerable amount of overhead. Another issue is that if you get the XML from the server, there is no simple way to handle that data on the client side. Yes, you have the XML DOM model, but this is not a simple object to work with. Just to make things a bit easier, we have put together a module that will help you to handle XML returned from the server called **XMLRS.bas** and you can read more about it in Chapter 12. Let us first look at the simplified server implementation:

```
Public Function GetAllXML() As Variant

   Dim laco As Connection
   Dim lars As Recordset
   Dim last As Stream

   ' Create objects
   Set laco = CreateObject("ADODB.Connection")
   Set lars = CreateObject("ADODB.Recordset")
   Set last = CreateObject("ADODB.Stream")

   ' Open Connection
   laco.CursorLocation = adUseClient
   laco.ConnectionString = CONNECTION_STRING
   laco.Open

   ' Open Recordset
   lars.CursorType = adOpenKeyset
   lars.LockType = adLockReadOnly
   Set lars.ActiveConnection = laco
   lars.Open "SELECT * FROM Article"

   ' Return XML (from Recordset via Stream)
   lars.Save last, adPersistXML
   GetAllXML = last.ReadText

End Function
```

You can see that we use the ADO Stream object to get the Recordset in XML format back to the client. And here is how the same call that we showed for the other ways would look like using this method:

```
Dim ls As String
Dim litm As ListItem

' Clear and fill ListView from server object
lvwRecordset.ListItems.Clear
ls = pcfoCatalog.GetAllXML()
XMLRSOpen ls
```

```
Do While Not XMLRSEOF
  Set litm = lvwRecordset.ListItems.Add(, , XMLRS("ArticleNo"))
  litm.SubItems(1) = XMLRS("Description")
  litm.SubItems(2) = XMLRS("Price")

  XMLRSMoveNext
Loop
XMLRSClose
```

You can see that using this module (XMLRS.bas), you can handle the XML data much in the same way as you would with a normal Recordset. The module is far from complete, but will give you an idea of how this could be done. The main advantage with the XML method is that you have a much looser coupling between the server and the client. There are many server environments that will be able to create XML data and this way you could handle the returned data in a generic way.

Updating data from server components

In the previous samples, you have seen how to retrieve data from the server. That is probably the most common scenario. However, you will need to update the information on the server too. Of course you can do this by passing a parameter value to a server component that updates the database for you – the most efficient way of doing it. If we have a server method implemented like this:

```
Public Function UpdatePrice(ByVal ArticleNo As String, ByVal
Price As Double) As Variant

  Dim laco As Connection

  ' Create objects
  Set laco = CreateObject("ADODB.Connection")

  ' Open Connection
  laco.CursorLocation = adUseClient
  laco.ConnectionString = CONNECTION_STRING
  laco.Open
  laco.Execute "UPDATE Article SET Price=" & Price & " WHERE
ArticleNo='" & ArticleNo & "'"
  ' Return success
  UpdatePrice = True

End Function
```

... you could then do the following from your Pocket PC:

```
pcfoCatalog.UpdatePrice "3R11101", 30
```

As you can see, this is a very efficient way of doing it. You will not have any state on the server, you will simply pass a minimum of data and you have as much as possible of the business logic left on the server where you want it.

Sometimes, you may want to get the data from the server and update some data. You may not be able to easily determine which data has changed. In this case you would use a Recordset and then return the updated Recordset to the server for updating. Let's look at how this could work. We start with the server implementation:

```
Public Function GetRecordset(ByVal SQLString As String) As
Variant

  Dim laco As Connection
  Dim lars As Recordset

  ' Create objects
  Set laco = CreateObject("ADODB.Connection")
  Set lars = CreateObject("ADODB.Recordset")

  ' Open Connection
  laco.CursorLocation = adUseClient
  laco.ConnectionString = CONNECTION_STRING
  laco.Open

  ' Open Recordset
  lars.CursorType = adOpenKeyset
  lars.LockType = adLockBatchOptimistic
  Set lars.ActiveConnection = laco
  lars.Open SQLString

  ' Disconnect Recordset from connection and close it
  Set lars.ActiveConnection = Nothing
  laco.Close

  ' Return Recordset
  Set GetRecordset = lars

End Function
Public Function UpdateRecordset(ByVal RecordsetToUpdate As
Variant) As Variant

  Dim laco As Connection
  Dim lars As Recordset
  Dim i As Integer
```

```
' Create objects
Set laco = CreateObject("ADODB.Connection")

' Open Connection
laco.CursorLocation = adUseClient
laco.ConnectionString = CONNECTION_STRING
laco.Open

' Open Recordset
Set lars = RecordsetToUpdate
Set lars.ActiveConnection = laco
lars.UpdateBatch

' Return success
UpdateRecordset = True

End Function
```

And with these two methods available on the server, we could do the following in eVB:

```
Dim rs As CFMTS.Recordset

' Get Recordset
Set rs = pcfoCatalog.GetRecordset("SELECT * FROM Article WHERE
ArticleNo="3R11101'")

' If found, update
If Not rs.EOF Then
  rs("Price").Value = 30
End If

' Update Recordset
rs.UpdateWithNoRefresh
pcfoCatalog.UpdateRecordset rs
```

And as we mentioned before, there will be a greater demand for bandwidth due to all the roundtrips that this method creates. MtsAgent will also be using up resources by keeping track of state on the server side for each client performing such activities. The more resources required to manage state that you keep on the server, the less your application will scale. But you knew that already.

MtsAgent conclusion

You have seen that we have simply implemented what we needed on the server and then accessed it from the Pocket PC using MtsAgent. Is that possible for all kind of COM objects? The answer is amazingly, Yes! And the server components don't even have to be registered with MTS/COM+ even if we assume that you would like to do this to build a solid solution. It means, however, that you can test your components both inside and outside MTS/COM+, which is a good thing. It also means that you can access server components that have not been modified to fit into MTS/COM+ and that is another good thing.

 Tip

It's important for you to know that you can only access components through their automation (IDispatch) interface. This means that you cannot access different interfaces on the same object and only the default interface will be available to Pocket PC users through MtsAgent. If you haven't implemented interfaces in your VB 6.0 server components, you will not have any problems, since the publicly declared methods will be part of the default interface and also available through automation. On the other hand, if you have worked with interfaces, you will probably have to create new "facade" objects with a default interface that publishes the methods of the other interfaces that you need to access from Pocket PCs.

When you access all these components, you can be assured that with MtsAgent you have support for all standard parameter and property types (16bit integer, 32bit integer, Single, Double, Currency, Date, String, Boolean, Variant, and Byte). And all parameters passed by reference can be modified; even optional parameters are supported. If you write a VB 6.0 (COM) component on the server that has a method with the **ParamArray** keyword, it will enable you to work with a variable number of parameters.

As we have already seen, arrays are supported as both in/out parameters and return values. As you have also seen, objects are supported as both in/out parameters and return values. For an object to be passed as a parameter it must exist on the server; that is, it must be a CfMts object. You have already seen two of the CfMts objects; the **CfMts.Object** object and the **CfMts.Recordset** object. The only one we haven't mentioned is the **CfMts.Field** object, and you might guess what that is for. If you want to read more about these objects, we recommend the CEfusion documentation. There is no support for named parameters but you can use indexed properties.

In MtsAgent there is special support for collections. Returning a collection as an output parameter or return value transfers the entire collection at once. If you want to pass a collection created on the Pocket PC, you can use the **OSIUtil.Collection** object. You can also use **OSIUtil.Collection** to return a keyed collection from the server. When you return an **OSIUtil.Collection** we refer to it as a static or disconnected collection. That is, adding or removing members of the collection won't affect the server side collection. In fact, the MtsAgent does not persist an OSIUtil.Collection returned from your COM object. All other collections returned from the server, such as ADO collections are dynamic or connected collections. Adding or removing members will update the collection on the server.

As you have seen in our samples above, you should always declare the return values (and output parameters) as Variants. Output parameters and return values other than Variants can only be used with eVC. This is actually a limitation of eVB as all variables are of type Variant, so eMbedded VB always passes variables as by reference Variants.

The bottom line is that you should be able to use the exact same syntax with the **CfMts.Object** object in an eVB application, as you would use in a VB 6.0 application that uses late binding. The one exception is when you create the object. So, if an object isn't working as anticipated, the first debugging step should be to try it in desktop VB. This will determine whether the problem is in the syntax used, or in the **CfMts.Object** objects. When doing this test in VB 6.0, use CreateObject and assign the result to a variable of type Object. In other words, don't declare variables as a particular type. We want to make sure late binding rather than early binding is used.

Using the ADO Agent

The ADO Agent (CfAdo) enables access to any ODBC or OLEDB provider that is available from the remote server. The object model implemented by **CfAdo** mimics the Microsoft server side original ADO object model. The **CfAdo** object model includes the objects given in Table 7.1.

Table 7.1   Objects included with CfAdo object

Object	Description
CfAdo.Connection	Used to establish a connection with a database.
CfAdo.Recordset	Used to open a set of records from an SQL statement.
CfAdo.Field	Represents a column of data with an common data type.
CfAdo.Error	Contains information about any errors that have occurred.

The following list contains the methods and properties of the **CfAdo.Recordset** object and it illustrates how similar the **CfAdo** the server side ADO is.

● Properties
  – ActiveConnection
  – BOF
  – CursorType
  – EOF
  – LockType
  – Source
  – State
● Methods
  – AddNew()
  – CancelUpdate()
  – Close()
  – Delete()
  – GetRows([Rows], [pStart], [pFields])
  – Move(NumRecords, [Start])
  – MoveFirst()
  – MoveLast()
  – MoveNext()
  – MovePrevious()
  – Open([Source],[ActiveConnection],[CursorType],[LockType],[Options])
  – ReQuery([Options])
  – Update()

Creating a Data Source Name

To open a connection to an ODBC/OLEDB source you need to specify an appropriate connection string. Figure 7.10 shows the server side ODBC Data Source Administrator that is used to create Data Source Names (DSN).

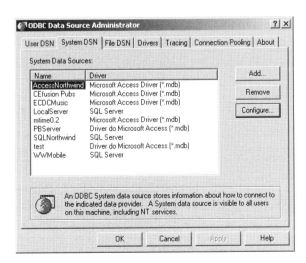

Figure 7.10 Creating a server side DSN

The selected DSN in the screen shot is the Microsoft Access version of the Northwind database.

Note

To access a database with the ADO Agent you will need to have the Microsoft Data Access Components (MDAC) installed on the remote server. Also, note that the connection string can be any valid ADODB ConnectionString meaning you don't have to first create a server side DSN.

Connecting to Microsoft Access

The following sample (see Sample 7.2 on the CD) opens a connection to the Microsoft Access Northwind database. The sample project is available on the CD-ROM.

The **cfAdo Connection** and **Recordset** objects are used to populate the list view with names from the remote Customers table.

```
Private Sub pRefreshCustomerList()

' Known bugs:
' Version    Date   Who Comment
' 00.00.000 010315 ASJ Created
'*****************************
' Variables
Dim cfcnADO As CFADO.Connection
Dim cfrsADO As CFADO.Recordset
Dim strConnectionString As String
Dim litm As ListItem
Dim strSQL As String

    ' Clear ListView list
    lvwCustomer.ListItems.Clear
    lvwCustomer.Sorted = False

    ' Make listview invisible to improve performance
    lvwCustomer.Visible = False

    ' Set connection string and SQL statement
    strConnectionString = "DSN=AccessNorthwind"
    strSQL = "SELECT CustomerID, CompanyName, ContactName,
Phone FROM Customers"

    ' Create connection and recordset object
    Set cfcnADO = CreateObject("cfADO.Connection")
    Set cfrsADO = CreateObject("cfADO.Recordset")
```

```
    ' Open connection and recordset
    cfcnADO.Open strConnectionString
    cfrsADO.Open strSQL, cfcnADO, adOpenForwardOnly,
adLockReadOnly

    ' Populate listview
        Do While Not cfrsADO.EOF
            Set litm = lvwCustomer.ListItems.Add(, "K" &
cfrsADO("CustomerID"), cfrsADO("CompanyName"))
            litm.SubItems(1) = cfrsADO("ContactName")
            litm.SubItems(2) = cfrsADO("Phone")
        cfrsADO.MoveNext
    Loop

    ' Close recordset and connection
    cfrsADO.Close
    cfcnADO.Close

    ' Clean up
    Set cfcnADO = Nothing
    Set cfrsADO = Nothing

    ' Set full row select
    lvwCustomer.SetFocus
    SetFullRowSelect GetFocus()

    ' Make first customer default
    lvwCustomer.SelectedItem = lvwCustomer.ListItems(1)

    ' Make listview visible
    lvwCustomer.Visible = True

End Sub
```

The award-winning user interface enables the user to select a customer in the list view and update the customer's phone number (see Figure 7.11).

Figure 7.11
Customers from the remote Access database

The code that updates the customer phone number uses an UPDATE statement and looks like this:

```
Private Sub cmdSave_Click()
' Add order
' Known bugs:
' Version   Date   Who   Comment
' 00.00.000 010315 ASJ   Created
'*****************************
' Variables
Dim strSQL As String
Dim strCustomerID As String
Dim strConnectionString As String
Dim cfcnADO As CFADO.Connection
Dim cfrsADO As CFADO.Recordset

    strCustomerID = Mid(lvwCustomer.SelectedItem.Key, 2)

    ' Set connection string and SQL statement
    strConnectionString = "DSN=AccessNorthwind"
    strSQL = "UPDATE Customers Set Phone = '" & txtPhone.Text &
"'"

    strSQL = strSQL & " WHERE CustomerID = '" & strCustomerID &
"'"

    ' Create connection
    Set cfcnADO = CreateObject("cfADO.Connection")

    ' Open connection
    cfcnADO.Open strConnectionString

    cfcnADO.Execute strSQL

    ' Close connection
    cfcnADO.Close

    ' Clean up
    Set cfcnADO = Nothing

    ' Update list view
    lvwCustomer.SelectedItem.SubItems(2) = txtPhone.Text

End Sub
```

ADO Agent conclusion

The **CfAdo** creates and uses server side ADO objects. Most of the errors you will see when developing using the **CfAdo** objects are being returned from the server objects. Errors returned from the server generally mean you are trying something that is not allowed in desktop ADO. To determine whether the error is coming from the server or client objects, you can run the ADO Agent in debug mode. You should be able to see the error message being passed back to the client. Another debugging method is to try your eVB code in a desktop VB application. In general, anything that throws an error in a desktop VB application will throw an error in your Pocket PC application.

The ADO Agent will enable you to reach any ODBC and OLEDB compliant data source including SQL Server, Oracle, Access, and Excel.

Using the File Agent

The File Agent (**CfFile**) enables the transferring of text and binary files between the Pocket PC and the server. The Pocket PC natively supports a number of file formats including text, Word, and Excel files. Files of these formats can be created on the server and passed to the Pocket PC, or created on the Pocket PC and passed to the server, using **CfFile**.

The second significant feature of **CfFile** is the ability to call remote server side scripts from the Pocket PC. Server side scripts typically automate common tasks related to network administration, database maintenance, backups, etc. Server side scripts can be developed in VBScript, a language you already know from having learned Visual Basic and eMbedded Visual Basic.

Receiving files from the Pocket PC

Managing files with **CfFile** is a snap. The **CfFile** object implements a **Send** and a **Receive** method that accepts the parameters **LocalPath** and **RemotePath**. The property **LocalPath** defines the Pocket PC folder and **RemotePath** defines the server folder. You can define these locations as parameters in **Send** and **Receive** methods, as well.

The following sample (see Figure 7.12 and **Sample 7.3** on the CD) illustrates how to send files from the server to Pocket PC and from the Pocket PC to the server. The sample allows the user to:

1 Receive a text file from the server to the Pocket PC.

2 Execute a server side script that first creates an Excel file, which then is received at the Pocket PC.

3 Send a camera shot from the Pocket PC to the server (the Pocket PC in this sample is thought either to be equipped with a camera or to be accompanied by a stand-alone digital camera).

Figure 7.12   The
Send and Receive
options

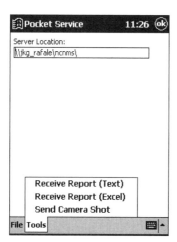

The code that pulls the text file from the server to the Pocket PC or executes the server side script and then pulls down the Excel file to the Pocket
PC looks like this:

```
Public Sub PullBackupReport(ByVal FileType As String)
'****************************
' Pulls backup report from server
'
'History:
' Version    Date    Who  Comment
' 00.00.000 010124  AS    Created
'****************************
' Declaring variables
Dim cfFile As cfFile.Transfer

    ' Creating CEfusion objects
    Set cfFile = CreateObject("CFFILE.Transfer")

    Select Case FileType
      Case "Text"

            ' Set Properties
            cfFile.LocalPath = "\Program Files\Pocket
Admin\copierservice.txt"
            cfFile.RemotePath =
frmCfAdministrator.txtBackupReport.Text & "\copierservice.txt"
            cfFile.AutoRunScript = False

            ' Receive file
            cfFile.Receive

      Case "Excel"
            ' Set properties
```

```
            cfFile.LocalPath = "\Program Files\Pocket
Admin\copierservice.xls"
            cfFile.RemotePath =
frmCfAdministrator.txtBackupReport.Text & "\copierservice.xls"
            cfFile.AutoRunScript = True
            ' Receive file AFTER the script has been run
            cfFile.Receive , , , "ExcelFile.vbs"

    End Select

    ' Clean up
    Set cfFile = Nothing

End Sub
```

You can see how the paths are defined before the **Receive** statement executes. Figure 7.3 shows a text file received from the server.

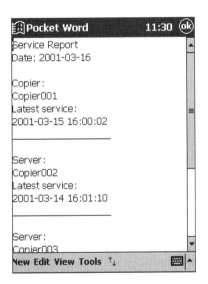

Figure 7.13   The latest service information

Pocket Word launches when the user taps on the file that has been received from the remote server.

Executing server side scripts

CfFile can be used to execute remote server side scripts. The code above includes the line:

```
cfFile.Receive , , , "ExcelFile.vbs"
```

This statement receives the Excel file that has the following remote path:

```
cfFile.RemotePath = frmCfAdministrator.txtBackupReport.Text &
"\copierservice.xls"
```

The cool thing to observe is the parameter "**ExcelFile.vbs**" in the **Receive** statement. The fact is that before the **Receive** statement is executed, there is no Excel file ("**copierservice.xls**") on the server. Instead, the script "**ExcelFile.vbs**" executes first on the server and creates the file on the server. The **Receive** execution waits until the remote script finishes before trying to receive the file. The script file "**ExcelFile.vbs**" is a simple text file located on the server and looks like this:

```
Option Explicit
' VBScript that creates an Excel-file and saves it on the
network.
' Known bugs:
' Version    Date    Who Comment
' 00.00.000 010315 ASJ Created
'****************************
' Variables
Dim mobjOffice

' Create the Excel-object
Set mobjOffice = CreateObject("Excel.Application")

' Turn off messages and other settings
mobjOffice.DisplayAlerts = False
mobjOffice.Visible = False

' Add and save new Workbook
mobjOffice.Workbooks.Add
mobjOffice.ActiveWorkbook.SaveAs
("\\jkg_rafale\ncnms\copierservice.xls")

' Populate sheet with data.
' This code will need to be replaced with calls to
components/databases.
mobjOffice.Range("A1").Value = "Service Report"
mobjOffice.Range("A2").Value = "Date:"
mobjOffice.Range("B2").Value = "=NOW()"
mobjOffice.Range("A4").Value = "Copier"
mobjOffice.Range("B4").Value = "Latest Service"
mobjOffice.Range("A5").Value = "Copier 001"
mobjOffice.Range("A6").Value = "Copier 002"
mobjOffice.Range("A7").Value = "Copier 003"
mobjOffice.Range("A8").Value = "Copier 004"
mobjOffice.Range("B5").Value = "3/15/2001 16:00"
mobjOffice.Range("B6").Value = "3/14/2001 16:01"
```

```
mobjOffice.Range("B7").Value = "Service Ongoing"
mobjOffice.Range("B8").Value = "3/14/2001 16:24"
mobjOffice.Range("A1").Select
mobjOffice.Range("A1:B5").Select
mobjOffice.Selection.Font.Bold = True
mobjOffice.Columns("A:B").EntireColumn.AutoFit
mobjOffice.Range("A1").Select

' Save and close workbook
mobjOffice.ActiveWorkbook.Save
mobjOffice.ActiveWorkbook.Close

' Quit Excel
mobjOffice.Quit

' Clean up
Set mobjOffice = Nothing

AfAgent.SetScriptResult 0, "OK"
```

The user can view the Excel file on the Pocket PC once the script is executed, and the Excel file is received (see Figure 7.14).

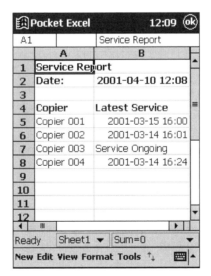

Figure 7.14   A newly backed Excel file!

Note

The default folder \CEfusion\Scripts will be used if you don't specify the folder in which the script is located. The Microsoft Visual Basic Scripting engine must be installed before you can use the **CfFile RunScript** command. If you are using Microsoft Internet Explorer, then scripting is already installed on your system. To read more about server side scripting see the homepage for Microsoft Windows Script Technologies at: **msdn.microsoft.com/scripting/**

Sending files from the Pocket PC

In this sample, there is a file called "**camerashot.jpg**" in the Pocket PC. The use of digital cameras in combination with Pocket PCs is growing rapidly. We assume in this sample that the field technician has just shot a picture of a broken part in a copier machine to be able to forward the picture to the manufacturer.

The code that sends the picture to the server from the Pocket PC looks like this:

```
Public Sub PushPicture()
'****************************
' Pushes picture from Pocket PC
'
'History:
' Version   Date   Who   Comment
' 00.00.000 010124 AS    Created
'****************************
' Declaring variables
Dim cfFile As cfFile.Transfer

    ' Creating CEfusion objects
    Set cfFile = CreateObject("CFFILE.Transfer")

    ' Set properties
    cfFile.LocalPath = "\Program Files\Pocket
Admin\camerashot.jpg"
    cfFile.RemotePath = frmCfAdministrator.txtBackupReport.Text
& "\camerashot.jpg"
    cfFile.AutoRunScript = False

    ' Send file
    cfFile.Send

    ' Clean up
    Set cfFile = Nothing

End Sub
```

Figure 7.15 shows the remote server folder contents, and you can see the three files:

- copierservice.txt – There from the beginning
- copierservice.xls – Created by the server side script
- camerashot.jpg – Sent from the Pocket PC

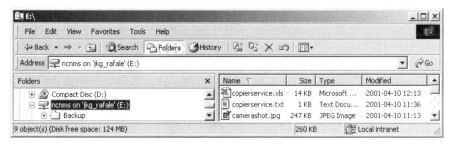

Figure 7.15   All files in one remote place!

The **Send** method has similar functionality to the **Receive** method, which allows it to automatically call a remote script file. The difference here is that with the **Send** method, the script is called *after* the file has been transferred from the device to the server. (With the **Receive** method, the script is called *before* the file is transferred from the server to the device.) For example, this would allow you to stuff an image into a server-side database, after you transfer it to the server.

The CfFile object can also call remote scripts without having a file transferred, using the **RunScript** method.

File Agent conclusion

The File Agent is a nifty little chap. Even though most enterprise development relates more to components, databases, and queues (and increasingly so) we still face situations where file transfer is an efficient method of passing data. The **CfFile** object's ability to execute server side scripts makes it even more useful.

Using the MQ Agent

Message queuing is perhaps the most important system integration facilitator, even surpassing component remoting. Systems, sub-systems, and applications use queues to send and receive messages between each other. The system integration goals that message queuing delivers on present a lesser degree of vulnerability and higher degree of portability.

Asynchronous and loosely-coupled integration is less vulnerable than the synchronous and tightly-coupled integrated enabled by calling remote components or databases. This is true because if the called system is for some reason unavailable, the calling user or application is left without being able to even pass information to it.

In synchronous system dependencies, if one sub-system is down the whole system is down. Message queuing guarantees the ability to send and receive information regardless of the state in other sub-systems.

Message queuing also increases the overall system portability as sub-systems and applications can easily be changed or even replaced without breaking the integration rules.

Consider using message queuing when you cannot afford message loss or interruption, when senders cannot wait for responses before continuing with other tasks or when sending and receiving occurs at different times.

The discussions presented here about message queuing are nowhere near the full story, although they do provide a general positioning in relation to system integration. Check out your favorite online (or off-line, for that matter) bookstore, and you will find a lot of cool books on the subject of message queuing.

You can safely assume that since the CfMq object is designed to mimic the server side MSMQ objects, the portability to the Windows CE MSMQ implementation is good. The MQ Agent (**CfMq**) communicates with the remote server Microsoft Message Queuing (MSMQ) technologies and provides Pocket PC applications guaranteed message delivery and priority-based messaging.

The **CfMq** object can be set to work synchronously (**Dependent** mode) or asynchronously (**Independent** mode). Select the mode before the **Open** method is called.

- In **Dependent** mode you must have a direct connection to the server. Both **Send** and **Receive Access** modes are valid. One additional feature of the **CfMq** implementation is the support for multi-message transaction when running in **Dependent** mode and the ability to directly open, read from, and write to remote queues on the server.

- In **Independent** mode, message delivery is handled through the **MQ** "**Tray Application**," implemented as a CEDB database. You can only **Send** messages (Receive Access mode is not valid).

Note

Microsoft provides its own Windows CE MSMQ implementation. We choose to showcase Odyssey Software's implementation, partly because it is less complex to use from eMbedded Visual Basic and partly because it is an important piece of CEfusion Enterprise Edition. You can read more about Microsoft's implementation at these two URLs:

- Message Queuing Overview and Resources
  www.microsoft.com/ntserver/appservice/exec/overview/MSMQ_Overview.asp

- Microsoft Windows CE 3.0 Message Queuing Service
  msdn.microsoft.com/library/techart/wce3appserv_msmq.htm

Creating the MSMQ Queue

The first thing to set up in a message queuing scenario is the MSMQ Queue, to be performed on the remote server. Follow these steps to create the queue required to follow the next sample:

1 Install **Message Queuing**. Follow the guidelines in the Windows 2000 help file under the section *Installation overview for Message Queuing*.

2 Start **Computer Management** from the **Administrative Tools** menu.

3 Create a public queue called **PocketService**.

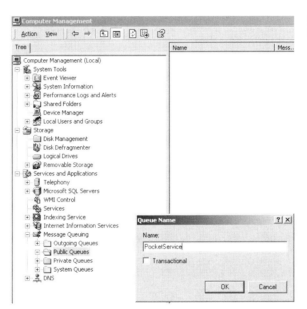

Figure 7.16 Creating the MSMQ Queue

Sending and receiving messages from the server

The following sample (see **Sample 7.4** and subfolder **VB6** on the CD) is a Visual Basic 6.0 project and uses Microsoft MSMQ components. The sample application enables a customer service representative to send and receive urgent service orders to field technicians at ACME Copier Inc. The application also facilitates receipt of messages from the field technicians at the customer service department.

Figure 7.17 illustrates the user interface that implements this functionality.

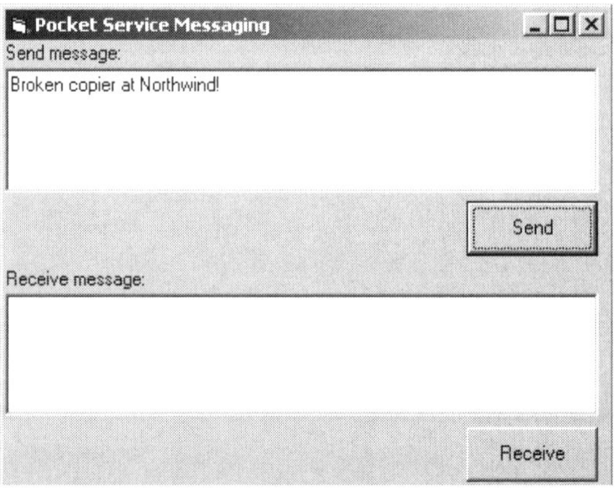

Figure 7.17   Pocket
Service Messaging on
the server

The sample code that enables the user to send messages looks like this:

```
Private Sub cmdSend_Click()
'****************************
' Sends message to queue
'
'History:
' Version    Date    Who   Comment
' 00.00.000 010124   AS    Created
'****************************
' Declaring variables
Dim qinfoSend As New MSMQQueueInfo
Dim qSend As MSMQQueue
Dim qmesMessage As New MSMQMessage
Dim strSend As String

    ' Set properties
    qinfoSend.PathName = ".\PocketService"

    ' Send to queue
    Set qSend = qinfoSend.Open(MQ_SEND_ACCESS, MQ_DENY_NONE)

    qmesMessage.Label = "Urgent Service Order"
    qmesMessage.Body = txtSend.Text

    ' Send to queue
    qmesMessage.Send qSend

    ' Close queue
    qSend.Close

End Sub
```

Once the user has sent the message, it appears in the queue as shown in Figure 7.18.

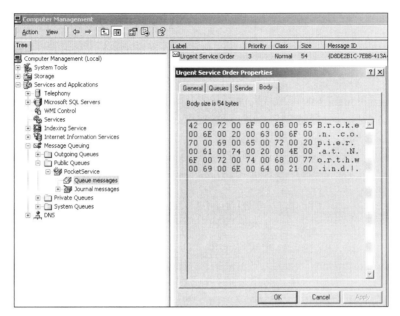

Figure 7.18
Message stored in MSMQ

A great advantage to message queuing, in comparison to component remoting or direct database access, is the management features found in the **Message Queuing** portion of **Computer Management**.

Sending and receiving messages from the Pocket PC

The field technician can receive the messages from Customer Service, by using their Pocket PC. The following user interface (see Sample 7.4 and sub-folder **PocketPC** on the CD) enables sending and receiving messages from the Pocket PC using the **CfMq** object (see Figure 7.19).

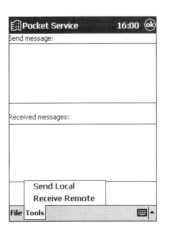

Figure 7.19   Pocket PC messaging

The code that receives messages from the server looks like this:

```
Public Sub ReceiveQueue()
'****************************
' Receives queue
'
'History:
' Version    Date     Who   Comment
' 00.00.000 010124   AS    Created
'****************************
' Declaring variables
Dim CfMq As CfMq.MsgQueue

    On Error Resume Next

    ' Creating CEfusion objects
    Set CfMq = CreateObject("CFMQ.MSGQUEUE")

    ' Setting Independent to True indicates that all messages
    ' will be first persisted in a local queue and then will be
    ' transferred to the server by the MQ Tray Application when
    ' connectivity is available
    CfMq.Independent = False
    CfMq.Access = MQ_RECEIVE_ACCESS
    CfMq.PathName = ".\PocketService"

    ' Open queue
    CfMq.Open

    ' Clear textbox
    frmCfMq.txtReceive.Text = ""

    ' Loop through queue
    Do While True
       ' Receive
       CfMq.Receive
       If Err.Number <> 0 Then Exit Do

       ' Set text box
       frmCfMq.txtReceive.Text = frmCfMq.txtReceive.Text &
CfMq.Body & vbCrLf

    Loop

    ' Clean up
    Set CfMq = Nothing

End Sub
```

The queue loops through and the messages are pulled down to the Pocket PC. The code that sends messages from the Pocket PC to the server looks like this:

```
Public Sub SendQueue()
'****************************
' Sends queue
'
'History:
' Version   Date    Who  Comment
' 00.00.000 010124  AS   Created
'****************************
' Declaring variables
Dim CfMq As CfMq.MsgQueue

    ' Creating CEfusion objects
    Set CfMq = CreateObject("CFMQ.MSGQUEUE")

    ' Setting Independent to True indicates that all messages
    ' will be sent directly to the Server.
    CfMq.Independent = False
    CfMq.Access = MQ_SEND_ACCESS
    CfMq.PathName = ".\PocketService"

    ' Open queue
    CfMq.Open

    'Set Label and Body properties
    CfMq.Label = "Urgent Service Order Reply"
    CfMq.Body = frmCfMq.txtSend.Text
    CfMq.Priority = 1

    ' Send Message
    CfMq.Send

    ' Clean up
    CfMq.Close
    Set CfMq = Nothing

End Sub
```

You notice that the **CfMq** object is quite straightforward to use. The MSMQ similarities are obvious.

Figure 7.20   Sending
and receiving
messages

Finally, take a look at Figure 7.21 which shows the server application once
it has received the message from MSMQ.

Figure 7.21
Response from the
field technician

MQ Agent conclusion

The MQ Agent plays an important role in many Pocket PC applications
because it makes it possible to reach remote MSMQ Queues, with little
effort. This is the last agent we cover in this book, and although we know
there are lots of additional details to reveal it is our hope that you have
been inspired to install the free developer license of Odyssey Software
CEfusion found on the CD and try all this out yourself! Yours may be the
next really cool mobile enterprise application!

The web anywhere

In this chapter we will examine how Pocket PCs can be used as an online thin clients. One of the major advantages the Pocket PC has over other mobile platforms is that it supports standard HTML. This means that the Pocket PC can access most of the internet and the World Wide Web.

We will look at how we can build online web applications that support Pocket PCs, and other devices as well. We will also go through the available options, from the simple approach of programmatically transforming content depending on client all the way to a multi-channel architecture.

8.1   Supporting multiple types of clients

When building web applications we have grown used to supporting a limited number of web browsers on the PC. We have standardized most of the web sites to support Microsoft Internet Explorer and Netscape Navigator and the most common choice has been to support their respective versions 4 and above. A "least denominator" approach is usually applied to address the problem of supporting multiple types of browsers.

There are a number of advantages to using this approach that derive from the fact that we end up with only one page source. For simple needs, this might be an excellent solution resulting in low maintenance costs for the web site. However, the consequence is also that we have to be careful not to use any of the more interesting features of the web browsers since they might not be supported on all of them. Another issue is the fact that the same browser might be implemented in different ways on different platforms. But in general it was enough just to support these two browsers and you were doing all right.

Today there is a radical change going on. Users need to access the web pages from other things than a normal PC. Currently, this might be some kind of a mobile device, like a Pocket PC, but in the future (now?) an increasing number of users will be accessing your web site from their TV, their handheld "surfpad" or even their mobile phone. You don't want to serve these new users with your "least denominator" approach that slaughters your application's functionality.

> 66 You don't want to serve these new users with your 'least denominator' approach that slaughters your application's functionality. 99

If you want to create a web site that is perfectly usable from all these devices, you will end up with something very, very simple. And then all your previous users, the ones who became used to browsing your site from a PC, will be really disappointed. Another problem is that not even using the simplest form of HTML will get your site to these users, since some devices do not even support HTML. They might support some other modern content scripting language that is not 100 percent compatible with HTML.

What do you do if you want to support all these new clients and still provide them with rich experience? There are basically two different answers to this question depending on how structured you would like your solution to be. The answers are:

- **Programmatic Content Transformation** – Here you will actually add code to support different clients
- **Stylesheet-based Content Transformation** – If this is your choice, you add different style sheets to support different clients

In the rest of this chapter, we will go through both of these answers and as we have said before, the truth is not "or/else" but "both/and" thinking. In your real life solutions, you will probably use a little of both as they have their respective advantages.

8.2 Programmatic content transformation

If you have a lot of content already available, this approach will allow you to start right away. You can work through your web pages one by one and add support for different clients. You might also create just a portion of your site to support for multiple types of clients. This is actually a very common approach today as many newspapers and other information sites use a special URL for Pocket PCs and other devices. The advantage is that you can start with what is most important and get that multi-channel support up as quickly as possible. Just the fact that you support multiple types of clients, and especially mobile clients, and even for only a part of your content, will raise some extra attention among your users. And as we all know, attention is the scarcest resource in the e-economy.

Web application platforms

The discussion and the samples you'll find here assume that you are using Microsoft web server (IIS) and ASP. Even if the code can only be used in this environment, you can apply most of the logic to whatever web server environment and programming language you are using.

Who is the client?

To transform content depending on the client capabilities, the first thing we have to know is the type of device or computer that is attempting to view your site. Each web browser sends information in their HTTP requests that identifies what they are. This information can then be used to provide them with different content. The information is available as an HTTP header in the request, and in ASP, running on IIS, you have this information available through the **Request** object. The **Request** object contains a collection called **ServerVariables** and one of its members is the **HTTP_USER_AGENT** value. We can use the following code to get that information:

```
UserAgent = Request.ServerVariables("HTTP_USER_AGENT")
```

We will get different replies depending on what client we are using. If you are curious (as we are) you can create an ASP page with the following simple line of code:

```
<% =Request.ServerVariables("HTTP_USER_AGENT") %>
```

And then you can use different types of clients to see how they identify themselves. If you browse to that page with a Pocket PC, the response would be:

```
Mozilla/2.0 (compatible; MSIE 3.02; Windows CE; 240x320)
```

If we use this information in our ASP pages, we could have a variable indicating that we have a Pocket PC client at the other end. The code would do something like this:

```
IsPocketPC = (InStr(UserAgent, "Windows CE") > 0)
```

If you have a mobile phone with MME or if you download the free MME emulator from Microsoft, along with browser, to the page that you created, you will see that it responds like this:

```
Mozilla/1.22 (compatible; MMEF20; Cellphone; Generic Small)
```

The string "Generic Small" is in the emulator, replacing whatever skin you are currently using. If you use the Sony phone, this string will be replaced with "Sony CMD-Z5." Following the example for the Pocket PC, we could know that there is an MME client using our page, by setting a variable like this:

```
IsMME = (InStr(UserAgent, "MME") > 0)
```

There is actually more information that the client sends to the server and to be absolutely sure that the client is using a Pocket PC, you can look at another of the **ServerVariables** member (HTTP header) called **HTTP_UA_OS**. With the following code, you can find out.

```
IsPocketPC = InStr(Request.ServerVariables("HTTP_UA_OS"),
"POCKET PC") > 0
```

For a more complete discussion on determining clients, please see the white paper **Designing Web Sites for the Internet Explorer for Pocket PC** at **www.microsoft.com/mobile/developer/PIE_dev.asp**. Since this is enough for us to move on with the transformation of the content, we will stop the discussion here.

Transforming content

We will start by showing you a quite common web application page – an order entry form. In Microsoft Internet Explorer 5.5, the page looks like Figure 8.1 (see Sample 8.1 on the CD).

Figure 8.1   Order entry form sample in Internet Explorer for the PC

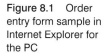

And the somewhat simplified source of this page looks like this:

```
<HTML><HEAD><TITLE>New Purchase Order</TITLE></HEAD>
<BODY><FONT FACE="Tahoma">

<!-- LOGO -->
<TABLE BORDER="0" CELLSPACING="0" CELLPADDING="0" WIDTH="100%">
  <TR>
    <TD VALIGN="top" WIDTH="100%"><IMG SRC="images/line.gif"
      WIDTH="100%" HEIGHT="42"></TD>
    <TD VALIGN="top" WIDTH="93"><IMG SRC="images/logo.gif"
      WIDTH="93" HEIGHT="42"></TD>
  </TR>
</TABLE>
<TABLE BORDER="0" CELLSPACING="0" CELLPADDING="0"
  WIDTH="100%"><TR><TD VALIGN="top" WIDTH="100">

<!-- MENU -->
<B>Menu:</B><BR>
<A HREF="">Home</A><BR>
<A HREF="">About Us</A><BR>
<A HREF="">Order</A>
</TD><TD VALIGN="top">
<H1>New Purchase Order</H1>
<P><B>
  Fill in the information and create new Purchase Order.
</B></P>

<!-- MAIN -->
<H2>Purchase Order Information</H2>
<FORM ACTION="submit.asp" METHOD="POST">
<TABLE BORDER="0" CELLSPACING="1" CELLPADDING="3">
  <TR>
    <TD VALIGN="top"><B>Customer:</B></TD>
    <TD VALIGN="top"><INPUT TYPE="text" NAME="Customer"
VALUE=""></TD>
  </TR>
  <TR>
    <TD VALIGN="top"><B>Order No:</B></TD>
    <TD VALIGN="top"><INPUT TYPE="text" NAME="OrderNo"
VALUE=""></TD>
  </TR>
  <TR>
    <TD VALIGN="top"><B>Our Ref:</B></TD>
```

```
            <TD VALIGN="top"><INPUT TYPE="text" NAME="OurRef"
      VALUE=""></TD>
        </TR>
        <TR>
          <TD VALIGN="top"><B>Customer Ref:</B></TD>
          <TD VALIGN="top"><INPUT TYPE="text" NAME="CustRef"
      VALUE=""></TD>
        </TR>
        <TR>
          <TD VALIGN="top" COLSPAN="2"><INPUT TYPE="submit"
       VALUE="Create"></TD>

        </TR>
      </TABLE>
      </FORM>
      </TD></TR></TABLE>

      </FONT></BODY></HTML>
```

If you browse to this page with the Internet Explorer for the Pocket PC, and even if you use the **Fit to Page** option on the device, you will get horizontal scroll bars and you will have to use both horizontal and vertical scrolling to see the whole content of the page. As you might have discovered, it is not very efficient to navigate horizontally with the stylus, and that is therefore something that we would like to avoid. We will have to do something about that.

> As you might have discovered, it is not very efficient to navigate horizontally with the stylus, and that is therefore something that we would like to avoid.

On the page, the menu is placed in an almost standardized way as a left-hand column. This column (also somewhat standardized) is created using an HTML table. To use the screen space more efficiently, since we have a much smaller screen on a Pocket PC, we would prefer to have the menu options laid out on a single row horizontally instead. The left-hand column works great on PCs, since the browser window is often wider than it is tall.

The opposite is true on a Pocket PC and therefore we would like to save as much width as possible. By placing the menu choices on a single line, we avoid using unnecessary horizontal space (we don't need the menu column on the left) and convert it to compact vertical space (a single line) instead. We start by adding code to get information about the client that we learned before:

```
' Device Indicators
UserAgent = Request.ServerVariables("HTTP_USER_AGENT")
IsPocketPC = (InStr(UserAgent, "Windows CE") > 0)
IsMME = (InStr(UserAgent, "MME") > 0)
IsThin = (IsPocketPC Or IsMME)
```

With these variables available, we could change the menu code to look something like this:

```
<% If Not IsThin Then %><B>Menu:</B><BR><% End If %>
<A HREF="">Home</A><% If IsThin Then %> <% Else %><BR><%
End If %>
<A HREF="">About Us</A><% If IsThin Then
%> <%Else%><BR><%End If%>
<A HREF="">Order</A>
```

Using the same technique, we could remove the table that creates the extra column for the menu. Also, the first logo row could be changed to a simple logo on a Pocket PC client by:

```
<% If Not IsThin Then %>
  <TABLE BORDER="0" CELLSPACING="0" CELLPADDING="0"
WIDTH="100%">
    <TR>
      <TD VALIGN="top" WIDTH="100%"><IMG
        SRC="images/line.gif" WIDTH="100%" HEIGHT="42"></TD>
      <TD VALIGN="top" WIDTH="93"><IMG
        SRC="images/logo.gif" WIDTH="93" HEIGHT="42"></TD>
    </TR>
  </TABLE>
<% ElseIf IsPocketPC Then %>
  <IMG SRC="images/logo.gif" WIDTH="93" HEIGHT="42"><BR>
<% End If %>
```

You could even remove unnecessary content for MME clients by:

```
<H2>Purchase Order Info<%If Not IsThin Then%>rmation<%End
If%></H2>
```

An interesting case is when you want to enter information on a web page in a Pocket PC. If you leave INPUT fields without any SIZE attribute, you will probably get a field that is wider than the screen, resulting in the dreaded horizontal scrollbar showing up again. Therefore, we recommend that you include a SIZE attribute for Pocket PC clients. It would look something like this:

```
<INPUT TYPE="text" NAME="Customer" VALUE=""<% If IsThin Then
Response.Write(" SIZE=""10""") %>>
```

With these changes, let us see how this looks in the Pocket PC now (Figure 8.2).

Figure 8.2   Order entry form sample in Internet Explorer for Pocket PC

We are now free from the horizontal scroll bar and that is going to save us some valuable browsing time. As you have seen, we have even added support for MME clients, and therefore we will take a look at how the MME emulator views the same page (Figure 8.3).

Figure 8.3   Order entry form sample in MME

For a complete example, please see the **ordermulti.asp** file in the sample on the CD.

More structure

You have now realized that you can easily update your existing pages with client type-specific content. You could start going through your pages to insert these transformation snippets everywhere. One important note is that not all your content is real content. Several parts of your page are the same for many different pages like headers, logos, menus, and so on. We guess that you realize this, and also that you have done something about reusing common content between pages. But if you have not, this is the time to save some time updating of your pages.

One approach to reusing content (or structure) on several pages is to use server-side includes. This means that you place a part of your ASP page in a separate file and include it on each page that should contain it. In our simple example above, one such part is the top of the page. The top of the page includes both the logo and the menu. It is likely that a complete web application will include the same header, so we move this code to a separate file and call it **top.asp**. The next thing we would like to do is to include this page in our original page. We do this with the following code:

> **"**One approach to reusing content (or structure) on several pages is to use server-side includes.**"**

```
<!--#INCLUDE FILE="top.asp"-->
```

Now, you have not only prepared yourself for simple changes to the logo and menu on all pages (by simply changing the **top.asp** file) but you have also prepared your pages to accept new clients in the future. If you add support for a new client, you will simply add the client determination code for this client, change the logo and menu to support the new client, and you are all done! This will surely impress your boss since he or she is starting to realize that your company's web site will have to support future clients that may not have emerged on the marketplace yet.

As you have seen, many of your existing web applications can be modified to support more fully Internet Explorer for the Pocket PC. This approach is suitable for an iterative approach to supporting multiple types of clients, and it means that you can start by converting only a part of your content to see how it works. You will then be able to collect user feedback and work together with the users of these new clients to create well-suited content for them. In the next section we will discuss a more radically different way of handling the problem, but the solution described in this section could very well work as a way to learn more before you convert all content on your site.

Our suggestion is that you start modifying your web applications today. Ask a few of your users equipped with Pocket PCs if they would be interested to test your site from their devices – and off you go. Someone will most probably find it very useful and soon perhaps this may well be your next project.

8.3   Stylesheet-based content transformation

If you have decided that you want to support multiple types of clients using your web application in a solid, structured, and futuristic way, you have come to the right place. You are now in multi-channel land and we will take you on your first tour. You have left the reasoning (from the previous section). Let's return to your site the way it actually is today.

> **"**You are now in multi-channel land and we will take you on your first tour.**"**

In this section you will now see how you can separate content and presentation in a structured way. In so doing, you will therefore learn how to use XML (Extensible Markup Language) and XSL (Extensible Stylesheet Language). We will not go through any theoretical discussion about these technologies; instead we will show you how you can make them work for you.

XML is how you communicate your content and XSL is responsible for transforming that content into the HTML that the different types of clients will see. You can keep your XML in static files and use XSL to transform it, but if we are talking about web applications your content most likely resides in a database somewhere. But the data in the database will probably need to pass the business logic that you have implemented in your components. We will therefore focus on the needs of transforming content from a database, via business logic components, to different types of clients. Moving forward, Microsoft will probably focus on providing a user interface control-based transformation model called *Mobile Forms*. In this model, each control is rendered differently on different clients depending on their capability. You can read more about this in Chapter 12.

Multi-channel strategy

Figure 8.4 illustrates the basic structure of a multi-channel system.

Figure 8.4 Simple multi-channel system overview

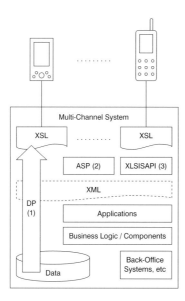

As in any multi-tiered application, the data is stored either in a database or comes from some back-office system (like an ERP package). The different applications are always reached through the business logic components. The addition we make to this common architecture is that we separate the content created by the applications (XML) from both the application itself and the presentation of that content (XSL).

You can see that the XML is not actually stored anywhere since it is derived from the back-end source (database or back-office system) and can simply be viewed as a way to present content in a standardized way. Finally, the client presentation is created using stylesheets customized for each client – each channel.

We have chosen to show only the relevant clients for the samples that you will use here, but of course the idea is to support even channels that are not mobile. The same approach could be used to support clients like webTVs, WAP phones, and so on, as well as normal PC browsers.

The fact is that the group of users who are using more than one device is steadily growing. Even more interesting is that this group will grow in size faster than the single device users. The consequence is that not only do we have to support multiple devices; we will have to support single users using multiple devices. These users will require that the content and functionality available in different channels (using different devices) are consistent.

The same user may even use the same service on different channels (devices) depending on various factors. These factors include the location of the user, the user's preference in different situations, etc. The conclusion is that we need an integrated user experience. An integrated user experience means that the user might be using her handheld device to browse for interesting items to purchase during her free time during the day. When she gets home, she might order some of those items from her laptop or desktop PC. And a few days later, she might want to check the order status of her purchase from her mobile phone.

The solution is not only to provide content in different channels but also to integrate them to support the users' combination of differing needs. The different channels also need to be managed in a consistent way. Corporations will not only have to focus on supporting different channels, but will also need to have a strategy on how those channels will complement each other. We can start talking about a channel mix management. This will not only be the combination of the company's products and services (their "offer") but also be the combination of integrated channels to support the offer.

In Figure 8.4 you saw that we numbered some of the system components, and that is the order in which we will go through the different ways to transform content.

Multi-channel database publishing (using SQL Server 2000)

We will start with something that shows the idea, but is far from the channel mix management strategy that we talked about above. Because SQL Server 2000 has the capability to return XML directly, we can set this up in a similar way by setting up a virtual root in your IIS (see the SQL Server 2000 documentation). When you have done so, you can use an URL like this:

```
http://localhost/ppdexml?SQL=SELECT+*+FROM+Article+WHERE+Price<
50+FOR+XML+AUTO&root=Articles
```

The ISAPI plug-in in IIS makes us able to refer to the database through a virtual root (**ppdexml**) and we simply add a SQL query statement as a parameter (**SQL**). Since the browser does not accept spaces in the URL, we have to replace them with plus signs (+) or we could also use another notation (using **%20** for each space). We also have to add the special SQL keywords (**XML AUTO**) to the SQL statement. Finally, we have to provide the plug-in with information about what root node to use in the output XML using a second parameter (**root**). The URL above will produce the following result in IE5.5 (see Sample 8.2 on the CD):

```
<?xml version="1.0" encoding="utf-8" ?>
<Articles>
   <Article ArticleID="{99772458-CC14-44EA-864F-0E6B3BA512CA}"
ArticleNo="3R11101" Description="Paper Multipurpose 4024"
Price="25" Stock="1065" Picture="mp4024.jpg" Comment="Ideal for
important internal documents, Xerox Premium Multipurpose is an
87 bright, blue-white product, specifically engineered to
improve productivity on your copier, laser or inkjet printer,
plain-paper fax machine or offset press. Our exacting
specifications will result in more machine up-time, reduced
service costs and less wear to your equipment – with lower
levels of paper dust and improved image quality over
competitive sheets. Premium Multipurpose 4024 Papers carry a
99.99% jam-free guarantee, providing you with increased
reliability and optimum performance." LastUpdate="2001-02-
13T17:03:14.260" />
   <Article ArticleID="{8D05540D-7E2A-40D4-8363-148BE6B996FA}"
ArticleNo="123123" Description="Paper Standard" Price="20"
Stock="2743" Picture="papers.jpg" Comment="The most important
characteristics of papers are legibility, durability and the
ability to pass through a copier or printer without jamming."
LastUpdate="2001-02-13T17:06:34.920" />
</Articles>
```

You can see that each row results in an **Article** element with all the fields as XML attributes and all rows included in the root element **Articles** (that was provided as a parameter). With this simple functionality you can actually do a lot. If we want to transform this content into something more readable, we could add an XSL file to the URL. We start by looking at the XSL file:

```
<?xml version="1.0"?>
<xsl:stylesheet xmlns:xsl="http://www.w3.org/TR/WD-xsl">
  <xsl:template match="/">
  <HTML><HEAD><TITLE>ACME Copier</TITLE></HEAD>
  <BODY><FONT FACE="Tahoma">
    <IMG SRC="/PPDE/images/largelogo.jpg" ALT="ACME logo"
ALIGN="right" WIDTH="315" HEIGHT="105" VSPACE="0" HSPACE="0"
BORDER="0"/>
    <H1>Article Catalog</H1>
    <P><B>
      Following is the article list:
    </B></P><BR CLEAR="all"/><BR/>
    <TABLE BORDER="0">
      <xsl:for-each select="*/Article">
        <TR>
          <TD VALIGN="top"><IMG><xsl:attribute
name="SRC">/PPDE/pictures/<xsl:value-of
select="@Picture"/></xsl:attribute></IMG></TD>
          <TD VALIGN="top"><B><xsl:value-of
select="@Description"/></B><BR/>
                          <FONT SIZE="2"><xsl:value-of
select="@Comment"/><BR/>
                          Article No: <xsl:value-of
select="@ArticleNo"/></FONT><BR/>
                          Price: <B><FONT
COLOR="red">$<xsl:value-of select="@Price"/></FONT></B>
                          <A><xsl:attribute
name="HREF">/PPDE/PO/cart.asp?ArticleID=<xsl:value-of
select="@ArticleID"/>
                          </xsl:attribute><IMG
SRC="/PPDE/images/add.gif" ALT="Add to Order" ALIGN="top"
WIDTH="99" HEIGHT="21" HSPACE="50" BORDER="0"/></A>
          </TD>
        </TR>
        <TR><TD COLSPAN="2"><BR/></TD></TR>
      </xsl:for-each>
```

```
      </TABLE>
      </FONT></BODY></HTML>
      </xsl:template>
</xsl:stylesheet>
```

If we name the above file **article.xsl**, and then change the URL to look like this:

```
http://localhost/PPDEXML?SQL=SELECT+*+FROM+Article+FOR+XML+AUTO
&ROOT=Articles&xsl=article.xsl
```

We will have a page looking like Figure 8.5.

Figure 8.5 Article catalog using database publishing

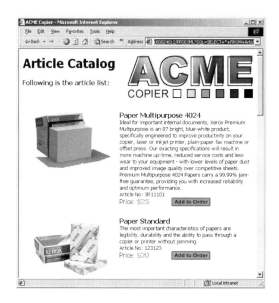

Nice, isn't it? We have now done what could maybe be called multi-channel database publishing. Whenever we change the database content, we will instantly have the content changed on our web site.

If we add another XSL file (called **pocketpc.xsl**) with the following content:

```
<?xml version="1.0"?>
<xsl:stylesheet xmlns:xsl="http://www.w3.org/TR/WD-xsl">
  <xsl:template match="/">
  <HTML><HEAD><TITLE>ACME Copier</TITLE></HEAD>
  <BODY><FONT FACE="Tahoma">
    <IMG SRC="/PPDE/images/logo.jpg" ALT="ACME logo"
WIDTH="208" HEIGHT="68" VSPACE="0" HSPACE="0" BORDER="0"/>
    <H1>Article Catalog</H1>
```

```
    <P><B>
       Following is the article list:
    </B></P><BR CLEAR="all"/><BR/>
    <TABLE BORDER="0">
      <xsl:for-each select="*/Article">
        <TR>
          <TD VALIGN="top"><IMG><xsl:attribute
name="SRC">/PPDE/pictures/<xsl:value-of
select="@Picture"/></xsl:attribute></IMG></TD>
        </TR>
        <TR>
          <TD VALIGN="top"><B><xsl:value-of
select="@Description"/></B><BR/>
                          <FONT SIZE="2"><xsl:value-of
select="@Comment"/><BR/>
                          Article No: <xsl:value-of
select="@ArticleNo"/></FONT><BR/>
                          Price: <B><FONT
COLOR="red">$<xsl:value-of select="@Price"/></FONT></B>
                          <A><xsl:attribute
name="HREF">/PPDE/PO/cart.asp?ArticleID=<xsl:value-of
select="@ArticleID"/>
                          </xsl:attribute><IMG
SRC="/PPDE/images/add.gif" ALT="Add to Order" ALIGN="top"
WIDTH="99" HEIGHT="21" HSPACE="50" BORDER="0"/></A>
          </TD>
        </TR>
        <TR><TD COLSPAN="2"><BR/></TD></TR>
      </xsl:for-each>
    </TABLE>
  </FONT></BODY></HTML>
  </xsl:template>
</xsl:stylesheet>
```

and then change the URL to this:

```
http://localhost/PPDEXML?SQL=SELECT+*+FROM+Article+FOR+XML+AUTO
&ROOT=Articles&xsl=pocketpc.xsl
```

browsing it with our Pocket PC, the page would look like Figure 8.6.

Figure 8.6 Article catalog in Internet Explorer for Pocket PC

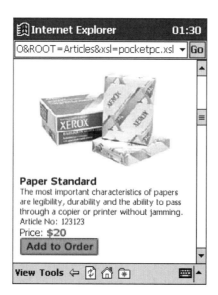

We now have exactly the same content presented in two different ways depending on the stylesheets that we created. This is really the tool that we need to build a more solid solution.

8.4 Multi-channel web applications (using ASP, components, and ADO Recordsets)

Even if using SQL Server 2000, as we did above, is a quick way to get started, this is probably not the way we would like to build our web applications. Since the data is usually not enough, we would like to go through the business logic tier (components) before we publish our content.

If we go back to building solid Microsoft Web Solutions Platform (formerly known as Windows DNA), we usually use the ADO Recordset as a data container. We use the ADO Recordset as the "floating state" between tiers and use the special DCOM abilities that it has to even "float" between physical machines. Since most of our business components already use the ADO Recordset, we would like to leverage that when transforming our applications into multi-channel web applications.

The question then is whether and how ADO Recordsets support XML. The interesting news is that the XML support in ADO Recordsets is not really news. It has been around for some time (since version 2.1 and Windows NT) and the current version (2.6) has the ability to both save the XML as a file and to a stream. Interestingly the ADO Recordset can even be created from an XML source, but that is not the focus of our exercise here (see Sample 8.3 on the CD).

To get XML from an ADO Recordset, you use the **Save** method with the second parameter set to **adPersistXML**. The first parameter is the destination that can be both a file and a stream. If we do this:

```
rs.Save "C:\test.xml", adPersistXML
```

...we would be saving the contents of the Recordset to a file in XML format. An example of using a stream as a first parameter, if we put the following code in an ASP page:

```
rs.Save Response, adPersistXML
```

...this will return the XML to the client requesting the ASP page. Let us take an example, and put the following into an ASP page:

```
<%
Option Explicit

'From adovbs.inc file:
'---- PersistFormatEnum Values ----
Const adPersistXML = 1

' Page variables
Dim conn
Dim rs

' Set page info
Response.ContentType = "text/xml"
Response.Expires = 0
Response.Write "<?xml version=""1.0""?>"

' Create and open Connection
Set conn = Server.CreateObject("ADODB.Connection")
conn.Open "Provider=SQLOLEDB;Data Source=(local);Initial
Catalog=PPDE;Trusted_Connection=Yes"

' Get Recordset
Set rs = conn.Execute("SELECT * FROM Article")

' Save to Response object
rs.Save Response, adPersistXML
%>
```

We simply open a connection to the database and create a Recordset object from a SQL query statement. And in this way we simply get the XML and return it to the user. This corresponds to the first of the SQL Server 2000 samples that we showed above. Let's look at what we get when we browse to this page with Microsoft Internet Explorer 5.5:

```
<?xml version="1.0" ?>
- <xml xmlns:s="uuid:BDC6E3F0-6DA3-11d1-A2A3-00AA00C14882"
xmlns:dt="uuid:C2F41010-65B3-11d1-A29F-00AA00C14882"
xmlns:rs="urn:schemas-microsoft-com:rowset"
xmlns:z="#RowsetSchema">
+ <s:Schema id="RowsetSchema">
- <rs:data>
  <z:row ArticleID="{99772458-CC14-44EA-864F-0E6B3BA512CA}"
ArticleNo="3R11101" Description="Paper Multipurpose 4024"
Price="25" Stock="1065" Picture="mp4024.jpg" Comment="Ideal for
important internal documents, Xerox Premium Multipurpose is an
87 bright, blue-white product, specifically engineered to
improve productivity on your copier, laser or inkjet printer,
plain-paper fax machine or offset press. Our exacting
specifications will result in more machine up-time, reduced
service costs and less wear to your equipment – with lower
levels of paper dust and improved image quality over
competitive sheets. Premium Multipurpose 4024 Papers carry a
99.99% jam-free guarantee, providing you with increased
reliability and optimum performance." LastUpdate="2001-02-
13T17:03:14.260000000" />
  <z:row ArticleID="{8D05540D-7E2A-40D4-8363-148BE6B996FA}"
ArticleNo="123123" Description="Paper Standard" Price="20"
Stock="2743" Picture="papers.jpg" Comment="The most important
characteristics of papers are legibility, durability and the
ability to pass through a copier or printer without jamming."
LastUpdate="2001-02-13T17:06:34.920000000" />

    .
    .
    .

  </rs:data>
  </xml>
```

We have removed some of the schema information and also the last data rows, as they all look the same. The observant reader notices that this looks somewhat similar to what SQL Server 2000 created for us. However, each row has the standard **z:row** element, but the fields are still XML attributes. If you want to look at the schema information, please try the **raw.asp** page in the Sample 8.3 folder on the CD. This sample page can be used to explore more about the XML format that is generated from ADO Recordsets.

As we agreed earlier, we want to have the business object doing the job for us, and return the result in an ADO Recordset. Now we will implement a method to return a simple Recordset that is named **GetAll** and looks like this:

```
Dim laco As Connection
Dim lars As Recordset

On Error GoTo ErrorHandler

' Create objects
Set laco = CreateObject("ADODB.Connection")
Set lars = CreateObject("ADODB.Recordset")

' Open Connection
laco.CursorLocation = adUseClient
laco.ConnectionString = CONNECTION_STRING
laco.Open

' Open Recordset
lars.CursorType = adOpenKeyset
lars.LockType = adLockReadOnly
Set lars.ActiveConnection = laco
lars.Open "SELECT * FROM Article"

' Disconnect Recordset from connection and close it
Set lars.ActiveConnection = Nothing
laco.Close

' Return Recordset
Set GetAll = lars

' Allow MTS transaction set to proceed
GetObjectContext.SetComplete

 Exit Function

ErrorHandler:
   ' Roll back MTS transaction set
   GetObjectContext.SetAbort

   ' Raise Error
   Err.Raise Err.Number, Err.Source, Err.Description
```

And if we have put this method on a business object called **PPDE.Catalog**, we can now use the following code in the ASP page:

```
<%
Option Explicit

'From adovbs.inc file:
'---- PersistFormatEnum Values ----
Const adPersistXML = 1

' Page variables
Dim poCatalog
Dim rs
```

```
' Set page info
Response.ContentType = "text/xml"
Response.Expires = 0
Response.Write "<?xml version=""1.0""?>"

' Create object
Set poCatalog = Server.CreateObject("PPDE.Catalog")

' Get Recordset
Set rs = poCatalog.GetAll()

' Save to Response object
rs.Save Response, adPersistXML
%>
```

So, this means that we can publish any components that create ADO Recordsets as XML. That is very interesting, but we need to be able to transform the XML into HTML since not many users appreciate reading the raw XML. Unfortunately, there is no such functionality in ADO. But of course it can be found in the XML DOM (Document Object Model).

The trick then is to find a way to get the XML into a XML DOM object. And it is here that another very interesting use of the destination (first) parameter to the Recordset **Save** method comes in handy. It cannot be used to save the Recordset data into an XML DOM object directly, but if we go via an ADO **Stream** object, we could pull it off. This is an example producing exactly the same result (XML) as before:

```
<%
Option Explicit

'From adovbs.inc file:
'---- PersistFormatEnum Values ----
Const adPersistXML = 1

' Page variables
Dim poCatalog
Dim past
Dim pXML
Dim rs

' Set page info
Response.ContentType = "text/xml"
Response.Expires = 0
Response.Write "<?xml version=""1.0""?>"

' Create object
Set poCatalog = Server.CreateObject("PPDE.Catalog")
```

```
Set past = Server.CreateObject("ADODB.Stream")
Set pXML = Server.CreateObject("MSXML2.DOMDocument")
pXML.Async = False

' Get Recordset
Set rs = poCatalog.GetAll()

' Save Recordset to XML DOM (via Stream object)
rs.Save past, adPersistXML
pXML.loadXML past.ReadText

' Write XML from XML DOM
Response.Write pXML.xml
%>
```

Everything looks the same up until we save the Recordset to the Stream object. Then we use the Stream object to load the XML DOM object (pXML). After this we could do whatever we want (that can be done in XML DOM) with the data. Here we have decided to just dump the **xml** property to the **Response** object, as it will create the same result as the previous samples.

The only missing piece in our multi-channel puzzle now is the XML DOM method **transformNode**. Using it we can transform a XML file into one XML DOM and an XSL file into a second XML DOM, to produce the desired HTML that we want.

```
<%@ LANGUAGE="VBSCRIPT" %>
<%
Option Explicit

'From adovbs.inc file:
'---- PersistFormatEnum Values ----
Const adPersistXML = 1

' Page variables
Dim poCatalog
Dim past
Dim pXML
Dim pXSL
Dim rs

' Set page info
'Response.ContentType = "text/xml"
Response.Expires = 0
'Response.Write "<?xml version=""1.0""?>"

' Create objects
Set poCatalog = Server.CreateObject("PPDE.Catalog")
```

```
Set past = Server.CreateObject("ADODB.Stream")
Set pXML = Server.CreateObject("MSXML2.DOMDocument")
Set pXSL = Server.CreateObject("MSXML2.DOMDocument")

' Turn off async mode
pXML.Async = False
pXSL.Async = False

' Get Recordset
Set rs = poCatalog.GetAll()

' Save Recordset to XML DOM (via Stream object)
rs.Save past, adPersistXML
pXML.loadXML past.ReadText

' Load XSL
pXSL.Load Server.MapPath("article.xsl")

' Transform XML/XSL to HTML
Response.Write pXML.transformNode(pXSL)
%>
```

You can see that we have created another XML DOM object (pXSL) where
we load the XSL file. Then we use that object to transform the XML DOM
holding the XML data from the Recordset. Now we have all the tools that
we need to transform the content for different clients. Using the same technique that we described before for finding out what the clients are, we can
now create an ASP file that looks like this:

```
<%
Option Explicit
Response.Expires = 0

'From adovbs.inc file:
'---- PersistFormatEnum Values ----
Const adPersistXML = 1

' Page variables
Dim poCatalog
Dim past
Dim pXML
Dim pXSL
Dim rs

' Create objects
Set poCatalog = Server.CreateObject("PPDE.Catalog")
Set past = Server.CreateObject("ADODB.Stream")
Set pXML = Server.CreateObject("MSXML2.DOMDocument")
Set pXSL = Server.CreateObject("MSXML2.DOMDocument")
```

```
' Turn off async mode
pXML.Async = False
pXSL.Async = False

' Get Recordset
Set rs = poCatalog.GetAll()

' Save Recordset to XML DOM (via Stream object)
rs.Save past, adPersistXML
pXML.loadXML past.ReadText

' Load XSL depending on client
If InStr(Request.ServerVariables("HTTP_UA_OS"), "POCKET PC") >
0 Then
 pXSL.Load Server.MapPath("pocketpc.xsl")
Else
 pXSL.Load Server.MapPath("article.xsl")
End If

' Transform XML/XSL to HTML
Response.Write pXML.transformNode(pXSL)
%>
```

In this way we can provide support for numerous types of clients, and the content (data) would always be in the same format. When we change something, like adding a new field, we only need to change the XSL for each client (assuming that you have already changed both the database and any related components).

We might even let the business object (component) do some of this work. It would be nice if all components had the possibility to supply both ADO Recordsets (as they have for a while) as well as XML directly. To gain speed (and even scalability) you could even do all of the above in a component, but then that component would actually be a part of the presentation tier, when instead it should be clearly separated from the business logic. Note also that then you have to update the component for each added client type that you want to support. You will find some nice way of solving all this because we have already made our point – you can now design solid multi-channel solutions leveraging your existing business logic, components, and knowledge.

> **❝** In this way we can provide support for numerous types of clients, and the content (data) would always be in the same format. **❞**

8.5   Multi-channel infrastructure (using XSL ISAPI Filter)

In the previous section we saw that we could use ASP pages to do multi-channel support for different clients. The approach is very straightforward and very familiar if you know ASP and XML/XSL to some extent. However, as we mentioned above, there is an issue when it comes to maintaining all those ASP pages.

You will have to update ASP pages (code) for each new client and you would have custom handling on each of the logical pages that your application contains. If you are creative, you would probably come up with something more structured with maybe a single ASP page acting as a gateway for your web application that handles all the XML/XSL transformations for your pages. But before you go ahead and build something like that yourself, you should really take a look at an interesting technology that Microsoft has made available called **XSL ISAPI Filter**. This is probably what you would have come up with anyway. It is mainly an implementation called an ISAPI Filter that filters all requests to pages with the extension **.xml** (for static) and **.pasp** (for dynamic). When you have set it up correctly, it will use an XML document to select different XSL files depending on attributes of the requesting client. The document will look like this:

```
<?xml version="1.0" ?>
  <server-styles-config>
    <device platform="Windows CE">
      <stylesheet href="pieStyle.xsl"/>
    </device>
    <device browser="IE" version="5.0">
      <stylesheet href="ie50Style.xsl"/>
    </device>
    <device browser="IE" version="3.0">
      <stylesheet href="ie30Style.xsl"/>
    </device>
  </server-styles-config>
```

To make this work, you have to update your **BROWSCAP.INI** file located in the C:\WINNT\system32\inetsrv folder. This file is actually a translator of the HTTP headers (USER-AGENT, and so on, that we looked at before) into attributes that can be used to select which XSL file to use for the transformation. You can also chain the XSL files to be handled in sequence. If you have a certain structure that you want for a certain page, you can create the basic structure with the first XSL and then use a second to transform it for a certain device. This is an example:

```
<device platform="Windows CE">
  <stylesheet href="SortByName.xsl"/>
  <stylesheet href="pieStyle.xsl"/>
</device>
```

And the input XML will first be transformed using the **SortByName.xsl** file; and that output will be transformed again using the **pieStyle.xsl** file. You can do this on at least 64 levels (!) which should be more than sufficient for most needs.

The selection can be made not only on device characteristics (as we saw above) but also on the XML document type. If the XML document (static or dynamic) has a defined DTD (internal to the document or external in a separate file), it can also be used to select different XLS files. Here is an example:

```
<?xml version="1.0"> <?configuration file:
<server-styles-config>

  <device platform="Windows CE">
    <doctype name="invoice">
      <stylesheet href="pieInvoice.xsl"/>
    </doctype>
    <doctype name="productDescrip, descrip">
      <stylesheet href="pieDescrip.xsl"/>
    </doctype>
  </device>

  <device browser="IE" version="5.0">
    <doctype name="invoice">
      <stylesheet href="ie5Invoice.xsl"/>
    </doctype>
 <doctype name="productDescrip, descrip">
      <stylesheet href="ie5Descrip.xsl"/>
    </doctype>
  </device>

</server-styles-config>
```

One of the more interesting features is that the XSL files get cached on the server. The performance gain is about ten times that of reading them from disk each time. Of course you can do this too, by storing your XSL files as text in the ASP Application collection, but again this is a much more structured way of doing it and the best part is that someone else is handling it (relieving you from maintaining it over time).

Another point worth mentioning is the ability to specify custom output encoding and post-processing support and even custom error handling.

The Microsoft XSL ISAPI Filter enables and simplifies server-side XSL formatting for multiple device types. It features automatic execution of XSL style-sheets on the server with the choice of alternate stylesheets based on browser device characteristics or XML document type, stylesheet caching for improved server performance, the ability to specify output encoding, post-processing support for certain cell phone markup languages, and customizable error messages.

The idea here is that you can, in a more controlled way based on XML, maintain a multi-channeled web application. Another point is that this technology will probably be a part of future products from Microsoft for handling multiple channels. To read more about Microsoft XSL ISAPI Filter go to: msdn.microsoft.com/Downloads/webtechnology/xml/xslisapi.asp

8.6   Conclusion

The main part of the transformation work is probably the creation of XSL pages for each client type, and that work will remain the same between all the different suggestions for supporting multiple types of clients, that we offer here in the second part of this chapter. We started with a very simple solution and worked up to a level where we have a more maintainable, and thereby more cost effective, solution to support multiple client types.

The alternative you choose will probably depend on what you want to do. The general recommendation is always to start small, launch, test, and iterate. Another recommendation is that you start working with these tools right away. You will most probably support multiple clients sooner or later and you might as well start the process now.

ACME Copier field service operation

In this chapter we will see how the people at ACME Copier have extended their processes to wherever their employees may be. We will look at what they might need while out in the field, moving about performing their work. We'll learn what is possible in the way of interactions with other internal departments and back office data too. And then we'll look at the architecture that produces the solution. In the following chapter we will guide you through the code for this sample. The application is available both as a ready-made installation and as source code on the CD.

Of course, we all know that ACME Copier is not real. But for us the people and situations at ACME have somehow come alive during our work on this book. Incorporated into the scenarios and solutions you'll read about and the sample code you'll work with is a lot of what we have seen in real-life scenarios and at companies in our own work.

We hope that you find ACME Copier a relevant example of how any company could make their workforce more productive and effective when on the move. We hope too, that these people inspire you to see how your company could take advantage of this new technology in your everyday business. And we present this material with the additional desire that you will be able to use this material in explaining to your sponsors (your management and other decision makers) how a real-life mobile solution could work.

9.1   How it works

We will now turn to the practical use of the Field Service Operational System at ACME Copier. We will start with the back-office functionality of creating a new service order and continue with the functionality for the service technician.

A new service order

It is Monday morning and the phone rings at the ACME Copier customer service. Bill, who is working in field service support, answers the phone. On the other end of the line is Kim at Northwind Traders. Kim has a problem with their Xerox copier on the third floor. "Okay," says Bill, "Just hold on and I will make up a service order for you. We'll get your copier fixed in no time." Bill starts the web application to enter a new service order. Designed as a "wizard," it helps Bill fill in the necessary information (see Figure 9.1).

Figure 9.1   New Service Order wizard, search customer page

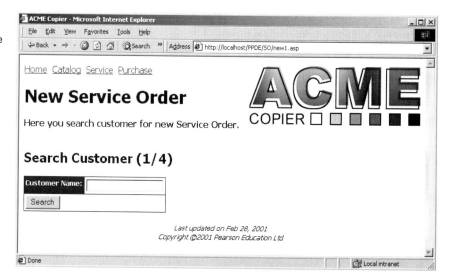

At his PC he enters "North" in the search page and presses the Enter key. After getting a list of search results, he selects Northwind Traders. He then sees a page to complete the service order request (see Figure 9.2).

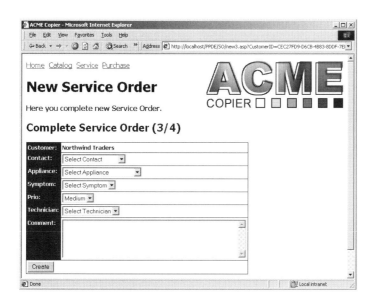

Figure 9.2   New Service Order wizard, complete service order page

He selects Kim in the contacts list and notices that she is the second contact. It is always the first contact who signed the contract with ACME Copier, and therefore Bill asks, "Kim, have you checked with Stephen that we should set up a service order to fix the copier?"

Kim is clear, "Yes, he asked me to call you just a minute ago."

"Okay, fine, I just have to check," Bill replies and is now about to select the copier model in question. He can see from the pull-down list that Northwind has several Xerox copiers and he has to ask Kim, "Do you have the appliance number of the copier?"

Since Kim has called before, she is prepared for this, and she promptly responds, "Yes, it's the 1111.22."

Bill makes the selection with a "Thanks" to Kim. Next, Bill is about to select what the problem type is and after asking Kim, he concludes that the printing quality has become blurred and makes that appropriate selection on the screen.

As Bill is making the last selection, Kim wonders, "How long will it be until it's fixed? We are really in trouble here."

And as he sets the priority to "High" he responds, "As usual it depends upon how busy the technicians are, but I've put a high priority on this. I know that Anne, who is a very qualified technician, will fix it as soon as she possibly can. Usually that is within the next day. She will probably be there tomorrow." Bill knows that Anne is the service technician who knows the Xerox printers best and she is also very fast. That is why Bill selects Anne as the designated service technician for the service order.

Bill is about to complete the service order request. He asks, "And is that all…?"

Kim answers, "Oh, I almost forgot. Can you ask Anne to bring a ream of the Multipurpose Sunset Pink copier paper?" Bill adds a comment to the service order about that with a "Yes, of course." The completed service order form now looks like Figure 9.3.

Figure 9.3   The Complete Service Order page filled in

Bill creates the new service order and when he receives the confirmation, the new service order is stored and ready to be forwarded to Anne. He tells Kim that the service order is created and that Anne probably will get in touch with her as soon as possible to confirm when she will arrive to take care of the copier.

Because Bill is working in-house, we have shown the above scenario from a normal PC browser. However, the system is built to enable multiple types of clients to access the web application. For example, if we would start the new service order from a Pocket PC, it would look like Figure 9.4.

66 We have shown the above scenario from a normal PC browser. However, the system is built to enable multiple types of clients to access the web application. 99

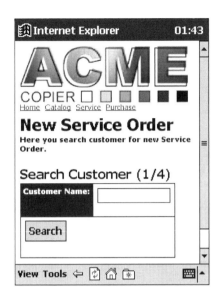

Figure 9.4   New Service Order wizard on Pocket PC

And on a phone using Microsoft Mobile Explorer, it would look like Figure 9.5.

Figure 9.5   New Service Order wizard in MME

And therefore Bill could also be doing his job from wherever he wants, say working at home occasionally. We can even take the back-office anywhere – isn't that cool?

9.2   Pocket Service Assistant

The off-line client that Anne, a service technician at ACME Copier, uses is called *Pocket Service Assistant* or Pocket Service for short. This is a client that she can use wherever she is and she can also connect with it and use it at the office. When she starts it, it looks like Figure 9.6.

Figure 9.6   Pocket
Service Assistant
splash screen

Synchronization

A number of times a day, Anne makes an online connection to her company's server to synchronize her Pocket PC application, Pocket Service. During synchronization, her completed service assignments are sent back to the office and new service orders are retrieved onto her device. Also, a load of other information (articles, numbers of parts in stock, look-up data, etc.) is also pulled off the server into her local database on the Pocket PC.

She is very mobile, so she most often uses her mobile phone hooked up to the Pocket PC to connect to the company's server. When she passes the office sometime during the day, she can also connect her Pocket PC directly to the company network using a network adapter or via a cradle attached to a PC, and make the synchronization then as well. Figure 9.7 is how synchronization looks.

Figure 9.7
Synchronization form

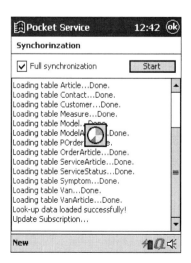

As you can see, she can make a full synchronization as well as just transferring all the completed service orders to the company server and getting new ones from the server.

Scheduling

After the synchronization is complete, she looks at her service order list to see what she should do next. Figure 9.8 is what she sees.

Figure 9.8   Service Order List

She notices that there is a new service order that arrived with the last synchronization. It looks like their Xerox copier at Northwind Traders is producing blurred copies again and that they are in a hurry (the first column indicated Priority=High). She quickly checks the calendar for today, and luckily for Northwind, the afternoon has a two-hour gap, between 2 p.m. and 4 p.m., where she could fit this in. She switches back to her service order list and makes a new Calendar appointment out of the Northwind service order. Figure 9.9 shows what appears when she taps the **Make Appointment** button.

Figure 9.9
Appointment created
from Service Order

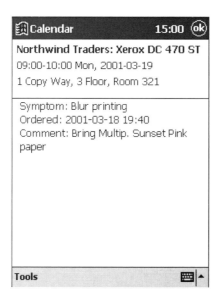

In the new appointment screen, she enters the correct time and notices that there was a comment attached to the service order about bringing a special kind of paper along as well. She quickly checks her van inventory and finds that she has at least one ream left. Great, she thinks, that saves me an extra stop at the company warehouse. She could also see that it was Kim at Northwind who sent the message, and she knows that Kim is an impatient customer. So she decides to send Kim an e-mail right away – just to keep her calm. When she taps the **Send E-Mail** button in the Service Order List window, Figure 9.10 shows what appears on the screen.

Figure 9.10
Automatically pre-
filled e-mail message
created using
information from
Service Order

Anne gets a ready to send an e-mail message with Kim's e-mail address, the symptom, and the appliance already filled in. She sends the e-mail and starts her working day by drinking a cup of coffee.

Completing a service assignment

In the afternoon, when Anne arrives on site at Northwind, she first has to find a contact person. Since she knows Kim, she tries to call her – and even the reception tries a few times without success. The clerk asks if there is someone else whom he could contact instead. Anne asks him to wait and then she selects the service order in the service order list (see Figure 9.8) and taps the **Show** button in the Service Order List window to get to the service order form (see Figure 9.19). When she taps the **Customer** button and then switches to the **Contacts** tab, so that she can see all the contact people at Northwind Traders as in Figure 9.11.

Figure 9.11
Customer contacts

Let's stop here at the customer form for a minute. On this form, Anne can get all kinds of information. She can check the address, phone numbers, and even check any comments on the customer. Contacts can be added, updated, and removed. And for each contact, she gets all the contact information, including telephone, fax, and mobile phone numbers (see Figure 9.12).

Figure 9.12   Contact details

She can easily send e-mail directly to the contact by tapping the **Send E-Mail** button. She can even add the contact to her Pocket PC Contacts if it is a frequent contact that she wants to be able to reach. When she taps the **Create Contact in Contacts** button, Figure 9.13 shows what appears on the screen.

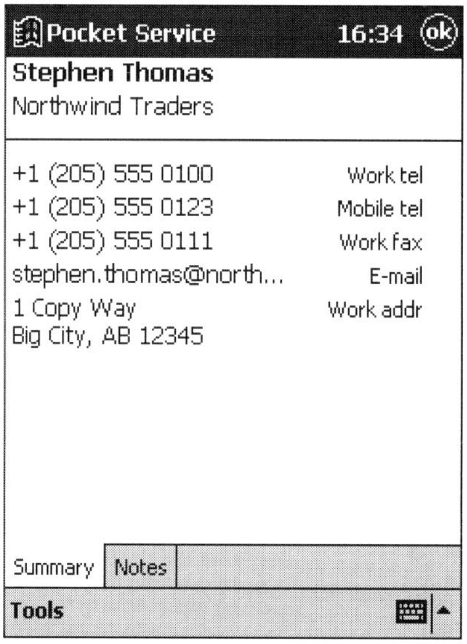

Figure 9.13   A contact in Pocket Contacts created from a contact in Pocket Service Assistant

If a new contact at Northwind Traders were entered, for example, the new contact will receive all the information that ACME Copier has on the contact and it even gets the company information.

Okay, let's get back to the receptionist at Northwind, who is waiting politely. Anne asks the clerk to try Stephen Thomas instead since he is actually the primary contact person for Northwind (she can see that in the priority column – the column with heading "P" in Figure 9.11).

Stephen answers the phone instantly and asks the clerk to let Anne in since she will probably find her way to the copier. The truth is that Anne has no idea were the copier is, but she does not need to bother Stephen with helping her. She knows how to find the right location for the copier. From the service order form she taps the **Appliance** button and can see the placement of the copier (Figure 9.14).

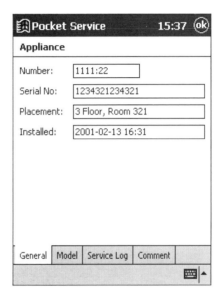

Figure 9.14
Appliance form

She gets to the third floor and finds room 321. She then taps (**OK**) to get back to the **Service Order** form. She taps the **Measure** tab and taps the **Job Start** button to select the time for starting the job.

She opens the printer and realizes that it has not been cleaned for a while and that the dirt may well be the cause of the problem. When she checks the **Service Log** tab, she notices that it has not been cleaned since it was installed. She also checks the **Model** tab for information on the specific copier (see Figure 9.15).

Figure 9.15 Model
tab on Appliance form

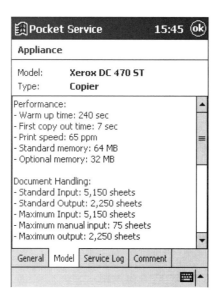

Figure 9.15 Model
tab on Appliance form

When she finishes cleaning the copier she records the steps she took on the service order and also taps the **Job End** button to provide the ending time, which will calculate the time for the job (see Figure 9.16).

Figure 9.16
Measure tab on
Service Order form

This is all she has to do to report her work! As she does this, Kim comes into the room. Kim is happy that Anne could get there so fast and delighted that she sent the e-mail to confirm when she was coming. That way, Kim could plan to meet up with her as she was fixing the copier.

"So, what was it?" asks Kim. Anne responds, "Well, it was just some dirt that blurred the copies. But I have cleaned it now." Kim wants one more thing: "Did you bring the paper?"

"Yes, I had one box in the van. Should I leave it with you?" says Anne. "Oh yes, please!" responds Kim.

Anne taps the **Articles** tab and taps the **New...** button to add the article to the service order. She gets to the **Add Article** form (see Figure 9.17):

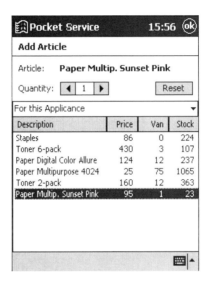

Figure 9.17   Add article form

Here she can search for the articles suitable for this copier and when she has them in front of her on the screen, she can select the paper that Kim wants. She could update the quantity, but since the default is one box, she just taps **OK** to add the new article. Now she has an updated list of articles on the service order (see Figure 9.18):

Figure 9.18   Articles tab in Service Order form

She can add more items, update, or remove articles as she pleases. Anne asks Kim if she is pleased with the service and on confirmation, she finishes the job by tapping the **General** tab, updates the job status, enters the meter reading on the copier (number of copies) and checks the **Ready?** check box (that turns into **Ready!** in green) (see Figure 9.19):

Figure 9.19   Service Order ready!

Now that Anne has checked the **Ready!** check box, it will be synchronized back to the office the next time she performs a synchronization. Usually that is at least once between each service job (using her mobile phone). That means that the back-office at ACME Copier can invoice the work and articles supplied just a few minutes after the work is completed at the customer's site.

9.3   Article catalog

Before Anne leaves, Kim stops her to ask if she can get more of the paper. Kim wants another two boxes. Anne does not have any more in the van, so she makes up an additional order for the additional boxes. She connects to ACME Copier's server with her mobile phone, which is attached to the Pocket PC and starts Internet Explorer for the Pocket PC. She has a favorite link to the Article Catalog web application and Figure 9.20 shows how it looks on her screen.

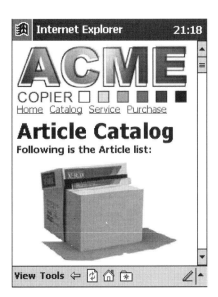

Figure 9.20   Online
Article Catalog on the
Pocket PC

For each item she finds a picture with its article denomination (short
description). She also gets a longer description as well as the article number
and even the article price (see Figure 9.21).

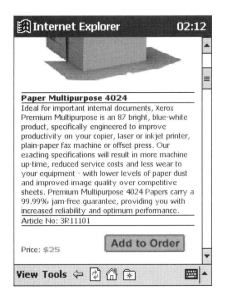

Figure 9.21   Article
details in article
catalog

The catalog is exactly the same web application that the back-office personnel at ACME Copier have access to, but why bother them when she can get
the information herself? She saves both colleagues' and her own time, and

most importantly, she saves the risk of someone else ordering the wrong article. ACME Copier thereby wins in three ways: (1) efficiency and productivity increases; (2) time and thereby money is saved due to the simpler process; and last but far from least (3) the accuracy of the product ordering improves because there are no intermediaries who can add mistakes.

9.4   A new purchase order

When she has found the article she is looking for, Anne can simply order it by tapping the **Add to Order** button in the catalog. She then gets to the Shopping Cart as shown in Figure 9.22.

Figure 9.22
Shopping cart

From here, Anne can go on and create the order by tapping the **Create Purchase Order** button. Similar to the Service Order web application that Bill used in the beginning of this chapter, the purchase order creation process is handled like a wizard. First Anne searches for the customer. She then selects the correct customer from the search results to obtain the purchase order completion page as shown in Figure 9.23.

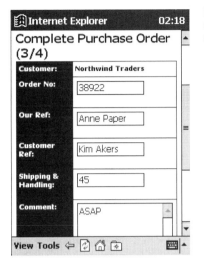

Figure 9.23
Complete Purchase
Order

She completes the order and receives a confirmation that the order is stored and will be handled immediately. She can even go back to check the estimated time of delivery once the order is saved. She does check. Before she leaves, she passes Kim's room and tells her that the boxes of paper are ordered, and that they are expected to arrive tomorrow. Anne leaves Kim with a smile on her face – it is great when there is a win/win situation between supplier and customer!

9.5   ACME Copier system architecture

Following is the description of the software architecture for the Field Service Operations System at ACME Copier. Following the basic guidelines described earlier about software architecture, here is the design that the people at ACME Copier came up with. As with all architectures, the system architecture must be based on the business needs. Therefore, most of the architecture is based on what we have described in the first section of this chapter. When we described the day for Bill and Anne, we actually went through the requirements for the system.

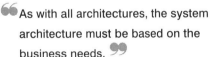 As with all architectures, the system architecture must be based on the business needs.

Note

It is important to remember that all architectures and systems have to have a well-defined scope. We realize that in this example there are a number of things that could be described as well. Those include integration with other back-office systems, service contract handling to create planned maintenance service order, as well as other things. We have decided to make the business principles below the scope of the architecture and solution described in the rest of this chapter.

Let's also review the business principles of the solution:

- Improve the service technician's productivity by increasing the time spent in service order and scheduled maintenance work.
- Increase customer satisfaction by cutting lag time between the time the service order was initiated to when the service technician shows up.
- Reduce customer service administration by removing all paper forms and notes carrying service order information.
- Reduce cost by improving Service Technician daily routes.
- Enable decision support (type of equipment, causes and frequency of failure, etc.)
- Pocket PC solutions must be easy to use.
- Pocket PC solutions must support both connected and disconnected scenarios.
- All solutions must be scalable so that they perform equally well for one service technician as for thousands.
- Solution must integrate well with current and future IT architecture at ACME Copier Inc.
- Maximize development efficiency by leveraging skill set already present at IT-department.

And these combined with the requirements are the input to the architectural work. We will not talk so much about the actual process that ACME went through to create the software architecture as it is well described in Chapter 3.

Conceptual architecture

Let's start with the conceptual part of the architecture. Based on the requirements from the service technicians and back-office personnel, ACME Copier came to the conclusion that the overall architecture for the field service operation would look like Figure 9.24.

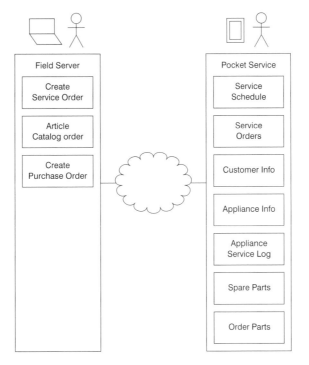

Figure 9.24
Conceptual
architecture overview

The back-office personnel (Bill) basically need two different main function-alities from the solution. Here is a short description of them:

- Create Service Order: Service orders are created in two ways. (1) By the system itself as a consequence of the maintenance contracts that cus-tomers have for specific appliances, and (2) by back-office personnel who get calls for assistance from customers on unscheduled events (break-downs, etc.). The functionality we're describing here in this chapter only covers the latter.

- Article Catalog: This contains both the ability to browse available prod-ucts and also to add articles to a "shopping cart," which can later be turned into a new purchase order.

- Create Purchase Order: This simply creates a purchase order with articles picked from the Article Catalog. The output from this transfers into an order management system.

For the service technician (Anne), there are a number of functionalities needed. Here is a short description of those:

- Service Schedule: Service technicians should be able to handle their mainte-nance schedules themselves. Their maintenance schedules should be able to integrate with some calendar functionality already available in their device.

- Service Orders: This is the main part of this system's functionality. The purpose here is to provide the service technician with a tool to help her before, during, and after the service is provided. It should be possible to register measures, time necessary for the service tasks, and to add articles used for service, and so forth.

- Customer Information: It is important always to have customer information available where and when it's needed. ACME Copier service technicians do therefore carry most of the customer information, which is easily updated with their Pocket PCs.

- Appliance Information: Equally as important as customer information, the service technician needs the product information about the copiers (and other appliances) available at any time. This includes specification data, installation date, serial number, etc.

- Appliance Service Log: It is also important for the service technician to be able to follow up on previous services performed on each appliance. This includes both scheduled and ad hoc repair services; also all services, including those performed by other service technicians.

- Spare Parts: These are articles that are used during service and that are readily available from the service technician's van, can be added to the service order and are invoiced later with the service order invoice.

- Order Parts: Items that are not available instantly (not in the van), can be ordered as a purchase order directly by the service technician.

As shown by the cloud in Figure 9.24, there should be a connection between the back-office system and the service technician system on a handheld device. This connection includes the ability to access functionality directly from the handheld device and also synchronization of information between the server and the client.

Logical architecture

If we move on to the logical architecture, the overview would look like Figure 9.25. On the server side, ACME Copier came to the conclusion that they would implement the back-office functionality as web applications. The catalog and purchase order functionality were placed in one web application, and the service order functionality in another. A point with developing web applications was that these could be accessed from both the in-house back-office personnel as well as the service technician out in the field. Both these web applications use a common tier of business logic implemented as components. A number of objects were needed:

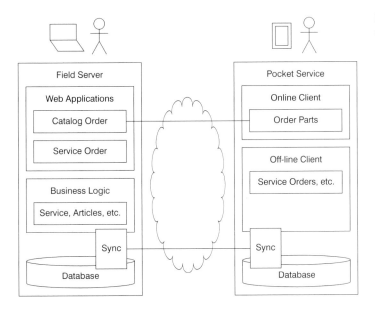

Figure 9.25   Logical architecture overview

- Catalog: Takes care of the functionality surrounding handling catalog information. This might have been called the article object, but we would like to emphasize that business logic is divided due to business needs, not due to database design.

- Customer: Handles customer-related functionality.

- ServiceOrder: Responsible for all functionality related to handling and creating new service orders.

- PurchaseOrder: Handles all functionality related to handling and creating purchase orders.

- Synchronization: Responsible for all synchronization functionality.

In Figure 9.25 you can see that the synchronization functionality involves both business logic (an object) as well as synchronization handled by the database directly (replication). There are several reasons for this:

1 Some data is just too critical to transfer without any logic (mostly lookup data like symptoms, measurements, etc.).

2 Some data need business logic when handled (like submission of service orders).

3 We would like to show all the different ways of handling the synchronization between the server and the client (this last reason does not have anything to do with ACME Copier or their architectural needs).

On the client side, they concluded that there was a need for a standard thin web client. This would preferably be a client that did not need any additional hardware or gateways and that could read standard HTML. The service technicians would also need an off-line client for handling service orders when in the field.

ACME Copier realized that the vision of "always connected" was still a long way off and did not want to depend on wireless wide area networks for service technicians to do their job. As on the server, the synchronization was handled both by the off-line client as well as by the database natively.

Physical architecture

And to complete the architectural roundtrip, Figure 9.26 shows the physical architecture overview.

Figure 9.26 Physical architecture overview

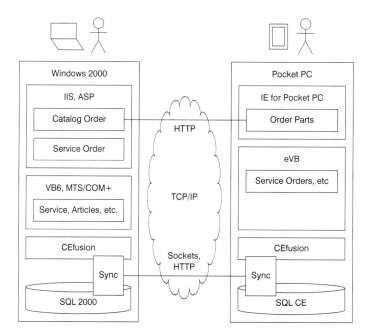

Now we are at the level where we actually select the physical components of the architecture. With "physical" we mean products and other things like servers, network adapters, and other hardware. We also mean things that are not really physical, too, such as software and network protocols.

If we start with the server side, you can see that this is a fairly pure Microsoft solution with Windows 2000 Server hosting the server functionality. The web applications are built with IIS and ASP. The ASP pages use the COM components written in VB 6.0 and running in MTS/COM+. The data is stored in SQL Server 2000 with some of the synchronization functionality handled through its replication capabilities. Also, for some of the business logic-related synchronization functionality, the middleware from Odyssey Software called CEfusion is used (see Chapter 7 for more information). Even if ACME Copier currently is using only a fraction of this software's capabilities, they have invested in it for the future. It's also true that there were not many other options if they wanted a standard solution.

On the handheld device, ACME Copier came to the conclusion that the Pocket PC would be the appropriate choice for a number of reasons:

1 It has a standard web browser that could handle normal HTML and did not require any additional hardware (gateways, etc.).

2 It is capable of handling large amounts of features and data which is necessary to handle the off-line functionality.

3 It has a solid database (SQL Server CE) that supports SQL and also has a native support for replication build in.

4 The database middleware (ADO) is similar to the one used on the server which means that code could be reused.

5 Since most developers at ACME Copier already knew the Microsoft tools (like VB 6.0), they were already well on their way to building Pocket PC applications with eVB.

6 Our book is about Pocket PCs! For the online/thin client functionality, ACME is using Internet Explorer for the Pocket PC. For the off-line client, they decided to build an eVB application themselves.

They like to say that they did it, even if it was a number of wizard consultants who actually did most of the job. From eVB they use both the CEfusion middleware components as well as the functionality built into the database. They used SQL Server 2000 for Windows CE as the database.

> 66 They like to say that they did it, even if it was a number of wizard consultants who actually did most of the job. 99

The "Sync" component is not very well described in Figure 9.26, but if you look at the chapters on SQL Server for CE (Chapter 6) and CEfusion (Chapter 7) you will see that they include figures of how their architecture works. In brief we can state that SQL Server CE handles most of the pure transfer of data while CEfusion handles the synchronization that involves business logic to some extent. SQL Server CE uses HTTP to do the replication while CEfusion uses sockets.

To complete the physical architecture, Figure 9.27 shows what each service technician is equipped with.

Figure 9.27 Physical architecture for service technician

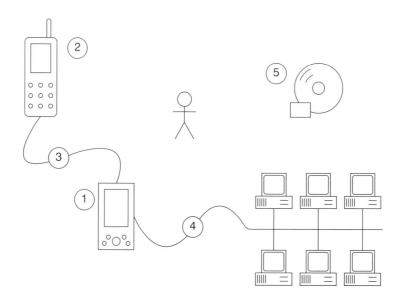

First of all, they have a Pocket PC (1 in the diagram) and a mobile phone (2 in the diagram). They have a connector between the Pocket PC and the mobile phone (this is 3 in the figure). Also, to connect to the company network they have a network adapter with cable (shown as 4). Because ACME Copier realizes the value of having happy employees, they have equipped all their employees with extra memory cards (5), purely for the technicians' own discretion. Anne uses her 512 MB memory card to store a full-length video, one hour of MP3 music, and a number of great Flash comics that she loves to watch, and show customers. She even has some space left for commercial and educational videos that she can show customers: videos showing the newest copiers, some of the new copiers' features, as well as troubleshooting steps they can perform themselves.

❝Because ACME Copier realizes the value of having happy employees, they have equipped all their employees with extra memory cards (5), purely for the technicians' own discretion.❞

Some companies believe that business applications are everything that the employees need, and some firms even attempt to stop employees from using their tools by "locking" them to perform a single task. Even if the thought is based on honest focus on core business, this is purely destructive and never good for business. ACME Copier has, through measurements, found that their employees are more productive, innovative, and even more focused on what is best for the company if they have fun at work. They have found that having fun is good for business.

Actors and use scenarios

Here is a description of the different professional roles (actors) who use the system:

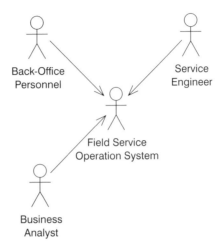

Figure 9.28   System actors

In our discussion here, we have only seen the functionality for the two top-most roles (Bill and Anne), but there are other roles that ACME Copier had thought of already.

One interesting role is the business analyst. Persons performing in this role would probably be interested in doing work with business intelligence data on all the information that is collected in this system. For example, since each service technician reports the meter readings on each machine that they service and all services are registered, one could easily create some analysis of how long it should be between planned maintenance service to minimize unscheduled and therefore more costly repair visits. We have not covered this functionality in the architecture but we have placed the information in SQL Server 2000 with its built-in analysis capabilities (OLAP, etc.), so we know that we could support this functionality in the future.

Here are some of the use cases, or user scenarios, as some prefer to call them. First, let's look at the use cases for the back-office personnel (Figure 9.29).

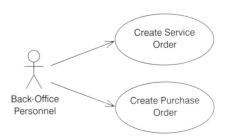

Figure 9.29   Back-office personnel use-cases

And then we see how it looks for the service technician (Figure 9.30).

Figure 9.30   Service technician use cases

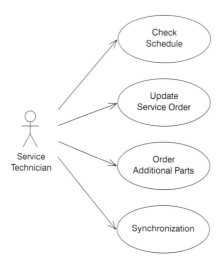

And once we have the use cases in place, we might as well show you an example of a scenario diagram. We have chosen a simplified scenario for the Order Additional Parts (wizard) (Figure 9.31).

Figure 9.31   Sample scenario

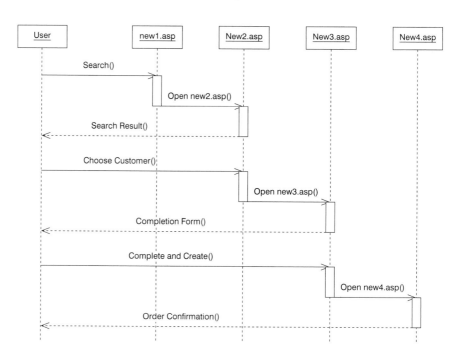

It is truly a good practice to document use cases and scenarios this way. It enables a clear communication between the users and the developers, and can always be used as a blueprint of the solution as you build (or have built).

System overview

Figure 9.32 Sample model

Figure 9.32 is a model of the implementation.

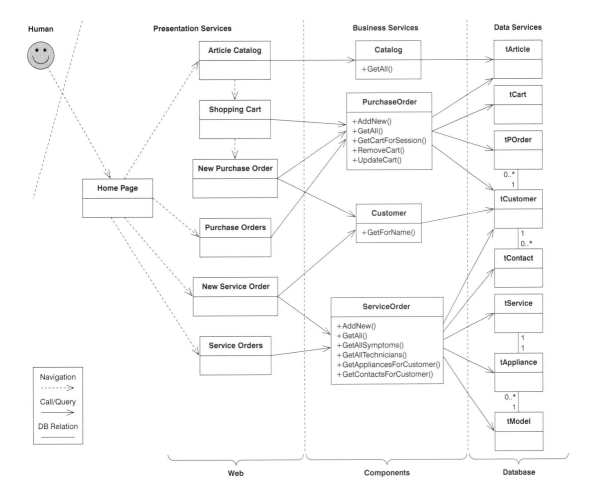

Figure 9.32 is actually a mix of two different UML diagrams, but it gives a nice overview of what the system looks like. You can see three relationships at once. You get to view all of the navigation between ASP pages in the presentation services, you can see the calls made from pages to objects and components to tables, and then you also get the relationship between the table in the database. If you happen to like this model, you are welcome to use the same technique as the model file is on the accompanying CD in Microsoft Visio format.

The model only includes the tables used by the business objects, but if you want the complete database, Figure 9.33 shows the data model from SQL Server.

The data model is normalized and all relationships have been implemented to ensure referential integrity. All fields are showing except a few on some of the look-up tables.

Figure 9.33
Database model

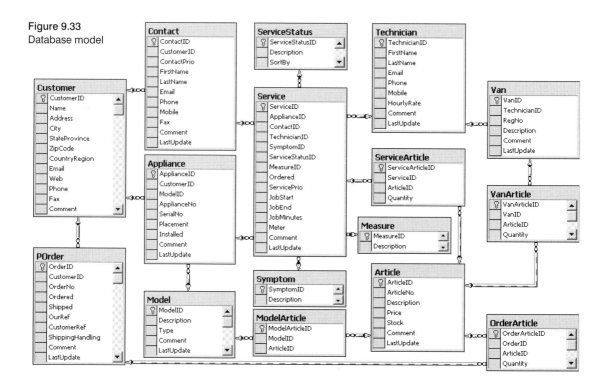

9.6　Conclusion

We have now seen the major part of how the ACME Copier Field Service Operations System is used. We have seen both the use of the back-office with a web application, as well as the service technician's use of both the online client using Internet Explorer for the Pocket PC and the off-line client using an application implemented in eVB.

Then we have looked at how the architecture design was made according to best practices and also according to the demands of the system. In the architecture we have seen the transition from conceptual, via logical to physical implementation with selected hardware and software. We have also looked at how the system could (should) be documented (mostly using UML). We hope that this background will give you a good understanding of the purpose of the system, and also that it will serve as an introduction to the next chapter were we walk you through parts of the implementation in detail.

Inside ACME Copier's system

In this chapter we will look behind the scenes at the system we saw in action in Chapter 9. We will look at the most important parts of the implementation. The point here is to show you how the various techniques fall into place when compiled into a complete enterprise application.

We will guide you through the sample code much in the same order as we observed interactions with the system in Chapter 9, to make it easier for you to go back and see how it actually worked when used. We hope that this code will be useful for you when you start building your own enterprise applications and that the context provided will make it easier for you to see how the different features fit together.

10.1   A new service order

As you saw in Chapter 9, the new service order web application is built with ASP pages running in IIS that call business logic built with VB 6.0 and which in turn runs as a COM+ application in Windows 2000 Server.

First page – new1.asp

The ASP pages are built to enable multiple clients to access the web application and if we look at the source code for the first page of the new service order wizard, **new1.asp**, it looks like this:

```
<%@ LANGUAGE="VBSCRIPT" %>
<%
Option Explicit
Response.Expires = 0
%>
<!--#INCLUDE FILE="../include/global.asp"-->

<!DOCTYPE HTML PUBLIC "-//IETF//DTD HTML//EN">
<HTML><HEAD><TITLE>ACME Copier</TITLE>
<LINK REL="stylesheet" HREF="../css/acme.css" TYPE="text/css">
</HEAD><BODY><FONT FACE="Tahoma">

<!--#INCLUDE FILE="../include/top.asp"-->
<H1>New Service Order</H1>
<% If Not IsMME Then %><P><B>
  Here you search customer for new Service Order.
</B></P><% End If %><BR CLEAR="all">

<H2>Search Customer (1/4)</H2>
<FORM ACTION="new2.asp" METHOD="POST">
<TABLE BGCOLOR="navy" BORDER="0" CELLSPACING="0"
CELLPADDING="0"><TR><TD>
<TABLE BORDER="0" CELLSPACING="1" CELLPADDING="3">
  <TR BGCOLOR="white">
    <TD BGCOLOR="navy" VALIGN="top"><FONT
COLOR="white"><B>Customer Name:</B></FONT></TD>
    <TD VALIGN="top"><INPUT TYPE="text" NAME="CustomerName"
VALUE=""<% If IsPocketPC Then Response.Write(" SIZE=""10""")
%>></TD>
  </TR>
  <TR BGCOLOR="white">
    <TD VALIGN="top" COLSPAN="2"><INPUT TYPE="submit"
VALUE="Search"></TD>
  </TR>
</TABLE>
</TD></TR></TABLE>
</FORM>

<!--#INCLUDE FILE="../include/bottom.asp"-->

</FONT></BODY>
</HTML>
```

A number of server-side include files are used to simplify the creation of similar pages. We will come back to those in a minute. If you look closely to the text beneath the main heading (the <H1> tag), you see that if **IsMME** is True, this text will not be sent to the client. The IsMME variable is set in the **global.asp** include file. This is how an ASP page can consider different types of clients and send the most appropriate content to each one.

Another example is the use of **IsPocketPC** that adds a size attribute to the input field if **IsPocketPC** is True. The reason for checking what type of client that requests the page is to avoid getting a page in response that otherwise would be too wide for Pocket PC clients and thereby creating a horizontal scroll bar in Internet Explorer for the Pocket PC – something that we want to avoid. Okay, how do we set the **IsMME** and **IsThinClient** variables? Let us look at that part of the **global.asp** page:

```
<%
' Device Indicators
Public IsPocketPC, IsMME, IsThinClient
IsPocketPC = (InStr(Request.ServerVariables("HTTP_USER_AGENT"),
"Windows CE") > 0)
IsMME = (InStr(Request.ServerVariables("HTTP_USER_AGENT"),
"MME") > 0)
IsThinClient = (IsPocketPC Or IsMME)

' Web Root
Public Const WEBROOT = "/PPDE"
%>
```

We look at a property on the **Request** object (**ServerVariables**) that holds information about the HTTP headers sent by the client. One of those values (**HTTP_USER_AGENT**) tells us who the client is. We use this information to set Boolean variables (like IsMME) for each client type. As you can see, we have also included a common variable (IsThinClient) for clients other than normal browsers (Internet Explorer, Netscape, etc.).

 Tip

You can read more about browser sniffing in Chapter 8.

We also set a constant containing the virtual directory name to make it dynamic (you can move the virtual directory without changing more than this variable).

If we look at one of the other include files, **top.asp**, it looks like this:

```
<% If Not IsThinClient Then %>
  <IMG SRC="<% =WEBROOT %>/images/largelogo.jpg" ALT="ACME
logo" ALIGN="right" WIDTH="315" HEIGHT="105" VSPACE="0"
```

```
HSPACE="0" BORDER="0">
<% Else %>
  <% If IsPocketPC Then %>
    <IMG SRC="<% =WEBROOT %>/images/logo.jpg" ALT="ACME logo"
WIDTH="208" HEIGHT="68" VSPACE="0" HSPACE="0" BORDER="0">
  <% ElseIf IsMME Then %>
    <IMG SRC="<% =WEBROOT %>/images/smallogo.jpg" ALT="ACME
logo" WIDTH="97" HEIGHT="34" VSPACE="0" HSPACE="0" BORDER="0">
  <% End If %>
<% End If %>
<A HREF="<% =WEBROOT %>/">Home</A> 
<A HREF="<% =WEBROOT %>/Catalog/">Catalog</A> 
<A HREF="<% =WEBROOT %>/SO/">Service</A> 
<A HREF="<% =WEBROOT %>/PO/">Purchase</A>
```

Here you find some more examples of using the client indicator variables. On the top of the web page, actually one of three possible different logo files load depending upon the client type. The **largelogo.jpg** file is used on normal browser clients and a smaller version simply called **logo.jpg** appears on Pocket PC clients. Finally, on MME clients, an even smaller, black and white image displays, that is called **smallogo.jpg**.

We will not cover the last include file, **bottom.asp**, since it only includes the copyright notice at the bottom of the page.

Second page – new2.asp

We now move to the next page, new2.asp, where the user arrives when clicking on the **Search** button in the new1.asp page. This page shows the customer search results, and the source looks like this:

```
<%@ LANGUAGE="VBSCRIPT" %>
<%
Option Explicit
Response.Expires = 0

' Server side includes
%>
<!--#INCLUDE FILE="../include/global.asp"-->
<%

' Page variables
Dim poCustomer
Dim pars ' Recordset
%>
```

```
<!DOCTYPE HTML PUBLIC "-//IETF//DTD HTML//EN">
<HTML><HEAD><TITLE>ACME Copier</TITLE>
<LINK REL="stylesheet" HREF="../css/acme.css" TYPE="text/css">
</HEAD><BODY><FONT FACE="Tahoma">

<!--# INCLUDE FILE". ./include/top.asp"-->
<H1>New Service Order</H1>
<% If Not IsMME Then %><P><B>
  Here you select customer for new Service Order.
</B></P><% End If %>

<H2>Select Customer (2/4)</H2>
<% Set poCustomer = Server.CreateObject("PPDE.Customer")
   Set pars =
poCustomer.GetForName(Request.Form("CustomerName"))
   Set poCustomer = Nothing %>
<TABLE BGCOLOR="navy" BORDER="0" CELLSPACING="0"
CELLPADDING="0"><TR><TD>
<TABLE BORDER="0" CELLSPACING="1" CELLPADDING="3">
<% If Not IsMME Then %>
  <TR BGCOLOR="navy">
    <TD VALIGN="top"><FONT
COLOR="white"><B>Customer</B></FONT></TD>
 <% If Not IsThinClient Then %>
    <TD VALIGN="top"><FONT COLOR="white"><B>
E-Mail</B></FONT></TD>
    <TD VALIGN="top"><FONT COLOR="white"><B>Web</B></FONT></TD>
    <TD VALIGN="top"><FONT
COLOR="white"><B>Comment</B></FONT></TD>
  <% End If %>
 </TR>
<% End If %>
<% Do While Not pars.EOF %>
  <TR BGCOLOR="white">
    <TD VALIGN="top"><A HREF="new3.asp?CustomerID=<%
=StripGUID(pars("CustomerID").Value) %>&CustomerName=<%
=pars("Name").Value %>"><% =pars("Name").Value %></A></TD>
    <% If Not IsThinClient Then %>
    <TD VALIGN="top"><A HREF="mailto:<% =pars("Email").Value
%>"><% =pars("Email").Value %></A></TD>
    <TD VALIGN="top"><A HREF="http://<% =pars("Web").Value
%>"><% =pars("Web").Value %></A></TD>
    <TD VALIGN="top"><% =pars("Comment").Value %></TD>
  <% End If %>
  </TR>
```

```
<%  pars.MoveNext
    Loop
    pars.Close
    set pars = Nothing %>
</TABLE>
</TD></TR></TABLE>

<!--#INCLUDE FILE="../include/bottom.asp"-->

</FONT></BODY>
</HTML>
```

This page uses the **Customer** business object to find customers matching the supplied search string (passed to this page in the **Request. Form** ("CustomerName") field) using the method **GetForName**. The **GetForName** method returns an ADO Recordset with the matching customers and a table filled with the customer data on each row. As you can see, not all of the columns are sent to the client if it is not a normal browser, since we do not want Pocket PC (and MME) clients to get a table that is too wide (saving the user from horizontal scrolling). Each client name gets a link to the next page in the wizard (new3.asp) with the customer ID and name as page parameters.

Third page – new3.asp

If you go on to this page, its source looks like this:

```
<%@ LANGUAGE="VBSCRIPT" %>
<%
Option Explicit
Response.Expires = 0

' Server side includes
%>
<!--#INCLUDE FILE="../include/global.asp"-->
<%

' Page variables
Dim poServiceOrder
Dim pars ' Recordset
Dim psCustomerID
Dim psCustomerName

' Init
psCustomerID = Request.QueryString("CustomerID")
psCustomerName = Request.QueryString("CustomerName")
```

```
%>
<!DOCTYPE HTML PUBLIC "-//IETF//DTD HTML//EN">
<HTML><HEAD><TITLE>ACME Copier</TITLE>
<LINK REL="stylesheet" HREF="../css/acme.css" TYPE="text/css">
</HEAD><BODY><FONT FACE="Tahoma">

<!--#INCLUDE FILE="../include/top.asp"-->
<H1>New Service Order</H1>
<% If Not IsMME Then %><P><B>
 Here you complete new Service Order.
</B></P><% End If %>

<H2>Complete Service Order (3/4)</H2>
<FORM ACTION="new4.asp" METHOD="POST">
<TABLE BGCOLOR="navy" BORDER="0" CELLSPACING="0"
CELLPADDING="0"><TR><TD>
<TABLE BORDER="0" CELLSPACING="1" CELLPADDING="3">
  <TR BGCOLOR="white">
    <TD BGCOLOR="navy" VALIGN="top"><FONT
COLOR="white"><B>Customer:</B></FONT></TD>
    <TD VALIGN="top"><B><% =psCustomerName %></B>
        <INPUT TYPE="hidden" NAME="CustomerID" VALUE="<%
=psCustomerID %>">
        <INPUT TYPE="hidden" NAME="CustomerName" VALUE="<%
=psCustomerName %>">
      </TD>
    </TR>
<% Set poServiceOrder =
Server.CreateObject("PPDE.ServiceOrder") %>
    <TR BGCOLOR="white">
      <TD BGCOLOR="navy" VALIGN="top"><FONT
COLOR="white"><B>Contact:</B></FONT></TD>
      <TD VALIGN="top"><SELECT NAME="ContactID" SIZE="1">
        <OPTION VALUE="0" SELECTED>Select Contact</OPTION>
        <% Set pars =
poServiceOrder.GetContactsForCustomer(psCustomerID)
          Do While Not pars.EOF %>
        <OPTION VALUE="<% =pars("ContactID").Value %>"><%
=pars("FirstName").Value + " " + pars("LastName").Value + " ("
+ pars("ContactPrio").Value + ")" %></OPTION>
          <% pars.MoveNext
            Loop
            pars.Close
```

```
          Set pars = Nothing %>
      </SELECT></TD>
    </TR>
    <TR BGCOLOR="white">
      <TD BGCOLOR="navy" VALIGN="top"><FONT
COLOR="white"><B>Appliance:</B></FONT></TD>
      <TD VALIGN="top"><SELECT NAME="ApplianceID" SIZE="1">
        <OPTION VALUE="0" SELECTED>Select Appliance</OPTION>
        <% Set pars =
poServiceOrder.GetAppliancesForCustomer(psCustomerID)
        Do While Not pars.EOF %>
        <OPTION VALUE="<% =pars("ApplianceID").Value %>"><%
=pars("ApplianceNo").Value %> (<% =pars("Description").Value
%>)</OPTION>
        <% pars.MoveNext
        Loop
        pars.Close
        Set pars = Nothing %>
    </SELECT></TD>
    </TR>
    <TR BGCOLOR="white">
      <TD BGCOLOR="navy" VALIGN="top"><FONT
COLOR="white"><B>Symptom:</B></FONT></TD>
      <TD VALIGN="top"><SELECT NAME="SymptomID" SIZE="1">
        <OPTION VALUE="0" SELECTED>Select Symptom</OPTION>
        <% Set pars = poServiceOrder.GetAllSymptoms()
          Do While Not pars.EOF %>
        <OPTION VALUE="<% =pars("SymptomID").Value %>"><%
=pars("Description").Value %></OPTION>
        <% pars.MoveNext
          Loop
          pars.Close
          Set pars = Nothing %>
     </SELECT></TD>
    </TR>
    <TR BGCOLOR="white">
      <TD BGCOLOR="navy" VALIGN="top"><FONT
COLOR="white"><B>Prio:</B></FONT></TD>
      <TD VALIGN="top"><SELECT NAME="ServicePrio" SIZE="1">
        <OPTION VALUE="H">High</OPTION>
        <OPTION VALUE="M" SELECTED>Medium</OPTION>
        <OPTION VALUE="L">Low</OPTION>
```

```
      </SELECT></TD>
    </TR>
    <TR BGCOLOR="white">
      <TD BGCOLOR="navy" VALIGN="top"><FONT
COLOR="white"><B>Technician:</B></FONT></TD>
      <TD VALIGN="top"><SELECT NAME="TechnicianID" SIZE="1">
        <OPTION VALUE="0" SELECTED>Select Technician</OPTION>
        <% Set pars = poServiceOrder.GetAllTechnicians()
          Do While Not pars.EOF %>
        <OPTION VALUE="<% =pars("TechnicianID").Value %>"><%
=pars("FirstName").Value + " " + pars("LastName").Value
%></OPTION>
        <% pars.MoveNext
         Loop
         pars.Close
         Set pars = Nothing %>
      </SELECT></TD>
    </TR>
<% Set poServiceOrder = Nothing %>
    <TR BGCOLOR="white">
      <TD BGCOLOR="navy" VALIGN="top"><FONT
COLOR="white"><B>Comment:</B></FONT></TD>
      <TD VALIGN="top"><TEXTAREA ROWS="5" <% If Not IsThinClient
Then Response.Write("COLS=""50""") Else
Response.Write("COLS=""16""") %>
NAME="Comment"></TEXTAREA></TD>
    </TR>
    <TR BGCOLOR="white">
      <TD VALIGN="top" COLSPAN="2"><INPUT TYPE="submit"
VALUE="Create"></TD>
    </TR>
  </TABLE>
  </TD></TR></TABLE>
  </FORM>

  <!--#INCLUDE FILE="../include/bottom.asp"-->

  </FONT></BODY>
  </HTML>
```

After storing the passed parameters from the previous page (**Request. Querystring** items CustomerID and CustomerName), this page uses the business object **ServiceOrder** to get the required information to complete the service order.

First, it gets the contacts for the chosen customer (**GetContacts ForCustomer** method) and adds them to a combo box. In the same way the appliances for that customer are retrieved (**GetAppliancesForCustomer** method) and populated in a combo box. Then, the look-up data for the different symptoms are also placed into a combo box (**GetAllSymptoms** method). The priority combo box is hard-coded but all the available service technicians are listed in the last combo box. Finally, you can see that the **Comment** field sizes differently depending on the client type. When the user (in this case Bill) has made all appropriate selections and presses the **Create** button, he receives the last page in the new service order wizard (new4.asp).

Fourth page – new4.asp

The last page, has the following source:

```
<%@ LANGUAGE="VBSCRIPT" %>
<%
Option Explicit
Response.Expires = 0

' Server side includes
%>
<!--#INCLUDE FILE="../include/global.asp"-->
<%

' Page variables
Dim poServiceOrder
%>
<!DOCTYPE HTML PUBLIC "-//IETF//DTD HTML//EN">
<HTML><HEAD><TITLE>ACME Copier</TITLE>
<LINK REL="stylesheet" HREF="../css/acme.css" TYPE="text/css">
</HEAD><BODY><FONT FACE="Tahoma">

<!--#INCLUDE FILE="../include/top.asp"-->
<H1>New Service Order</H1>
<% If Not IsMME Then %><P><B>
 This is the New Service Order confirmation.
</B></P><% End If %>

<H2>New Service Order Confirmation (4/4)</H2>
<%
  Set poServiceOrder = Server.CreateObject("PPDE.ServiceOrder")
  poServiceOrder.AddNew Request.Form("ApplianceID"),
```

```
Request.Form("ContactID"), _
                        Request.Form("TechnicianID"),
Request.Form("SymptomID"), _
                        Request.Form("ServicePrio"),
Request.Form("Comment")
  Set poServiceOrder = Nothing
%>

<P>The new Service Order for Customer <B><%
=Request.Form("CustomerName") %></B> has been saved!</P>

<!--#INCLUDE FILE="../include/bottom.asp"-->

</FONT></BODY>
</HTML>
```

And here the supplied values are stored using the **ServiceOrder** business object (**AddNew** method) after which the user simply gets a confirmation of the newly created service order.

10.2   Pocket Service Assistant

Now we turn our focus to the off-line client of the ACME Copier solution. This application is mainly implemented in eVB using a SQL Server CE database and some CEfusion functionality as well. The off-line client is called Pocket Service Assistant. Hereafter we will refer to it as Pocket Service.

Synchronization

The synchronization functionality is intentionally implemented using a number of different replication techniques. The reason for using different techniques is not that the ACME Copier had to use them all, but rather for us to illustrate the different available options in connecting the Pocket PC to a server to synchronize data.

> The reason for using different techniques is not that the ACME Copier had to use them all, but rather for us to illustrate the different available options in connecting the Pocket PC to a server to synchronize data.

Most of the functionality was implemented in the **Synchronization** form in the Pocket Service application (see Figure 10.1):

Figure 10.1
Synchronization form
in Pocket Service

We use three different techniques to synchronize:

- SQL Server CE RDA: This technique "pulls" tables from a SQL Server 2000 on a Windows server down to the Pocket PC.

- SQL Server CE Merge Replication: When you use this to replicate tables down to the Pocket PC, you will be able to merge changes made on both the server (SQL Server 2000) and on the Pocket PC (SQL Server CE).

- CEfusion MTSAgent: Here we use the CEfusion middleware to use components on a server. We implement methods on the server component both to "pull" information from the server to the Pocket PC, as well as to "push" back information via other methods.

 Tip

The SQL Server CE RDA and merge replication methods are used only if the user selects **Full synchronization** (the check box on the Pocket Service Synchronization form in Figure 10.1).

SQL Server CE Remote Data Access

This is the simplest way to get data from a server to a Pocket PC, provided that the server is running SQL Server 2000. You first have to set up the server to accept connections. That procedure is described in Chapter 6. When the server is set up, here is the code from the **Synchronization** (frmSync.ebf) form:

```
Dim lrda As SSCE.RemoteDataAccess

On Error Resume Next

 ' Drop tables
paco.Execute "DROP TABLE Appliance"
paco.Execute "DROP TABLE Article"
paco.Execute "DROP TABLE Contact"
 ' .
 ' .
 ' .
paco.Execute "DROP TABLE Van"
paco.Execute "DROP TABLE VanArticle"

On Error GoTo 0

' Close connection
paco.Close

' Create the RDA Object
Set lrda = pw32.CreateObject("SSCE.RemoteDataAccess.1.0")

' Set RDA properties
lrda.InternetURL = "http://SERVERNAME/sqlce/sscesa10.dll"
'lrda.InternetLogin = "userid"
'lrda.InternetPassword = "password"
lrda.LocalConnectionString =
"Provider=Microsoft.SQLSERVER.OLEDB.CE.1.0; Data
Source=\PSA.sdf"

' Pull the database
If Not pPullTable(lrda, "Appliance") Then Exit Sub
If Not pPullTable(lrda, "Article") Then Exit Sub
If Not pPullTable(lrda, "Contact") Then Exit Sub
 ' .
 ' .
 ' .
If Not pPullTable(lrda, "Van") Then Exit Sub
If Not pPullTable(lrda, "VanArticle") Then Exit Sub

' Remove objects
Set lrda = Nothing
```

We are assuming that the SQL Server CE database exists and is opened, because we first need to remove the SQL Server CE tables before we can "pull" them from the server. The "pulling" does not, as the name may imply, mean that the tables on the server are affected in any way. If the tables exist, we will generate a runtime error. However, if the table does not exist (the first time), we will get an error on the "DROP TABLE …" statement sent to the database. Therefore we have to turn error handling on (On Error Goto Next) to prevent the application from stopping if that happens.

> **Note**
>
> We are using the free **OSI Utility Collection** from Odyssey Software object to create all objects since it removes a memory leak problem in the normal **CreateObject** function. You can read more about the problem on the Microsoft Developer Network (MSDN) web site (**msdn.microsoft.com**). This function does not load the enumerations as the normal **CreateObject** does, so therefore you have to load each object that you want to use one time, which in turn loads the enumerations. We do that in the **LoadEnum** function in the **basGlobal.bas** module like this:

```
Dim lact As ADOXCE.Catalog
Dim lrda As SSCE.RemoteDataAccess
Dim lrep As SSCE.Replication
Dim lcfo As CFMTS.object
Dim lpoa As PocketOutlook.Application

' Create utility library (CreateObject without memory leak)
Set pw32 = CreateObject("OSIUtil.Win32")

' Load objects and destroy
Set lact = CreateObject("ADOXCE.Catalog.3.1"): Set lact = Nothing
Set lrda = CreateObject("SSCE.RemoteDataAccess.1.0"): Set lrda = Nothing
Set lrep = CreateObject("SSCE.Replication.1.0"): Set lrep = Nothing
Set lcfo = CreateObject("CFMTS.Object"): Set lcfo = Nothing
Set lpoa = CreateObject("PocketOutlook.Application"): Set lpoa = Nothing
```

And after this has been done once, you can use the **pw32** object anywhere in your application to create objects without wasting memory.

You can see that it is quite simple to set up the RDA object with an HTTP connection to the server. And if you have enabled Anonymous access or are using Windows Authentication on the virtual root where you installed the SQL Server CE Server Agent, you don't even have to set the username and password on the RDA object.

In a real-world scenario, the Pocket PC client would probably have to log on to the server as an authenticated user and then have the appropriate access to the virtual root. It is in the **pPullTable** function that the real work is done, so let us have a look at that:

```
' Pull table
lrda.Pull TableName, "SELECT * FROM " & TableName,
HOST_CONNECTION_STRING, TRACKINGOFF, TableName + "_Error"

' Check error
If lrda.ErrorRecords.Count > 0 Then
  pShowErrors lrda.ErrorRecords
  pPullTable = False
  Exit Function
End If
```

The approach is straightforward. You just supply the desired name in the local database and the SQL query to retrieve data (parameters 1 and 2). You also have to specify whether the pulled tables are to be tracked for changes (parameter 4). Changes can later be pushed back to the server using the **Push** method on the RDA object. You also have to supply a name for an additional table used for storing any errors during the "pull" (parameter 5). Lastly, you supply a host connection string (parameter 3). Here's how it's done:

```
"Provider=SQLOLEDB;Data Source=(local);Initial
Catalog=PPDE;Trusted_Connection=Yes"
```

There is nothing unusual about this. Note however, that we are using the "Trusted_Connnection=Yes" parameter to allow for Windows accounts to be authenticated within SQL Server 2000. You have to set up the Windows account to have rights in SQL Server. This parameter is also necessary if you are using Anonymous access (actually using the Windows account named IUSR_<machinename> that also has to be assigned rights in SQL Server).

The RDA objects (actually all SQL Server CE objects) use their own error handling and put all errors in a collection called **ErrorRecords**. If you want to get the full error description, you have to parse this collection. Here is the code to do that:

```
Dim lErrRec As SSCEError
Dim lparam As SSCEParam
Dim ls As String

For Each lErrRec In ErrColl
  ls = ls & "Source: " & lErrRec.Source & vbCrLf
  ls = ls & "Number: " & Hex(lErrRec.Number) & vbCrLf
  ls = ls & "NativeError: " & lErrRec.NativeError & vbCrLf
  ls = ls & "Description: " & lErrRec.Description & vbCrLf
  For Each lparam In lErrRec.Params
    ls = ls & "Param" & " = " & lparam.param & vbCrLf
  Next 'lparam
```

```
    ls = ls & vbCrLf
Next 'lErrRec

MsgBox ls, vbInformation, App.Title
```

The collection includes some interesting information and is well worth the time to implement. This is actually all we do with SQL Server CE RDA in the Pocket Service application. Basically we use RDA to pull down lookup data from the server.

All tables, except the **Service** and **Technician** table, use this method of transport. Actually, we even use this method for bringing the structure of the **Service** table to the client when we create the database the first time.

SQL Server CE merge replication

The SQL Server CE merge replication is similar to the same functionality available in SQL Server 2000. It enables merging of the changes made both on the server and on an off-line client.

When changes conflict, they are resolved using a "resolver" and you have different default resolvers to choose from. One resolver can take the last change made, whether it is on the server or on the Pocket PC, another can always favor the server or the Pocket PC, and so forth. You can even develop your own custom resolver.

We have chosen to only set up one table for merge replication and that is the **Technician** table. The idea is that both the back-office personnel and the technician can change this information and their respective changes will be synchronized. First, we have to set up the server with a publication of the **Technician** table. You'll find a description of that procedure in Chapter 6. When you use merge replication on the client you set up a subscription for the client and then you synchronize that subscription. The code in Pocket Service to set up and synchronize a subscription on the **Technician** table looks like this:

```
Dim lrep As ssce.Replication

' Create the Replication Object
Set lrep = pw32.CreateObject("SSCE.Replication.1.0")

' Set Internet properties
lrep.InternetURL = "http://SERVERNAME/sqlce/sscesa10.dll"
'lrep.InternetLogin = "userid"
'lrep.InternetPassword = "password"

' Set Publisher properties
lrep.Publisher = "SERVERNAME"
```

```
lrep.PublisherDatabase = "PPDE"
lrep.Publication = "PPDE"
lrep.PublisherSecurityMode = NT_AUTHENTICATION
'lrep.PublisherLogin = "userid"
'lrep.PublisherPassword = "password"

' Set Subscriber properties
lrep.SubscriberConnectionString =
"Provider=Microsoft.SQLSERVER.OLEDB.CE.1.0; Data
Source=\PSA.sdf"
lrep.Subscriber = "Anne Paper"

' Create the new anonymous subscription
If Create Then lrep.AddSubscription EXISTING_DATABASE
'CREATE_DATABASE

' Perform the first synchronization to download the initial
' snapshot by calling the Initialize, Run Terminate methods
On Error Resume Next
lrep.Initialize
If lrep.ErrorRecords.Count > 0 Then
  pShowErrors lrep.ErrorRecords
Else
  On Error Resume Next
  lrep.Run
  If lrep.ErrorRecords.Count > 0 Then
    pShowErrors lrep.ErrorRecords
  End If
  lrep.Terminate
End If

' Remove objects
Set lrep = Nothing
```

We are using a parameter to the (Create) function to choose whether we set up or just synchronize the subscription. You can see that we are using the same logic as for SQL Server CE RDA when initializing the HTTP connection to the server.

And the same comments that we made on security concerning RDA also apply here. For the **Publisher**, we are using Windows authentication and we have named the subscription the same as the database (PPDE); but you would probably choose different names. We use the same connection string and we have named the subscription the service technician's name. In a real-world scenario, you would probably set this name with some local information on the Pocket PC (i.e. from the registry were it has been stored during installation). The only thing that differs between creating and synchronizing a subscription is the use of the **AddSubscription** method. Because we already have a database created, we choose to add the subscription to the existing database. But, as you can see in the code comment, you could use another parameter to create the database as you add the subscription. The error collection also works the same way as for RDA.

CEfusion MTSAgent

The last synchronization method is the one used by the service technician during the day. This handles only one single table, the **Service** table, and its purpose is to send service orders back and forth between the server and the Pocket PC. Since this is something that the service technician would like to do several times a day and considering the fact that the normal connection during daytime is by a cellular phone, we have to use the most efficient way of transporting the data (through the business logic components on the server). The CEfusion MTSAgent is an excellent supplier of such functionality. It uses a very efficient technique to connect the Pocket PC to components on the server and also a very efficient protocol to transfer data between the two. As always when you want to use the most solid solution, it involves some extra work and the CEfusion MTSAgent is no exception.

> As always when you want to use the most solid solution, it involves some extra work and the CEfusion MTSAgent is no exception.

A key decision that has to be made is how to package the information transferred back and forth. This is not an easy decision, and we recommend that you take the time to consider this carefully before you decide. In the ACME Copier solution, we have chosen the recommendation from Odyssey Software (creators of CEfusion) to use variant arrays to package data.

Let us start with the necessary implementation on the server side. We need three methods to synchronize the service orders, and they are:

- **SendService:** Transfers service orders from the Pocket PC to the server.
- **GetService:** Pulls service orders from the server to the Pocket PC.
- **GetServiceCount:** Provides the Pocket PC with information on how many service orders to expect. This is the number of times the application then will call the **GetService** method.

We want to see the server perform as the master, so we always send before we get. The logic is that if anything sent affects something that will be received, that modification should happen on the server before we receive new things. In the ACME Copier solution this never happens, but in a real-world scenario this is a good practice to use. We will start with the code for the **SendService:**

```vb
Public Function SendService(ByVal ServiceRows As Variant) As
Variant

  Dim laco As Connection
  Dim lars As Recordset
  Dim i As Integer

  On Error GoTo ErrorHandler

  ' Create objects
  Set laco = CreateObject("ADODB.Connection")
  Set lars = CreateObject("ADODB.Recordset")

  ' Open Connection
  laco.CursorLocation = adUseClient
  laco.ConnectionString = CONNECTION_STRING
  laco.Open

  ' Open Recordset
  lars.CursorType = adOpenKeyset
  lars.LockType = adLockBatchOptimistic
  Set lars.ActiveConnection = laco
  lars.Open "SELECT * FROM Service WHERE ServiceID='" +
ServiceRows(0, 0) + "'"

  ' Parse arrays and update Recordset
  If Not lars.EOF Then
    For i = 1 To UBound(ServiceRows)
      lars(i).Value = ServiceRows(i, 0)
    Next 'i
    lars("Status").Value = SERVICE_STATUS_INSERVER
    lars.UpdateBatch
  End If

  ' Close objects
  lars.Close
  laco.Close

  ' Return Recordset
  SendService = True

  ' Allow MTS transaction set to proceed
  GetObjectContext.SetComplete

  Exit Function

ErrorHandler:
```

```
' Roll back MTS transaction set
GetObjectContext.SetAbort

Err.Raise Err.Number, Err.Source, Err.Description

End Function
```

We start by opening the ADO **Connection** and filling the **Recordset** with the currently received service order. We then parse the passed Variant array and update the **Recordset**. We finish the update by setting a flag indicating that the service order is now transferred from a service technician back to the server. Finally, we do some cleaning up and the standard transaction and error handling code.

Let us look at the **GetServiceCount** implementation (we have now removed some of the standard data, error and transaction handling code that you saw from the previous code snippet):

```
Public Function GetServiceCount(ByVal TechnicianID As String)
As Variant

  ' Open Recordset
  lars.CursorType = adOpenKeyset
  lars.LockType = adLockReadOnly
  Set lars.ActiveConnection = laco
  lars.Open "SELECT COUNT(*) FROM Service" + _
            " WHERE Status=" + CStr(SERVICE_STATUS_TOFIELD) + _
            " AND TechnicianID='" + TechnicianID + "'"

  ' Return Count
  GetServiceCount = CInt(lars(0))

End Function
```

And the SQL query simply counts the number of service orders that this service technician (parameter) should receive. Also it makes the data selection provided that the status of the service order indicates that it should be transferred to the Pocket PC. Finally, the count is returned. And we go on to look at the **GetService** implementation (again, without some of the standard code):

```
Public Function GetService(ByVal TechnicianID As String) As
Variant

  ' Open Recordset
  lars.CursorType = adOpenKeyset
  lars.LockType = adLockBatchOptimistic
  Set lars.ActiveConnection = laco
```

```
lars.Open "SELECT * FROM Service" + _
         " WHERE Status=" + CStr(SERVICE_STATUS_TOFIELD) + _
         " AND TechnicianID='" + TechnicianID + "'"

' Return Count
If Not lars.EOF Then
  lars("Status").Value = SERVICE_STATUS_INFIELD
  lvRows = lars.GetRows(1)
  GetService = lvRows
  lars.UpdateBatch
End If

End Function
```

Here we actually get the service order row and before we send it off to the Pocket PC, we update the status and save the row again. Note how convenient the **GetRows** method is when doing the conversion to Variant array – it is really a snap!

Now, it's time to look at the code in the Pocket PC to communicate with the component implementing these methods on the server. We will start with the main synchronization code in Pocket Service. This code is run on all types of synchronizations (if "full synchronization" were selected or not) and looks like this:

```
Dim lcfoSync As CFMTS.object
Dim lsSQL As String
Dim liServiceCount As Integer
Dim i As Integer

' Create the host object
Set lcfoSync = pw32.CreateObject("CFMTS.Object")
lcfoSync.ObjectName = "PPDE.Sync"

' Open Recordset
lsSQL = "SELECT * FROM Service WHERE Status=" +
CStr(SERVICE_STATUS_TOSERVER)
pars.Open lsSQL, paco, adOpenForwardOnly, adLockReadOnly

' Send Service Orders
Do While Not pars.EOF
  If Not pSendService(lcfoSync) Then
    pars.Close
    Exit Sub
  End If
  'pars.MoveNext
```

```
Loop

' Close Recordset
pars.Close

' Open Service Recordset for update
pars.Open "Service", paco, adOpenDynamic, adLockOptimistic,
adCmdTableDirect

' Get number of Service Orders to receive
liServiceCount = lcfoSync.GetServiceCount(psTechnicianID)

' Receive Service Orders
If liServiceCount > 0 Then
  For i = 1 To liServiceCount
    If Not pGetService(lcfoSync) Then
      pars.Close
      Exit Sub
    End If
  Next 'i
End If

' Close Recordset
pars.Close

' Remove objects
Set lcfoSync = Nothing
```

First, you can see how the CEfusion MTSAgent object is created, and by setting the **ObjectName** property on that object, you can tell it what object to go look for on the server. We then get all the service orders that are to be sent to the server (according to the **Status** field). We loop through these and call the **pSendService** function. We open the **Service** table again, but this time for updating.

Note how we have to supply the **Open** method on the Recordset object with a table and not a SQL statement to be able to update to the Recordset. We also provide a special option (**adCmdTableDirect**) to make it work. We then get the number of service orders to receive using the **GetServiceCount** method on the server object and loop that number of times and call the **pGetService** function (provided that we get a successful return value).

Note

You might be wondering why the **MoveNext** method on the Recordset is commented or used. In the **pSendService** function there is a **GetRows(1)** function call that does this automatically.

The code for the **pSendService** function looks like this:

```
' Send
If Not lcfoSync.SendService(pars.GetRows(1)) Then
  pLog "Error!", True
  Exit Function
End If

' Delete sent Service Orders
paco.Execute "DELETE FROM Service WHERE ServiceID='" +
pars("ServiceID").Value + "'"
```

Sending Recordsets as variant arrays is as simple here on the Pocket PC as we saw before that it was on the server. The parameter (1) to the **GetRows** method means that only the current row will be sent (and as noted before, this also moves the row point forward one step). This function also removes the transferred rows from the **Service** table. Now, we will look at the **pGetService** implementation:

```
Dim lvRows As Variant
Dim i As Integer

' Get
lvRows = lcfoSync.GetService(psTechnicianID)

' If OK, parse array and update Recordset
If Not IsEmpty(lvRows) Then
  pars.AddNew
  For i = 0 To UBound(lvRows)
    pars(i).Value = lvRows(i, 0)
  Next 'i
  pars.Update
End If
```

Here you can see the call to the server component (**GetService**) with the service technician identification as the parameter. And on return, we check that the call went well by checking that the returned value was not **Empty**. If everything was fine, we create a new row, update each column from the Variant array and update the new row.

And that concludes the walk-through of the different synchronization options implemented in the ACME Copier solution.

10.3   Scheduling

An interesting part of the scheduling section in Chapter 9 showed some features that you can do if you use the POOM (Pocket Outlook Object Model) in your eVB applications. The first thing that Anne did was to create an appointment from a selected service order (see Figure 10.2).

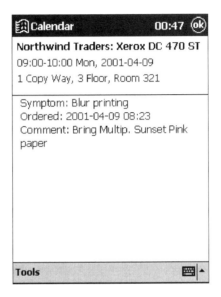

Figure 10.2
Appointment from
Service Order

This was done by the following code (behind the **Make Appointment** button on the **Service Order List** (frmMain.ebf) form):

```
Dim lpoa As PocketOutlook.Application
Dim lAppointment As PocketOutlook.AppointmentItem
Dim lsSQL As String
Dim lsComment As String
Dim lsLocation As String
Dim i As Integer
Dim loid As Long

If lvwItems.SelectedItem Is Nothing Then
  MsgBox "You have to make a selection in the list first!",
vbInformation, App.Title
  Exit Sub
End If

  ' Get Comment
lsSQL = "SELECT Comment FROM Service WHERE ServiceID='" & _
```

```
            Mid(lvwItems.SelectedItem.Key, 2) & "'"
pars.Open lsSQL, paco, adOpenForwardOnly, adLockReadOnly
lsComment = pars(0).Value
pars.Close

' Get Location (Customer.Address, Appliance.Placement)
lsSQL = "SELECT C.Address, A.Placement" & _
        " FROM Service S, Appliance A, Customer C" & _
        " WHERE S.ApplianceID=A.ApplianceID" & _
        " AND A.CustomerID=C.CustomerID" & _
        " AND S.ServiceID='" & Mid(lvwItems.SelectedItem.Key,
2) & "'"
pars.Open lsSQL, paco, adOpenForwardOnly, adLockReadOnly
lsLocation = pars(0).Value & ", " & pars(1).Value
pars.Close

' Create Pocket Outlook application object
Set lpoa = pw32.CreateObject("PocketOutlook.Application")

' Logon to Pocket Outlook
lpoa.Logon Me.hWnd

Set lAppointment = lpoa.CreateItem(olAppointmentItem)

' Set appointment properties (Subject = Customer: Appliance)
i = lvwItems.SelectedItem.Index
lAppointment.Subject = _
    lvwItems.ListItems(i).SubItems(1) & _
    ": " & lvwItems.ListItems(i).SubItems(2)
lAppointment.Body = _
    "Symptom: " & lvwItems.ListItems(i).SubItems(4) & vbCrLf & _
    "Ordered: " & lvwItems.ListItems(i).SubItems(5) & vbCrLf & _
    "Comment: " & lsComment
lAppointment.Location = lsLocation
'lAppointment.Start = Now
'lAppointment.End = Now

' Save appointment and get it again to display (have to do
this!)
lAppointment.Save
loid = lAppointment.oid
Set lAppointment = Nothing
Set lAppointment = lpoa.GetItemFromOid(loid)
lAppointment.Display

' Remove objects
Set lAppointment = Nothing
```

We need to have one item selected in the ListView to do this, so:

1 We first check that one item at least has been selected. Then we go and get the **Comment** column from the current service order (using the **Key** property of the currently selected list item).

2 We also want the location for the new appointment and we therefore get the **Address** column from the **Customer** table and the **Placement** column of the **Appliance** table.

3 Then we get down to business by creating a new **AppointmentItem** object and set the various properties on the new object (most directly from the ListView).

4 Finally we would like to display the new appointment to enable the service technician to set it to a suitable time for the appointment. You would suspect that this is what the **Display** method on the **AppointmentItem** object would do, and you are right. The problem is that you cannot call **Display** after you have made changes to the object. It has to be newly created or directly retrieved from the Pocket Outlook object store. We therefore have to save the new appointment first, save the object ID (property **oid**), get it back again using the object ID and now we can display it.

Another similar thing that was shown in Chapter 9 was the ability to send an e-mail directly from the **Service Order List** (frmMain.ebf) form. This is the code that hides behind the **Send E-Mail** button on that form:

```
Dim lsSQL As String
Dim lsEmail As String
Dim lsSubject As String
Dim i As Integer

If lvwItems.SelectedItem Is Nothing Then
  MsgBox "You have to make a selection in the list first!",
vbInformation, App.Title
  Exit Sub
End If

' Get Contact e-mail address
lsSQL = "SELECT C.Email FROM Service S, Contact C WHERE
S.ContactID=C.ContactID AND S.ServiceID='" &
Mid(lvwItems.SelectedItem.Key, 2) & "'"
pars.Open lsSQL, paco, adOpenForwardOnly, adLockReadOnly
lsEmail = pars(0).Value
pars.Close

' Subject = Symptom on Appliance)
```

```
i = lvwItems.SelectedItem.Index
lsSubject = lvwItems.ListItems(i).SubItems(4) & " on " &
lvwItems.ListItems(i).SubItems(2)

' Create new e-mail
Call Shell("iexplore.exe", "mailto:" & lsEmail & "?Subject=" &
lsSubject)
```

We start by doing the same list item check as before in the ListView control. Then we get the e-mail address for the customer contact that is registered on the service order. We also obtain the symptom and the appliance identification number from the ListView directly.

The real magic is on the last row. There we use a custom implementation of calling the **CreateProcess** Windows CE API with the application as the first parameter and the command line (parameters) as the second. We simply create a "mailto:" link with a "subject" parameter. If you want to check out the **Shell** implementation, you will find it in Chapter 5.

There is actually another example of POOM integration, and that is the ability to convert the customer contacts from the customer records into Pocket PC contacts. The code behind the **Create Contact in Contacts** button on the **Contact** (frmContact.ebf) is:

```
Dim lpoa As PocketOutlook.Application
Dim lContact As PocketOutlook.ContactItem
Dim lsSQL As String
Dim loid As Long

' Create Pocket Outlook application object
Set lpoa = pw32.CreateObject("PocketOutlook.Application")

' Logon to Pocket Outlook
lpoa.Logon Me.hWnd

' Create Contact item
Set lContact = lpoa.CreateItem(olContactItem)

' Set Contact properties
lContact.FirstName = txtFirstName.Text
lContact.LastName = txtLastName.Text
lContact.BusinessTelephoneNumber = txtPhone.Text
lContact.MobileTelephoneNumber = txtMobile.Text
lContact.BusinessFaxNumber = txtFax.Text
lContact.Email1Address = txtEmail.Text
lContact.Body = txtComment.Text

' Get Customer data
lsSQL = "SELECT Name, Address, City, StateProvince, ZipCode,
CountryRegion FROM Customer WHERE CustomerID='" & psCustomerID
```

```
        & "'"
pars.Open lsSQL, paco, adOpenForwardOnly, adLockReadOnly
lContact.CompanyName = pars("Name").Value
lContact.BusinessAddressStreet = pars("Address").Value
lContact.BusinessAddressCity = pars("City").Value
lContact.BusinessAddressState = pars("StateProvince").Value
lContact.BusinessAddressPostalCode = pars("ZipCode").Value
lContact.BusinessAddressCountry = pars("CountryRegion").Value
pars.Close

' Save appointment and get it again to display (have to do
this!)
lContact.Save
loid = lContact.oid
Set lContact = Nothing
Set lContact = lpoa.GetItemFromOid(loid)
lContact.Display

' Remove objects
Set lContact = Nothing
```

The approach is very similar to creating appointments (like we did above). We start by creating the **PocketOutlook.Application** object, logging on, and creating a new **ContactItem** object.

Then we set the properties of this new object and we get the values from the form controls. The reason for this is that you want to be sure that the current values are used to create the new contact. If the user has just changed the contact's e-mail address and then wants to create a new contact, she would like the current value in the control to be used and not any stored value.

The logic here is also that the user will not be able to escape the dialog box without saving the data. We have chosen the approach not to allow the user to cancel updates (called "autosave"), thus ensuring that the changed values will be preserved. If you want to provide a **Cancel** button, you should remove the **(OK)** button on the top right and replace it with a normal **OK** button next to the **Cancel** button. This will steal some screen space from your forms, which is the price your users will have to pay for the ability to undo their changes.

Completing a service assignment

We will start by showing how the application is launched. When Anne taps the Pocket Service application icon in the **Programs** folder, what happens? Well, the first thing that happens is that the shortcut in the **Programs** folder starts the Pocket Service eVC launcher application that in turn starts the intermediate file for the eVB application (**PSA.vb**). Once we are there, we have reached the code in the Pocket Service eVB project.

We have chosen a **Sub Main** as the starting point of the application. There are several reasons for this:

- We do not want any form to be responsible for overall logic like creating global objects (yes, we know what you are thinking – that global variables are generally not a good thing), opening the connection to the database (oh yes, here too – that you should not keep a connection to the database live during the lifetime of the application), and loading **Enums** due to the memory leak problem with **CreateObject**, etc. (see, that the main reason why).

- We want to be able to start up with different forms. If the database does not exist, we will be moved to the **Synchronization** form directly for a first full synchronization to be performed.

- No form has to be loaded before execution begins.

- We want to show a cool (but totally unnecessary, just for fun) splash screen!

This is the code for **Sub Main:**

```
Dim lreg As OSIUTIL.Registry
Dim lcfoSync As CFMTS.object
Dim lsEmail As String
Dim ls As String

' Show splash
frmSplash.Show
frmSplash.Refresh

' Create the database objects
Set paco = CreateObject("ADOCE.Connection.3.1")
Set pars = CreateObject("ADOCE.Recordset.3.1")

' Load enumerations on all objects (to be) used
LoadEnums

' Get e-mail address from User Information
Set lreg = pw32.CreateObject("OSIUtil.Registry")
lreg.OpenKey hKeyCurrentUser, "ControlPanel\Owner", False
On Error Resume Next
ls = lreg.GetValue("Owner")
If Err = 0 Then ' No value in registry
  lsEmail = Mid(ls, 284)
End If
On Error GoTo 0
lreg.CloseKey
```

```
' Get TechnicianID from Registry
lreg.OpenKey hKeyLocalMachine, "Software\ACMECopier", True
On Error Resume Next
ls = lreg.GetValue("TechnicianID")
If Err <> 0 Then ' No value in registry
  On Error GoTo 0
  ' Get e-mail address
  lsEmail = InputBox("Enter E-mail:", App.Title, lsEmail)

 If Len(lsEmail) > 0 Then
   ' Create the host object
   Set lcfoSync = pw32.CreateObject("CFMTS.Object")
   lcfoSync.ObjectName = "PPDE.Sync"

   ls = lcfoSync.GetIDforEmail(lsEmail)
   If Len(ls) > 0 Then
   lreg.SetValue "TechnicianID", ls
  Else
  ' Show message, remove splash and end application
   MsgBox "E-Mail not found!", vbInformation, App.Title
   frmSplash.FormClose
   App.End
  End If
  Set lcfoSync = Nothing
 Else
   ' Remove splash and end application
   frmSplash.FormClose
   App.End
 End If
End If
psTechnicianID = ls
lreg.CloseKey
Set lreg = Nothing

On Error Resume Next

' Open connection
paco.Open CONNECTION_STRING

' If it doesn't exist
If Err <> 0 Then
  Err.Clear
  On Error GoTo 0
  If vbYes = MsgBox("No database found!" & vbCr & _
```

```
                              "Create new database?", _
                              vbQuestion Or vbYesNo, App.Title) Then
         ' Close splash
         frmSplash.FormClose
         ' Open Sync form and create database
         Call frmSync.ShowForm(Nothing, True)
       Else
         ' Remove splash and end application
         frmSplash.FormClose
         App.End
       End If
     Else
         ' Show main from
         frmMain.Show
         ' Refresh splash
         frmSplash.Show
     End If
```

We start by showing the splash screen over the full screen and then we create the global objects for connecting to the database. Even though we do not believe in having global variables at all, we did this originally due to the memory leak problem in the **CreateObject** function. These objects are used in most forms throughout the application, so there are really some code lines to be saved here. We have already looked at the **LoadEnum** function (see previous section) and its purpose to take care of the **CreateObject** memory leak problem using the free **OSIUtil** component from Odyssey Software.

And here is the code to handle identification of the service technician. When the application runs the first time, the user will be asked to supply their e-mail address. The suggested e-mail address is retrieved from the **Owner Information** in the Pocket PC (set using **Start > Settings > Personal > Owner Information**). We use that to call the server object to get the ID of the technician. If the ID is not found, the application stops. If the ID was found, we store it in the registry (where it will be picked up from then on) and drop the objects for connecting to the server and for registry reading. Note that there must be a connection to the server the first time the user starts the application.

Next, we open the connection to the database, and we are also not very happy about keeping the connection open to the database during the application's lifetime. But we are winning some performance through not having to open the connection all the time. Also, in contrast with the server side, we do not have the scalability issues that we have there. It's not as important to release connections as soon as possible on a Pocket PC with one user.

If the database does not exist (we get an error message on opening it), we offer the user to create a new database. If she accepts, we move her directly to the **Synchronization** (frmSync.ebf) form. If she does not, the application ends.

Note that we pass the **Service Order List** form (frmMain.ebf) to the **Synchronization** form's **ShowForm** method. The reason is that when the **Synchronization** form closes, it will show the **Service Order List** form. If the database opens, the **Service Order List** form is loaded as the first form. The splash screen in refreshed to remain visible until the user taps it. This way, the complete work of loading the application will be done the millisecond the user taps the splash screen.

 Tip

> If you replace **frmSplash.Show** with **frmSplash.FormClose** the splash will be removed as soon as the **Service Order List** form is loaded. You should then also remove the text from the splash screen that asks the user to tap the screen to start the application.

Since we are at the **Service Order List**, we might as well check out some of its code. From Chapter 9 we saw that the ListView fills after making a selection in the ComboBox. Even though we could have loaded one of the choices from the beginning, we opted to leave this to the user to make the application respond as quickly as possible. The ComboBox include choices for different states of the service order that the service technician can use to keep order in her life. Because we want to make the application as data driven as possible, we load the ComboBox choices from the database. There is a look-up table called **ServiceStatus**. It contains the possible states that a service order can have. Here is how the ComboBox loads:

```
' Add ComboBox choices
cmbSelect.Clear
cmbSelect.AddItem "Make your selection:"
cmbSelect.AddItem "All"
lsSQL = "SELECT Description FROM ServiceStatus WHERE SortBy > 0
ORDER BY SortBy"
pars.Open lsSQL, paco, adOpenForwardOnly, adLockReadOnly
Do While Not pars.EOF
  cmbSelect.AddItem pars("Description")
  pars.MoveNext
Loop
pars.Close
cmbSelect.ListIndex = 0
```

The first choice is actually only a prompt and will not generate any result in the ListView and the second is hard-coded to return all service orders in the database. Then we fill in the list from the **ServiceStatus** table and note that we use the **SortBy** field for two purposes.

The first purpose is as a field to sort the options because we probably want the choices presented in a specific order (and not the order they were inserted into the database, such as alphabetically, etc.).

The other reason to use the **SortBy** field is as an indicator of current service order status. When a status is no longer available, we just give it a **SortBy** value less than zero and it will not show up in any ComboBoxes. The reason we do not want to remove it altogether is that old service orders might use these codes, and we do not want to break the referential integrity of the database.

The ComboBox selection code looks like this:

```
Select Case cmbSelect.ListIndex
  Case 0
    Exit Sub
  Case 1
    pFillListItems ""
  Case Else
    pFillListItems " AND SS.SortBy=" & CStr(cmbSelect.ListIndex
- 1)
End Select
```

And as you can see, we are adding a string to the **pFillListItems** function, so we need to see that function to understand what this means:

```
Private Sub pFillListItems(ByVal Selection As String)

' Load ListView for Items.
' IN: Selection, selection string (added to WHERE-clause)
' Known bugs:
' Version Date Who Comment
' 00.00.000 010205 CFO Created
'***************************************************************
  Dim litm As ListItem
  Dim lsSQL As String

  ' Show hourglass
  Screen.MousePointer = vbHourGlass

  ' Hide ListView to increase speed
  lvwItems.Visible = False
```

```
' Open Recordset
lsSQL = "SELECT S.ServiceID, S.ServicePrio, C.Name
CustomerName," & _
        " M.Description Appliance, SS.Description
ServiceStatus," & _
        " SM.Description Symptom, S.Ordered," & _
        " ME.Description Measure, S.JobStart, S.JobEnd," & _
        " S.JobMinutes FROM Service S, Customer C, Appliance
A," & _
        " Model M, ServiceStatus SS, Symptom SM, Measure ME"
& _
        " WHERE S.ApplianceID=A.ApplianceID" & _
        " AND A.CustomerID=C.CustomerID AND
A.ModelID=M.ModelID" & _
        " AND S.ServiceStatusID=SS.ServiceStatusID AND" & _
        " S.SymptomID=SM.SymptomID AND
S.MeasureID=ME.MeasureID" & _
        Selection
pars.Open lsSQL, paco, adOpenForwardOnly, adLockReadOnly

' Clear list and get item rows
lvwItems.ListItems.Clear
Do While Not pars.EOF
  Set litm = lvwItems.ListItems.Add(, "K" +
pars("ServiceID"), pars("ServicePrio").Value)
    litm.SubItems(1) = pars("CustomerName").Value
    litm.SubItems(2) = pars("Appliance").Value
    litm.SubItems(3) = pars("ServiceStatus").Value
    litm.SubItems(4) = pars("Symptom").Value
    litm.SubItems(5) =
FormatDateTimeNoSec(pars("Ordered").Value)
    litm.SubItems(6) = pars("Measure").Value
    litm.SubItems(7) =
FormatDateTimeNoSec(pars("JobStart").Value)
    litm.SubItems(8) =
FormatDateTimeNoSec(pars("JobEnd").Value)
    litm.SubItems(9) = NullStr(pars("JobMinutes").Value)
  pars.MoveNext
Loop

' Close recordset
pars.Close
```

```
' Show ListView
lvwItems.Visible = True

' Remove cursor
Screen.MousePointer = vbArrow

End Sub
```

Oh, yes, this is really something that you will do a lot. You will go and get things in the database and fill ListView controls. Have no doubts about that! You have done it before on the PC, and now it is time to do it again. You can see that we simply add the parameter (**Selection**) from the ComboBox selection code to the SQL query statement. And the selection now makes more sense.

We can now see that the **SS.SortBy** is the **SortBy** field from the **ServiceStatus** table. This means that we will only get service orders for the selected status code (if one was selected). We then fill the ListView with the Recordset columns. Note that we have to prefix the ListView Key with a **K** because it does not accept anything else but a letter as the first character. We want to put the **ServiceID**, which is a GUID and has the form {**00000000-0000-0000-0000-000000000000**} where the zeros are filled in with hexadecimal values.

GUIDs as primary keys

We use GUIDs as primary keys in all tables. There are four main reasons for this:

Reason 1: On most tables we need to have something that is truly unique. Traditionally we might have used a long integer value and incremented it for each new row. There are a number of problems with that. You have to know how to get the next number (e.g., by using the SQL MAX() function), you have problems with filling gaps that arise from removed rows, or there might be someone else who is adding rows at the same time, etc. In the Pocket Service application we have a great example. On the service order, the service technician can add article rows to the service order. Those rows will later be synchronized to the company server and merged with other service order article rows. To avoid conflict with long integer identity columns, you really have to come up with a smart solution. This way, we are able to create unique records off-line that will stay unique when synchronized – that is very powerful!

Reason 2: We know that we always have one field that is the primary key to a table. All of you who have made referential integrity between tables with multiple field keys know what we are talking about. It is not very easy and adds unnecessary complications to the database.

Reason 3: We get unique keys that are never visible. Even if we have other fields that make a row unique, there is a valid point in hiding the relevant key from the user, since this will never change. Sometimes we assume things to be unique, when over time, they end up not being unique.

Reason 4: When we want to set up database synchronization (like merge replication), the database will add GUIDs to all rows if they do not already exist. This means that you will have two different unique keys assigned to your rows when you only need one.

No default properties

You can also see that we are always using the properties on all objects, constantly avoiding default properties. The reason is that in the upcoming development tools (VS.NET) you will have to provide them anyway. You might as well start now to prevent having to go through your code later. There are a number of things that you can do to prepare your code for VS.NET, and we recommend you to follow the excellent articles on MSDN on the subject.

SQL revival

A consequence of the fact that we do not have any business services tier (with components) is that we need to brush up some of those SQL techniques that we once knew. In the code above, you can see an example of a SQL query that joins a number of tables. The format presented above is not very easily readable, so let us format it a bit to make it readable:

```
SELECT  S.ServiceID, S.ServicePrio, C.Name CustomerName,
        M.Description Appliance, SS.Description ServiceStatus,
        SM.Description Symptom, S.Ordered,
        ME.Description Measure, S.JobStart, S.JobEnd,
        S.JobMinutes
FROM    Service S, Customer C, Appliance A,
        Model M, ServiceStatus SS, Symptom SM, Measure ME
WHERE   S.ApplianceID=A.ApplianceID AND
        A.CustomerID=C.CustomerID AND
        A.ModelID=M.ModelID AND
        S.ServiceStatusID=SS.ServiceStatusID AND
        S.SymptomID=SM.SymptomID AND
        S.MeasureID=ME.MeasureID
```

You can now see that there was not so much to it. We are joining a number of tables the simplest possible way to get a lot of information about the service order on the first form of the application. Note that the syntax is very similar to what you can do on SQL Server 2000 at the server. You can rename displayed columns by just adding a new name after the field name (with or without the **AS** keyword). The same is true for the naming of tables (with or without the **AS** here too).

Actually most of the syntax works and there are just some minor differences. For example, you cannot use the old, shorthand format for outer joins (using the *= and =* construct in WHERE clauses). Another is that you cannot use sub queries as a table source. You just have to try the statement in the SQL Server CE Query Analyzer (ISQL) on the Pocket PC to be sure that it works.

Anatomy of a data-aware form

The first form is not really representative of the normal structure of a data-aware form, so let us take a look at the **Options** form (frmOptions.ebf) (see Figure 10.3).

Figure 10.3 Options form

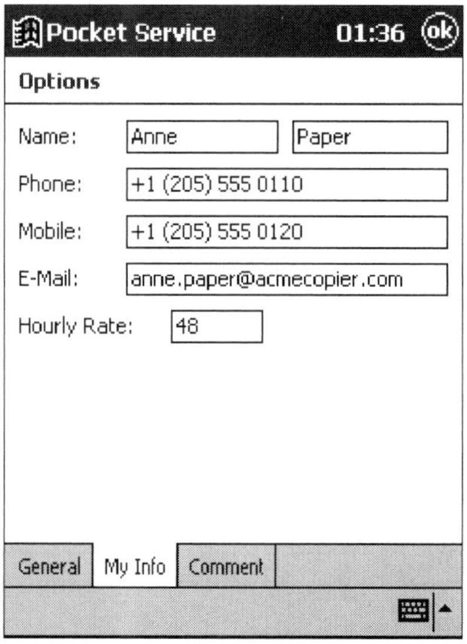

The form is probably very common in most applications and in Pocket Service it is mainly used for updating the service technician's own information. Let us see how the code in the form is structured by listing the methods in order:

- **ShowForm**: This is the only function called from outside the form and it is used to initialize the form (controls, etc.).
- **Form_Load**: Initializes things that are only initialized once as this function is always run only once in an application, since there is no way to unload forms.
- **pLoadControls** Initializes things that have to be initialized each time the form is shown.
- **TabStrip_Click**: An example of control events that are handled in the middle of the form code.
- **Form_OKClick**: Activated when the user taps the **(OK)** button in the title bar and handles the closing (validating, saving, etc.) of the form.
- **PValidateControls**: Validates that the control data is ready to be saved.
- **PSaveControls**: Saves the control values to the data store.
- **PResetControls**: Cleans things up for hiding the form, like emptying listviews and other controls containing large amounts of data.

If we start off with the **ShowForm** method, it looks like this:

```
Private pfrmParent As Form
Public Sub ShowForm(ByVal ParentForm As Form)

    ' Initialize form
    Screen.MousePointer = vbHourGlass
    Set pfrmParent = ParentForm
    Me.Visible = False
    pLoadControls
    Me.Visible = True
    Me.Show
    pfrmParent.Hide
    Screen.MousePointer = vbArrow

End Sub
```

We have included the declaration of the **pfrmParent** variable on the form level since it is used in this method to store the passed form from the parent. The parent would use this line to call this form:

```
Call frmOptions.ShowForm(Me)
```

The first thing that happens in the **ShowForm** method is that we turn on the hourglass cursor to let the user know that something is happening. If the loading of the form is very quick, the user will not be able to see the cursor anyway. We then save the passed form parameter in our form variable (we will use it when closing the form). We then make this form invisible to stop the screen from showing strange images while the form is loading and we call the **pLoadControls** function to do the job.

We can then make the form visible again and show it (we run the code in **Form_Load**) after which we hide the calling form. The reason for hiding the parent form (even if it will be in the background anyway) is that we want the application to show up in the **Running Program List** only once. We finally turn the cursor off and then we are done. The user can now see the new form.

Note

You can reach the Running Program List by tapping **Start** > **Settings** > **System** > **Memory** > **Running Programs**.

In this particular form, there is no code in the **Show_Form** event because there is nothing to initialize that can only be done once. Examples of things that are done in this method are the creation of ListView column headers, loading of images from the file system, etc. We therefore move on to the code in the **pLoadControls** method:

```
Dim lsSQL As String
Dim i As Integer

' Open Technician Recordset
lsSQL = "SELECT * FROM Technician WHERE TechnicianID='" +
psTechnicianID + "'"
pars.Open lsSQL, paco, adOpenForwardOnly, adLockReadOnly

' Load misc controls
txtFirstName.Text = pars("FirstName").Value
txtLastName.Text = pars("LastName").Value
txtPhone.Text = pars("Phone").Value
txtMobile.Text = pars("Mobile").Value
txtEmail.Text = pars("Email").Value
txtHourlyRate.Text = pars("HourlyRate").Value
txtComment.Text = Space2Empty(pars("Comment").Value)

' Close Recordset
pars.Close
```

This code is very typical of what you will find in this method. It opens a Recordset with data that is passed to each of the controls in the form. The use of the global variable with the ID of the technician may not be so common, because the SQL query will normally contain a parameter passed to the form with the ID to be shown. In the code for loading the comments TextBox, you can see a special function that is needed to load data of the type **NTEXT** from the database (Space2Empty). We cannot assign empty strings to fields of this type, so we have to add a space each time we save and remove that space (if it is there) when we load the value back into the control again. You will see later that when saving the comment we need a similar function for handling the conversion from TextBox to database field (Empty2Space).

Now that we have finished loading data, it is important that we close the Recordset again. This is important because we use the same global variable to load all Recordsets, and if we later try to call the **Open** method on the Recordset without first having called **Close**, we will get a runtime error. We move on to the code in the **Form_OKClick** method:

```
' Check for save
If pValidateControls Then
  ' Save, clean up and leave
  pSaveControls
  pfrmParent.Show
  pResetControls
  Me.Hide
End If
```

As we mentioned before, this code is called when the users taps the (OK) button on the right in the title bar. This method handles closing the form. It starts with checking that the controls are valid to save to the database. If so, it saves the control data to the database and shows the form that called this form (remember that we saved the passed form in a form-level variable). It resets the controls that contain large amounts of data and finally hides this form. If the controls were not valid, we simply return without either saving or closing the form. If we look at the **pValidateControls** method, it looks like this:

```
Dim ls As String

' Check controls
If Len(txtFirstName.Text) > 20 Then ls = ls + "First name too
long (max 20 char)!" + vbCrLf
If Len(txtLastName.Text) > 20 Then ls = ls + "Last name too
long (max 20 char)!" + vbCrLf
If Len(txtPhone.Text) > 20 Then ls = ls + "Phone too long (max
20 char)!" + vbCrLf
If Len(txtMobile.Text) > 20 Then ls = ls + "Mobile too long
(max 20 char)!" + vbCrLf
If Len(txtEmail.Text) > 50 Then ls = ls + "E-Mail too long (max
50 char)!" + vbCrLf
If Not IsNumeric(txtHourlyRate.Text) Then ls = ls + "Hourly
```

```
rate invalid!" + vbCrLf
'If Len(txtComment.Text)...

If Len(ls) > 0 Then
  MsgBox "Error in validation:" + vbCrLf + ls, vbInformation,
App.Title
  pValidateControls = False
Else
  pValidateControls = True
End If
```

Here we check the validity of all the control data and if we find any errors, we build an error string with suggestions to the user on how to fix the problems. We return an indication of the validation success to instruct **Form_OKClick** to continue with the save, or abort the saving and close the form. We move on to the **pSaveControls** method:

```
' Open Technician Recordset for update
pars.Open "Technician", paco, adOpenDynamic, adLockOptimistic,
adCmdTableDirect
pars.Find "TechnicianID='" + psTechnicianID + "'"
If pars.EOF Then
  MsgBox "Couldn't find Technician! (this shouldn't happen)",
vbInformation, App.Title
  pars.Close
  Exit Sub
End If

' Save controls
pars("FirstName").Value = txtFirstName.Text
pars("LastName").Value = txtLastName.Text
pars("Phone").Value = txtPhone.Text
pars("Mobile").Value = txtMobile.Text
pars("Email").Value = txtEmail.Text
pars("HourlyRate").Value = txtHourlyRate.Text
pars("Comment").Value = Empty2Space(txtComment.Text)
pars("LastUpdate").Value = Now
pars.Update
pars.Close
```

Note that we open the Recordset with a table as the argument and not as a SQL query statement. The reason for this is that ADOCE (version 3.1) does not support updates on Recordsets created from SQL statements. You also have to add an option at the end (**adCmdTableDirect**) to make it work.

Since you cannot add a WHERE clause to the Recordset, you use the **Find** method on the Recordset to filter the rows that you want. After the **Find** method is called, the Recordset will only include the rows that meet the search criteria and therefore we can check the **EOF** property for success in finding the wanted row. If all works fine, we go on to save all the control data to the Recordset fields. We finish off by updating the Recordset to the database and remember to always close the Recordset again. Finally, we will have a look at the single line of code in the **pResetControls** method:

```
txtComment.Text = ""
```

It empties the TextBox control containing the comment on the service technician. As this could be a large amount of text, we clear it here to save some memory while the form is hidden.

Some code highlights

In this section we will just browse through some interesting details of the sample code because we think that they deserve mentioning. The first issue involves the **About** form. You will probably provide one with your application, and it is really here where you will market yourself as an excellent application developer. To simplify the implementation of the About form and also to ease maintenance and reusability of the form, we suggest that you use the properties on the eVB project to display in the About form. You can do this with code similar to:

```
' Set labels
lblProductName.Caption = App.ProductName
lblLegalCopyrightCompanyName.Caption = App.LegalCopyright & " "
& App.CompanyName
lblComments.Caption = App.Comments
lblAuthor.Caption = App.FileDescription
```

And when you need to update the information about your application, you can simply edit the project properties (in the eVB IDE you click **Project > Project1 Properties > Make** and look under **Version Information** where all this information is available for updates.

You might recall that we discussed that forms cannot be unloaded during an application's execution. That means that the **Form_Load** event will be called only once during your application's lifetime. Therefore, you will include only things that are supposed to run once in the **Form_Load** event.

Let us take a common, but tricky, scenario. When we want to load a ListView in a form, we usually start by setting the column headings in the opening of the form. You might think that this will only happen once, and therefore you add this code to the **Form_Load** event. You are partly right. Usually when we add column headers to ListView controls, we also set the column width because it's usually done that way.

But as the user can change the column width (but not the names of the headers), so we want to restore that width each time the form shows (and not only the first time it is loaded). What we have to do is to separate the code for setting column header names, and code for setting column widths. In **Form_Load** we do:

```
' Clear and add ListView headings
lvwItems.ColumnHeaders.Clear
lvwItems.ColumnHeaders.Add , , "First"
lvwItems.ColumnHeaders.Add , , "Second"
lvwItems.ColumnHeaders.Add , , "Third", , lvwColumnRight
```

... and in the **pLoadControls** function (that is run each time the form is activated):

```
' Set not sorted and ListView headings width
lvwItems.Sorted = False
lvwItems.ColumnHeaders(1).Width = 300
lvwItems.ColumnHeaders(2).Width = 1500
lvwItems.ColumnHeaders(3).Width = 700
```

We hope that this example will help you to think twice about where to place your initialization code.

When you have a form that includes sub items of some sort, like the Customer form with Contacts in Pocket Service, you will want to have a structured way of adding, editing, and removing sub items. The implementation of the buttons in the Customer form looks like this:

```
Private Sub cmdNewContact_Click()

    ' Open Contact form
    Call frmContact.ShowForm(Me, "", psCustomerID)

End Sub
Private Sub cmdEditContact_Click()

    ' Check if any selected
    If Not (lvwContacts.SelectedItem Is Nothing) Then
      ' Show Contact Form
      Call frmContact.ShowForm(Me,
Mid(lvwContacts.SelectedItem.Key, 2), psCustomerID)
    Else
      MsgBox "You have to make a selection in the list first!",
```

```
vbInformation, App.Title
  End If

End Sub
Private Sub cmdDelContact_Click()

  ' Check if any selected
  If Not (lvwContacts.SelectedItem Is Nothing) Then
    If vbYes = MsgBox("Delete Contact '" +
lvwContacts.ListItems(lvwContacts.SelectedItem.Index).SubItems(
1) + "'?", vbQuestion Or vbYesNo Or vbDefaultButton2) Then
        ' Remove Contact
        pars.Open "Contact", paco, adOpenDynamic,
adLockOptimistic, adCmdTableDirect
        pars.Find "ContactID='" +
Mid(lvwContacts.SelectedItem.Key, 2) + "'"
        If Not pars.EOF Then
        pars.Delete
      Else
        MsgBox "Couldn't find Contact! (this shouldn't happen)",
vbInformation, App.Title
      End If
      pars.Close
      'lvwContacts.ListItems.Remove
lvwContacts.SelectedItem.Index
      ' Fill Contact list
      pFillListContacts
    End If
  Else
    MsgBox "You have to make a selection in the list first!",
vbInformation, App.Title
  End If

End Sub
Public Sub UpdateContactList()

' Update Contact list (used from Contact form).
' Known bugs:
' Version Date Who Comment
' 00.00.000 010205 CFO Created
'*************************************************************
****************

 ' Fill Contact list
 pFillListContacts

End Sub
```

Above, you can see that we are passing the **ContactID** (a GUID) to the Contact form as the second parameter (the first is always the parent form) and if that parameter is empty, we know that this is a new contact. We therefore need to know the **CustomerID** (also a GUID) to add the new contact to (foreign key in the **Contact** table).

When we edit and remove contacts, we use the **ContactID** inserted as the **Key** on each item in the ListView with contacts. And this is another great advantage of using GUIDs before primary keys consisting of multiple table fields. Finally you see that we have a public function that can be called from the Contacts form to update the list if any changes (additions) have been made. In the Contacts form we can also use the passed parameter (ContactID) to determine what title we should set on the Contact form (**Add Contact** or **Edit Contact**).

How about error handling?

There are probably loads of things that we have not shown in this sample walk-through, but let us just mention some of the things that we have thought about and left out on purpose.

The most important thing that we left out is error-handling code. There are many ways that you can do this, and it is not very different from how you would do it on the PC (with VB 6.0). As many programmers have developed their own approach to error handling, we have decided not to suggest any particular method. We have included it where it was necessary to make the application run (like trapping errors on opening the database, or when reading the registry, etc.).

But do not think that we consider error handling to be unimportant. If your application does not handle all the errors that happen, however excellent a programmer you may be, your users will lose the use of a terrific application. And unhappy users are not good references.

One recommendation: When you choose your error handling approach, aim mostly for using the **On Error Resume Next** construct. One reason is that it's the only way you can do it in eVB and another reason is that your code will be easier to adapt to the new constructs for error handling that you will see in the next generation of development tools from Microsoft (VS.NET). The main approach then will be the **Try...Catch...Final** construct that is somewhat similar to the On Error Resume Next currently available in eVB.

How about printing?

In the ACME Copier sample we want to show that we are moving towards a more paperless process in enterprise applications. However, we know that many real-life scenarios demand that you still need to have various things printed out on paper. There could be many reasons for this; legal mandates might be the most common. Even if we have not shown any printing code in the Pocket Service sample, it can easily be added using a third-party tool from FieldSoftware called PrinterCE (**www.fieldsoftware.com/PrinterCE.htm**). Using this tool, printing from eVB applications is pretty straightforward. To print simple text, you would:

```
Dim PrinterCE1
Set PrinterCE1 = CreateObject("PrEngineCE.PrinterCE")

PrinterCE1.SelectPrinter
PrinterCE1.DrawText "Hello World"
PrinterCE1.EndDoc
```

Depending on which version you choose, you would even be able to print bar codes, pictures, and so forth. You are even able to print in color. The main issue when it comes to printing is that you have to decide on the way to connect your Pocket PC to the printer. The two most common options are to use infrared or a serial connection.

On FieldSoftware's web site you will find the various printers that they support – and there are quite a number to choose from. There is even a trial version available to get you started at once.

How about multiple language support?

We have not made any special efforts in supporting multiple languages in our Pocket Service sample. You could add this support. There are two main options available to do so:

- Resource files for each language
- Source code translation tool

And the first option is probably the most commonly used method. It means that you will create a resource file for each language. The problem with this approach is that you have to set all your control values (captions, and that sort of thing) from code. The main side effect of this approach is that your application will be slower since setting properties (even form captions and the like) consumes important performance that you need on a Pocket PC.

The second option really means that you run your completed source code through an extractor that finds all the language specific texts in your code (control properties included) and puts them into a database. Then you will use a translation tool to update the text replacements for different languages. Finally, run a generator that takes your original source code and the translation database as input and creates new source code for each language.

In this manner you will have multiple versions of your source code (one for each language) that you have to build separately. But you will not have to update each version of the source code over time. If you add new code to your original project, you will simply run the extractor again, complement with the new translations, and do a new generation. One such tool is Whippleware's VB Language Manager found at: **www.whippleware.com/vblm.htm**

Want to see more?

We are convinced there are other things that you will find useful and interesting in the Pocket Service code, but we will not go through any more of them here. Instead, we recommend that you look through the complete code in the **\ACME Sample\Client\PSA** folder on the accompanying CD.

10.4   Article Catalog

To conclude the walk-through of the scenarios that you saw in Chapter 9, we will now look at the implementation of the Article Catalog (see Figure 10.4).

Figure 10.4   Article catalog

The Article Catalog is built using a multi-channel strategy and therefore is ready to be used from several devices. The difference with the previous samples (like the Service Order creation) is that this solution is based on data in XML format from the business logic (component) tier transformed using stylesheets (XSL) for different clients. If we start on the server side, we implement the **GetAllXML** method like this:

```
Dim laco As Connection
Dim lars As Recordset
Dim last As Stream

' Create objects
Set laco = CreateObject("ADODB.Connection")
Set lars = CreateObject("ADODB.Recordset")
Set last = CreateObject("ADODB.Stream")

' Open Connection
laco.CursorLocation = adUseClient
laco.ConnectionString = CONNECTION_STRING
laco.Open

' Open Recordset
lars.CursorType = adOpenKeyset
lars.LockType = adLockReadOnly
Set lars.ActiveConnection = laco
lars.Open "SELECT * FROM Article"

' Return XML (from Recordset via Stream)
lars.Save last, adPersistXML
GetAllXML = last.ReadText
```

And we are using the ADO Stream object to get the XML data directly from the Recordset and pass it back to the client. The client in this case is an ASP page that looks like this:

```
<%
Option Explicit
Response.Expires = 0

' Page variables
Dim poCatalog
Dim pXML
Dim pXSL
%>
<!DOCTYPE HTML PUBLIC "-//IETF//DTD HTML//EN">
<HTML><HEAD><TITLE>ACME Copier</TITLE>
<LINK REL="stylesheet" HREF="../css/acme.css" TYPE="text/css">
</HEAD><BODY><FONT FACE="Tahoma">

<!--#INCLUDE FILE="../include/top.asp"-->
<H1>Aricle Catalog</H1>
<% If Not IsMME Then %><P><B>
  Following is the <% End If %>Article list:
</B></P>
```

```
<%
  ' Create Catalog object
  Set poCatalog = Server.CreateObject("PPDE.Catalog")

  ' Create XML and XSL objects
  Set pXML = Server.CreateObject("MSXML2.DOMDocument")
  Set pXSL = Server.CreateObject("MSXML2.DOMDocument")

  ' Turn off async mode
  pXML.Async = False
  pXSL.Async = False

  ' Get XML from Catalog object
  pXML.loadXML poCatalog.GetAllXML()

  ' Multi-channel switch
  If IsPocketPC Then
    pXSL.Load Server.MapPath("pocketpc.xsl")
  ElseIf IsMME Then
    pXSL.Load Server.MapPath("mme.xsl")
  Else
    pXSL.Load Server.MapPath("standard.xsl")
  End If

  ' Send back transformed HTML
  Response.Write pXML.transformNode(pXSL)
%>

<!--#INCLUDE FILE="../include/bottom.asp"-->

</FONT></BODY>
</HTML>
```

Even if some of the irrelevant parts of the page are removed, you can see that the basic structure of the page is very similar to what we saw in the beginning of this chapter. However, the last part of this page is very different. We start by creating the Catalog business object (where the **GetAllXML** method is implemented) and also the two XML DOM objects – one for the XML and the other for the XSL. To do what we want to do, we have to turn off the default asynchronous mode of the XML DOM objects.

The most interesting part is where we select the different XSL files, depending on the current client. We use the variables that we talked about in the first part of this chapter and then we load the XSL from disk. The last and most powerful thing we do is to transform the XML using the XSL with the **transformNode** function.

10.5   New purchase order

The implementation of the purchase order functionality is very similar to what we saw in the New Service Order section in the beginning of this chapter, and therefore we will not go through this part in detail. The functionality was primarily provided to make the ACME Copier sample complete. In a real-world scenario, you would probably use a standard product like Microsoft Commerce Server 2000 to implement ordering scenarios.

More information

The most important tip is to urge you to take the time to go through the samples provided on the CD. There are a lot of details on it that we have not described here that you will find useful in your forthcoming projects.

10.6   Conclusion

In Chapter 11, we will talk about something we all fear and love: distributing applications. Our discussion will take on this challenge step by step, to complement the system we've explained thus far.

Distributing applications

In this chapter we will look at ways that you can make your excellent applications available to your mobile users. We will start by looking at how you package your application into an installation package that can be distributed as a PC installer and also for web distribution. We will look at how you can add a nice-looking icon to your eVB application, since it is not possible to add one natively (only using eVB). We will show you how to update the installation information (extension .inf) file with things that the application install wizard will not perform automatically.

11.1 Creating an installation

When you have finished building your application, you will want to create an installation that can be deployed on your user's devices. In eVT you are equipped with something similar to the VB 6.0 Package and Deployment Wizard called Application Install Wizard. The steps to create an installation package for an eVB application are:

- Make (compile) an intermediate file.
- Run Application Install Wizard to create installation files.
- (Optional) Include additional controls and libraries in your installation.
- (Optional) Create an eVC launcher application to associate your application with an icon.

● (Optional) Include the eVC launch application in your setup files.

● (Optional) Create a standard Help file for your application.

● (Optional) Create an e-book for your application.

● Package setup files into single self-extracting, auto-executable archive.

● (Optional) Set up your application for web distribution.

The different steps are covered in the following sections.

Make the intermediate file

When you have implemented and tested your application, you create the intermediate file (with extension **.vb**) by selecting the menu option **File > Make Project1.vb**. You then select the destination folder for the intermediate file. That's all there is to it.

Note that the intermediate file that is created when you run your program is identical to the file created with the **Make** menu option. You could therefore copy the file from your device (real or emulator) to a suitable folder to build your installation package there.

Run Application Install Wizard

You start the Application Install Wizard from the eVB IDE by selecting the menu option **Tools > Remote Tools > Application Install Wizard**. First, you will select the project file (**Project1.ebp**) and then the intermediate file (**Project1.vb**). Then you will choose where to put the output files from the installation. This is the folder where all installation files will be placed, and probably a dedicated subfolder to your normal development folder.

Then select which platforms that your application should support. It is best to always create installations for all possible platforms; so the norm is to check all processor types. Next you will have to add the controls used by your applications. Usually the Application Install Wizard will find the appropriate controls itself, so you will just go on to selecting if you have any additional data files. Usually this includes the image files that you need to have in the installation folder. Lastly, you will choose the installation folder, name of the application, and the description as it will appear during installation and your company name. Then start the creation of the installation files.

After the wizard is finished, you will have the structure shown in Figure 11.1 generated beneath the folder you choose for your installation output files.

Figure 11.1   Setup
folder structure

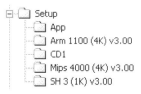

In the **CD1** folder is all that you need to install the application. The **.vb** file is placed in the **App** folder and then there is one folder for each processor type that you selected in the wizard. In each folder, you find the files that are processor-specific, which means that the files contain compiled code.

Including additional controls and libraries (DLLs) in your installation

Including the S309PictureBox

When you are about to deploy your applications that use the S309-PictureBox control, and if you are using the eVB Application Installation Wizard, the S309PictureBox control will not be added to the setup. You will have to add this control yourself by updating the **.inf** file and rebuilding the installation cabinet (extension .cab) files.

In short, the updates to the **.inf** file are:

- Add S309PictureBox.ocx to the CESelfRegister key in the [Default-Install...] section for each processor type.
- Add a "S309PictureBox.ocx=3" key to the [SourceDisksFiles...] section for each processor type.
- Add a "S309PictureBox.ocx,,0x80000000" key to the [Files...] section for each processor type.

And then you will copy the S309PictureBox.ocx for each processor type to the corresponding setup folder. Finally, rebuild the cabinet files with the command line supplied in the Readme.txt file created by the Application Installation Wizard and replace the old files in the CD1 subfolder.

Distributing applications based on SQL Server CE

The Help file that accompanies SQL Server CE has a short called *Redistributing SQL Server CE*. This chapter explains which components you need to include with your application to redistribute SQL Server CE:

- Ssce10.dll
- Msdadc.dll
- Msdaer.dll
- Msdaeren.dll
- Adoce31.dll
- Adoceoledb31.dll
- Adoxce31.dll

The following can be read in the same Help file regarding the rights to redistribute applications based on SQL Server:

> *SQL Server CE is licensed as part of SQL Server 2000 Developer Edition. Unlimited deployment of SQL Server 2000 Windows CE Edition to devices is covered by the SQL Server 2000 Developer Edition license, provided that these devices operate in a stand-alone mode – not connecting to or using the resources of any SQL Server not present on the device.*
>
> *Otherwise, when devices running SQL Server CE connect to or utilize the resources of a SQL Server not on the device:*
>
> *The SQL Server being connected to or utilized must be licensed in a per-processor fashion.*
>
> *Note: This applies to SQL Server 2000.*
>
> or
>
> *The device must have a SQL Server Client Access License (CAL).*
>
> *Note: Because per-processor licensing is not available for versions of SQL Server prior to SQL Server 2000, devices connecting to or utilizing the resources of SQL Server version 6.5 and SQL Server version 7.0 databases require CALs.*

11.2   Create eVC launch (icon) application

If you are not satisfied with the standard icon for your application, here is a way that you can create a small eVC application that has the singular purpose of containing an icon and also to launch your eVB application.

Launch eVC and choose menu option **File > New** and select **WCE Pocket PC Application**. Give the project the same name as your eVB application (as usual we will use the **Project1** example). In the application wizard select the option **Simple Windows CE Application**.

Now the wizard has created almost all we need except the launcher code. All you need to add is the code for calling the **ShellExecuteEx** Windows CE API in the **WinMain** function (unfold the class tree on the left). This is the code you should add:

```
SHELLEXECUTEINFO sei;
TCHAR tFile[255];

  if (lpCmdLine[0]==0) wsprintf(tFile,TEXT("\\Project1.vb"));
           // Hard-coded full path to .vb file (not
recommended!)
       else
          wsprintf(tFile,lpCmdLine);
             // Command Line parameter is better
      ZeroMemory(&sei, sizeof(sei));
      sei.cbSize = sizeof(sei);
      sei.lpFile = tFile;
      return ShellExecuteEx(&sei);
```

Because the eVB application (**Project1.vb**) is associated with the **pvbload.exe**, the **ShellExecuteEx** will load the pvbload.exe file with the **Project1.vb** as a parameter (just as if we were tapping the **Project1.vb** file from the Start menu or Programs folder).

Next, you will add an icon. You probably need an icon with both resolutions 16×16 as well as 32×32 pixels. You can import an existing icon by selecting menu option **Insert > Resource** and select **Import**, or you can simply create a new one by selecting **New** in the same dialog. You do not need to name the icon – the Pocket PC will find it anyway.

Now, all you have to do is compile the application for the target platforms (select them one-by-one in the **Active Configuration** ComboBox in the WCE Configuration Toolbar. Use the **Release** suffix for each processor type) and select menu option **Build > Build Project1.exe**. The compiled executable files will be located in subfolders named after the respective processor and build type (release or debug). The next thing to do is to copy the launch application that you have built to the device (real or emulator). Then try it to see how it works. Looks much better with a custom icon, doesn't it?

11.3   Include eVC launch application in setup files

If you have choosen to create an eVC launch application, it's time to update the installation files to include these files. This is a trickier business than you might expect. What we will show you here works without any other third-party tools. However, there are a number of great installation builder packages that will solve this problem for you. For the brave – let's just do it!

First of all, you need to copy each version of the compiled eVC launch applications, **Project1.exe** (for ARM, MIPs, and SH3), to the appropriate sub-folder for each processor. All resulting in the following paths/files created:

```
\Arm 1100 (4K) v3.00\Project1.exe
\SH 3 (1K) v3.00\Project1.exe
\Mips 4000 (4K) v3.00\Project1.exe
```

Now, you must update the **.inf** file located in the folder that you previously chose to put the installation output files. The file is named as your application (**Project1.inf**). Open this file in Notepad. In the **.inf** file, edit the following:
Change:

```
[Shortcuts]
%AppName%,0,"Project1.vb"
```

To:

```
[Shortcuts]
%AppName%,0,"Project1.exe"
```

The shortcut will thereby point to the eVC launch application instead of the **.vb** file. As we saw earlier, the eVC launch application will in turn launch the eVB application. But the effect will be that the shortcut will get the icon from the eVC launch application instead of the standard eVB icon.

You then have to add the launch application to the [SourceDiskFiles…] section for each processor, like this:

```
[SourceDisksFiles.Arm 1100 (4K) v3.00]
Project1.exe=3

[SourceDisksFiles.SH 3 (1K) v3.00]
Project1.exe=3

[SourceDisksFiles.Mips 4000 (4K) v3.00]
Project1.exe=3
```

This is where the installation program will look for the file. For this reason you will place each version of the eVC application (for each processor) in the same folder as the other files generated by the Application Install Wizard.

Finally, you add the .exe reference to the [Files.App] section like this:

```
[Files.App]
PSA.exe
```

This section tells the installation program which files to put in the chosen installation folder – regardless of what processor section they are defined in.

The Readme.txt file in the folder where the .inf file is located contains a command line that can be used to rebuild the cab files (using the **cabwiz.exe** utility). Copy and paste it to the Start, Run Dialog or execute at a DOS prompt. Copy the .cab files generated to the CD1 folder. This should complete the process.

11.4   Creating Help files

One very important part of your complete application is to assist your users with helpful hints and information. Usually we do this by providing a Help file. We will guide you through the most important steps of creating a Help file for your Pocket PC application.

The Pocket PC Help

If you are in the Today screen and tap Start and Help, you will open Help on your Pocket PC. What actually happens is that the Help system browses through the \Windows\Help folder that contains shortcuts and dynamically creates the menu that you are presented with. The list links to Help files installed on your system. The linked shortcuts point at HTML files in the \Windows folder and that is the place where you should add your own file. To be in the list you should:

1 First create the HTML file, place it in the \Windows folder.

2 Then make a shortcut to that file and place the shortcut in the \Windows\Help folder. The shortcut can easily be created manually or by adding a shortcut to the [**Shortcuts**] section of the .inf file.

To create the HTML file, you need to put in some more effort.

Help file creation

To create a Pocket PC Help file, which is really a plain HTML file, you need to either write the HTML directly in any editor, or you might use your standard WYSIWYG HTML editor of choice. We will show you the samples below in HTML and you will find your way to do this in your own tool.

In any case, you will write content that is compliant with HTML 3.2. (Or rather, that is compliant with *most* of HTML 3.2.) You can forget doing really fun things like scripting, Dynamic HTML (DHTML) and XML. But you will be doing some new things like special HTML comments that are interesting for the Help system.

A sample Help file

Let us start by looking at the beginning of a Help file:

```
<HTML>
<HEAD>
<META HTTP-EQUIV="Htm-Help" Content="PSA.htm#Main_Contents">
<TITLE>Pocket Service Help</TITLE>
</HEAD>
<BODY BGCOLOR=#ffffff TEXT=#000000>
<!-- PegHelp -->

<P><A NAME="Main_Contents"></A><B>Pocket Service Assistant
Help</B></P>
<P></P>
General
<P>
<A HREF="PSA.htm#About">About Pocket Service</A><BR>
</P>
How to use Pocket Service
<P>
<A HREF="PSA.htm#OpenServiceOrder">Open Service Order</A><br>
</P>
Pocket Service Dialogs
<P>
<A HREF="PSA.htm#ServiceOrderList">Service Order List</A><BR>
<A HREF="PSA.htm#ServiceOrder">Service Order</A><BR>
<A HREF="PSA.htm#Article">Article</A><BR>
<A HREF="PSA.htm#Customer">Customer</A><BR>
<A HREF="PSA.htm#Contact">Contact</A><BR>
<A HREF="PSA.htm#Appliance">Appliance</A><BR>
<A HREF="PSA.htm#Synchronization">Synchronization</A><BR>
<A HREF="PSA.htm#Options">Options</A><BR>
</P>

<P><FONT SIZE=2>Copyright &copy;2001 Pearson Education Ltd. All
rights reserved.</FONT></P>

<BR CLEAR=all>
<!-- PegHelp --><HR>

<!-- ******************** Topic Break
********************* -->

<P><A NAME="About"></A><B>About Pocket Service</B></P>
```

```
<!-- CS topic for About dialog -->
<P>
<IMG SRC="..\Program Files\PSA\logo.bmp">
</P>
<P>
Pocket Service Assistant is a sample project provided with the
book "Pocket
PC Development in the Enterprise" and its purpose is simply to
show various
functionality available in eMbedded Visual Basic.
</P>

<BR CLEAR=all>
<!-- PegHelp --><HR>

<!-- ********************* Topic Break
********************* -->
```

Figure 11.2 is how the first page will look.

Figure 11.2 Help file sample

The first important thing to notice is that you have to include the **<META>** tag that points to the main topic in the Help file. That main topic must also be called exactly **Main_Contents**. The reason is that the **View** menu in the Help system will make a jump to a tag with this name when selected.

The next interesting thing is the special HTML comment <!-- **PegHelp** --> that is actually used by the Help system to determine where each topic ends. There should be one directly after the <BODY> tag and after each topic. As you can see, there is a common practice to place a <HR> just after each topic break (<!-- **PegHelp** -->) as it makes it easier to view the different topics in an HTML browser. The Help system will not show the horizontal rules anyway.

Another practice is to add a <!-- ****** Topic Break ****** --> comment after each topic break. The reason is the same as the <HR>, but in this case it's for editing in HTML. The Help system uses neither the <HR> nor the <!-- ****** Topic Break ****** --> and therefore are not really needed in the Help file. Yet another practice is to include a comment for each of the topics that are used as "context sensitive" Help in your application. You can see an example of this above in the <!—**CS topic for About Dialog** --> comment in the code above.

The next thing that you may notice is that you have to include the Help file name with the anchor name in each link. And of course you are free to create links to other Help files as well.

In Help's About topic you may notice that we have included an image (the ACME Copier logotype). The logotype image is in bitmap (.bmp) format as this and the older bitmap (.2bp) are the only ones supported by the Help system. You cannot currently use GIF or JPEG images in your Help files. The default location for images is the **Windows** folder and that is why we have added two dots before the actual path. The path that the Help system will use in this case is **Windows\..\Program Files\PSA\logo.bmp** that is the same as **Program Files\PSA\logo.bmp**. The reason we are doing this is mainly that we do not want to clog up the \Windows folder with application-specific image files.

About creating Help files

As always with Pocket PC applications, we want to minimize the space and when it comes to Help file creation, it means that you should:

- Always write very efficiently to get as much information through in as few words as possible (Use **File > Open** in favor of **Open the File menu and tap Open**).

- Try to use as few images as possible, and when you do, consider making them black and white.

- Use as few HTML tags as possible – you really want the text to come through, not the formatting.

That said, you have to consider the fact that none of your users will be carrying instruction manuals with them anymore and your Help file has to provide enough text to Help them really solve the problems they have when using your application. One of the more common mistakes you can make is to build the Help file to reflect the structure of the application (one topic for each form, etc.) and not the usage patterns. Try to include a "How to" section in your Help file that guides your users through the most common task that they will perform with your application.

You can find more infomation on creating Help files at: www.microsoft.com/TechNet/wce/technote/cehelp3.asp

Installing Help files

To make the Help file you have created a part of your installation, you will update the .inf file to both install the Help file and create a shortcut for the Help file. To add the file to the installation, you place it in the same folder as your .vb file that would normally be named **App**. Then you add a reference to the **[SourceDisksFiles]** section like this:

```
[SourceDisksFiles]
Project1.htm=1
```

And to create the shortcut, you would add this to the **[Shortcuts]** section:

```
[Shortcuts]
%AppName%,0,"Project1.htm", %CE2%\Help
```

To copy the file to the Windows directory, insert an entry in the **[Files.Windows]** section (if there is no [Files.Windows] section, you will have to add it too):

```
[Files.Windows]
Project1.htm
```

Creating Help e-books

You may want to complement your application with an e-book that can be read by the Microsoft Reader included with all Pocket PCs. This could be implemented in a simple "readme" style, but could also be any valid documentation that you would like to provide your users with. A number of common business documents are:

● Error tracking documentation

● Product documentation

● Conditions

- Contracts
- Policies
- Guidelines

You'll want to provide the Help files as an e-book because you will get a number of enhancements over providing a plain Pocket Word documents or even an HTML file. The two most important are:

- Reader is optimized for reading. You have a number of functions that you need when reading something, such as turning pages, adding annotations, searching for words or phrases, and locating definitions for words in a dictionary, etc.
- The text will be easier to read due to the included ClearType technology. This technology makes letters and text look smoother on a LCD screen, and therefore enhances the reading experience.

We will now look at some of the options that you have in creating an e-book for your application. We will start with the easiest and move on to ways that will add more control (and work) to the process of making e-books.

Note

If you want the best-looking document, a general recommendation is to use the font Frutiger Linotype. Frutiger Linotype is the only ClearType font included with Microsoft Reader.

Using the Word Add-in

Microsoft has provided a free tool to create e-books for their Microsoft Reader software. These e-books will also work with the Reader in Pocket PC as they use a similar file format. This is probably the easiest way to create e-books: Start by downloading the Add-in for Microsoft Word, carefully following instructions on the download page. Find it at: www.microsoft.com/ Downloads/Release.asp?ReleaseID=23533

When the software installs, you simply open any Microsoft Word document that you would like to transform into an e-book and click the **File > Read...** menu option (or the Reader icon on the toolbar). This will take you through a wizard that creates the e-book for you. You will choose a name for your e-book, an author name, the name of the e-book file (with the extension .lit), and also the location to create the e-book file. After the wizard is done, you can simply copy the file to your Pocket PC. When you open the Reader on the Pocket PC the new file will appear as a readable book.

When you open the book, you will notice that the title page of the e-book has the Microsoft Word logo. This is one of the consequences of using this simple way to translate documents. We will not go further into it here, but even if you are able to create e-books with some of the more advanced features this way (table of contents, pictures, etc.), there are some limitations on what you can do using the Word Add-in method. However, it is truly the fastest way to get something converted to an e-book and may very well work as your prototype version of your e-book. We use the term "prototype" as this is not really something that we would reuse to build a real e-book.

Using OverDrive's ReaderWorks

The best way to create e-books for your Pocket PC users is to use some of the third-party tools available on the market. One of the most popular tools is probably OverDrive's ReaderWorks at **www.overdrive.com/readerworks/software/**

The ReaderWorks tool comes in two versions:

- Standard version that is free and has the basic functionality to create e-books for Pocket Reader.
- Professional version (called Publisher) that is commercially available and has extra functionality that you need to create a full featured e-book (cover page art, etc.).

If you are creating professional e-books for your applications we clearly recommend that you get the professional version, although the free standard version can be used to create pilot versions of your e-book. We use the term "pilot" because an e-book created with this tool can really be used to create the final e-book.

We will now take you through the basic steps of creating an e-book file:

1 Prepare source text files.

2 Set properties of e-book.

3 Create/import table of contents.

4 Set cover page images (requires Professional version).

5 Insert marketing data (requires Professional version).

As you may suspect, the most important step in creating an e-book is to prepare the source text files. There are many ways you could do this and you should aim at having your source content in HTML files. The reason is that ReaderWorks can use this or plain text file format, but HTML provides you with more features regarding layout.

Many applications can export in HTML format, so this should not be a problem for you. You can export any Word document into HTML and use it directly as a source file in ReaderWorks. You may not like all the formatting that you get, and that is when you have to start looking at what is correct HTML in source files for Reader.

Here are links to additional useful information.

- A list of allowed HTML tags in the Help file of ReaderWorks: www.overdrive.com/readerworks/support/usermanual/AppD.asp

- We highly recommend that you install the Office HTML Filter tool from Microsoft: officeupdate.microsoft.com/2000/downloadDetails/Msohtmf2.htm It will clean the HTML files from some of the unnecessary content created by Microsoft Word when saving in HTML format. Depending upon the original document, you'll have more or less editing to do before your e-book will look good.

- Many useful tips on the support page at ReaderWorks: www.overdrive. com/readerworks/support/tips.asp

You can choose to create your source files as one single file for the whole book, or you could divide the different chapters into separate files. This has some impact on creating tables of contents, as you will learn soon. The most important thing when creating source files is to keep them as simple as possible. The purpose of the Reader software is to make straightforward book reading easier, and if you add too much fancy formatting (colors and so forth) you will lose some of the reading experience.

Next, you will set the different properties of your e-book. Here you can set things like book title, author name, subject, language, etc. The point of setting these properties is that you will have this information embedded into the book file and it can also be used to categorize your book. Search engines in digital bookstores can later use this information to find your book. You are not required to enter any of this information, but the title will be provided by ReaderWorks anyway (name of first file in the source file list) and should probably be changed.

The next step is to create the table of contents, and ReaderWorks will help you with its built-in **TOC Wizard.** If you have the different chapters in separate files, the wizard will simply create a link in the table of contents to each file and name the link as the file name of the chapter. If you have the entire e-book in a single file, the wizard will use the HTML heading tags inside the file (<H1>, <H2>, <H3>, and so forth) for creating a table of contents. Since the table of contents will include links to the different chapters, the wizard will add IDs to the HTML heading tags in the file and will therefore need to make changes to your source file. In the wizard, you will also be able to choose different styles for your table of contents. You will even be able to create your own style that you can use for different e-books. When the wizard is done, it has created an HTML file that it will later use to create the e-book.

The features that you can only take advantage of with the Professional version, are creating the cover page images and adding marketing data, and these processes are quite straightforward. When it comes to images, you simply create the images in any favorite image editing. The recommended image sizes for the cover page art is:

- Desktop Cover Page: 510×680 pixels (3:4 aspect ratio)
- Desktop Thumbnail: 99×132 pixels (3:4 aspect ratio)
- Desktop Title Image: (spine): 82×680 pixels
- PocketPC Cover Page: 480×240 pixels (2:1 aspect ratio)
- PocketPC Thumbnail: 45×90 pixels (2:1 aspect ratio)

And the image format can be JPEG, GIF, or PNG. Entering marketing data is quite similar to what you did with the properties before and should not create any problems for you.

As we mentioned earlier, the editing of the source files is the main effort in creating a good-looking e-book. An iterative approach while constantly building the e-book and viewing it in Reader on the Pocket PC is probably the best approach to finding out how to do the right formatting.

You can find more info on creating e-books on:

www.overdrive.com/readerworks/support/tips.asp

Package setup files into setup.exe

The last step is to package the setup files into a single archive file that the users can run that extracts itself and starts the installation automatically. The tool we have been using for this is WinRAR (available at this site: www.rarsoft.com/). The first thing to do is to create an archive (ZIP) containing all the files in the **CD1** folder. Then, open this newly created archive in WinRAR, select toolbar button **Add Archive Comment** and enter the following text into the Comment dialog:

```
Silent
Setup=Setup.exe
TempMode
```

Then, select menu option **Commands > Convert archive to SFX** and just select **OK** in the dialog box asking you to select SFX module. You have now created a self-extracting auto-starting installation executable – are you a hero or what?!!

Web distribution

When you have finished with the creation of your installation, you will have to decide on a way of distributing your application to your users. There are several options here. The options that you have without using any third-party tools are:

● Distribute a self-extracting **setup.exe** file that the user can run from her PC and it will install to the Pocket PC via ActiveSync

● Put the installation cabinet files (.cab) on a web site for direct installation using Internet Explorer for the Pocket PC

And you already saw earlier in this chapter how to create the **setup.exe** file, and to distribute it you can send it as an e-mail to the recipients or you may set up a link on a web page where the users can download and run the file on their PCs.

The second option above presents an interesting way for your users, because it enables them to accomplish installation without having to use their PCs to install the application. The only requirement is that they have an online connection (wired or wireless) that they can use. Using Internet Explorer for the Pocket PC, users could go to a page that could look like Figure 11.3.

Figure 11.3   Web setup sample

And when they tap one of the links (which really links to a .cab file) the installation will start automatically. You have to provide a link for each device type, or at least groups of devices, based on processor type. Let us take a look at the source code for such a page:

```
<%
Option Explicit
Response.Expires = 0

' Server side includes
%>
<!--#INCLUDE FILE="../include/global.asp"-->

<!DOCTYPE HTML PUBLIC "-//IETF//DTD HTML//EN">
<HTML><HEAD><TITLE>ACME Copier</TITLE>
<LINK REL="stylesheet" HREF="../css/acme.css" TYPE="text/css">
</HEAD><BODY><FONT FACE="Tahoma">

<!--#INCLUDE FILE="../include/top.asp"-->
<H1>Web Setup</H1>
<P><B>
  Here you can install directly from your Pocket PC.
</B></P>

<H2>Pocket Service Assistant</H2>
<P>This is the offline client for managing Service Orders</P>
<TABLE BGCOLOR="navy" BORDER="0" CELLSPACING="0"
CELLPADDING="0"><TR><TD>
<TABLE BORDER="0" CELLSPACING="1" CELLPADDING="3">
  <TR BGCOLOR="navy">
    <TD VALIGN="top"><FONT
COLOR="white"><B>Proc/ver</B></FONT></TD>
    <TD VALIGN="top"><FONT
COLOR="white"><B>Comment</B></FONT></TD>
  </TR>
  <TR BGCOLOR="white">
    <TD VALIGN="top"><A HREF="files/PSA.Arm 1100 (4K)
v3.00.CAB">Arm 1100 v1.0</A></TD>
    <TD VALIGN="top">Compaq iPAQ users</TD>
  </TR>
  <TR BGCOLOR="white">
    <TD VALIGN="top"><A HREF="files/PSA.Mips 4000 (4K)
v3.00.CAB">Mips 4000 v1.0</A></TD>
    <TD VALIGN="top">Casio Cassiopeia users</TD>
  </TR>
  <TR BGCOLOR="white">
    <TD VALIGN="top"><A HREF="files/PSA.SH 3 (1K)
v3.00.CAB">SH3 v1.0</A></TD>
    <TD VALIGN="top">HP Jordana users</TD>
```

```
    </TR>
  </TABLE>
  </TD></TR></TABLE>

  <!--#INCLUDE FILE="../include/bottom.asp"-->

  </FONT></BODY>
  </HTML>
```

As you can see, there is little magic in this page. Over time, you just have to add new links for new versions released and place the new files in the **files** subfolder. The .cab files that you use are exactly the ones that generate when you build your installation using the **cabwiz.exe** utility.

Using this approach, installation of your application can in practice be managed from anywhere where there is web connectivity. The goal here is "self service," and this way, each time there's a new release each technician could receive an e-mail containing a link to the download page.

11.5   ACME Copier Pocket Service Assistant installation

On the accompanying CD we have completed the above process for the ACME Copier **Pocket Service Assistant** application. We started by creating the intermediate file and then ran the Application Install Wizard that created most of what we needed. Then, we created the eVC launch application containing the following code:

```
TCHAR tFile[255];

  if (lpCmdLine[0]==0) wsprintf(tFile,TEXT("\\Program
Files\PSA\PSA.vb"));
              // Hard-coded full path to .vb file (not
recommended!)
      else
        wsprintf(tFile,lpCmdLine);
          // Command Line parameter is better
    ZeroMemory(&sei, sizeof(sei));
    sei.cbSize = sizeof(sei);
    sei.lpFile = tFile;
    return ShellExecuteEx(&sei);
```

We then updated the **.inf** file to look like this:

```
[Version]
Signature="$Chicago$"
CESignature="$Windows CE$"
```

```
Provider=%CompanyName%

[SourceDisksNames]
.1=,"Application Files",, App

[DefaultInstall]
CopyFiles=Files.App, Files.Windows
CEShortcuts=Shortcuts

[Shortcuts]
%AppName%,0,"PSA.exe"
%CompanyName% %AppName%,0,"PSA.htm",%CE2%\Help

[CEStrings]
InstallDir=%CE1%\%AppName%
AppName="Pocket Service"

[Strings]
CompanyName="ACME Copier"

[DestinationDirs]
Shortcuts=,%CE11%
Files.App=,%InstallDir%
Files.Windows=,%CE2%
Files.Arm 1100 (4K) v3.00=,%CE2%
Files.SH 3 (1K) v3.00=,%CE2%
Files.Mips 4000 (4K) v3.00=,%CE2%

[SourceDisksFiles]
PSA.vb=1
splash.bmp=1
logo.bmp=1
PSA.htm=1

[DefaultInstall.Arm 1100 (4K) v3.00]
CopyFiles=Files.Arm 1100 (4K) v3.00
CESelfRegister=MSCEListView.dll,MSCEPicture.dll,MSCETabStrip.dl
l,MSCEMenuBar.dll,osiutil.dll,vbscript.dll,pvbhost2.dll,pvbform
2.dll,pvbdecl.dll

[CEDevice.Arm 1100 (4K) v3.00]
ProcessorType=2577

[SourceDisksNames.Arm 1100 (4K) v3.00]
3= ,"Arm 1100 (4K) v3.00 Files",,Arm 1100 (4K) v3.00

[SourceDisksFiles.Arm 1100 (4K) v3.00]
pvbhost2.dll=3
```

```
vbscript.dll=3
pvbload.exe=3
MSCETabStrip.dll=3
MSCEListView.dll=3
pvbdecl.dll=3
MSCEMenuBar.dll=3
osiutil.dll=3
MSCEPicture.dll=3
pvbform2.dll=3
PSA.exe=3

[DefaultInstall.SH 3 (1K) v3.00]
CopyFiles=Files.SH 3 (1K) v3.00
CESelfRegister=MSCEListView.dll,MSCEPicture.dll,MSCETabStrip.dl
l,MSCEMenuBar.dll,osiutil.dll,vbscript.dll,pvbhost2.dll,pvbform
2.dll,pvbdecl.dll

[CEDevice.SH 3 (1K) v3.00]
ProcessorType=10003

[SourceDisksNames.SH 3 (1K) v3.00]
3= ,"SH 3 (1K) v3.00 Files",,SH 3 (1K) v3.00

[SourceDisksFiles.SH 3 (1K) v3.00]
pvbload.exe=3
MSCEMenuBar.dll=3
pvbdecl.dll=3
pvbform2.dll=3
pvbhost2.dll=3
vbscript.dll=3
MSCEPicture.dll=3
osiutil.dll=3
MSCETabStrip.dll=3
MSCEListView.dll=3
PSA.exe=3

[DefaultInstall.Mips 4000 (4K) v3.00]
CopyFiles=Files.Mips 4000 (4K) v3.00
CESelfRegister=MSCEListView.dll,MSCEPicture.dll,MSCETabStrip.dl
l,MSCEMenuBar.dll,osiutil.dll,vbscript.dll,pvbhost2.dll,pvbform
2.dll,pvbdecl.dll

[CEDevice.Mips 4000 (4K) v3.00]
ProcessorType=4000
```

```
[SourceDisksNames.Mips 4000 (4K) v3.00]
3= ,"Mips 4000 (4K) v3.00 Files",,Mips 4000 (4K) v3.00
[SourceDisksFiles.Mips 4000 (4K) v3.00]

pvbform2.dll=3
MSCETabStrip.dll=3
MSCEPicture.dll=3
MSCEListView.dll=3
pvbhost2.dll=3
vbscript.dll=3
pvbload.exe=3
pvbdecl.dll=3
MSCEMenuBar.dll=3
osiutil.dll=3
PSA.exe=3

[Files.Arm 1100 (4K) v3.00]
pvbhost2.dll,,0x80000000
vbscript.dll,,0x80000000
pvbload.exe
MSCETabStrip.dll,,0x80000000
MSCEListView.dll,,0x80000000
pvbdecl.dll,,0x80000000
MSCEMenuBar.dll,,0x80000000
osiutil.dll,,0x80000000
MSCEPicture.dll,,0x80000000
pvbform2.dll,,0x80000000

[Files.App]
PSA.vb
splash.bmp
logo.bmp
PSA.exe

[Files.Windows]
PSA.htm

[Files.SH 3 (1K) v3.00]
pvbload.exe
MSCEMenuBar.dll,,0x80000000
pvbdecl.dll,,0x80000000
pvbform2.dll,,0x80000000
pvbhost2.dll,,0x80000000
vbscript.dll,,0x80000000
```

```
MSCEPicture.dll,,0x80000000
osiutil.dll,,0x80000000
MSCETabStrip.dll,,0x80000000
MSCEListView.dll,,0x80000000

[Files.Mips 4000 (4K) v3.00]
pvbform2.dll,,0x80000000
MSCETabStrip.dll,,0x80000000
MSCEPicture.dll,,0x80000000
MSCEListView.dll,,0x80000000
pvbhost2.dll,,0x80000000
vbscript.dll,,0x80000000
pvbload.exe
pvbdecl.dll,,0x80000000
MSCEMenuBar.dll,,0x80000000
osiutil.dll,,0x80000000
```

And as you can see, we have added the different versions of the eVC launch application and also the Help file shortcut. The changes that were made after the Application Install Wizard ran are in bold. The **.inf** file format is far from obvious, and even though there is some information to be found in the eVT online Help, it is not very easy to understand completely the format. Therefore, you will benefit from buying some of the installation and distribution applications available on the market.

Other tools

So far, we have shown you the things you can do with the standard toolset. As you can see, it can take you quite far. However, there is a whole market for these tools, and just to help you find alternatives, we have included some of the options that you have:

- **InstallShield Software Corporation InstallShield Professional – Standard Edition 6.22:** This tool makes it possible to create PC-to-device, PC Card, and web installations, all in a solid installation creation package. www.installshield.com/solutions/pocket_pc/pocket_1.asp

- **Wise Solutions InstallMaster 8:** With this tool you can also create PC-to-device, PC Card, and web installations in a solid installation creation package. www.wisesolutions.com/imaster.htm

- **Odyssey Software ViaXML Device Services:** This free framework (requires ViaXML) will enable central distribution of software with a special client installed on the Pocket PC. The only requirement on the client side is some software and that the device be connected to a network. Then applications and upgrades can be "pushed" onto the device and even forced to install. A number of other remote administration features are available for retrieving information from the devices (battery life, memory, files, etc.). www.odysseysoftware.com/viaxml_overview.html#8

● **Extended Systems XTNDConnect Server 2.5:** Manage data and applications on mobile devices with backup/restore, installation, configuration, and reporting capabilities. This is a comprehensive package with the installation features just a part of it.
www.extendedsystems.com/ESI/Products/Mobile+Data+Management+Products/Server-Based+Synchronization/

● **CEWebInstallX** allows for complex installation of applications using ActiveSync. This package allows for the automated installation and updates to critical files without requiring the steps that a standard installation does on the desktop. www.doctorce.com/cewebinstallx_features.htm

Since all of the tools have their pros and cons, which are beyond the scope of this book to discuss, we hope that you will take the time to evaluate each of them.

11.6   Conclusion

The first experience a user has with an application is the installation procedures. A poorly designed and working application installation does not speak very well about you or your application. If you have installed any new PC games lately, you have noticed the gaming experience starts during the game installation. Cool graphics, music, and other types of "fireworks" build the user's expectations and communicate the great capabilities of the game being installed. Business software is not, in any significant measure, lagging behind. Most commercial software on the Windows platform has a great looking as well as functional installation.

Through the information here, we very much hope that you have been inspired to make your Pocket PC application installations look good as well as be functional.

.NE(x)T steps

In this chapter we will look at what to expect in the future. We will discuss the progress of mobile solution development in general and also what is happening with the Pocket PC and its supporting tools. We will talk about Microsoft's .NET initiative and the impact for mobile solutions. We will introduce you to Web Services (using SOAP) and even show you how you can use this technology right away.

As you are probably already aware, this business is moving extremely fast. Hopefully not too much of what is said here will be redundant when you read it (it is very hard to tell as we write this). In summary, there is a truly exciting time ahead and best of all – you will be ready when the changes come!

12.1　What will change?

What will *not* change? As always, reality will either surpass our wildest dreams – or, it will get even worse than we expect. However, some things can be expected: increasing bandwidth, more powerful devices, more demanding users, higher demands on services, and so on. To avoid making the scope of this chapter too vast, we would like to focus some of the new thoughts on the future of system architecture, and some of the more interesting technology changes. We would also like to show you how you can use this technology right now.

A new web

Evolution (in the sense of using technology) seems to take one step forward and two steps back. The current internet architecture mirrors the old mainframe model. We have central logic and data storage, and very thin, simple clients. For those of us who had been working with client/server applications for several years, and were just turning to multi-tiered applications, this was hardly what we were dreaming about.

We really wanted something more solid than old terminal emulation, however flashy it may have looked. The amazing fact that made it all happen was that most clients were willing to pay more for something that had less functionality.

If we were proposing a web solution, there was suddenly no demand for per-field validation (now they were fine with only one validation per page), responsiveness (users could wait for seconds to get the new page where before they complained that it took one second to get to the next dialog box), or efficient user interaction (they were perfectly fine with jumping between pages in an unorganized manner where previously they had complained that the dialog structure was too complex).

We could continue, but hopefully you get the point. Users and buyers were willing to pay more for less and that is an opportunity that few on the selling side neglected. But in the end what we got was the old mainframe, however better looking; it was still the old mainframe. An important reason behind the client/server backlash was the pain that came with distributing and maintaining client/server applications, sometimes referred to as the "DLL Hell" (having the right combination of DLLs on all target PCs) as well as other configuration management issues for distributed applications.

To understand what is happening right now, you have to look at the reasons why client/server was more popular than the mainframe for most applications. Most of the first client/server applications connected desktops and mainframes. Many of them also made connections between different mainframes (or mini computers) and a local data store that integrated that data into something that was far more useful than the sum of the parts.

The PC was the point of integrations. The reason for data integration was mainly that the cost of doing the integration on the mainframe side was too high. Some corporations today have a well-defined application integration framework. Probably they have some protocols that they have decided on and probably some databases act as "masters" for certain type of information. Some may even have the infrastructure for doing the integration in a standardized way. Usually this is some kind of messaging system. This means that inside the company, most of the impor-

> ❝The PC was the point of integrations.❞

tant integration is solved. But they have not made the link to customers or even partners. If they have any integrated system services at all, it is still in-house and most of the integration is made in the web server itself.

The web server is now the point of integration. The interesting question is how the focus will shift as we go forward. One part of the industry, the one that has become rich selling "hard steel" in the back-end, is still focusing on the mainframe model. If you allow the simile it is like the old communistic model where the government (mainframe) knew every-thing and the citizens (clients) were stupid and passive.

> 66 The web server is now the point of integration. 99

At the other end of the scale we have the fully distributed model (demo-cratic) where each client acts like both a client and a server. The probable answer is, as we have said before, that it will be "both/and" rather than "or/else." We will have mainframes doing what they are best at, but they will be forced to "open up" their services in an integration-friendly way. At the other end we will see more clients, even handheld clients (even wear-able clients), acting as both clients and servers. This is currently known as P2P (peer-to-peer) and there are already products available that can operate in this manner on a Pocket PC. As peer-to-peer gains more ground, we will be able to use local services (off-line

> 66 The Pocket PC will be the new point of integration. 99

applications, calendar, etc.) as well as remote services in a mix that we com-bine ourselves. The Pocket PC will be the new point of integration.

Q Authors Andy and Christian, do you think that any of the delegations focusing on the mainframe model want to think about fully distributed scenarios like P2P (Napster, etc.)?

A No, since it is the complete opposite of all that they believe in. In the distributed scenario the only winners are the users, and if device manufacturers and device software suppliers give them the tools to create fully distributed applications, the major players are in trouble – serious trouble.

When it comes to current technology, we can conclude that TCP/IP, HTTP, and HTML are de facto standards. Whatever solution we build will most probably include all three of these acronyms, which represent core web technologies. Another acronym that is the next to join them as "core stan-dards" is XML. XML is well on the way to becoming de facto standard for data representation and interchange and is already widely use. XML enables what we would like to call data integration to distinguish it from application integration.

The next extremely important web technology to join the others is SOAP. The purpose of SOAP, which is based on XML, is to enable applica-tion integration beyond system and company borders. The currently available services that are based on SOAP are called Web Services from Microsoft and other vendors. Connected to SOAP is UDDI (Universal Description, Discovery, and Integration), which is an upcoming standard for description and discovery of the available web services. Any already existing or newly created component can be published as a public/private service over the internet, and since the SOAP standard is vendor and operating system independent, it can reside on any physical platform. Microsoft and other companies will provide some core/base services.

We have to move away from the proprietary "single-product solutions" as all current packages (SAP R/3, Office, etc.) on all levels will probably be split up into separate web services that can be used alone or in an integrated way. Also, the integrated solutions will be a mix of web services from different vendors and packages. Therefore the old "shop" thinking will be obsolete. No more "vendor shops" (IBM, etc.), "package shops" (SAP, etc.) or even "system integrator shops" (Accenture, etc.). As competition could come down to the web service level, the information cost (marketing) will far exceed the production cost (implementing the service). All the small players will have the ability to act very fast, and will put pressure on the larger players. Maybe Marx was right in saying that the "critical means of production" (nowadays our knowledge in our brains) will be owned by the workers themselves.

> **❝As competition could come down to the web service level, the information cost (marketing) will far exceed the production cost (implementing the service). ❞**

12.2　Microsoft .NET

You have probably already heard many times of the Microsoft .NET strategy. The changes that come with .NET are significant to say the least. We will discuss the implications for mobile applications. The driving idea in .NET is to connect the inner workings of stand-alone web sites, currently with no collaboration between them.

Today there is not a significant amount of service integration between different web service providers. And the standards that we have been able to standardize on are the basic network protocol (TCP/IP) and the communication protocol (HTTP). But there is not a standard for exchanging data and services between providers. There is no standard for doing application integration between different web sites. For example, there is no way that we can get the current exchange rate from our own web site to provide our prices in local currency for the visitor. We have to build the currency support ourselves.

These are the main messages that Microsoft is sending out with .NET: Get Connected! Don't do everything yourself – use what others have already done! Open up your business to partners and customer! We could probably think of a few more, but this covers what we think are the most important aspects of .NET.

To support the vision Microsoft has worked hard to standardize the tools you need to accomplish this. Also, they are building in support for XML, SOAP, and Web Services into their new products. Even Microsoft itself realizes that this new web will turn them from product manufacturers to service providers. As we mentioned before, they have already announced that they will be offering core/base services for authentication, notification and messaging, personalization, XML-based data storage, calendar, directory/search functions, dynamic delivery of software and services, and much more. Microsoft is forced to actually change their overall business model and many corporations will have to do the same.

A core part of Microsoft .NET is the ambition to enable ubiquitous application integration, enabling applications that reside on different platforms to call each other in a standardized way. With Web Services, you can make component methods available over HTTP using XML to format the communicated data. The standard for doing this is SOAP and is currently subject to standardization by the W3C.

Web Services will change the way we perform application design. As we can integrate functionality that is available anywhere on the internet into a single, customized application, we will end up with the possibility to create something very powerful. It could be a web application (making the web server the point of integration) but could also be a (fat) client application, which would combine the best of both worlds – a powerful user interface and a wealth of services available from anywhere. This is a perfect match for a Pocket PC due to its Windows-based (rich) user interface, and compared to a personal computer, relatively low capacity (memory, screen size, and so on).

Since most services will transport low amounts of data, you can add wireless scenarios to this and end up with a very powerful solution to make existing functionality available anywhere.

Web Services = win/win/win

The question is of course how we will all benefit from this new technology? And who will benefit? You can be sure that Microsoft itself is planning to benefit from all this. Actually, their change of business model reflects that they see huge business benefit in providing services rather than products. But is this just something invented to increase the revenue of Microsoft and other vendors focusing on the same technology? The answer is a firm NO!

> The buyers (corporations) will not be locked in by a platform; rather competition will be on the more relevant service level.

As Web Services become a ubiquitous technology (in the meaning vendor-independent), technology will make the buying side stronger. The buyers (corporations) will not be locked in by a platform; rather competition will be on the more relevant service level.

As each service provider competes with the quality and price of the service, anyone can start competing. Ask yourself; how probable is it that Microsoft or any other large vendor will provide a better Swedish spell checking service than a small company in Sweden focusing only on this task? If I can choose to use any spell checker service from my word processor, why would I settle for the standard service if it were charged for like any other available on the internet? The result is that the buyers (corporations or even single users) will gain more power and freedom that with the help of competition will lead to higher quality services at a lower price. Buyers and users are also winners.

For software developers and system designers the benefits are obvious. They can start looking at the internet as a large bin of reusables. All published web services will be an available and readily usable part of a new application. Why design, build, test, and deploy a basic service (like currency exchange or even translation) when someone else before has not only built it, but also made it available online through any internet connection.

That is a huge leap forward for software reuse. Even if the quality of the web service will be an important issue, some entity making their business out of providing such indicators will probably resolve this issue. Another issue will be the agreements between service providers and service consumers and the solution will probably be reused from how outsourcing services resolve it today. They use something called an SLA (Service Level Agreement). An SLA states things like uptime, response time, how to handle support, and so on.

Another benefit for software developers is the fact that they can use multiple platforms and development tools to create these web services. They can stick with whatever language they are fond of and can still reuse other web services no matter what language was used or the platform originally targeted. Reuse will be possible cross platform and across language boundaries – something that has rarely happened before. The software community is a winner as well.

> **❝ Reuse will be possible cross platform and across language boundaries – something that has rarely happened before. ❞**

We can conclude that not only vendors are winners, so also are corporations, users, and developers. Even the internet itself is a winner since we will start to utilize its true potential – to be our global digital nervous system. This vision is within reach and will become a reality in the crossroads of mobile solutions and the internet.

12.3   Web Services today

Well, you probably wonder, can it be done today? The answer is, actually, yes, but as always with future technology you have to add some tweaks and you may have to make changes when the technology is mature. Let us start by showing you how it can be done with just eVB and the technology available in your Pocket PC. Then we will look at how it can be done with the help of a third-party product called Pocket SOAP. Finally, we will look at another third-party product called ViaXML to assist us in creating even more sophisticated Web Services applications.

Do it yourself

So let's go through some of the typical ways you might enhance your applications today to incorporate this exciting new approach.

How to call Web Services

On your PC, get one of the Microsoft SOAP Toolkits (1.0 or 2.0) and make Web Services calls from any language using a SOAP client object (in SOAP Toolkit 1.0 called ROPE [Remote Object Proxy Engine].). The SOAP client object provides the core functionality and infrastructure for Web Service development and implementation using a familiar programming paradigm. It allows a client to access a Web Service as if it were a local COM object. On your Pocket PC, however, there is no SOAP client implementation available from Microsoft yet. We say "yet" because we believe that Web Services (SOAP) and even other parts of .NET will be available for the Pocket PC in the future.

Meanwhile, you could use the simplified SOAP client implementation that we have provided below and start using Web Services in your Pocket PC applications today.

Note

The SOAP specification (in version 1.1) is still just a proposed standard and will probably change. The sample code provided below (and on the accompanying CD) will probably need to be updated if or when it changes.

What can Web Services do?

Let's begin by exploring what Web Services enable us to do. If you know that a Web Service exists somewhere on the internet, you could use that functionality from within your Pocket PC application (see Sample 12-1 on the CD). To complement the SOAP Toolkit 1.0, Microsoft has set up a number of sample Web Services. One of these allows a user to get the current price for a stock ticker symbol in real time over the internet and to do that you use this code:

> ❝If you know that a Web Service exists somewhere on the internet, you could use that functionality from within your Pocket PC application. ❞

```
Dim ls As String
Dim lavParam(2, 2) As Variant

' Set parameters
lavParam(0, 0) = "Symbol": lavParam(0, 1) = "MSFT"
lavParam(1, 0) = "description": lavParam(1, 1) = "any company"

 ' Make SOAP call
ls = SOAPCall("urn:Foo", _
              "http://www.soaptoolkit.com/soapdemo/services.asp", _
              "GetStockQuote", lavParam, "", False)

 ' Show result
 MsgBox ls
```

Some comments on the code:

● Since eMbedded Visual Basic lacks the ParamArray option for function parameters, we have to put the parameters in a two-dimensional Variant array manually.

● The SOAPCall function takes six parameters:

   1 Namespace URI (Universal Resource Identifier) and is not used in this example.

   2 Listener URL, to the "listener" of the Web Service. The Listener is the web page that the request will be posted to and is defined in the services description. Usually the Listener URL is an ASP page but there is also a more efficient ISAPI implementation available (see the "More information" section at the end of the chapter for links to read more about SOAP).

   3 Method name to call.

   4 Parameters to the method in a two-dimensional array.

   5 SOAPAction string to be set in HTTP header.

   6 A true/false value indication if the XML payload (sent and received) should be displayed while making the call (in this case using the check box on the form).

Due to the SOAPCall function implementation in the SOAPClient.bas module, calling Web Services is fairly simple. Let's look into the SOAPClient.bas module some more. Here is some simplified code for actually making the SOAP call (from within the SOAPCall function):

```
' Set Payload
lsRequest = & _
"<S:Envelope
xmlns:S='http://schemas.xmlsoap.org/soap/envelope/'" & _
" xmlns:SOAP-ENC='http://schemas.xmlsoap.org/soap/encoding/'" & _
" S:encodingStyle='http://schemas.xmlsoap.org/soap/encoding/'"
& _
" xmlns:xsd='http://www.w3.org/1999/XMLSchema'" & _
" xmlns:xsi='http://www.w3.org/1999/XMLSchema-instance'>" &
vbCrLf & _
"<S:Body>" & vbCrLf & _
" <m:" & Method & " xmlns:m='" & Namespace & "'>" & vbCrLf
If Not VarType(Arguments) = vbInteger Then
  For i = 0 To UBound(Arguments, 1) – 1
    lsRequest = lsRequest & " <" & Arguments(i, 0) & ">" & _
              Arguments(i, 1) & "</" & Arguments(i, 0) & ">"
& vbCrLf
  Next 'i
End If
lsRequest = lsRequest & " </m:" & Method & ">" & vbCrLf & _
"</S:Body>" & vbCrLf & _
"</S:Envelope>"

' Create XML HTTP object
Set loXMLHTTP = CreateObject("Microsoft.XMLHTTP")

' Make request to SOAP service/method
loXMLHTTP.Open "POST", Listener, False, "", ""
' (set header info)
If Len(SOAPAction) > 0 Then
  loXMLHTTP.setRequestHeader "SOAPAction", SOAPAction
Else
  loXMLHTTP.setRequestHeader "SOAPAction", Namespace & "#" &
Method
End If
loXMLHTTP.setRequestHeader "Content-Type", "text/xml"
loXMLHTTP.Send lsRequest
```

```
' If OK, get response
If Len(loXMLHTTP.responseXML.XML) > 0 Then
  lsResponse = loXMLHTTP.responseXML.XML

  ' Find type of call and if "Function" send back return value
  If Len(lsResponse) > 0 Then
    SOAPCall = GetReturnValue(lsResponse, Method)
  Else
    SOAPCall = ""
  End If
Else
  MsgBox loXMLHTTP.responseText
End If
```

Some comments on the code:

● The lsRequest variable is filled with the actual request payload (in XML). This is mostly hard-coded XML text, except for the method name and parameter values.

● We're using the XMLHTTP component available on all Pocket PCs to make the actual call.

● The GetReturnValue function extracts the return value from the response payload (in XML). If an error occurs, an error message is returned.

The GetReturnValue function uses XMLDOM component (available on all Pocket PCs) to parse the response XML string. And even if the SOAPClient .bas module does not implement all the functionality of the PC-implementation provided in the SOAP Toolkits, the most important functionality is there – to enable calls to Web Services.

In most business applications, there is a need to transfer data between the server and a client application. In a traditional Microsoft Web solution platform (again, formerly known as Windows DNA) the normal choice for doing data transfer would be to use the ADO Recordset object. Since it used a special type of "marshalling" (object transfer), it could be transferred to the client without holding any "state" (resources) on the server. Because of this, many existing systems have implemented many components to return data in the form of ADO Recordsets.

66 A way to transfer those ADO Recordsets over SOAP. 99

If we want to leverage the investment in those components and still have the benefits of the application integration possibilities with Web Services, we need a way to transfer those ADO Recordsets over SOAP.

This is usually not a problem on the server side since it is probably using ADO (2.1 or later), which support Recordset persistence. However, on the Pocket PC some differences exist in the ADO implementation. The most important difference is that ADOCE (version 3.1) does not currently support persistence, and especially not in XML (Extensible Markup Language) format.

Another difference is that ADOCE does not support the Recordset marshalling that we mentioned above. Therefore, it does not support the dynamic creation of "disconnected" (without a live connection to the data source) Recordsets. With the current implementation of ADOCE (version 3.1) we have to find another way of handling data returned from Web Service (SOAP) calls. We will come back to that later.

Let us start by looking at the server-side code:

```
Public Function GetXML(ByVal SQLString As String, _
                      ByVal MaxRecords As Long) As String
    Dim laco As Connection
    Dim lars As Recordset
    Dim last As Stream

    On Error GoTo ErrorHandler

    ' Create objects
    Set laco = CreateObject("ADODB.Connection")
    Set lars = CreateObject("ADODB.Recordset")
    Set last = CreateObject("ADODB.Stream")

    ' Open Connection
    laco.CursorLocation = adUseClient
    laco.ConnectionString = CONNECTION_STRING
    laco.Open

    ' Open Recordset
    lars.CursorType = adOpenKeyset
    lars.LockType = adLockReadOnly
    If MaxRecords > 0 Then lars.MaxRecords = MaxRecords
    Set lars.ActiveConnection = laco
    lars.Open SQLString

    ' Disconnect Recordset from connection and close it
    Set lars.ActiveConnection = Nothing
    laco.Close

    ' Return XML (from Recordset via Stream)
    lars.Save last, adPersistXML
    GetXML = last.ReadText

    ' Allow MTS transaction set to proceed
    GetObjectContext.SetComplete

    Exit Function

ErrorHandler:
```

```
' Roll back MTS transaction set
GetObjectContext.SetAbort

' Raise Error
Err.Raise Err.Number, Err.Source, Err.Description
End Function
```

As you can see, this is just a standard data retrieval function. The only major difference being that it returns the persisted Recordset as XML. This function is implemented in a server COM object, and you would make it available as a Web Service. Depending on what SOAP Toolkit you are using you will have to run different "wizards," but it is pretty straightforward and you find good tips in the documentation.

Note

The XML format for persisting ADO Recordsets (we have used ADO version 2.6) will probably change and then the sample code provided will probably need to be updated. Please visit the authors' web site at: **www.businessanyplace.net**

Now, let us look at the client side code to call this new Web Service that we have created:

```
Dim ls As String
Dim lavParam(2, 2) As Variant
Dim litm As ListItem

' Set parameters
lavParam(0, 0) = "SQLString": lavParam(0, 1) = "SELECT * FROM
Article"
lavParam(1, 0) = "MaxRecords": lavParam(1, 1) = "4"

' Make SOAP call
ls = SOAPCall("http://tempuri.org/message/", _
              "http://localhost/soap/PPDE.asp", _
              "GetXML", lavParam, _
              "http://tempuri.org/action/Catalog.GetXML", _
              False)

' Clear and add ListView headings
ListViewCtrl1.ColumnHeaders.Clear
ListViewCtrl1.ColumnHeaders.Add 1, , "ArtNo", 700
ListViewCtrl1.ColumnHeaders.Add 2, , "Description", 1450
ListViewCtrl1.ColumnHeaders.Add 3, , "Price", 850,
lvwColumnRight

' Clear and fill ListView from XML (with Recordset Emulation)
```

```
ListViewCtrl1.ListItems.Clear
XMLRSOpen ls
Do While Not XMLRSEOF
  Set litm = ListViewCtrl1.ListItems.Add(, ,XMLRS("ArticleNo"))
    litm.SubItems(1) = XMLRS("Description")
    litm.SubItems(2) = XMLRS("Price")
  XMLRSMoveNext
Loop
XMLRSClose
```

You can see that the call is very similar to the previous call that we made to the sample Web Service provided by Microsoft. In addition, we have added the possibility to populate a ListView control by using a special module called XMLRS.bas (see Figure 12.1).

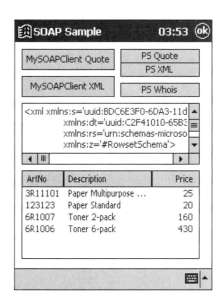

Figure 12.1   SOAP Sample

The purpose of this module is to simulate the handling of a Recordset, but instead of using an actual Recordset, it uses a XML DOM object. This XML DOM object gets loaded from the response from the Web Service in the XMLRSOpen function. Here is how that function looks:

```
' Create DOM object
Set poXML = CreateObject("Microsoft.XMLDOM")

' Load string
psXML = XML

' Load DOM
poXML.loadXML psXML
```

```
' Position data nodes
Set poDataNodes =
poXML.documentElement.selectNodes("//rs:data")
Set poDataNodes = poDataNodes.Item(0).childnodes
```

The psXML variable will contain the ADO Recordset XML representation and the poXML variable is the XML DOM object holding the Recordset data. The poDataNodes variable will hold the XML elements of all the Recordset data rows. We now have an object that holds all the data rows in the Recordset, and that's what we need to start navigating the data. That is done with the XMLRSMoveFirst and XMLRSMoveNext functions. Let's have a closer look at the code in XMLRSMoveNext function:

```
' Check not EOF
If Not XMLRSEOF() Then
  ' Increase pointer
  piRecordPos = piRecordPos + 1
End If
```

To follow the logic, let's look at the code in function XMLRSEOF:

```
' Check EOF
If piRecordPos > poDataNodes.length - 1 Then XMLRSEOF = True
```

What we need now, is the way to extract the actual data which is done in function XMLRS:

```
' Check if field number or field name
If IsNumeric(FieldID) Then
  ' Get Field Data
  XMLRS = poDataNodes(piRecordPos).Attributes(FieldID).Text
Else
  ' Get Field Data
  XMLRS = _
 poDataNodes(piRecordPos).Attributes.getNamedItem(FieldID).Text
End If
```

As you can see, we are allowed to supply both a field name (as we have done in the form code) as well as an ordinal number of a field.

If you look closer at the XMLRS.bas module, you'll note that we have just supplied the necessary functions for this sample. The idea is to get you started. Of course more of the ADO Recordset functionality could be implemented as well. Since the module uses the XML DOM object, you will need some XML skills to do it. Of course this is not a solid "enterprise" solution to the problem. On our wish list for ADOCE is that in the future the Recordset (or some similar construct) should have the XML support needed to do without our XMLRS.bas module. As the code provided is meant to allow for minor changes if (when) that capability is provided, your invested time and effort will not be wasted.

Okay, we have written the "plumbing" part of making Web Services work for you. Now it's up to you to do the fun part: create great applications that make use of Web Services. Today, there are not too many Web Services available on the internet, so you may have to implement some of your own at first. One interesting Web Service already available from Microsoft is called TerraService. TerraService is used for putting dynamics maps into your web or Windows applications.

If you would like to keep track of new Web Services as they become available, check out the Microsoft UDDI site at http://uddi.microsoft.com/. The goal of UDDI is to create a global repository of Web Services that can be used to find the desired functionality – even in real time from an application – and is supported by all major players including Microsoft, IBM, Sun, Oracle, and more than 100 others.

We believe that all of the .NET features will be available for Pocket PC in the not-too-distant future. Then there will be support for Web Services integrated in the operating system as well as in the development tools. Calling Web Services will be as easy as calling any local components and most applications will be built integrating multiple services. It will probably include something similar to the "disconnected" ADO Recordsets with XML support.

We even believe that the actual packaging of ADO Recordset data (XML) into the SOAP calls will be transparent to the developers. You will then have both the option to modify the XMLRS.bas to conform with the new XML structure of Recordsets. Or you can just update the code to replace the XMLRS functions with Recordset functionality. The first wave will probably be company-internal, with application integrating services from multiple systems, followed by full integration of services from multiple service providers all over the internet.

The Pocket PC, with its slim size, is well suited to take advantage of the power that distributed Web Services can bring. You can now deliver not only the content but also the power (functionality) of the web to your users, even wirelessly. We hope that you think this is as exciting as we do – this will really change the way we think about providing integrated solutions. And when all those great Web Services show up, you will be ready to take them anywhere. Expect to see more developer articles on Microsoft's PocketPC dot com site (**www.microsoft.com/pocketpc/** on this subject, as Web Services are at the very core of the .NET strategy.

> 66 The Pocket PC, with its slim size, is well suited to take advantage of the power that distributed Web Services can bring. 99

Getting some help

Well, now that you have seen the inside of how SOAP works, let's see how to make things simpler for you. A nice way to get some help on how to use Web Services from your Pocket PC applications, is to use a third-party product called Pocket SOAP. We have placed a copy of Pocket SOAP software at your convenience on the accompanying CD. You'll also find it available for downloading at: **www.pocketsoap.com/**

If we look at the previous sample, here is how the code would look to accomplish the same thing on the Pocket PC:

```
Dim lenv As PocketSOAP.Envelope
Dim lhtt As PocketSOAP.HTTPTransport
Dim lsResponse As String
Dim lsRequest As String

' Init Envelope
Set lenv = CreateObject("PocketSOAP.Envelope")
lenv.MethodName = "GetStockQuote"
lenv.URI = "urn:Foo"

' Set parameters
lenv.CreateParameter "Symbol", "MSFT" ', "xsd:string"
lenv.CreateParameter "description", "any company" ',
"xsd:string"

' Set request
lsRequest = lenv.Serialize

' Make SOAP call
Set lhtt = CreateObject("PocketSOAP.HTTPTransport")
lhtt.Send "http://www.soaptoolkit.com/soapdemo/services.asp",
lsRequest
lsResponse = lhtt.Receive

' Parse response
lenv.parse lsResponse

  ' Show result
MsgBox lenv.Parameters.Item(0).Value
```

And as you can see it is somewhat similar to what we did before. But instead of having to include the SOAPClient.bas module in our projects, we just need to set a Reference to the Pocket SOAP Type Library and we are ready to go. Of course, you could always put this code into your own SOAPCall function to simplify the call even more. It should be noted that if you do not supply the parameter type, all parameters will default to "string."

Let's turn our attention to how the second Web Service call (to retrieve a Recordset in XML format) would look with Pocket SOAP:

```
Dim lenv As PocketSOAP.Envelope
Dim lhtt As PocketSOAP.HTTPTransport
Dim ls As String
Dim litm As ListItem

' Init Envelope
Set lenv = CreateObject("PocketSOAP.Envelope")
lenv.MethodName = "GetXML"
lenv.URI = "http://tempuri.org/message/"

' Set parameters
lenv.CreateParameter "SQLString", "SELECT * FROM Article"
lenv.CreateParameter "MaxRecords", "4"

' Make SOAP call
Set lhtt = CreateObject("PocketSOAP.HTTPTransport")
lhtt.SOAPAction = "http://tempuri.org/action/Catalog.GetXML"
lhtt.Send "http://localhost/soap/PPDE.asp", lenv.Serialize

' Parse response
lenv.parse lhtt.Receive

' Get result
ls = lenv.Parameters.ItemByName("Result").Value

' Clear and add ListView headings
ListViewCtrl1.ColumnHeaders.Clear
ListViewCtrl1.ColumnHeaders.Add 1, , "ArtNo", 700
ListViewCtrl1.ColumnHeaders.Add 2, , "Description", 1450
ListViewCtrl1.ColumnHeaders.Add 3, , "Price", 850,
lvwColumnRight

' Clear and fill ListView from XML (with Recordset Emulation)
ListViewCtrl1.ListItems.Clear
XMLRSOpen ls
Do While Not XMLRSEOF
  Set litm = ListViewCtrl1.ListItems.Add(, ,
XMLRS("ArticleNo"))
    litm.SubItems(1) = XMLRS("Description")
    litm.SubItems(2) = XMLRS("Price")
  XMLRSMoveNext
Loop
XMLRSClose
```

We strongly recommend you use a tool like Pocket SOAP since you probably will not want to put your energy into implementing SOAP on a low level. However, it is always good to know the reasoning behind it to make better use of the technology.

Pocket SOAP has been tested with a number of different server implementations, and is probably a more stable solution than the eVB code module (SOAPClient.asp) we have supplied in the previous section. Pocket SOAP have been tested with the following server-side implementations:

● Microsoft SOAP Toolkit December Release (also known as ROPE)
● Microsoft SOAP Toolkit v2.0 beta 2
● Microsoft Visual Studio.NET Beta 1
● Apache SOAP v2.0 and up
● DevelopMentor's Keith Brown's SOAP/Perl 0.25
● SOAP::Lite
● UserLand Software's Frontier
● 4s4c (same author as Pocket SOAP)

Just to show you an example of calling an already existing Web Service, and to give you an idea of what will come in the future, here is a code sample that works like the standard **Whois** service:

```
Dim lenv As PocketSOAP.Envelope
Dim lhtt As PocketSOAP.HTTPTransport
Dim lsResponse As String
Dim lsRequest As String
Dim ls As String

' Get domain name
ls = InputBox("Enter Domain:", App.Title, "pocketsoap.com")

' Init Envelope
Set lenv = CreateObject("PocketSOAP.Envelope")
lenv.MethodName = "whois"
lenv.URI = "http://www.pocketsoap.com/whois"

' Set parameters
lenv.CreateParameter "name", ls

' Set request
lsRequest = lenv.Serialize

' Make SOAP call
Set lhtt = CreateObject("PocketSOAP.HTTPTransport")
```

```
lhtt.Send "http://soap.4s4c.com/whois/soap.asp", lsRequest
lsResponse = lhtt.Receive

' Parse response
lenv.parse lsResponse

' Get and show result
txtText.Text = lenv.Parameters.Item(0).Value
```

When you enter a domain name in the InputBox, you will get the response loaded into the TextBox. If you look around at sites like **XMethods** (**www.xmethods.com**/), you will find that there are actually people already building them. There are currency exchange services, news services, book price quotes, eBay price watchers, etc., and there are more and more services focusing on solving real business problems. Just take the samples that we have provided and try to use some other Web Services – you will probably find some of them quite useful. You might even include them in your next Pocket PC application.

12.4   No server or all servers?

Let us say that we could actually provide services on all clients, services that other clients could access. What if there were no servers? Building on the success of Napster and similar services, we think that corporations will realize the power of distributing the business services rather than requiring all services to be centralized.

Imagine that the accounting department had the necessary services to submit a travel bill. They would not only be responsible for the manual service, but also the automatic (self service) service. It would mean that they would actually decrease their manual work by implementing (themselves or by help of others) a better automatic service. The possibilities are huge! As we have said before it is not "or/else" but "both/and" that is the rule and we will see servers in the future too. The point is that there are a number of services that could actually be distributed, and some services are actually perfect for distributing. We will look at one such service in the next section.

P2P messaging

You have built messaging, right? Well it really is a new name for something we have all done for a while – chatting. But all those messenger (chat) services operate from a centralized architecture. Is it really efficient that we send all text to the server that then redirects it to the other people on the same chat session? Not really. One problem is that if we talk mere bandwidth, we would have to send the same text first to the server and then back to the receiver again, which doubles the bandwidth requirements. What if we could connect the sender and receiver directly? What if we could provide P2P services on our Pocket PCs?

Actually, we can. Thanks to the guys over at Odyssey Software (www.odysseysoftware.com), creators of the product ViaXML, we can do P2P on the Pocket PC today. Their ViaXML product allows you to expose and call mobile Web Services, which can make the Pocket PC act both like a client and a server concurrently.

Hey, you might think, but that would require a web server on my Pocket PC, would it not? Yes, it would, and that is exactly what the ViaXML product does. It does not contain a full-featured web server that you can use for displaying content, but it is rather an embedded HTTP Listener that allows you to make your Pocket PC a Web Service provider. The ViaXML HTTP listener can be directly embedded into your application, and multiple instances of the listener can be running at the same time.

 It does not contain a full-featured web server that you can use for displaying content, but it is rather an embedded HTTP Listener that allows you to make your Pocket PC a Web Service provider.

> **Note**
>
> As of May 2001 ViaXML implements the XMLRPC specification for Web Services (XMLRPC is the predecessor to SOAP, with .NET, Win32, Java, and PERL implementations – for more information visit **www.xmlrpc.org**). This means that today you cannot directly call SOAP services on the internet using ViaXML without transforming XMLRPC calls into SOAP through XSLT. However, Odyssey is currently working on adding native SOAP support to ViaXML. According to Odyssey Software, all code using ViaXML to call XMLRPC-based web services will call SOAP services with minimal changes.

We will now look at an example that Odyssey Software put together called InkMessenger. And the main application form looks like Figure 12.2.

Figure 12.2
InkMessenger peer-to-peer sample

This application enables the client (and server) to send and receive messages from other clients directly. Messages could be both text and something drawn. You have a list of friends that you can direct your messages to (and receive from). This brings up a very interesting question. How do I know which people in my defined community, have the same application (InkMessenger) running?

Well this is actually one of the biggest issues when it comes to P2P, and the solutions are many. One solution is to have an online directory that I can connect to and retrieve information about other users. This is actually the model that Napster uses.

The directory is accessible in real time, and the same approach has been chosen for the InkMessenger application. Here, the directory is implemented as a set of exposed web services that allow registration and real-time lookup of device, owner, and application information on a central server. The underlying storage of the directory information is a simple Microsoft Access database (could be any ADO accessible data store, like SQL Server, as well). This dynamic mobile directory is called DirectoryFX, and is one of Odyssey Software's application frameworks delivered with ViaXML. With this software set up, you can start messaging away with your other Pocket PC peers.

One issue here is that you can only access the peers that are connected to the same directory, and to make this truly powerful you would probably like to go and search for other Web Services, like directory services, somewhere. This is the whole point of UDDI. With UDDI, Microsoft and a load of other huge corporations are trying to create the white and yellow pages of Web Services. If we are lucky, they will succeed. We would then be able to go to the UDDI site and search for the specific Web Service that we were interested in. We would maybe even be able to search for different InkMessenger directories hosted by different servers. In the meantime, P2P is here today for Pocket PCs, and enterprises can begin to evaluate how P2P empowers their business strategies.

Things to come

Note

Please understand that the following paragraphs are our own interpretation of the mobile aspects of the .NET initiative (**www.microsoft.com/net**). Do not regard our interpretations as commitments from Microsoft.

If you are like us (curious), you would probably like to know more about what is in the pipeline regarding Microsoft .NET and the Pocket PC platform. One thing is for sure; Microsoft is hard-core about supplying us (Pocket PC developers and users) with as many as possible .NET features that will be available on the PC platform. The Microsoft mobile mission states that developing mobile applications should be familiar to enterprise developers, requiring minimal additional effort to take applications anywhere. This includes areas such as:

- Single set of Web Services for a server side and client side application
- Network transparency
- Consistent data access methods
- Consistent tools and development model
- Applications that provide out-of-the-box functionality and can be extended

And as you may understand, there will be some drastic changes from the way we build mobile applications today. Our interpretation of the "single set" of Web Services for server and client is that you will be able to consume Web Services on a Pocket PC in a native way. By "native way," we mean that it will be like using any component (DLL) on your Pocket PC today. The fact that the "component" is remote on a server somewhere on the internet will be irrelevant for both the user and the developer. We hope that you will also be able to host Web Services on your Pocket PC and that you will be able to provide Web Services over the internet from your hand – that's really cool! This will also enable you to do peer-to-peer interaction with other Pocket PC users. It will then be possible to build applications that make use of services on other Pocket PCs as well as your own, and others may call your Pocket PC to use functionality that you provide. In such an environment, your Pocket PC will truly become the point of integration.

> ❝The fact that the 'component' is remote on a server somewhere on the internet will be irrelevant for both the user and the developer.❞

> ❝In such an environment, your Pocket PC will truly become the point of integration.❞

We think that network transparency means that you will be able to access both wired and wireless networks in a seamless way. You will no longer have to bother with new protocols or gateways, you will simply be using the good old TCP/IP networking that you have grown used to over the past web years.

Connectivity will be a native part of the Pocket PC platform with integrated support for using the device as a mobile phone. It means that you can find a person in the Pocket PC's Contacts and call him and start talking through the device itself. No more "two-body" configurations with the need for an old mobile phone. Those old mobile phones can probably be recycled in a nature-friendly way somewhere. Just kidding! The truth is, as we have stated many times in this book, that it will be "both/and" rather than "or/else." We can all be certain that in the future there will be more devices, with different capabilities, that you will have to support when building your applications.

That we will have consistent data access methods is something we have seen already in Chapter 6, and we can only assume that the consistency with the PC version of the data access methods will be even higher.

The tools too

The consistency in the tools and development model is even more interesting. This actually means that you are likely to have a single toolset for building applications on the PC platform as well as the Pocket PC platform. We think that you can look forward to seeing a development environment that will be able to develop solutions for multiple devices. An IDE that will even be able to select a profile for the target devices you are building for, and it will adapt itself to show only the available features on those target devices.

You will also see a slight shift in the way that you build multi-channel support in your applications. Rather than building different stylesheets (XSL) for each client (device), you will be using intelligent controls (much like the VB/eVB controls) that will change depending on the device the application is running on. It means that you will not have to maintain an increasing number of stylesheets to support more and more devices.

The controls that are provided from Microsoft (and probably a growing number of third-parties) will also be extendable. Due to all the new features that you will have in VS.NET (such as inheritance), you will be able to build on the provided controls to create user interfaces that not only look good on most devices, but ones that also have built-in understanding of your application logic. You can inherit a control and in the new control that you create, you also include simple business logic, like validation. One example is that you can create a text box for e-mail addresses that includes the validation of e-mail addresses. When that control is deployed on multiple devices, it would probably look different but it will have the same logic attached to it. To be more business specific, you could have an article number text box that knows how an article number should look, a customer category combo box that knows how to load all valid categories, etc.

> 66 You will be able to build on the provided controls to create user interfaces that not only look good on most devices, but ones that also have built-in understanding of your application logic. 99

The controls come in two flavors; one for online (web) scenarios and the other for off-line scenarios. The online controls are hosted on a web server and adapts to the client by sending different flavors of HTML (or even other markup languages, like WML) to the client depending on its capabilities. The capabilities tracking have been extensively refined since the good old **BROWS-CAP.INI** file that we discussed in Chapter 8. The off-line controls are installed in different versions on the target device (just like the VB/eVB controls already today) and have generally richer capabilities than the online controls. The new thing is that these controls will also be common across different platforms and build on the same basic framework both on PCs and Pocket PCs.

The controls are truly one of the most valuable "out-of-the-box functionality" that you will get. Another interesting part of what you get with the platform is not really "out-of-the-box" but rather "out-of-the-net." We are talking about all the ready-made Web Services that Microsoft (and surely numerous others) will provide to ease your life as an enterprise developer. From Microsoft, you will get services for identification (Passport), credit information (myWallet), notification (myNotifications), storage (myDocuments), positioning (myLocation), contacts (myContacts), calendar (myCalendar), and so on.

And you will be able to use them natively in your applications. Think about that. If we provide just one simple example; how many times have you spent time in developing a web application on how to identify the user? If you buy into the Passport Web Service, you will not think about this problem again.

Let us look at a generic figure of what we have been talking about (Figure 12.3).

Figure 12.3 Logical application framework

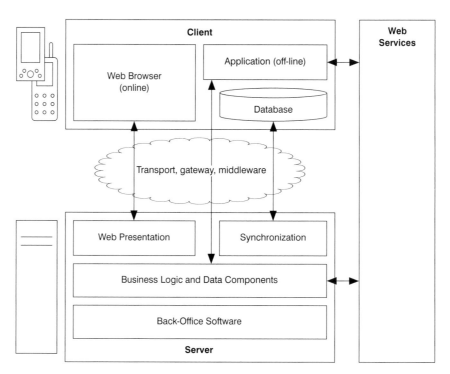

In Figure 12.3 you can see a basic framework for supporting multiple clients (channels) as well as utilizing server, client, and "public" (internet/web) services. You can see that the framework supports both online (web) and off-line applications.

And if we look at the same figure for the current available toolset, it would look like Figure 12.4.

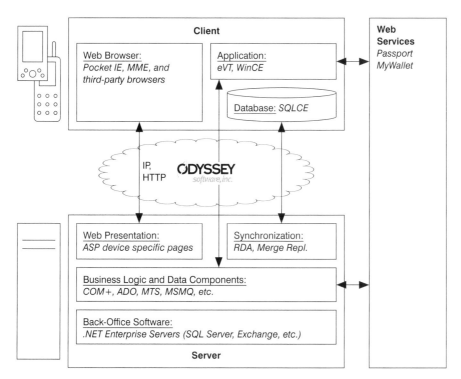

Figure 12.4 Physical Pocket PC framework with today's products and technologies

As you can see, the Pocket PC is almost all of the clients (not really a phone yet, but soon) and it is really a design issue whether we want to use the Pocket PC as an online client, as an off-line client, or both! The latter is probably the most likely scenario since different parts of a complete enterprise architecture will be suitable to deploy using different client requirements.

We can see that Microsoft has most of the pieces in place already, even if some parts are weaker than others. As you have seen in this book, we have to build either device-specific ASP pages in our web applications, or we have to use stylesheets with all the maintenance that comes with that.

You can also notice that Odyssey Software is missing one important part in the platform today – the ability to call server components with its CEfusion product. In Microsoft .NET the ability to call server components (not Web Services) is called **remoting**, and that will enable us to call server components much in the same way as we have done for a while on the PC when we use DCOM. As you can see, there isn't any specific gateway product so we are using IP (CEfusion) or HTTP (SQL Server CE, SOAP, web applications) in most cases.

Now it is time to move on to the way we see a likely .NET version of the same figure (Figure 12.5).

Figure 12.5 Physical Pocket PC framework with tomorrow's products and technologies

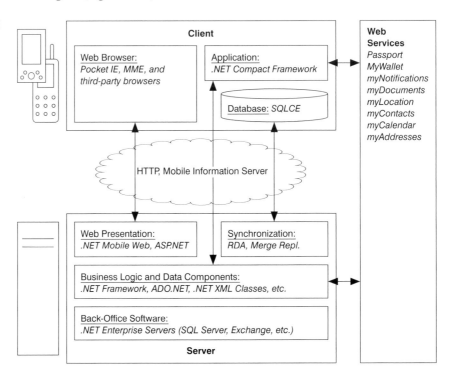

We can see that there are a lot of things that have changed in the boxes in the figure. We now have support for building mobile web applications and can take advantage of the new features (like the web controls that we were talking about above). We also have a lot of new functionality on the server side as well as a load of new "public" (internet/web) services. Most of the data storage story is the same with SQL Server for CE on the device and RDA/Merge Replication on the server. However, there will be a new ability to synchronize your local data (e-mail, calendar, contacts, etc.) directly with the server similar in function to ActiveSync, but without the PC. This functionality will be delivered with the Mobile Information Server, which you notice has been added as a gateway product.

But the really cool stuff is bound to happen on the client side. As you can see, we will have a subset of the .NET Framework called the .NET Compact Framework and with it, we think, comes things like ADO.NET, ASP.NET, etc. Hopefully, you will be able to create local web applications with ASP.NET.

But doesn't that mean then that there will actually be a web server on the device, you might ask? And the answer again is, Yes! As you may recall, we started this section by telling you that you will be able to provide web services from your device. That would not be possible if you didn't have a web server, since the Web Services protocol (SOAP) is dependent on the HTTP protocol that is provided by web servers.

If you think about it, having a .NET Compact Framework on the device also means that you can write Pocket PC applications in any language. You will be able to write Pocket PC applications in C# in the not-too-distant future. You might even be able to write them in any of the other languages that will be supported in VS.NET. Why not build applications for Pocket PC in Smalltalk?

> **❝** You will be able to write Pocket PC applications in C# in the not-too-distant future. **❞**

If we transform the .NET Framework into something like a .NET Compact Framework on the Pocket PC device itself, it could look like Figure 12.6.

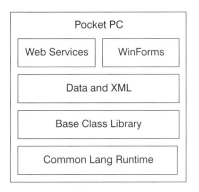

Figure 12.6 Device architecture

With the CLR and technologies like CTS and CLS, we can have a common platform for running our applications written in various languages. We can have common types and functionality for managed code and components. We can have the same platform for building applications and components, as we will have on the server.

You would therefore be able to write Pocket PC components in VB. Porting our code from PC to Pocket PC will be even easier. Data will be easier to share between servers and mobile devices.

XML is at the core of this sharing, and because of this, we will still be able to write great off-line applications based on the same framework as on the server/PC side (WinForms). For memory reasons, we will probably not have the full set of the framework, but the most important subset. And a nice feature is that the development environment will probably adapt to a "profile" that you select for targeting devices. If you set the profile to target Pocket PCs, only the relevant features will be available for you as a developer.

12.5   Conclusion

At this point, I hope you agree with us that there's power in distributed applications and that the technology to make them come true is on its way. Even though all pieces are not in place yet, you have seen that you can start using parts of .NET already today. By doing so, you will benefit in two ways. First, and most importantly, you will start thinking of your applications as part of something bigger (doesn't that sound almost poetic?) and that will change the way that you design your applications. And second, you will be ready to utilize the technology as it becomes available and later matures. There is no doubt in our minds that Web Services will change a lot of things – you are now ready to explore the full potential on your own. What are your .NE(x)T Steps?

More information

If you want to read more about:

- Microsoft .NET visit
  www.microsoft.com/net
- SOAP, visit the MSDN SOAP Developer Resource page at:
  msdn.microsoft. com/soap/
- UDDI at:
  uddi.microsoft.com/
- Pocket SOAP at:
  www.pocketsoap.com/pocketsoap/
- For sample Web Services at XMethods go to:
  www.xmethods.com/

Conclusion: Suggestions for beginning your first mobile solution

Isn't it great? You have seen that developing mobile solutions for the Pocket PC is something that you already knew how to do, and now hopefully you feel well prepared to do it. You are now equipped to take on your first project, and try out your new knowledge.

You are now ready to start finding your first Pocket PC project and the magic rule when working with new technology is to iterate. Below you will find some simple steps you can follow. You should remember to create a little, try a little, and sell a little. The key in iteration is to embrace the feedback that you get, go back and make changes, and then get more feedback. Just continue on the path that deliver results. This is where you find success.

Step 1   Identify a great mobile opportunity

You can start with the ideas from the **What does this mean for me** section from Chapter 2. An easy win is probably to look at some paper-based processes and some business operations that could also create some strong business cases. Supporting management to take faster (and better) decisions anywhere will always be interesting if you are looking for strong supporters of your project. You always have to take the "Does it matter?" test. You have to make sure that you are convinced that your solution meets a compelling need and that the people that could benefit from the solution understand this need. Build a sales pitch! Practice it! Make sure that you can explain your idea in two minutes if necessary. You will have to sell your idea constantly.

In this stage you have to note an important detail. In contrast to conventional practice, we recommend not telling your boss first. Often we are told in business to gain management's support to go forward with a new idea, but never go to the boss before you have the buyer's commitment and preferably even the grassroots support from people that are potential participants in creating the solution.

Step 2   Talk to the buyer

Meet with the buyers and present your idea. Spread among the potential users and supporters your personal conviction of the greatness of the idea. Ask them to refine the idea with their knowledge about the need that your solution satisfies. Talk to the business people and ask them what they would be most interested in seeing. Draw some screen shots on a whiteboard and make them build further on your idea. There are actually two important reasons for talking to the buyer:

1 You get the input for building a showcase, which you'll read about below.

2 The buyer gets emotionally involved in your idea, which will help you to gain support for it.

The buyer getting emotionally involved is the first step to a sale and you will probably get more leverage over time.

Step 3   Build a showcase

It is time to make use of this book's sample code. Reuse as much as you can. You should not try to reinvent everything yourself. Build something that can be used in a presentation and don't spend too much time on what is behind the forms and its controls. However, there is a point to include a small portion of each feature that you plan to be part of the full implementation. For example:

- If you have at least a part of your information in SQL Server for Windows CE, you can say that your solution utilizes a solid off-line database.
- If you can create an appointment from your application, you can say that you have integrated with the PIM functionality in the Pocket PC.
- If you call a server component with business logic to support the solution, you can say that you have integrated with existing systems.

Make it look spectacular! Design definitely counts, and if you don't have the artistic abilities yourself, try to engage someone with such skills. If you are able to include great-looking pictures or images (logos are always right) and even sound, don't miss the opportunity. But always try to keep it as simple as possible and in conflict between simplicity and flashy features, go for simplicity. We hope that you will find some ideas from the samples that we have provided.

Step 4 Build a value proposition

To create a business case could be a huge effort, but we suggest that you find the basic value proposition by listing all the benefits and group them by:

1 Measurable cost-savings benefits that can be expressed in money. Quantification cannot be over-stressed.

2 Measurable benefits that cannot be directly associated to a monetary profit.

3 Immeasurable benefits.

And of course, you should focus on them in the above order. You will want to show as much hard-core profits, or savings, as possible. And then you should not be too optimistic when stating the costs. Try to imagine what or how the buyer's objections and concerns might be and find the arguments you need to reply.

Step 5 Present your showcase and value proposition

It's show time! Take your time to prepare the presentation. One great way of presenting a showcase is to set it up as a role play.

Locate and place all the necessary equipment in place and try to add some great extra features. If you are using a PC viewer software like Virtual CE (on the CD), you could set up a wireless network connection to be able to walk around the audience during the presentation to make them "touch" the showcase themselves.

Value propositions are best presented after the showcase walkthrough and should be as brief as possible. The point is to show the profits and costs, preferably in dollar amounts. And then you want to show all the additional benefits, not necessarily measurable. A tip is to take concrete examples with the number of hours or days that one person will save, etc.

Another way of thinking about the presentation is to actually publish your idea, showcase, and value propositions. If it is internal, publish a few pages on the intranet and make sure that you get a headline on the internal site's homepage. If it is a showcase for your clients, try to get it published on your company web site and send them the URL to examine themselves. Why not put a ready-made installation of the showcase online for them to try out themselves.

Step 6   Launch the project

Now it is time to go and talk to your boss. With the buyers already supporting the idea, he will have some easy work getting the deal on paper. He will forgive you that you didn't come to him first when he starts counting his bonus increase. You will also be able to give him some input on the things that you need to get going – a new Pocket PC, a network CF card, and the like.

To define the work that has to be done, use the Pocket PC Solution Definition Method from Chapter 3. There you will find the activities to insert into your project plan and schedule. Remember that even in execution, you should iterate. Think of the implementation as a series of prototypes, or rather, pilots that you can continue to build further on. Don't always wait until you get it "right" because that could take too long. And keep in mind that execution by definition drains emotions, so try to keep that initial energy and feeling of success alive – celebrate your effort regularly!

And off you go!

Now it is time for us to let you fly on your own. We have brought to you what we think you will need in making your first mobile project a success. And remember that we will be here to assist you along the way. Just send us an e-mail or visit **www.businessanyplace.net**. We are eager to hear how things go for you. And please share your efforts and results with us. We would be happy to put your solutions, and even your showcase projects, online!

Pocket PC Development in the Enterprise CEfusion™ Offer

Odyssey Software is pleased to offer you a free ($495 value) permanent single user development license for CEfusion™, our powerful mobile and wireless application data access infrastructure for rapidly building and developing rich mobile enterprise applications for Pocket PCs and other Windows CE devices. Whether you're powering ACME Copier Inc. or thousands of mobile workers at a Fortune 100 business, Odyssey Software technology will get you where you need to be.

As you've already heard from Andreas and Christian, CEfusion™ extends the core Windows DNA data access technologies – ADO, MTS/COM+, and MSMQ – to the mobile application environment, enabling real-time, online, interactive access or application-controlled synchronization with centralized data and business logic over any wireless LAN or WAN, wired or dial-up connection.

In order for us to provide you the free license key included with your purchases of *Pocket PC Development in the Enterprise*, just go to the URL below:

http://www.odysseysoftware.com/PocketPCDevOffer

If you're interested in mobile web services and peer-to-peer computing, download a fully functional 30-day evaluation license of ViaXML at:

http://www.odysseysoftware.com/viaxml_eval.html

Index